DELMORE SCHWARTZ

THE LIFE OF
AN AMERICAN POET

JAMES ATLAS

 A DISCUS BOOK/PUBLISHED BY AVON BOOKS

Acknowledgment for permission to quote copyrighted material is made to New Directions for *In Dreams Begin Responsibilities* by Delmore Schwartz, copyright © 1938 by New Directions Publishing Corporation; *Shenandoah* by Delmore Schwartz © 1941 by New Directions Publishing Corporation; *Genesis* by Delmore Schwartz, copyright © 1943 by New Directions Publishing Corporation; *The World Is a Wedding* by Delmore Schwartz, copyright © 1948 by Delmore Schwartz; *Vaudeville for a Princess* by Delmore Schwartz, copyright © 1950 by New Directions Publishing Corporation. To Doubleday & Co., Inc., for two poems from *Summer Knowledge*, "During December's Death" and "Seurat's Sunday Afternoon along the Seine," copyright © 1958, 1959 by Delmore Schwartz. To the University of Chicago Press for quotations from *Selected Essays of Delmore Schwartz*, copyright © 1970 by the University of Chicago. To the Viking Press, Inc., for quotations from *Humboldt's Gift*, copyright © 1975 by Saul Bellow; to Mrs. T. S. Eliot for quotations from letters of T. S. Eliot to Delmore Schwartz; to James Laughlin for quotations from letters of James Laughlin to Delmore Schwartz. To Holly Stevens and Alfred A. Knopf, Inc., for quotations from *The Letters of Wallace Stevens*, edited by Holly Stevens, copyright © 1966 by Holly Stevens. Auden's letter to Schwartz, copyright © 1976 by the Estate of W. H. Auden, is reprinted by permission.

AVON BOOKS
A division of
The Hearst Corporation
959 Eighth Avenue
New York, New York 10019

First Discus Printing, November, 1978

DISCUS TRADEMARK REG. U.S. PAT. OFF. AND IN OTHER COUNTRIES, MARCA REGISTRADA, HECHO EN U.S.A.

Printed in the U.S.A.

FOR ANNA FELS

Contents

Preface

SAMUEL JOHNSON has supplied a shrewd defense of biographies that have as their subject a person whose contemporaries are still alive to provide testimony about him: "If a life be delayed till interest and envy are at an end, we may hope for impartiality, but must expect little intelligence; for the incidents which give excellence to biography are of a volatile and evanescent kind, such as soon escape the memory . . ." Delmore Schwartz, who died just over a decade ago, had a particular genius for exciting "interest and envy," so perhaps there is an advantage in writing about him now, while those qualities flourish in the memories of his friends.

Anatole Broyard, in a review of *Humboldt's Gift*, Saul Bellow's fictional portrait of Schwartz, objected to the way Bellow made him seem "a toothless lion, caged by circumstance, tamed by the captivity of the human condition . . . I knew Delmore Schwartz," Broyard declared, offering his own explanation of how Schwartz "transcended both his art and his history and drew solely on his 'spiritual nature.'" The late Philip Rahv, reviewing a posthumous collection of Schwartz's essays introduced by Dwight Macdonald, complained that Macdonald was "deficient in the comprehension of his friend's difficult and extremely problematical character," and "quite unaware of Schwartz's inner life." But Schwartz's close friend William Barrett revealed in *his* version of Schwartz (a memoir in *Commentary*) that Rahv had not "told the whole story," for Schwartz and Rahv "had come to loathe each other." What more could a biographer wish for in the way of volatility, interest—that is, in Johnson's usage, bias—or envy?

"The stockmarket of American success can be as unpredictable as Wall Street," Barrett marveled, noting the resurgence of interest in Schwartz over the last few years—a resurgence to which his own memoir has contributed, along with Bellow's novel, John Berryman's Dream Songs devoted to Schwartz, and in a more general sense, Irving Howe's *World of Our Fathers*, which comprises the history of Schwartz's generation. But he has been more talked about than read; only the celebrated short story "In Dreams Begin Responsibilities" and a few poems continue to be anthologized, and it is not often remembered now that he was once known as the most promising writer in America. When his first book appeared in 1938 (he was twenty-four at the time), T. S. Eliot, Ezra Pound, Allen Tate, John Crowe Ransom, Wallace Stevens, and William Carlos Williams all praised it highly; for Tate, it was "the only genuine innovation we've had since Pound and Eliot." A decade later, when *The World Is a Wedding*, a collection of short stories, appeared, many critics declared it the definitive portrait of their generation. And the same sort of critical acclaim is heard on occasion even now; Morris Dickstein, writing in a recent *Partisan Review* about that generation, called Schwartz "its most fascinating and least appreciated prophet."

The literary world of the 1930's and 1940's was less dispersed than it is now; everyone seemed to know everyone else, and so to write about Schwartz is to write about a whole milieu, that of the New York intellectuals once classified by Irving Howe as the only genuine intelligentsia America has ever had. In "The New York Intellectuals," his famous essay on that group so tentatively linked by temperament, style, or simply Jewishness, Howe noted their common attraction to "the idea of the Jew (not always distinguished from the idea of Delmore Schwartz)." Schwartz, Howe implied in his wry parenthesis, figured so prominently in the literary landscape that whatever special characteristics he possessed became identified with a whole temper: that of the alienated Jew, the radical, the *poète maudit*, the modern intellectual hero. It was his misfortune to be metonymous, the very embodiment of an entire generation's traumas and opinions. What lends resonance to his attitudes, what gives them a sort of historical authority, is how many others shared them; not only Jewish intellectuals and critics (Lionel Trilling, Alfred Kazin, Harold Rosenberg, Clement Greenberg, Philip Rahv), but novelists (Isaac Rosenfeld and Saul Bellow), non-Jewish writers (Dwight Macdonald, Mary McCarthy, F. W. Dupee, Wil-

liam Barrett), and poets (Robert Lowell and John Berryman) were associated with Schwartz at one time or another, and all of them had affinities with at least one of the
manifold components of his sensibility.

Of these, there were perhaps too many for his own good;
Schwartz was often faulted for being so involved in various
literary projects, so *public*, that he really had no stable
personality. There was, however, one situation in which he
could express the "intricate inner life, a kind of unremitting self-reflexive internal labor" that was, in Rahv's view,
fundamental to his character. Schwartz's work, both published and unpublished, is almost wholly autobiographical,
a tendency of unambiguous value to his biographer. He
wrote tirelessly about himself, scrutinizing and interpreting
every detail of his past with an obsessiveness that surpassed
Rousseau's—and also with a comic brilliance, an élan that
made these private researches his most original theme.

Still, biographers must naturally approach their own
subjects' confessions with caution in gathering evidence
about their lives; wherever possible, corroboration from
other sources must be sought, and such external sources
are fewer now than in earlier days, when the epistolary
habit flourished. (Perhaps nothing has been more detri-
mental to biography than the telephone.) Schwartz himself
wrote and received hundreds of letters, but their number
seems slight when compared with the vast correspondence
of Henry James or Virginia Woolf. The documentation
that survives, while ample, is by no means complete; a
good many letters and papers vanished in the chaos of
Schwartz's last years, and none of the letters he wrote as a
child have been recovered. His very contemporaneity
makes for a certain thinness of evidence; had he lived
longer ago, the practices of a more self-consciously literary
era would perhaps have left even richer sources for a biographer to draw upon.

Few writers contemplate the prospect of their future
biography without apprehension, and some ensure through
rather drastic measures that their biographer will not have
an easy time of his task. Willa Cather and W. H. Auden
instructed recipients of their letters to burn them, while
Henry James went a step further, consigning his correspondence of several decades to a roaring fire. Delmore
Schwartz, far less circumspect than these suspicious au-

thors, preserved virtually every scrap of paper he ever
scribbled on; but he, too, seems to have brooded over the
possibility that a biography might eventually be written of
him, as he revealed in an ambiguous journal entry of 1942:
"Biographies written of you. It is different with everyone;
with the great poet. *Not* moral." It was natural for him to
except great writers, for no one was a more assiduous
reader of biographies than Schwartz, who mastered every
known fact about the lives of his literary heroes and recounted them at great length in his verse journals.

In his letters to his friend and publisher James Laughlin,
the question of biography becomes a repetitive motif. On
many occasions, Schwartz expressed the fear that his letters would be read, and refused to "abandon [his] natural
reticence" unless Laughlin promised to return them. Any
letters intimating salacious episodes were to be "committed
to the flames." Schwartz delivered his most explicit warning to posterity in a message scrawled on the envelope that
contained his correspondence with Laughlin: "Letters from
D.S. to J.L. 1937–1940. Not to be opened until death.
God have mercy on him who disturbs the privacy of these
two minds." There was, however, one exception, a letter
from 1951 in which he considered the future consequences
of his epistolary revelations:

> It was pleasant to learn that you expected our cor-
> respondence to be read in the international salons and
> boudoirs of the future. Do you think they will be able
> to distinguish between the obfuscations, mystifica-
> tions, efforts at humor, and plain statements of fact?
> Will they recognize my primary feelings as a cor-
> respondent—the catacomb from which I write to you,
> seeking to secure some compassion? Or will they just
> think that I am nasty, an over-eager clown, gauche,
> awkward, and bookish? Will they understand that I
> am always direct, open, friendly, simple and candid to
> the point of naivete until the ways of the fiendish
> world infuriate me and I am forced to be devious,
> suspicious, calculating, not that it does me any good
> anyway?

This was the task he set for his biographer, to elicit from
the various poses and personae the true sensibility they

concealed. It is no longer acceptable, given the ascendancy of psychoanalysis, to believe in the testaments of individuals about themselves; yet in this letter, Schwartz provided a vivid self-portrait of his dauntingly complicated character.

PART ONE
1913-1945

———•———

The ground on which the ball bounces
Is another bouncing ball.

The wheeling, whirling world
Makes no will glad.

Spinning in its spotlight darkness,
It is too big for their hands.

A pitiless, purposeless Thing,
Arbitrary and unspent,

Made for no play, for no children,
But chasing only itself.

The innocent are overtaken,
They are not innocent.

They are their fathers' fathers,
The past is inevitable.

1

———•———

DELMORE SCHWARTZ had a particular fondness for stories about the origin of his first name. Sometimes he would insist he had been named after a delicatessen across the street from the house where he was born, sometimes that his mother had been fond of an actor who was named Frank Delmore. In still other versions, the name was taken from a Tammany Hall club, a Pullman railroad car, or a Riverside Drive apartment house. Delmore—no one ever called him by his last name—possessed a tireless, mythologizing imagination, a genius for eliciting general laws from the particular scenes of his life, and he made his name the subject of a grand historical drama.

> —Return with me, stand at my point of view,
> Regard with my emotion the small event
> Which gave my mind and gave my character,
> Amid the hundred thousand possibilities
> Heredity and community avail,
> Bound and engender,
>   the very life I know!

he declaimed in *Shenandoah*, a verse play about the naming of a Jewish child. That play, like Delmore's unpublished novels, like the thousand-page poem *Genesis*, like virtually everything he wrote, examined the forces that converged to form his identity.

Delmore must have been one of the most self-conscious writers who ever lived. "His only subject was himself—quite undisguised," he once confided in his journal, and he conceived of his own experience as "fabulous at every point," celebrating his "detailed and avid memory, his endless tracking down of motives." All his life, Delmore exulted in the drama the past could be made to yield; in journals,

poems, verse autobiographies, and stories, he returned to
his vibrant childhood in New York—"Scenes of my life
and of the lives which made me / And the immense powers, Europe, America, / And the metropolis which broke
their hearts," as he recalled it in *Genesis*. In "The March
Beginning," an ecstatic, *Iliad*-like catalogue of his mother's
friends, his father's business associates, and his neighbors
in the Washington Heights area of New York where Delmore grew up, he found their very names euphonious:
"The Siegels and Rose Grauer / And Mrs. Berkowitz";
"The Kottles, the Davises, / Helene, her mother, and
Irving, / The sister, her husband, their dog"; "Mrs. Gui-
chester who had lovers like Molly Bloom." Delmore was
fascinated by these ordinary lives, and made them emblems
in his work of what was "general, true, particular, and
rich."

Most social milieus eventually find their chroniclers, and
Delmore was to be widely acknowledged as the master
portraitist of his parents' generation. "The cut-glass bowls
on the buffet, / They are the works of art of these rising
Jews," he noted in *Shenandoah*; and he could have mentioned the linen napkins, the fine lace, the clutter of well-
polished secondhand furniture that were features of the
typical middle-class Jewish home. In Delmore's home, as
in a thousand others, the Old World had been re-created.
Jewish cuisine, the tea drunk from tall glasses, in many
homes even a samovar: these were the customs of a foreign
people, anomalous in America and yet remote from their
ancestral homes. In his late twenties, exhilarated by the
success his first volume of poetry had brought him, Delmore proclaimed himself "the poet of the Atlantic migration, that made America"; it was this event that had
dominated his past and formed the collective sensibility of
his generation.

The protagonist of this epic story was to be Delmore
himself, the child of "Europe, America, and Israel," and he
seized on his name as a convenient symbol for the dis-
parate forces that had made him what he was. Its prosaic
source was a neighbor of the Schwartzes who decided to
call her own child Delmore. Rose Schwartz, thinking it "a
beautiful name," declared, "If I ever had a son, I'd call him
Delmore." But the truth of its origin mattered less to him
than what it represented: a vivid instance of the conflict

between American values and his parents' aspirations. Like Walter and Elsie Fish in Delmore's play, who find the name Shenandoah so appealing, the Schwartzes bowed before "the dominion of the Gentile world" in choosing a name they thought to be typically American; but the name they chose was so incongruous that it served only to reveal —in their son's later estimate—their precarious grasp of the New World.

In the many ways, though, their grasp was surprisingly tenacious, given the circumstances of their arrival in America. Delmore's grandfather, Joseph Nathanson, had worked in his father-in-law's wheat mill in Botosani, Roumania, until one night, after some quarrel over a business matter, he announced he was going to America. Crammed into steerage, he lived on herring, black bread, and tea for two weeks, until the ship landed at Ellis Island. Six months later, he sent for his family, and on the eve of the new century, Hannah and her four children embarked from Hamburg. Joseph had started out selling marble counters for soda fountains, but before too long he went into the business of renting and selling pushcarts, an important trade in those days; within a few years, he owned a clothing store in the garment district.

Joseph settled his family on Willett Street in the heart of the Lower East Side, not far from the Schwartz family, who had come over a decade earlier. Louis Schwartz left his family's home in a village in the Roumanian province of Bessarabia when he was only thirteen, and three years later, in 1893, he sent for his younger brother Harry. For a while they were partners in a newspaper stand on the Lower East Side, but Harry was even then an enterprising businessman who sold chicken livers on the side, roasting them like chestnuts over a brazier. It wasn't long before the two boys had become prosperous enough to send for the rest of the family: their parents, a sister, and two younger brothers, Phil and Max.

By the time he was in his mid-twenties, Harry Schwartz had gone from selling insurance for the John Hancock Company to dealing in real estate. It was the time of the great real-estate boom in New York, during the century's first decade, when immigrants who had next to nothing were scraping together sufficient capital to make their first investments. Mortgages were not difficult to obtain, unions were poorly organized, and the growing population increased the demand for housing, so that it was possible, given a measure of daring and luck, to become affluent in no time.

Harry, a high-strung and charming young man, had just the sort of impatient temperament that enabled one to succeed in the business world, and within a few years he had made a great deal of money. For a time he was in partnership with his brothers Phil and Louis, developing land in Plainfield, New Jersey, when it was still a crossroads; later on, he went into business by himself, engaging —if one is to believe his inventive son—in some unorthodox practices. One story Delmore loved to tell was about how Harry would hire assistants to distribute cards on which a simple puzzle had been printed to "greenhorns" (those just off the boat) in the immigrant-filled ghettos. Whoever solved these puzzles could claim a prize at Harry's office. Once he had lured them in, Harry would give a persuasive sales pitch, encouraging his potential clients to buy land that generally turned out to be situated in the swamps and marshes of New Jersey.

Whatever the truth of this story, Harry was in a business that played on the hopes of newly arrived immigrants, for whom "private property" was the symbol of all they valued: stability, permanence, a place of their own in America. "Men like Jack Green," Delmore wrote in *Genesis* of a character very like his father, "knew well that they had brought with them from Europe / The peasant's sense that land was the most important thing and the owner of land / A king!" Real estate was a strategic line to be in, and Harry Schwartz had made himself a wealthy man by the time he met Rose Nathanson in 1909, when he was nearly thirty and she was twenty-two.

Rose was a strikingly beautiful woman then, with dark, penetrating eyes and auburn hair, and Harry was quite handsome; one of his more literary neighbors thought he resembled Rochester in *Jane Eyre*. "Tall, dark, dynamic," proud of his affluence, he liked to wear fine clothes; his suits were tailor-made, his shoes polished until they shone, the collars of his white shirts new and stiff. But he wasn't easy with his success; it both exhilarated and frightened him, since he dreaded that what had been so quickly won could be just as quickly lost. Pacing up and down a room, argumentative and full of energy, he would calculate how much money he had made that day. Still, Harry Schwartz had a less abrasive side that was attractive to women, a sensual nature that seemed to charm them, for he went from one affair to another—even though "it was the image of a domestic life presided over by Eva [Rose] which attracted him more than anything else," Delmore noted in *Genesis*. This image, combined with occasional seizures of remorse over his infidelities, prevented Harry from breaking off their courtship; finally, in one of his impatient moods, he obtained a marriage license and hastened with Rose to City Hall, ignoring her objections that such a casual ceremony was "against the custom and norm of their kind of people."

Soon afterward, the Schwartzes moved to an elegant apartment on Eastern Parkway in Brooklyn, a wide, tree-lined boulevard in a pleasant residential neighborhood. Rose was delighted to be married, and proud of the fine furniture that graced her new home. She was always boasting to the neighbors about "my Harry, my Harry," and looked forward to having a family of her own. But it wasn't long before her husband, "the prey of his own appetites and passions," renewed his philandering, a habit which made Rose all the more eager to have children; perhaps, her mother suggested, a child would awaken Harry's sense of responsibility. But Rose needed surgery that would enable her to conceive, and since Harry was reluctant to have children, she proceeded on her own to sell a French war bond—the gift of an uncle overseas—to finance her operation. This was all done behind her husband's back, while he was away on a business trip; Rose was a strong-willed, stubborn woman who never hesitated when she wanted her way. Once she was pregnant, Harry suddenly became enthusiastic about fatherhood, and for a time it seemed as if her calculations would succeed.

In later life, when Delmore learned that he owed his birth to a deception, he came to look on his very existence as problematic, the result of a devious struggle between his parents—two "egodoms," as he later referred to them, doomed forever to oppose each other. With an Aristotelian eye for the turning points in the drama of his life, he regarded certain episodes as bearers of such "pity and terror" that the whole of his experience stood revealed in them. Vergil's *Felix qui potuit rerum cognoscere causas* was one of his favorite axioms, from which it followed that he should consider his birth the most crucial episode of all; and since Freud and· Marx were his intellectual heroes, it was necessary to turn from the private theater of his parents' marriage to an examination of the forces of history. Years later, he looked up the files of *The New York Times* to learn what else had happened on December 8, 1913, the day of his birth, and reported his findings in a draft of *Genesis*.

President Wilson addressed the suffragettes in the afternoon,
An admiral died, there was trouble at Vera Cruz, the
Trouble of an imperial capitalism, but for the whole world
It was chiefly the wasted turning of another day.

.

"She spoke always of her own life or of the lives of her friends; of what had been; what might have been; of fate, character and accident; and especially of the mystery of the family life, as she had known it and reflected upon it." Thus did Shenandoah Fish characterize the monologues his mother decided as she sat around the kitchen in Delmore's story "America! America!" Like Shenandoah, Delmore in his youth listened with avid attention to the stories his mother—whose garrulity rivaled her son's—related in a querulous, animated voice. The complicated saga of her father-in-law's desertion from the Roumanian Army during the Russo-Turkish War; her parents' courtship in the Old World; her father's death of a heart attack in Kramer's restaurant on Forsyth Street: Delmore possessed a phenomenal memory for every detail of these distant episodes, and rehearsed them over and over in his work, convinced that "each event lies in the heavy head forever" and that he had inherited Rose Schwartz's narrative gifts; "My mother's rhetoric / Has charmed my various tongue," he once noted in his journal. Equipped by temperament and rare powers of recollection to conquer experience, Delmore billed himself as a "Tiberius of Washington Heights."

When he was twenty-six, Delmore made an outline of crucial scenes from his past in preparation for what was to have been a long narrative poem entitled "The Story of a Heart." The earliest images of consciousness, "seeing snow,

sex behind a bungalow garage, father swimming at sea-
shore, eating Idaho baked potato in Father's office": these
were the "events" he remembered from his earliest years.
One seemed especially portentous: the moment when his
symbol-making powers first became apparent. A late fragment of autobiography called "The Birthday, the Metaphor," written when Delmore had begun to cultivate a sort
of willful innocence in his prose, provides the most extensive account of his awakening to poetry.

> When I was three years of age, we lived in a Brook-
> lyn apartment, and the living room was at right angles
> to an avenue on which a street-car shook its jangling
> voyage. Placed often on the window-sill to be amused
> by the street (for how long now, the streets do not
> amuse me), I was particularly enchanted by this yel-
> low and red object, schooner, or caterpillar, moving
> one way and moving back again. It was very beautiful
> to me, it seems. The proof is that one day when a
> friend of my mother's, a lady named Mrs. Salmon,
> who had given me a spoon on my first birthday, came
> to visit us proudly with her son's fiancée, her beautiful
> daughter-in-law to be, I looked long at the young lady
> who was very pretty in a cold and blackhaired way
> and very shy (perhaps I am shy for this reason) and
> then delighted by the plump young baby (who filled
> her with such pleasant thoughts of futurity, perhaps),
> she kissed him, and he said out loud, with a lisp and
> yet with unheard thunder, announcing the whole ac-
> tivity and devotion of his life: STREET-CAR!

In that instant, Delmore recalled in another, still more
hyperbolic version of his epiphany, he "decided to become
a poet."

It was not only Delmore's precocity that made him an
attractive child. With his blond hair, his wide blue eyes,
and the markedly Slavic features so noticeable in some of
his early photographs, he appeared solemn and intense. In
one photograph taken in the company of his mother and
his younger brother, the children's resemblance to their
mother is remarkable; even their clothes, knickers and
baggy trousers that evoke the old country, contribute to
their foreign appearance. Later on, he came to find these

traces of an alien origin exotic, boasting of his "Tartar blood" and claiming to be a Bohemian in the geographical as well as in the literary sense.

Like his friend Robert Lowell, who at nearly the same age had observed, "Unseen and all-seeing," his family's unfolding tragedies, the five-year-old Delmore couldn't help but notice the deepening crisis of his parents' marriage. Harry was, as Delmore described him later, "naturally a very generous man and just as naturally cruel and ruthless when he felt himself injured or thwarted, his will or desire denied or blocked." He loved Delmore, and found it so unbearable to hear him cry that he used to turn on all the lights to console the weeping infant.

In 1916, just prior to the birth of their second child, Kenneth, the Schwartzes moved to a house on President Street in Brooklyn; and it was here, some three years later, that the disaster of their marriage revealed itself in a dramatic scene when they awakened their older son one night and demanded that he choose between them. This conflict of wills loomed over his entire childhood. Harry was always leaving on "business trips" to Florida, or storming from the house in a rage, while Rose invented schemes to lure him home. But when, lonely and full of remorse, he did return, they quarreled interminably while Delmore cowered in another room. Harry could never decide whether he wanted freedom or a family. On his own, living in hotel rooms, he pored grimly over the ledgers of his business, worried about his health, and brooded over his wife's imagined infidelities.

In her loneliness, Rose would torment her older son with lamentations on the sorrows of her existence. "Long-winded, verbal, self-righteous"—as Delmore later characterized his mother—the tireless *raconteuse* knew how to dramatize her grievances; one of Delmore's childhood friends compared her to Lady Macbeth. Early on, Delmore too acquired a flair for the dramatic; once, when his mother left the house in a rage, threatening to consult a lawyer, he ran down the hall and stood before the front door with his arms outspread in a desperate attempt to prevent her departure. But the Schwartz household was so emotionally charged that Delmore's unnatural passions were hardly even noticed; how could his childish sensibility hope to compete with the histrionics of such seasoned actors as his parents?

Nervous and discontented, Harry transferred his family from one apartment to another. From President Street they moved to a house on Ocean Parkway in Brooklyn where, after another tempestuous argument, the reluctant father abandoned his family again. Eventually he agreed to return home, but only on the condition that Rose move to a smaller apartment. Deluded, as always, by vain hopes, and perhaps welcoming still another opportunity to exercise the sense of martyrdom that was so much a part of her temperament, she complied, and Harry found an apartment for them in a grim building on 179th Street in Washington Heights. But as soon as they were settled in, he went back to the hotel where he had been living. From then on, he was home less than ever.

This was in 1921, when Delmore was seven, and the neighborhood they lived in, dominated by uniform blocks of apartment houses dating from the real-estate boom of the 1890's, has changed little since then. "Now Jews have come here most of all," Delmore observed in *Genesis*; "Prosperous, ambitious, concerned that their children / Should live near a park and play / With a 'better class' of children." But for the Schwartzes it was a step downward from the pleasant house on Ocean Parkway, and Delmore later came to look upon his uprooting as the first in a series of disenfranchisements that were to embitter his childhood. From the dark, cramped apartment on the fifth floor, he would gaze down on Broadway for hours, feeling the joylessness of his life.

> . . . he is there
> Upon the windowseat in his tenth year
> Sad separate and desperate all afternoon,
> Alone, with loaded eyes, as he looks down
> Upon the silent winter afternoon
> Silent the street and empty, Sunday's silence,
> Shaded and silent the store fronts under the boxed
>   apartment houses

William Barrett, in his fine memoir of Delmore, has said that a "decline in fortunes" was responsible for the "family migrations" that eventually landed Rose and her two young children in Washington Heights; but this is true only in a sense, for at the time of their separation Harry was, by any standards, a wealthy man. It was Rose alone whose fortunes had fallen, and even her situation was by no means as desperate as she made out, since Harry supported his family generously and without complaint. Rose was always insisting that he didn't provide enough for them to live on, but she still managed to take the children to summer resorts on the New Jersey shore; they spent one summer in Lakewood and another in Belmar, a name that intrigued Delmore for obvious reasons.

At P.S. 69, Delmore "climbed the ego's tower," skipping grades, excelling in geography, and beginning to read with enthusiasm. Even at the age of three, he could delight his father by reading the words on billboards and writing on the blackboard he had been given one Christmas. Proud of his distinction in school, Delmore on occasion exaggerated it for effect. When he prematurely announced his promotion to an advanced class, he was relieved to find "the lie confirmed, encouraging the habit."

Delmore's ambitions and excessive sensitivity provided a striking contrast to his brother Kenneth's even temperament.

> Fabulous, my life is Fabulous, full of
> Family, Nature, Society, and Sex . . .
> My brother, who grew up with me,
> Felt all these powers differently, and moved on
> And went to school, played in the street, made friends
> But never knew my hysteria . . .

he recalled in a notebook poem of the forties. Kenneth, when he was old enough, used to join his brother and the family's West Indian maid, Anna—known as "the Holy Terror" because of her aggressive management of their domestic affairs—outside their parents' bedroom door, where they would listen to the Schwartzes fighting; but he was a placid, uncomplicated child, and regarded the turmoil swirling about him with apparent equanimity.

Delmore struggled with his ambivalent feelings toward Kenneth all his life. More charitable than Proust, who could find no place for his brother in *A la recherche du temps perdu*, Delmore had a persistent habit of turning Kenneth into a girl in the otherwise autobiographical stories he wrote about his childhood. Still, his affection for his brother was intense; one of the earliest versions of *Genesis*,

when it was called "The Error," begins with a fantasy
about his brother's disappearance from the room where
they lie sleeping, and Delmore's frantic search for him in
the streets of New York—a fantasy that may have concealed a guilty wish for his brother to disappear.

In the summer of 1921, the dramatic battle between the
Schwartzes reached another, more desperate stage. One
day, during a period when his parents were separated,
Delmore was taken for a drive out to Long Island with his
mother, his aunt Clara, and some friends of the family. As
they were returning to the city, Rose spotted Harry's car in
the parking lot of a roadhouse café and demanded that her
friends pull over. Against their protests, she dragged Delmore into the dining room, where she found Harry with
another woman. There followed a loud burst of accusations before an audience of horrified patrons and waiters.
Clutching Delmore by the hand, Rose called the other
woman a whore, denounced her husband, and would only
cease her torrent of complaints when Harry, numb with
silent rage, led his small son from the restaurant.

Years later, in a letter to James Laughlin, Delmore announced his intention to end Book One of *Genesis* by
having the chorus "tell the protagonist that the roadhouse
denunciation will have an important effect on his later
life"; and it seems to have been the decisive confrontation
of his parents' marriage as well, for not long afterward,
Harry set about trying to get a divorce. Rose, however, was
adamant; she still held out hope he would return, and for a
long time refused to capitulate. There were endless discussions with lawyers, Rose using the children as bait to win
him back, while Harry raged against her tactics. He once
even offered to buy Delmore outright for $75,000.

In 1923, when Delmore was nine, his father abandoned
their home permanently and went off to live in Chicago,
selling his business to his brother at a loss in order to
escape his wife's harassment. Rose still had no intention of
granting a divorce, and on the rare occasions when Harry
came to New York to visit his sons, she would plead with
him to return home; eventually he resorted to meeting the
boys at his sister's house, or else arranged for them to stay
with him at the Biltmore.

Alone with his mother and younger brother in their
dreary railroad flat, Delmore was forced to contend with

Rose's "harshness, possessiveness, and nervousness," compounded by the frustration she took out on her older son, convinced he was "just like his father." Delmore always thought his mother favored Kenneth, but it was her older son whom she enlisted in the campaigns waged against her husband from afar. Delmore was ashamed of his mother's immigrant ways, "her brazen gaucheness and her lack of understanding of human nature"; her flawed English caused him such embarrassment that he dreaded going out to dinner because of the way she spoke to the waiters. But she knew how to elicit her son's "maudlin pity" by depicting for his benefit her hopeless situation, and would sit home alone, refusing to be placated, her only consolation the belief that she had been wronged by fate. An unpublished chapter of Delmore's famous story "The World Is a Wedding" provides a portrait of his mother, unmistakable despite his having identified her as the protagonist's aunt.

> Aunt Leah brought out the worst in him, she made him say the kind of things that she said, she made him rise to an intensity of accusation and denunciation of which he was ashamed, and which made him feel guilty, for he knew that there had been little in Aunt Leah's life, she had had nothing but frustration and disappointment, she had never had a good time or any satisfaction, and if this was her fault (and Richmond said just how it was her fault when he was angry), nevertheless it was true that she was very miserable and very unhappy and had nothing but an empty life.
>
> Aunt Leah knew that there was this center of pity and remorse in Richmond, and she used it, she appealed to it, and she made it grow, but Richmond's pity and remorse did not keep him from being brutal and violent in what he said to her.

In later life, Delmore attributed his "shyness and awkwardness" to "a mixture of vanity and not being brought up in the midst of a family with much social life." He spent a great deal of time with Rose's family, who lived nearby on Fort Washington Avenue, but they had problems of their own, and were, in any event, far more provincial than Rose herself. Her younger sister, Clara, lived at home with her mother and her brother Irving, who had trouble holding down a job; more often than not, he would squander what money he had on the horses. Only Hannah, Delmore's grandmother, a dignified, proud woman with a fine moral sense, seemed relatively serene. Delmore was devoted to Hannah, and drew an affectionate portrait of her in one of the stories in *The World Is a Wedding*, where she was described as having "an initimate experience of goodness." He called her "Baba" and she, proud of her grandson's scholarly disposition, called him "my professor." Hannah presided over the family's crises, mediating her children's continuous disputes, advising Rose on her dismal marriage, and plotting to find a husband for Clara, a millinery designer who had more or less resigned herself to a life of spinsterhood. (She finally married, some years later, a druggist named Benjamin Colle.)

The member of his family with whom Delmore came to believe he shared the deepest affinity was his uncle Carl, Rose's brother, who had died of rapid pneumonia in 1914, just a few months after his nephew's birth. Studious, quiet, and generally considered the most promising member of the family, Carl had worked hard even as a child, earning money for college by dragging a scale around the city streets for people to weigh themselves on at a modest fee. His death, which occurred just after he had completed his law exams at City College, left the Nathansons desolate. Delmore had no memory of his uncle, but Carl often appeared in his work as a sort of ally resurrected from the dead. Their posthumous bond was further strengthened when Delmore learned that Carl had spoken out against giving him the name that was to burden him all his life.

.

For American Jewish writers of Delmore's generation, Clement Greenberg has observed, literature offered "a means of flight, from the restriction and squalor of the Brooklyns and Bronxes to the wide open world which rewards the successful fugitive with space, importance, and wealth." By the time he was twelve, Delmore had embarked on this quest with precocious intensity, reading periodicals and borrowing books by Sinclair Lewis, O. Henry, and Alexandre Dumas from the public library in Washington Heights. At first, he was restricted to the children's room, but eventually he persuaded his mother to lend him her card so he could explain to the dubious librarian that he was taking books out on her behalf. Every Friday, he withdrew an armload of novels, and on weekends read far into the night, while Kenneth pulled the covers over his head in order to sleep. Rose would come in later to investigate and, after scolding her literary son, lift the blanket to find Kenneth drenched in sweat. She was always complaining that Delmore's reading habits raised their electricity bills. Nor did she approve of what he read; Shakespeare in particular she thought "old-fashioned." And when Delmore brought home a copy of Hart Crane's poem *The Bridge*, she couldn't understand why "such a small book" should have cost three dollars.

Delmore's eager accumulation of knowledge was by no means confined to literature. He had a mania for baseball, that "drama in which the national life performed itself," and acquired over the years a compendious store of statistics on the New York Giants, who rewarded his attentions by winning the pennant every year from 1921 ("My first year as a fan," he once noted) through 1924. The memory of that triumphant era never faded from his mind, and toward the end of his life he was still capable of dazzling an audience by recalling the Giants' lineup and batting averages of some forty years before. In a late notebook, he remembered the excitement that had overwhelmed him in 1927, when "suddenly, in the depths of melancholy, electrifying news transformed my entire attitude toward existence. The Giants had acquired Rogers Hornsby, the greatest hitter by far in the National League, from the St. Louis Cardinals." As a child, he would race to the newsstand on 181st Street for a glance at the standings, and he used to spend hours loitering in a radio store on Broadway to listen to some crucial game. Twenty years later, when Delmore was living at Yaddo, the writers' colony in Saratoga Springs, he stood in a field admiring "the immense winter sky, crowded with the stars in constellations, but desiring all the while to get to the *World-Telegram* and read of the winter baseball news."

The heroic appealed to his grandiose imagination. Like Hershey Green in an early prose draft of *Genesis*, Delmore "began to think of himself as becoming a great athlete, statesman, actor, drama critic, and intellectual"; and he had an opportunity to cultivate these various ambitions during two summers at the Pocono Camp Club in the Pocono Mountains of Pennsylvania. Unlike Camp Rondax in New Jersey, where Delmore and Kenneth spent the summers of 1923 and 1924 living in tents and roughing it, the Pocono Camp Club prided itself on the encouragement of more aesthetic activities; photography, arts and crafts, and theater were serious pursuits in this finishing school for the sons of European immigrants.

Delmore's pleasure in attending summer camp was somewhat dampened by the presence of his mother, who came along out of loneliness and performed menial chores in exchange for room and board. She followed her sons around all day, interfered with their activities, and embarrassed Delmore by her mild flirtations with the staff. It was not surprising that his counselor, a college student named Joseph Lotterman, thought him a "pale flower," introspective and overprotected by his mother; he seemed even then to be "fashioning within himself an inner life," Lotterman recalled—perhaps to escape the formidable shadow of his mother.

Delmore was in every respect the opposite of Herman Hochberg, who lived in the same cabin. Loud, brash, a pure product of the Brooklyn streets, Herman clashed with Delmore from the start, and their counselor soon saw that, without some formal resolution of their differences, there would be no peace all summer. So he decided to get Delmore a pair of boxing gloves and train him secretly to fight. After several weeks of this clandestine preparation, Lotterman arranged a bout to which the entire camp was invited. Despite his trainer's apprehension, Delmore came out fighting, and managed to hold his own. When the bout was halted a few minutes later, with neither party the winner, he was ecstatic.

Delmore's first appearance in print was in *The Poconola* (1926), "Published Fortnightly by the Campers of Pocono Camp Club," a handsome, well-printed journal that was far from amateurish in either format or content. Delmore was listed as an assistant editor, and contributed many of the lead stories. His most exuberant piece was a review of a show he himself had written, called *Pirate's Gold*, a "fearsome story" about "four wicked characters" plotting a treasure hunt.

The third act produced the greatest amount of fun. The discovery is made that the treasure, which is the object of everyone's search, is in the possession of a strange old man (Bert Blumencranz). Both groups find the old man at the same time and both claim the treasure. The honest group insist that they deserve the treasure because they are not pirates. The pirates claim that the others are pirates also, and then both groups agree that they have the necessary qualifications for a taxicab company in New York City.

Thus the play ended, in a gale of laughter and with promise for the suffering inhabitants of New York who are now stranded during the subway strike.

Either because of his accomplishments or because he was himself an editor of *The Poconola*, Delmore received prominent coverage in its pages. A versatile actor, he played a variety of parts, from "a gruesome magician" in the Poconolia Minstralia to the evil Doctor Doo-Nothing in *Pirate's Gold*. Probably the most prescient item in *The Poconola* turned up in Uncle Joe Lotterman's column: "That Socrates has returned to earth is the unshaken belief of Delmore Schwartz. And as proof, he points to himself as the individual in whom the wisdom of the great Athenian has come back again. Delmore is as insistent upon the fact that he is wise as many another is that he is Napoleon."

.

Genesis, a *Bildungsroman* on the grand scale, chronicled every vicissitude of Delmore's education, every development in his "fusing mind," with a comical solemnity. "As the term came towards its conclusion, because the globe turned on its axis and turned about the sun, making the days of man, exhausting the year," he wrote in a characteristic peroration, "Hershey knew he would fail in two subjects, but felt certain of passing the other three." Delmore may well have exaggerated his Hegelian consciousness of "world-feeling" in retrospect, but there is no reason to doubt his self-portrait of an adolescent devoted to meditating on the destinies of great men; his particular heroes were Lindbergh and Edison, who represented "the paradigm of his future success."

Excited by the grandeur of history, Delmore used the commonplace vehicles available in school to emulate a heroic ideal: classroom debates; the John Barrymore Dramatic Club (for which he wrote a play based on the story of Cyrano de Bergerac and supplemented by "ideas he had read about in a book by James Branch Cabell"); and the school paper, to which he submitted various didactic essays. In class, he was impatient and peremptory, traits mitigated by a sort of tactless generosity; once, out of pity for an unmarried teacher approaching middle age, Delmore offered to bring her a phonograph record he had at home called "Wedding Bells (Will They Ever Ring for Me?)."

In his last year of junior high school, Delmore read an article about Spengler in *The Haldemann-Julius Monthly*, and was appalled to learn that he had the misfortune to be living in the autumn of a declining civilization. If this was so, then where did he belong? Consulting the tables in *The Decline of the West*, he noted with consternation that "no one important had lived" after Plato and Goethe. Like Saul Bellow's Moses Herzog, reading Spengler at sixteen and discovering that he lived in an age of "spiritual exhaustion," Delmore cried out against the injustice of circumstance that had landed him in such an unpromising era; "by a naked fiat of will he would with his own life disprove Spengler and escape from the culture-machine of History."

Delmore's visionary fervor was occasionally muted by the suspicion that not all his literary impulses were spontaneous. He confided to his Pocono counselor Joseph Lotterman that he was bored by Shakespeare's plays, and in his autobiographical notes he recalled "trying to make [himself] appreciate *Lord Jim*." Aspiring to be "a sublime, creative boy," he lingered on Riverside Drive observing the melancholy winter landscape "and trying as before to force feeling and seeing." Delmore described these acts of self-imposed consciousness as "megalo" (from the Greek word meaning "large" or "abnormal"), by which he meant that his primary motive in striving to induce them was to win power and attention through the exercise of intellect. He would purchase a volume of Nietzsche "for megalo purposes," or have a "megalo conflict" with a classmate about the merits of H. L. Mencken.

For all his brilliance, Delmore was not a distinguished student, except in those classes where he was able to draw on his wide reading and verbal facility. In his second semester at Townsend Harris High School, a special school for gifted students, he failed three out of five subjects; only a feigned illness confirmed by a sympathetic physician enabled him to withdraw before he flunked out, and the following year he enrolled at the less rigorous George Washington High School. Nor was he enthusiastic about Hebrew School, where he was called upon to "learn by rote from teachers who spoke English certain passages in a dead language." The teacher lacked authority, he complained, and "looked like a shoe salesman." But he did conceive an admiration for the rabbi who came to lecture them on Sundays, and displayed a great gift for the sort of Talmudical argumentation that "could prove or disprove anything."

Many years later, Delmore produced a curiously optimistic portrait of what it had been like to grow up Jewish, "of the lower middle class and in a family of immigrants from Eastern Europe." To be a Jew in those days "was a matter of naïve and innocent pride," he claimed, "untouched by any sense of fear." And since it had provided him with a convenient symbol of alienation, "the fact of Jewishness has been nothing but an ever-growing good to me, a fruitful and inexhaustible inheritance." This retrospective expression of gratitude contradicts his account in *Genesis* of being set upon by a group of boys with a hose, who "suddenly turned it on Hershey, crying, / You are a Jew! You are a Jew!" Whether or not Delmore's own awakening to his Jewish identity was so traumatic, he found the distinction between Jews and non-Jews troubling; when a classmate intimated that the New York Giants were anti-Semitic, he went home and questioned his mother about what it meant to be a Jew. Neither of his parents was in any way religious, and Harry was openly cynical about such matters—"because he thought to be cynical was to be intelligent," Delmore observed; but he wanted his son to have a traditional Jewish education all the same, and so Delmore continued in Hebrew School until his thirteenth birthday, when he was bar mitzvah'd at the Temple of the Covenant on St. Nicholas Avenue in Washington Heights.

Julie Salomon (of the Salomons on whom the Baumann family was modeled in "America! America!") recalled Delmore's confirmation speech as a brilliant " 'philosophical' discourse." Afterward, there was a reception at the

Schwartz apartment, and Delmore stood on a chair to deliver an emotional toast to one whose conspicuous absence cast a shadow over the day: his father. Harry, lavish from afar, had sent a handsome check to cover the reception, but he had not been beside the altar during the crucial moment when Delmore received the blessing of the rabbi and "became a man."

As a child, Delmore conceived an immense admiration for his father; he saw him as a heroic figure who had mastered life by means of a defiant cynicism that protected him from the storm of emotions battering his son. Not that he wasn't aware of his father's vanity, which made him seem at times "a cruel and brutal man"; but even when Delmore himself became cynical about the American dream in later years, he never altered this authoritative image of his father, dressed in expensive Palm Beach suits, black and white shoes, with a Havana cigar in his mouth, "a tall powerful-looking handsome man who looked at others as if he owned the world."

When Rose begrudged him every nickel, Harry was indulgent with Delmore, sending him money and, on one occasion, hundreds of marbles—thus destroying at a stroke his efforts to collect them. Harry was proud of his son's intellectual accomplishments, but troubled by his morbid sensitivity; Delmore never forgot that his father had once referred to him as "a peculiar boy." The draft of a story called "A Remarkable Summer" begins:

> One would hardly expect a young boy to be so difficult.
> He was, it was true, a curious and strange boy, so uneasy and so shy that conversation with him was full of sudden leaps and elaborate excursions.
> He read too much, his father thought, he was withdrawn, he did not play with other boys, he wanted money to buy books—
> He insisted when his father questioned him tactfully that he *liked* to read—he smiled, speaking of his liking as if he had a secret understanding with some higher authority—

And in another uncompleted story, "The Rage of the Second Morning," Delmore depicted a scene on a beach where the handsome, well-dressed father looms over the "shy, withdrawn, unhappy, and nervous son," self-conscious and pale in his bathing suit.

Harry prospered in Chicago, where he became a partner in a firm appropriately called the Klipper Brothers, land developers who owned property near Gary, Indiana. But the more money he made, the more reluctant Rose was to grant him a divorce; not until 1927, four years after their separation, did she give in, and then only—if one is to believe *Genesis*—because Harry lured her into a spurious investment from which he agreed to rescue her on condition that she release him from their marriage. Another story Delmore told with bitter glee was about how his father had once sent a friend from Chicago to seduce his mother with the intention of entrapping her in an adulterous affair, thus establishing grounds for a divorce. It was no wonder that the boy likened his family to a play he had read in school, O'Neill's *Strange Interlude*.

Among the terms of their divorce was the provision that Delmore and Kenneth spend the summers with their father. Accompanied by his chauffeur behind the wheel of a sleek Lincoln, Harry would arrive in June to take his two sons away from the home where He—"it was as if the word were in capitals, and the name of a Demonic Being" —was more than ever the object of his ex-wife's interminable wrath. Dreading the lonely months ahead and vengeful as Medea, Rose would call upon God to destroy the profligate Harry Schwartz, while the two boys basked in anticipation of a luxurious summer in Chicago.

It was on the first of these journeys that Delmore discovered his father had remarried; Harry had arranged to meet his new wife in Albany so he would have time to break the news to the boys. From there they drove to Buffalo, and took a ferry across Lake Erie to Detroit, dining in an elegant salon on board where they were served "by white-coated Negroes, just as in Pullman dining cars." Harry bought some dice and they spent the evening gambling, while Delmore "thought of all the books he might buy with the money he was winning."

Harry lived in the Shoreland, a fancy residential hotel that still stands, overlooking Lake Shore Drive in Hyde Park. On weekends he would buy the boys clothes and sporting equipment from Marshall Field or take them to the best restaurants; his favorite was the Villa Venice in

Des Plaines. During the week, the chauffeur would accompany Delmore and Kenneth to Wrigley Field, where Harry always reserved a box. In the summer of 1929, Delmore arrived to find a brand-new white Chrysler Imperial with a rumble seat awaiting him. The chauffeur tried to teach him how to drive, but the very first time out he smashed into a truck while practicing on a side street. Since he was only fifteen, too young to obtain a driver's license, Delmore had to leave the car in Chicago when he returned to New York that autumn.

When Rose learned of Harry's marriage, she was furious. Frantic letters to Delmore followed: Who was this woman? Did Harry make more money than he admitted? Harry disapproved of the detailed bulletins his son—"mere violin of [his] mother's sick emotions"—wrote home, but was even more alarmed when Delmore, remorseful over having been found out, offered to spend the whole year in Chicago. The practical father found his literary son bewildering, and was impatient with Delmore's ideas. Poring over Spengler, Delmore explained that the West was dying; a ridiculous notion, retorted his father. "Things are getting better all the time!"

Despite their differences, Harry took pride in his son's accomplishments, boasting to his relatives that Delmore was "beyond his years." His letters were brief and awkward, but he never failed to express pleasure in the poems Delmore sent him. During the winter of 1930 he wrote from Miami Beach:

> Dear Delmore
> Just a line to acknowledge your letter and the enclosed. I enjoyed reading the poem immensely. I think its very good. I wish I could do it—and very happy you and Kenny are having a lot of fun playing Pool. It's not only fun, but good exercise.
> Please write me whenever you get a chance for I always enjoy getting mail from you.
> > Love to you both and Kenny
> > > Dad

In keeping with his exalted mythologizing of experience and history, Delmore had one great love in childhood, a girl named Rhoda who became a prominent feature of his

childhood recollections. Having first observed her in class
and at synagogue, Delmore finally approached her during
recess with an offer of chocolate; there ensued a passionate
courtship through the years of grammar school, and when
Delmore transferred from P.S. 69 to P.S. 115 as a result of
one of his family's innumerable moves, he felt crushed by
the prospect of separation. Later on, when he attended
George Washington High School, Delmore discovered that
Rhoda was enrolled there too, and told of waiting for her
after school, "posed like the Romantic, pale and miserable,
with a faintness like Dante's." This infatuation continued
until 1929, when he registered that his interest in her was
"fading" (though he also noted "still trying to get in R's
class"); but he seems to have regarded Rhoda as an image
of ideal early love, for he spoke of her to friends in college,
and wrote about her by name a decade later in the sequence of poems called "The Repetitive Heart" from his
first volume, *In Dreams Begin Responsibilities*. And as late
as 1942, when Delmore was twenty-eight, he tried to find
her address so that he could send her a copy of his book.

What was perhaps most significant in Delmore's account
of this "affair" was the literary characterization he gave it.
The "Romantic" pose, the self-conscious emulation of a
literary past: this was Delmore's model, as he noted in
Genesis:

> An ill-bred boy, bred as we have said before
> By the romantic ego, playing Timon, Hamlet,
> Byron, O the romantic day, after
> The French Revolution burned, when men
> Of sensibility, no longer held
> By their society at heart, ran off,
> Ran off to nature or themselves, their own
> Emotions, lakes and despair, seeking
> A dignity and mystery in Life,
> A sense of being which no longer ruled . . .

The notion of becoming a poet had been with him since he
was twelve, when he submitted his first poems (none of
which appear to have survived) to *The Nation* and *The
American Mercury*. Everyone in the neighborhood knew of
his ambition, and if there was any doubt, he would show

around a politely encouraging letter of rejection from H. L. Mencken.

It was obvious to some of his teachers that Delmore was a brilliant boy, and in particular to Mary J. J. Wrinn, "an Irish, red-faced woman with a terrible temper," as a classmate of Delmore's remembered her, who conducted the school's poetry club and would often argue with Delmore over his poems, which he was reluctant to revise. But she encouraged him in his writing, and was aware of his advanced knowledge of contemporary poetry. T. S. Eliot, who later became a terrible obsession of Delmore's, was on his mind even then. One afternoon he insisted on reading aloud, over the vociferous protests of the class, the whole of "Prufrock," a performance which made the editors of the high school yearbook observe that "T. S. Eliot is God, and Delmore Schwartz is his prophet."

A selection of Delmore's earliest poems can be found in *The Poet's Pack of George Washington High School*, a voluminous hardcover anthology of poems by "members of the Poetry Club and the Poetry Class 1927–1931." Of Delmore's four contributions, a sonnet entitled "The Saxophone" reveals that he had been reading Hart Crane; another, "Automobile," was more original in tone, exhibiting a fine dramatic intensity in measured quatrains. But none of them was equal to a still earlier poem, never published, that survives among his papers. Dated Anno Domini 1928, "New Year's Eve" displays a lavish imagination and the confused rhetoric endemic to fourteen-year-old poets; the poem is a loose "imitation" of Gérard de Nerval's *El Desdichado*.

> I am the eager and the unconsoled;
> The prodigal one from the home banished;
> My only star was hope, that star was bold,
> Was quick, and is dead; the green hope vanished!
>
> Am I Thought or Self, Blake or Rimbaud?
> The flower that stilled my questing eyes
> Was a part of sleep, and must suddenly go
> From me, Go, with thought's sunrise.
>
> In the immense night you that caressed
> The desolate brain with ariel snow,
> And the dry lips from the luminous breast

Give me the Dream for Real, and I'll go
And break with Time, and beyond arrest
Visit the tall countries that the holy know.

And outside the snow rests lightly
On the hard city, and the lean thin mountains
Stand up,—as if forever, with no indecision
And three o'clock, and still no vision,
And the street is unnatural with that moonlight
Fallen, or the stars' fall and congregation
And Sun, no sun but blond confusion

And soon will light translate the world to morning,
And I can build no morning of my world.

Delmore had set about mastering the principles of versification with remarkable diligence, and could now employ
them whether he had a theme in mind or not. The poetic
voice he was cultivating had already begun to sound like
that of a faintly weary, overly refined Modernist grandly
echoing the whole tradition of English poetry while striving
toward colloquialism.

Delmore's ambitiousness was by no means confined to
the life of the mind; he was competitive in everything he
did, and threw himself into sports with the same fierce
intensity that he brought to his literary activities, playing
tennis and baseball with a nervous energy that overcame
his physical awkwardness. He believed he had inherited his
father's nervous system, and it was true that, like Harry, he
was impatient and ill-tempered. One summer afternoon,
when he had come out onto the fire escape of their apartment on West 174th Street to smoke a cigarette, Jesse
Wallerstein, a boy who lived in their building, spotted him
from the street and called him a show-off; this innocent
remark prompted Delmore to rush down three flights and
flatten him with a single punch.

His autocratic manner in sports alienated the boys in the
neighborhood, but Delmore did have one close friend in
Julian Sawyer, a strange, haunted figure—"like someone in
the Inferno," a friend recalled, "tearing out his sinful self."
Sawyer was a devotee of Gertrude Stein, and when she
arrived in New York in 1934 he met her and fell to his
knees on the pier. Later he had a fanatical passion for the

theater, and could quote the whole of any Garbo script at will; his favorite pastime was to invite a few friends over and perform for them Gertrude Stein's opera *Four Saints in Three Acts* or T. S. Eliot's play *The Cocktail Party*, himself playing all the parts. Julian was openly homosexual, and pathetic in his adoration of Delmore, who treated him with a faint contempt.

Apart from Julian, Delmore found no one sympathetic to his interests and ideas. When he sat around the house, idle and bored, his mother would advise him, "Go knock your head against the wall." And when he went out, she would send him off with the sinister refrain "May you come home in your coffin" (a phrase that had reverberations in *Genesis*, where Hershey Green is told: "You lie in the coffin of your character!"). Embarrassed by her reproaches that he had no friends, he would inform her that he was on his way to a party and go off to the movies by himself. Thus began an addictive passion that he struggled against all his life. Fascinated by the "unself-consciousness" of Spencer Tracy and the solemn, orotund narration of the newsreel voice-over—which he compared to the Oracle at Delphi—Delmore found the orderly resolution of plot in movies consoling, for it assured him that life could be more comprehensible than his own experience. The cinema promised "appeasement of unrealized desires"; but it also provoked a sort of dread, and when he emerged from "the ghostly evening of the theater," it was only to find himself restored to the reality of an existence that offered few pleasures.

.

Harry Schwartz had a heart condition, and was always trying to prepare his sons for his death. Delmore could be assured of inheriting a hundred thousand dollars when he came of age, Harry would say, but that didn't mean he would never have to work for a living. Then, in October 1929, the stock market plummeted, and Harry arrived in New York with his chauffeur to see what could be salvaged of his fortune. Delmore and Kenneth went down to the Hotel Commodore to visit him, and he took them to a Broadway show—*Whoopee*, starring Eddie Cantor. The evening ended with a scene Delmore described in many versions of *Genesis*.

They were on Forty-Second Street right near Times Square. The white lights of Broadway shone down on them. The after-theatre traffic was full of blaring. It began to rain very hard as Jack Green said goodbye to Hershey and Roger through the open window of the cab while the cabdriver looked impatiently back at them. Hurriedly Jack Green asked Hershey if he wanted to go on a yacht trip through the Great Lakes next summer while Roger went to camp. Hershey said to his father that he had better get out of the rain which had begun to stream down his face. Jack Green brushed his face against Hershey's in a kind of kiss, an act which always embarrassed Hershey. The wetness and the sandpaper feel of his father's cheek remained with Hershey the rest of his life because Jack Green died before Hershey saw him again.

One Saturday morning the following June, Delmore was sitting home reading the baseball statistics when the phone rang; the moment his mother began to scream he knew his father had died. He was curiously unable to feel grief and, amid all the chaos and funeral arrangements, "permitted himself to wonder how the Giants were making out."

After the funeral, Delmore went forward reluctantly and peered into the coffin; overwhelmed by the fear of death that had haunted him through childhood, he stared down at his father, expecting to see the vigorous man of forty-nine he had last glimpsed six months before. But what he looked upon was "a fixed smile that seemed to him the most horrifying thing he had ever seen." At the cemetery, the rabbi recited a passage from Ecclesiastes:

> Or ever the silver cord be loosed, or the golden bowl be broken, or the pitcher be broken at the fountain, or the wheel broken at the cistern,
> Then shall the dust return to the earth as it was: and the spirit shall return unto God who gave it.
> Vanity of vanities, saith the preacher; all *is vanity*,

and they drove home to Washington Heights through a sudden summer rain.

2

—•—

THE APPARENT INDIFFERENCE to his father's death Delmore reported in a prose version of *Genesis* was belied by the crucial importance he gave it in a number of versified accounts. In the blank-verse journal he kept during the 1940's, he recalled how "the Depression came to strip the heir / Of hopes he had not chosen with his heart"; and in a verse passage of *Genesis*, he cried out with typical portentousness:

> you too,
> O New York boy,
> Fell with the market that October day,
> In new America in 1929!

When he did express sorrow over his father's death, it was invariably in terms of the disastrous event that occurred a few days later, when the executor Harry had appointed in his will arrived in New York with Delmore's car and some terrible news: the estate had turned out to be virtually worthless.

Delmore's claim—reiterated throughout his life—that his father had been a millionaire was no exaggeration; as a member of Homebuilder's Real Estate in Chicago, and the owner of a subdivision near Gary, Harry Schwartz did have a million dollars, at least on paper. But he had been hit hard by the Crash, and his fortune at the time of his death had dwindled to less than half of what it had been only a few months before. Even so, Delmore would have inherited a few thousand dollars, if not the considerable legacy his father had promised him, had it not been for the executor's dishonest dealings. When he showed up in New York, vague about what had happened and apparently drunk, the family became suspicious; and not long afterward they discovered that he was continuing to speculate with Harry's money without the consent of the Chicago Title and Trust Company officers, who controlled the estate. Once they learned of these practices, the bank forced him to resign on threat of prosecution, and Louis Earlix, a friend and business partner of Harry's, was appointed to supervise the estate. Earlix promptly tried to recover what was left, but a great deal of money had already been dissipated in taxes and real-estate claims. To make matters worse, Harry's attorney, who could perhaps have intervened, suffered a stroke three weeks after his client's death. Rose Schwartz, convinced that everyone connected with the estate was dishonest, went out to Chicago to investigate, but returned disappointed; whatever money remained was destined to be tied up indefinitely pending the settlement of various claims.

For many years Delmore continued to hope that he would eventually receive his legacy; as late as 1946, he was still corresponding with the Chicago Title and Trust Company and asking William Phillips, one of the editors of *Partisan Review*, to send him the ledgers of his father's business from the office where he had stored them. Over the years, he did inherit a few thousand dollars from time to time; but the fortune he had counted on was never to be his. It was a typical American story, he would tell his friends; if only he had been rich! Money would have spared him innumerable social humiliations; it would have changed his life. But the heir had been deposed by the vicissitudes of capitalism; the summers in Chicago, the chauffeur, the ten-dollar bill awaiting him on the breakfast table every morning were relagated to memory, and Delmore found himself imprisoned forever in the striving, anxious middle class.

In the many prose and verse drafts of *Genesis*, and in his autobiographical fiction, Delmore generally dwelled on the details of his vanished inheritance or the fanatical interest in baseball that distracted him from mourning during the summer following his father's death; but that terrible event found its way obliquely into the poems and parables he was writing in the early 1930's. "The Brother Poem," one of the many precursors to *Genesis*, contains the most explicit image of his grief.

Upon the blackboard of my pillowed eyes
I saw a circle drawn in thick white chalk,
And this was a hole and in this hole, deep down,
I saw my father lying in his coffin, and I
Felt nothing. Then I saw,
That this was no funeral chapel, but a morgue,
For floored there lay pale snow, or colder marble,
And then I saw that this was nothing. Then I knew
That I was in a hold, a coffin and a morgue
And nothing.

This resonant evocation of "nothing" expresses with grim concision the sorrow Delmore felt over his father's death. It was as if the only image of stability he knew had been wiped out, never to be recovered. Delmore had reposed such faith in his father that life without him seemed unimaginable, barren of love or certainty. It had been his father who encouraged him, who took pride in his accomplishments; and it had been his father who promised to liberate Delmore from the prison of Washington Heights. But Delmore could never bring himself to speak of his father's death in these terms, preferring to devise elaborate epistemological fables about abandonment and loss. *Having Snow*, a project conceived not long after his father's death, and which survives among his papers only in the form of notes, was to have treated the evanescent nature of experience; snow represented "the culmination of the year, the discovery of death," and thus could be made a convenient emblem of transience. And in "Domine Deus," still another variation on the motif of loss, Delmore envisioned coming home to find an ambulance parked in the street,

            its bell ringing and ringing,
    Like all the gongs of hell, and from that white
    Ambulance, my God! was carried, O Father!
    My only brother next to whom, sleeping
    And waking, my heart beat nineteen years, and he
    Was killed . . .

But the most intense—and direct—expression of grief occurs in a passage of *Genesis* when it was written as a novel, in a stammering ecclesiastical utterance of great rhetorical power; the moment Hershey Green learned "he was not a rich man's son" after all,

> everything in his life seemed to have vanished at one stroke, it was then that Hershey's whole being arose in one vast flood of eloquence and he began to utter or write, who knows which, the great work which would make him the Lindbergh, Moses, Siegfried, Odysseus, of America. It was then that he began to say everything which he thought was to be the foundation of the true state, the endless culture, the utter and everlasting world-feeling which was to characterize the civilization of mankind from that day to the end of eternity.
>
> This is what God said to him, this is how God saw him on that night in June 1930, when his work was finished. This is what he said to God and what God replied to him and how he heard God and how God saw and said.
>
> This is what Hershey explained and what God replied. This is what God explained and how Hershey felt, hearing. In the darkness, in the emotion of irreparable guilt and remorse, in the hysterical fear which brought about a total recall of memory, this is what Hershey said, trying to redeem himself.

Like Hershey, Delmore vowed to recover through poetry what he had lost through fate, and set about fashioning a brilliant future for himself.

.

Eager to escape from the constrictions of life at home, Delmore applied to several out-of-state colleges in the spring of 1931, but was turned down everywhere because of his erratic record. His average was only 75—equivalent to a C—but he had received honors grades in English, and his philosophy teacher, a Mr. Chapin, convinced his pupil was a genius, recommended him for the college-preparatory course at Columbia University. Delmore had acquired enough credits to graduate in mid-year, and that spring he enrolled at Columbia in four courses: French, mathematics, English, and philosophy. Early in the summer, he was admitted to the University of Wisconsin, and one day in the autumn of 1931 he went off in a cab with Rose and

Kenneth to Grand Central Station and boarded a train for the Midwest. "It was a true departure," he wrote of a young man on the way to college in one of the many unpublished novels about his youth, "for he departed with the hope and the illusion with which he went to each new place, the hope that he would please himself, and the illusion that everything in the new place would be new and different from what had been."

Wisconsin in the early 1930's was congenial to his dreams. "The aroma of Bohemianism" pervaded the campus, recalled one of Delmore's classmates in a memoir of those years. "Except for the gray mass of average students, 1931 was a year of vast experimentation, in which the experiences of the hip-flask decade were condensed into nine months." The Experimental College presided over by Alexander Meiklejohn, an administrator known for his progressive views, had provoked considerable controversy; William Ellery Leonard, a flamboyant poet and "apostle of freedom," whose flowing gray hair and black Windsor tie were symbols of a defiant spirit, was famous all over the country; and the Wisconsin legislature had become concerned enough about the university's libertarian ambience to start an investigation attended by a great deal of national publicity. No one was more eager than Delmore to participate in that atmosphere of "free love and bolshevism."

On arrival in Madison, he moved into Adams Hall on the pleasant campus, with its lakes and pines and rolling hills, and sat down to write the first of a series of long, extraordinary letters to his friend Julian Sawyer. From then on, he dispatched his brilliant, pompous, impassioned thoughts to Julian at the rate of two or three letters a week, chronicling his wide reading, transcribing passages from Baudelaire, Stendhal, a book in German on the Upanishads, and offering his own translations. The stunning arrogance with which he corrected Sawyer's grammar and lectured on literature appears to haved intimidated his correspondent (Sawyer's replies have not survived); but his hectoring tone concealed a nature as solicitous as it was dictatorial. From the start, it was obviously Delmore who was in charge, as he demonstrated in his first letter.

> I do not wish you to write any unconscious or conscious attempts at literature. The purpose of our

correspondence should be to keep burning the "home fires" of the relationship, (the bridge?) (the electrical current?) between us—not "apart from the night air and the traffic, and the jazz of the megapolitan world: taxis . . ." or "how beautifully stars shine in the forehead of each Wisconsin dusk"; O, no.

Once their mode of discourse had been established, he went on to describe his first weeks at Wisconsin.

I am very happy here. Does that interest you? Adams Hall, where I live, is an imitation of an Oxford college. It is divided into houses. Each house lives unto itself—in a particular section, has a special living room with a victrola, card-tables, magazines (the Nation and the New Republic!), a special dining table in the refectory, and is, in a real sense, a distinct and conscious group. There is, to make lists:

A young man of Boston who was present when Gershwin composed the 2nd part of the Rhapsody.

A young man who can discuss Aristotle and Kant intelligently; (my dear friend).

A subscriber to the Criterion.

Three Russian Communists, very passionate, in America to study civil engineering.

A Gentleman and a Musician who can play Bach on the 'cello, has victrola records of Mozart, Brahms, Haydn.

A concert violinist (quite theatrical).

Three versifiers, entirely stupid. But no one who has read Carlos Williams.

The library is a dream, has files of the Criterion, Dial, Bookman,—fourteen volumes of Pascal, and Pound, Eliot, H. Crane, Kenneth Burke even.

Madison is physically very beautiful: my room looks out on the lake, and many small birds, some red, some blue, waken me, as soon as light—, the woods full of fresh-water brooks, springs and creeks, deer, too, and rabbits, squirrels. And the long quiet streets, tree-lined (tall trees!), New England white houses,

The imitation of German beer gardens, (where everyone sings, and drinks),

The "quad": the internal lawn, park, of Adams Hall, where arguments are intense, sometimes reaching physical violence,

The whole provincial collegiate world.

But, best of all, most responsible for my emotion of happiness there is the sympathy, and friendliness of my reception, acceptance. For unconsciously, against my desire, an intellectual group is around me, looks toward me. Which is pleasing, and embarrassing, most of the boys being five and 7 yrs older than I am, Protestant, Catholic,—but I pose the questions, am the authority, and the kind of influence (through speech, I mean) that I do not want to be: everyone (the nine or ten) is reading Spinoza. I purpose a cleavage, that I may entirely devote myself to the clouds (such forms, I mean), Georgia O'Keeffe, the Picasso black storms, and the Wordsworthian lake, and walks. (Such is the pomposity of my soul.)

This sanguine appraisal of his popularity was belied by a note of loneliness in his correspondence, which he tried to dispel by binding Julian even closer to him. All his life, Delmore entangled his friends in relationships laden with unnatural ardor. He had a way of demanding their unqualified allegiance and then turning that allegiance into a powerful weapon with which to dominate their lives. His attachments were at times hysterical in their intensity; they resembled love affairs more than friendships. It was as if his immense need for solace and affection could express itself less guardedly with men than with women, since friendship circumscribed the limits of intimacy. Delmore belittled Julian's homosexuality, but he exploited it as well, and knew how to elicit his friend's erotic love without having to reciprocate it. Still, he invested a strange passion in their correspondence, praising Julian's "strong young mind purely moving AGAINST the world," addressing him as "my jewel, my plague," and celebrating the high purpose of their letters: "to keep clear fires burning, pile more wood on." Delmore's intention was not to be therapeutic—he was "too sick [himself] to be doctor yet"—but "to give you, as you demand I am very sure, a box-seat to the evening and morning of that which I see." To this end, his task was to write "major prose letters," not mere journalism.

Delmore was so elated by the high tone of their correspondence that he took to reading it aloud at Paratore's, a speakeasy he frequented. "You are becoming a valuable myth in my postures before the intellectuals," he advised his friend. But he continued to warn him against lyrical flights, offering the structure that "words are not used because they look nice, or sound good; they are used because they represent, with approximate exactitude, things that exist." And it was important for Julian not to praise him too much: "I am not a mechanism, nor a mould, nor a design, nor a carved effigy. My nostalgia is for heaven, which you know nothing about." Nor should Julian be too dependent on his friend's affections.

And if I really mean as much to you, as your vague, excited music suggests, I desire to destroy that excessive meaning. I am a very important person, but, quoting myself, I am not one of "the things that count." I am sinful in many ways—false, greedy, selfish—is it necessary to make some more lists? "All happiness or unhappiness solely depends upon the quality of the object to which we are attached by love." (Spinoza) Until "I die and go to Heaven," I will be a temporal and finite creature. The things that count are:
                as you say, the bridge, books, mornings, music —they have graduated to another state of being. I am a dealer in the things that count. Or, more accurately, I am the one dealer in the one thing that counts. But I always cause those who are near me more suffering than pleasure. I am an evil being.

This astonishing display of self-love mingled with self-hatred was typical of Delmore; the portentous, dictatorial voice would abruptly give way to self-indictments of a theological cast, in which he revealed that he was "damned." It was a conviction that both exalted and alarmed him. Writing these letters late at night and into the dawn (he liked to inform Julian of the exact hour of their composition), he described moods of excitement that turned to dread and a premonition of death: "You do not know what it is to fear that if the excitement in your mind, and mouth increases, you will become convulsive, very sick, and your body will die with an explosion."

He read *La Chartreuse de Parme* and decided he was the doomed Fabrice; translating a passage for Julian, he replaced the name of Stendhal's protagonist with his own, and was moved to write a poem about the novel.

I've drunk all night at the springs—
Whose taste is coolness—
Of Henri Beyle, and the slippery things
In the running currents were emotions:
Both fish and intellectual things!
Black print to hastening water?
See how I'm paid for my devotions;
A sweet change, and cheaply bought:
All night the fleeing fish were caught
Merely by bending over the water.
Love, Hate, Lust, Ambition seen!
Chill in my fingers, good to touch!
Sense is disordered by keen pleasure,
Apartness—for Art is such,
The hurting turn—is good to touch;
Is great, not mean.

In this poem, as in the letters, self-pity was tempered by a certain irony, the recognition that anguish was not the only component of poetry. His tears, he wrote Julian, were "intellectual tears," and he could be satirical about his obsessions, as when he explained that he liked apples "because the snow-white meat and ruddy cover" appealed to his intellect: "a metaphysical appetite, for I do not care for their taste." All the same, he hoped "to become in time someone very grand, and is sure he is someone very important still unflowered."

Delmore treated spiritual questions with a peculiar gravity in these letters. Once, he reported an hallucinatory visitation by Rimbaud in the middle of the night ("Rimbaud was here. He spoke to me of the magic study of happiness"), and on another occasion he complained, in a strange gloss on the Depression: "If the Christian religion were not sick in the minds of Americans, the greed and selfishness which creates hunger and unemployment would not be born. By changing the love of self to a love of God, such things will be destroyed." Announcing his farewell to the temporal world, the freshman mystic proclaimed: "I shall devote myself to vision alone."

Delmore at seventeen was a self-styled member of the avant-garde; he read *Hound & Horn*, studied Pound's *Cantos* as they appeared, and collected first editions of everything T. S. Eliot wrote. *transition* was especially important to him now that excerpts of *Finnegans Wake* were appearing in its pages, and he pored over each new installment with Talmudic zeal. For the rest of his life, Joyce was to be his literary hero, *Finnegans Wake* a work he read and annotated with such intensity that his copies would fall apart; he went through several in his lifetime. That year at Wisconsin he managed to obtain a finely bound pamphlet issued by Faber & Faber of "Haveth Childers Everywhere," an early chapter of *Finnegans Wake* when it was still called *Work in Progress*. He had also acquired the habit of transcribing by hand long passages of works that were significant to him, a practice that would continue through the very last days of his life. At Wisconsin, it was Pasternak's memoir, *Safe Conduct*.

Despite his shy and reclusive nature, Delmore was given to advertising the brilliant future in store for him. Transporting his poems around the campus in a satchel, he would announce to his classmates that the manuscripts he brandished before them were destined to earn his reputation as a great American poet. (Years later, he noted in a journal: "I have written the greatest poem in the English language! That is the way I used to speak when I was eighteen.") He could talk for hours about literature and philosophy, drawing upon an extraordinary store of information; but he had less taste for discussion than for monologue, a preference which soon wearied others.

The Arden Society, a poetry club conducted by the semanticist S. I. Hayakawa—at the time an instructor there in English—was apparently not impressed either with Delmore or with the poems he read to an audience of demure girls and earnest young men. He had been too shy to read at all on his first visit to the club—and with reason, for when he finally got up the nerve, an ominous silence followed his performance. Delmore began to explain that his work had to be read as well as heard; the subtler word associations could not be understood without studying the poems. One girl protested that poetry was meant to be read aloud. Delmore retorted that Hopkins was an exception; his poems were impossible to recite. Afterward, a friend kindly interpreted the silence and incomprehension of the others to mean that Delmore had "overawed" them. But Delmore himself felt (and he was probably closer to the truth) that he had perplexed his audience and made a poor impression.

Armed with a retrospective self-awareness, Delmore once began a novel about Wisconsin in which he described his "towering ambition" with a fine irony. He would sit in his room and not answer the door when friends knocked, in order to "impress the boys with his habit of solitude and concentration of study." If he was temperamental, it was "because of the great work in which he was involved." And yet his pride, as he well knew, was the result of "a recurrent suspicion that he was of an inferior station in life." (It must have been this suspicion that prompted him to claim on his college application form that his father's nationality was American, despite the unambiguous direction, "i.e. country in which he was born.") Moments of sublime inspiration, when he would drink Chianti in the speakeasies and hold forth eloquently to college girls, alternated with moments of despair, when the sense of "ecstasy and a new feeling for words" simply vanished. In those unhappy moods when he was "trying to feel," Delmore wondered if he had some deficiency of intellect or sensibility. But it was only that he tried too hard, and prematurely willed himself to acquire a sophistication beyond his years.

To Julian, he admitted the fraudulence of this worldly pose.

> . . . yr. friend becomes a bigger and better bluff all the time. Goes around like romantical (German 1800 style) genius, shows not his great poems (Having Snow, A Story of Light) or his great books (A Book For The Air, Life a True Poem, I Saw Eternity or Love in The Gentle Heart) but writes specially mysterious rhetoric t' impress young aesthetes of great institutions of learning.

And yet his ostentatious routines, embellished as they were by genuine accomplishments, impressed the faculty. Several English teachers, he reported to Julian, had asked him "to explain modern poetry to them" and invited him to dinner. His freshman English instructor had told him, "You don't belong here," and put him to studying Shakespeare on his own. He read aloud *The Waste Land* to "the congregation of the amazed," and held forth on Milton or Constant's *Adolphe* to the little band of auditors whom he thought of as "adolescents of the spirit."

In the role of Socrates, for which he had been known at the Pocono Camp Club, Delmore drew up a program of conduct and study which he disseminated among his friends.

1. To read a page of the dictionary every day.
2. To read a chapter in "Logic" (Aristotle) every day.
3. To tell no lies.
4. To use words as translations of reality, not as cheap band music.
5. To read a poem by Blake, Dickinson, Dante, Milton, every day (choosing one).
6. To read Spinoza for a half hour every day, look at Cézanne, Daumier, Rembrandt (choosing one).
7. To spend an hour writing one sentence with the goal: approximate perfection of precision.
8. To see no moving pictures, read no cheap books, listen to no catgut music at all.
9. To listen to Bach every day.
10. To be pure of insincerity, laziness, anger, procrastination, discourtesy, inconsideration, affectation, misunderstanding, absentmindedness, temporal desire, worry over time, vanity, sensitivity, dignity, loud speech, insulting commentary, irony, arrogance, pomposity, luxuriousness, sublimation, misapprehension, uncleanliness, bizarre dress, consideration of money, jealousy, hero-worship,—and thusward;
11. To accept the actions as transitory motions, to be re-expressed each day, to be known as indications, not consummations, not inflexible determinations—only implying suggestions.

> Summum of Sermons,
> Exhortations of D. Schwartz
> Sept. 21—Oct. 16, 1931

In his view, such exhortations were more than welcome; "God's truth, the young gentles, my colleagues, lap it up like milk and honey," he exulted to Julian. (Later on, he would lament that he was "a liar, pretender, cheat, lecher, sot, and a little tin Jesus to some unfortunate people who know him.")

Erratic as a student, Delmore drew on his arrogance and a fund of intuitive knowledge to get by. Once, in a notable show of bravado, he refused to answer an exam question on Stephen Vincent Benét because, as he wrote Julian, "I could not permit my mind to be profaned by such intellectual whorishness." So he wrote on Valéry instead, "making fifteen quotations in French" (which his instructor couldn't read, he added), and was given a C. Delmore appealed to another instructor: "So everyone spent three hours discussing Paul Valéry, and then adjourned to the Registrar's office where the mark was changed with much mock ceremony."

By January, Delmore was writing to Julian that he had made himself "unbearable" to everyone; "to know you is a calamity," one of his classmates had remarked. In a charitable mood, he confessed: "My gift for causing pain, my capacity for derogation and disparagement gives me much sadness." But this "orgy of insult" was all for the better, he claimed. "For it is necessary to surrender to that which is greater, and to resist that which is inferior. Resistance is not absolute denial, but the imposition of a controlling order."

·

Studying in his room late one Saturday night, Delmore heard a loud, drunken voice reciting Hart Crane's poem "The Wine Menagerie" from the steps of the library. "Invariably, when wine redeems the sight," the speaker began, and Delmore was so intrigued that he descended to the lawn in his pajamas and followed the anonymous declaimer to his room, where he knocked timidly, walked in, and finished the recitation. This other devotee of Crane turned out to be Maurice Zolotow, in later life the biographer of John Wayne and Marilyn Monroe. In those days, he was—in Delmore's words—a "voluble and dogmatic" Marxist given to rhapsodizing about the virtues of life in the Soviet Union. Delmore, preoccupied with New Edens

and True Republics, believed that "the new age ought to
come from above, from the ideas of intellectuals, from
some Moses who brought down the truth from Sinai."

Through Zolotow, Delmore made the acquaintance of a
circle of young men, mostly from New York, who regarded themselves as intellectuals and talked loudly about
books and politics in the dining hall, to the annoyance of
the more parochial Midwestern students. Among them was
a student by the name of Eugene Loveman, whom Delmore described as "a big tall boy with enormous ears and
an enormous head, who rejoiced at being in the university
as no one else did." Loveman was even more of a romantic
than Delmore, and spoke solemnly of their "Studentjahre,"
comparing Wisconsin to Heidelberg as they sat in the
Rathskeller on campus drinking beer. His enthusiasm was
inclusive enough for him to proclaim warmly that all his
friends were geniuses; Zolotow was a dramatic character,
Delmore a better poet than Swinburne, and Loveman himself so quick-witted that he vowed to master Sanskrit in a
month.

But Delmore soon quarreled with his new friends. It was
not enough that he emerged victorious from a rivalry with
Loveman over a girl named Fola; he had to dwell in public
on the details of his triumph, gathering his neighbors in the
dorm around to hear how Loveman had told Fola his
father was an important politician when he was only a
laundry-truck driver. And when a boy whom Delmore referred to as "a Bohunk from Chicago" had the temerity to
play the radio late one night while Delmore was in an
ecstasy of composition, he burst into a tirade of insults,
raging against the philistines ignorant of the realm of imagination in which he traveled.

Very soon I will have to stop hitting people [he
wrote Julian]. Already I have two knockouts to
repent—once because when a young lady called me,
she was told that I was up on the fourth floor, drunk.
I was up on the fourth floor, drinking, not drunk.
I am never drunk. Another time I became unexpectedly
savage because I was writing, and my dear friends
came to the door, and kept on knocking. After a while
I awoke to their world—but I did not want to let them
in. They knew I was in the room—from looking

through the keyhole! Finally I opened the door and started to hit everyone.

What he felt was not exactly remorse; in fact, he seemed pleased by what he had done: "Knocking a person out cold results in a delicious sensation of strength. . . . My pugilism is concrete. I've become the Real Thing now." Surely, though, his interpretation of the effect his outbursts had on others could not have been accurate: "I've antagonized no one, but impressed everyone very much."

Delmore had not done well academically in his first year of college. Just as in high school, he found it difficult to concentrate on his subjects, preferring to acquire a literary education on his own. Every evening, he had to struggle with his conscience about whether to study or go to the movies. More often than not, he would resolve to stay in his room; then, pleased with his resolution, reward himself by going after all. Sleeping late, attending classes sporadically, he still managed to get A's in all his English courses —although in one he had to appeal to his professor, since he had not read the required books—and passable grades in French and history; but he failed Latin and just scraped by in botany.

In June, Delmore went out drinking with a dissolute reporter the night before his last exam, and abruptly decided not to take the exam at all. The next morning he caught a bus to New York, expecting to return in the fall to the university that he would come to think of as "that Arcady of my youth."

3

———•———

No SOONER DID DELMORE walk in the door than his mother began scolding him because he had wired home for his fare. He was no longer the son of a rich man, she declared; Harry's estate was still in litigation, and he would have to reconcile himself to staying in New York from now on. Determined to make his own way, Delmore evolved an impractical scheme by which he hoped to earn his tuition: he would translate a book by Julien Benda.

Delmore's attraction to Benda is not at first glance easy to understand. An austere and reactionary classicist, Benda had fallen into relative obscurity after a brief moment of prominence during the Dreyfus affair, which he had protested with a fervor that rivaled Proust's. Only one book of his, *La Trahison des clercs*, had been translated into English; and Delmore probably read it soon after it appeared, in Richard Aldington's translation. This austere plea for disinterest and a retreat from the world on the part of *clercs*, or intellectuals, no doubt appealed to Delmore on the grounds of its reverence for scholarship as the highest end of man; and he was perhaps drawn to him by Eliot's advocacy in the pages of *Criterion*.

Delmore sent a copy of his translation to the author himself, and was gratified when Benda replied with a cordial note; but in the midst of the Depression no publisher could be persuaded to support such an esoteric venture, and all that came of it was a loan from Rose, in exchange for a note promising her whatever profits accrued from the translation. With this money, Delmore was at last able to retrieve his Chrysler Imperial from the garage where it had been stored since his father's death.

His uncle Irving took advantage of this new development by employing Delmore to drive him out to the suburbs where he collected rents for a real-estate agency. It was one of those rare periods when Irving had a job; known in the neighborhood as "Shake-Shake," he spent most of his time gambling on horses and reading turf sheets. After work, he and Delmore would cruise up and down Riverside Drive looking for girls. Apparently they had little luck, apart from one encounter with "a fat girl who said she was going to use the sex organs God gave her."

Irving was a difficult, petulant young man given to taking out his frustrations on his nephew. During the Depression, many people simply couldn't afford to pay their rent, and as the summer wore on, Irving became increasingly discouraged; and the more discouraged he became, the more he taunted Delmore about his intellectual pretensions. (Delmore had his revenge years later, when "The Child Is the Meaning of This Life," a cruel and witty novella about Irving, was published in *The World Is a Wedding*.) Finally, on a hot night in the middle of August, a violent quarrel broke out between them that ended with Irving breaking a mirror over Delmore's head and threatening to kill him. While neighbors gathered in the street, Delmore threw some clothes in a suitcase and went to stay for the weekend at a hotel on West Sixty-eighth Street. To support himself, he sold the car and was cheated in the deal.

With the approach of autumn, Delmore again begged Rose to send him back to Wisconsin, but she adamantly stressed her poverty, and he applied instead for admission to New York University, where he was accepted for the following term. In the months that followed, he vowed to take advantage of his leisure by producing a poem a day. Alarmed on his nineteenth birthday because he had so far failed to produce a masterpiece, he resolved "to work all the time to be great." It was a period of grace; he read *Anna Karenina* with intense pleasure in the New York Public Library, and went to the movies night after night.

Always eager to save money, Rose decided to move to Brooklyn, where rents were cheaper, and in September she found a house at 1752 East Seventeenth Street. Half of a brand-new two-family stucco dwelling in a quiet residential neighborhood with two floors and a winding staircase, this was the Schwartzes' most respectable home since their move from Brooklyn to Washington Heights a decade before. Even so, Delmore was unhappy at first in Brooklyn, and missed his friends in Washington Heights; but later that autumn he encountered Maurice Zolotow standing beside the speaker's platform at a political rally, and they renewed the friendship that had begun at Wisconsin. Zolotow had transferred to N.Y.U., and was living in Brooklyn with his family. He dragged Delmore along to meetings of the Flatbush Workers' Club and argued politics endlessly, still trying to convert his friend to Communism. Delmore was interested enough in politics to read *The New Republic* and take a progressive line, but he resisted Zolotow's proselytizing about how Communism was "a way of life." Delmore was drawn to Platonism, to the spiritual life of poetry, and the utopias of this world failed to attract him. Still, the determinist character of Marxism appealed to a mind that was always, like his mentor Spinoza's, in search of first causes.

That February, Delmore enrolled in the Washington Square College of N.Y.U. as a philosophy major, and through the spring he was more inspired than ever, delighted to be following a rigorous program of study at last. Among his professors were James Burnham and Philip Wheelwright, who had just published their *Introduction to Philosophical Analysis*. Burnham was then a prominent radical, active in support of Trotsky, and co-editor, with Wheelwright, of *Symposium*. Delmore found Burnham more congenial than Wheelwright, a New England Brahmin whose austerity and polish intimidated him; and Burnham, not one to give A's readily, always gave them to Delmore, who impressed him as a brilliant student, disciplined, hard-working, at ease with even the more technical philosophical questions.

No doubt the most significant influence on Delmore at N.Y.U. was Sidney Hook, whose seminar in contemporary philosophy he took during his second year. Delmore seemed to have an unerring talent for becoming acquainted with whatever person or idea happened at the time to be just on the verge of prominence; and Hook, in his early thirties then, was beginning to publish the studies of Marxism that were to be so influential among Delmore's generation—in particular *From Hegel to Marx*, a vigorous, impassioned work that appealed to Delmore primarily because of its cosmopolitan, polemical, erudite style. Hook's arguments possessed what he himself had found in Marx: "the poetry of passion." It was the style that would characterize *Partisan Review* in the coming years. Delmore always resisted politics whenever they threatened to encroach on what he thought of as the higher imaginative domain of literature, and Marx appealed to him less as a radical than as a determinist who had fashioned one of the great intellectual systems. Some years later, he wrote to the British critic Julian Symons:

> I am not, by the way, a Marxist, though Marx seems to me to have discovered all the connections—what is wrong is the *causal* direction, first productive relation, then value: one and the other are simultaneous and inseparable as a moment's introspection demonstrates: you can only *make* what you *want* to make.

This sort of conviction would have interfered with any serious claims to Delmore's being a Marxist; besides, Marxism was the prevailing mood on campus then, and he had to remain independent. If he had any political allegiance, it was to Trotsky, whose knowledge of literature impressed him; *Literature and Revolution* was one of his sacred texts. As for Hook, Delmore devised a Yeatsian couplet of homage: "It was his mind and not his looks / (Is that why some men study books?)." Walking with his teacher to the Fourteenth Street subway after class, he would expound a view of politics that owed less to Marx than to Franklin D. Roosevelt. "He sounded like an intelligent New Dealer," Hook recalled.

But Delmore was far more concerned in those years with religion than with politics. Ever since he had been introduced to the work of Maritain at Wisconsin, he had been cultivating the French Catholic's ideas with a peculiar earnestness that, for a time at least, had Hook convinced he was on the verge of converting to Catholicism. Hook warned his pupil against the dangers of too hasty a decision, and was relieved when Delmore announced, "Don't worry, Professor Hook, my father wasn't in real estate for nothing." Or, as he expressed it in his journal: "His father was in the realty business—he, however, was in the reality business." What appealed to him in Catholicism was its aesthetic component; he would have endorsed Gibbon's observation that "the Catholic superstition, which is always the enemy of reason, is often the parent of the arts." William Barrett had a solemn explanation for Delmore's religiosity; in his view, Delmore "ultimately accepted the religious position—one has to put it that vaguely . . . neither of us felt ultimately satisfied with a purely naturalistic view of the world." Some years later, Delmore offered his own, less theological reason; one of the principal attractions of religion, he confessed, was that it provided "some ground for disagreeing with Sidney Hook."

"You just want a father," Maurice Zolotow once accused Delmore apropos his belief in God; and it was true that he tended to populate his early poems with serene and kindly authority figures who had more in common with an ideal father than with a remote, omnipotent god. But his belief had a devout side as well, and early on Delmore acquired the habit of prayer, addressing Him in a formal manner. During his early twenties, he often had ideas for stories about God ("Driving in a car at night with brother, another car pulls up, and the Ancient Mariner instructs us in the nature and existence of God"), and he once had the protagonist of his Wisconsin novel declare: "I must try to understand the real cause for my belief & interest in God. It is not just the arguments. Perhaps it is because it makes life seem important. I do not really know why I believe in God."

Among the prose fragments that date from this period is a sort of Pascalian discourse on God.

Ladies and gentlemen! A strange and brilliant subject! The existence of God, no less! You turn away your interest; bored perhaps? It is not the modern topic. You are wrong. The existence of God, correctly understood, is very near to you. For if God does exist and you ignore Him, then think how much you are missing. Another being who knows everything and has been everywhere, who can help you in business, in love, and when you are blue. A gentleman of perfect taste who will appreciate your best efforts and frown upon your shortcomings. . . . All this and a great deal more you will be missing, if He exists and you do not look for Him.

. . . put on neat and well-brushed clothes, comb your hair, and admit that your sexual desires have sometimes been without conceivable extenuation, no matter what occurred during childhood.

It will not be a waste of time, even if it does turn out, in the end, that He does not exist.

Inevitably, the issue of God's existence returned Delmore to the issue of himself, and he ended this monologue with the warning: "It is better to spend a great deal of time trying to find out if God exists . . . while it is worse not to do so, for if one is wrong, then one will surely suffer, if only in self-contempt."

.

In class at N.Y.U., Delmore talked with great intensity ("prating voluble," as he characterized it later), high-handed in his displays of erudition and passionate about ideas. He was elitist in his thinking, dismissive of "hoi polloi," and he alienated other students with his open contempt for what he thought of as their simple-mindedness. In Hook's class there was "a burly, cynical wit" named Levine who resented Delmore's disputatious manner and was always baiting him; together they competed for Hook's attention, shouting one another down, until finally a fist fight erupted and Hook had to separate them. From then on, Delmore sat up front, Levine in back; it was like being in the second grade again, Hook protested.

Impatient with details, Delmore had a competitive attitude toward knowledge; whenever he heard someone talking about a book or idea that was new to him, he would rush off to the library to read up on it. But if he was impressionistic in his approach to philosophy, his achievements in it were genuine; the program at N.Y.U. was demanding in those days, and he took—apart from the introductory courses and Burnham's seminar in medieval philosophy—principles of aesthetics (with Wheelwright), and metaphysical analysis, earning A's in all of them. He also studied Greek for two years, and elected courses in the Renaissance, medieval and modern Europe, "economic behavior," and the philosophy of Communism and fascism. But he tended to rely on intuition rather than hard work; one of his classmates, Norman Jacobs, felt that he wasn't "studious in the most exacting sense, and lacked *Sitz-*

fleisch," the ability to sit down and master a text. He preferred to "transform philosophy into poetry." When it was a question of philosophy that touched on literature, as in Burnham's seminar on Aquinas and Dante, Delmore's fluency on occasion compensated for a deficiency in actual command of the texts.

Intent on making a name for himself, Delmore threw himself into campus activities. He was vice-president of the Philosophy Club, to which he lectured on Pascal, and founder of the Poetry Society, under whose auspices he moderated discussions with Burnham and other N.Y.U. professors. In his junior year, he arranged for William Carlos Williams to give a reading—and was delighted when the first thing Williams said to him was "Where's the can?" "It was a new period of intense excitement," he recalled in an unpublished novel about his years at N.Y.U., for "there were famous teachers at Stuyvesant [Delmore's name for N.Y.U.] and a sense of being close to the important tendencies in thought and in the arts."

Delmore's eager, strident, combative style was conspicuous among his classmates. To Norman Jacobs, he resembled Adonis, and embodied "the poetic temperament." He had "a sense of the demonic" about him, a tumultuous energy revealed in the rush of words that poured from him, the pale eyes, set wide apart on the broad expanse of his face, glinting as he talked. His moods could alternate without warning, from a silent, solemn deference to a sort of nervous intensity that spilled over into his gestures. William Barrett has given a vivid impression of him as he appeared in 1933.

> He was then quite thin, with an ivory pallor, odd-looking but very attractive . . . there was something very boyish and absolutely spontaneous in the way he got caught up in the excitement of a situation. There would come that curious hop, as if he couldn't stand still with glee, his arms flapping against his sides like a chicken's wings. He was awkward but very agile. In a later poem he caricatured his body as "the heavy bear that moves with me"; there was nothing bearlike or cumbersome in his movements then.

For all his awkwardness, Delmore possessed a certain social grace; he was, in his own way, attentive to people, wanting to flatter and amuse them, but without ever being obsequious. As Barrett noted, Delmore's anecdotes about others often had an edge of malice, but they also made their subject seem "a special and unique person, somebody whose great value was only enhanced by this or that harmless and slightly comic eccentricity." He was a great mimic, a confiding, intimate personality, and an able student of others' mannerisms. His comic gift drew inspiration from the Borscht circuit, American vaudeville, and the polemical style of a Russian intellectual, combined with a talent for dramatizing his own situation that enabled him to think of himself as representative of a whole historical era.

During the spring of 1934, Delmore reviewed *Ulysses*, Eliot's *The Use of Poetry and the Use of Criticism*, and a performance of Gertrude Stein's *Four Saints in Three Acts* in *The Washington Square Bulletin*. His review of *Ulysses*, despite its reverence for Joyce, was not without reservations; acknowledging it to be a difficult work, one that "requires a devotion, a concentration which is a moral act in itself," he went on to complain that

> the Odyssey parallel seems arbitrary, superimposed. In the difficulty of reading there is also the fact that to so great an extent the themes are stated in the terms of what a person thinks "to himself," and not in the traditional terms of action, speech or vision. In this way such a method contains the seeds of the destruction of the novel form for it leads away from drama and narrative, and towards lyric poetry.

The piece on Eliot revealed an interest in the poet's personality that was to become obsessive later on. "What Eliot [said] of himself," in terms of his literary preferences, was crucial to a full appreciation of these lectures, he insisted. "His criticism is a help to the understanding of his poetry," and in turn a reflection of his most inward beliefs. Here, too, as with Joyce, Delmore was not overly adulatory; although he declared Eliot to be "the best poet of our time," he reproached him for contradicting himself. How could the "remarkable consciousness of intention" Eliot claimed for "Sweeney Agonistes" be consistent with his assertion that poetry was "a spontaneous and unpremeditated outburst of words"?

Eliot had been in America to give the Charles Eliot

Norton lectures at Harvard the year before, and Delmore
attended addresses by him on two occasions: once at Columbia, where he spoke on Milton, and again in April,
when he gave a general talk on poetry at the New School.
"T. S. Eliot sat down," Delmore noted in his journal,
"scratched his leg at the garter, and looked with querulous
gaze at the ceiling's design. He was dressed in a dinner suit.
He adjusted his tie." Eliot's lectures, he recalled some
twenty-five years later, "only served to confirm what his
audience already felt: namely, that he was a very great
poet indeed and the greatest living literary critic." The
image Delmore formed then of a remote, oracular figure
was to remain an ideal long after he had become a bitter
critic of Eliot's work.

The thirties were the "Marxist decade" for intellectuals
of Delmore's generation, and William Barrett has since
become its principal historian, just as Delmore was its
chronicler in verse and fiction. Alienated, radical, uncertain of the future, they lived a marginal existence. No
longer "chained to the wheel of career and profession,"
Barrett wrote, "we could abandon ourselves to the delight
of irrelevant studies." In *The World Is a Wedding*, Delmore evoked the unhappier side of that era, when "hope
had worn thin like a cloth"; but when Barrett first knew
him, in the earlier years of the Depression, they prided
themselves on being intellectuals, as if it were a vocation in
itself. How much this attitude had to do with Marxism is
questionable, since revolution was never one of their most
urgent priorities; but at least Marx could explain their situation, if not its remedy. For that, they turned to literature
and philosophy.

One of Delmore's best stories, published in the 1937
New Directions anthology, provides a fine portrait of the
prevailing intellectual climate of those years. "An Argument in 1934" typifies the grandiose conversational style he
and his friends affected, in what he called "Biblical prose."

In the year of our Western culture 1934, Noah
Gottlieb went one Saturday morning to meet his
friend, Harry Morton.
2. Both young men were very much interested in

the history of thought and in the arts. It was this that
had brought them together.

3. They knew that they were intellectuals, but they
disliked the title. It had for them associations with the
previous decade.

4. Yet there is no other title to describe the part
they had chosen in Life. They were intellectuals, and
the way in which they made their living they detested
and merely endured.

5. "Yes, we are intellectuals," Harry had said to
Noah one day, "it is nothing if not an unpleasant
name. Yet, come to think of it, are not all the heroes
of Western culture intellectuals?"

Noah Gottlieb and Harry Morton could well have been
modeled on two other friends of Delmore's, Julian Breen
and Ben Hellman, a pair of neo-Thomists at N.Y.U. who
exercised considerable influence over him during his
undergraduate years. Hellman, like the Harry Morton of
Delmore's story, had a job at the New York Public Library, while Breen worked as an usher at Carnegie Hall
and peddled *Women's Wear Daily*. Breen lived with a girl
(whom he later married) on Sixth Avenue, and Delmore
was jealous of their sophisticated existence; Giotto prints
on the wall and a record player were luxuries in those
days.

He had more affinity with Barrett, who was poor himself
and shared Delmore's appetite for existential theory. Delmore and Barrett first met late in 1933, when both had just
turned twenty, at the "salon" of Florence Wolfson, the
daughter of a wealthy doctor who allowed her to entertain
friends in their large apartment on the Upper West Side, a
part of town Barrett and his friends referred to as the
Golden Ghetto. Barrett, then a graduate student at Columbia, was, in his own words, a "lugubrious bookworm" who
pored over literature and philosophy (it was in the latter
that he was eventually to make his reputation) with a zeal
that rivaled Delmore's, and by the following summer they
had become inseparable companions. Every night they
convened for dinner at the Foltis-Fisher cafeteria on West
Twenty-third Street, where Barrett professed not to see a
nickel's worth of difference between the forty- and forty-
five-cent dinners, and complained of the hard rolls which

"seemed to have been baked in express violation of the biblical warning, 'Who of you, if asked for bread, would give me a stone?' "

Among Delmore's other friends at N.Y.U. who shared in the *Zeitgeist* were the Koch sisters, Vivienne and Adrienne, and their younger brother, Sigmund, then a senior at DeWitt Clinton High School. (He later became a distinguished educator and psychologist.) Sigmund and a classmate, Alvin Schwartz, had decided to start a literary magazine to be funded by Sigmund's father, a jewelry manufacturer. Just as the first issue was about to go to press, Delmore heard about it through Vivienne and promptly offered his assistance. He managed to get two poems into the first issue, and by the second had established himself as one of the principal editors.

Sigmund wanted the magazine to reflect a Marxist viewpoint, but Delmore argued for a wider range of authors. Vivienne, too, was anxious to have a hand in the new publication, but soon found that Delmore's influence over Sigmund made it impossible for her to impose her own ideas. Finally, after prolonged negotiations, the first issue appeared in November 1934, with the usual introduction full of vague principles that promised a magazine "with a social emphasis." *Mosaic*, the editors wrote, "will seek to give clarity and definition to the complicated but vital question of a Marxian aesthetic."

Working out of a little room in Mr. Koch's store at 298 Broadway, they were astonished by their success in soliciting contributions for such an unknown journal. William Carlos Williams provided an article on Norman Macleod, then a well-known poet among readers of the little magazines; R. P. Blackmur offered some poems; and there was a polemic against Ezra Pound by Samuel Putnam, a minor literary figure of the day, announced in the pages of *The Washington Square Bulletin* as a "devastating attack." In a triumphant mood, the editors arranged a meeting with Macleod, in their eyes a celebrated older poet. One evening the Koch parents were sent away, a bottle of gin was procured, and the editors, in a state of high anticipation, put on their best clothes. The occasion proved a success; Delmore's poems were read aloud and praised, with an effect he related in his N.Y.U. novel: "Richmond tried to look serene amidst this praise, but he merely looked ex-

pressionless, often the result of any effort on his part at
serenity."

Mosaic lasted only two issues before its editors tired of
it, but the second issue was even more impressive than the
first. A young writer by the name of Paul Goodman gave
them a short story, R. P. Blackmur reviewed new collections by Spender and Auden, and Louis MacNeice submitted four poems. Even Pound put in a brief appearance,
with a reply to Samuel Putnam composed in the tedious
homespun dialect he reserved for correspondence. Delmore's contribution was a critical essay on the English poet
Joseph Gordon Macleod that praised his "mastery of language, his sensibility or awareness, and his fundamental
attitude." It was a very intelligent piece, and the editor of
Poetry singled it out for special praise in a notice of the
issue. Casual and erudite, Delmore showed himself at
home with Macleod's subtle paraphrases of the Latin of
Catullus and the Emperor Hadrian's lyric, "animula,
vagula, blandula"—Delmore himself was to adopt as the
epigraph to *In Dreams Begin Responsibilities*. The essay
closed with a list of some recent examples "of a break with
the contemporary style" to be found in the work of Mac-
Neice, Zukofsky, and Paul Goodman, and the suggestion
that poets should emulate Dante and the Elizabethan
playwrights by learning "to work within the sphere of the
audience's understanding."

•

The name of Paul Goodman would not have been
known to the readers of *Mosaic*, and he had to wait many
years longer than Delmore to achieve wide recognition.
When they met in 1934, Goodman had bettered Delmore
in one respect by acquiring a modest salon about him in
Washington Heights. It was only a matter of time, claimed
his admiring friends, before the plays and poems he was
writing so copiously would be recognized as masterpieces.

Goodman's childhood, like Delmore's, had been somewhat deprived; his father had abandoned the family before
he was born, and then his older brother had gone away,
leaving him in the company of his mother and his sister,
Alice. Even Goodman's mother was, in his own words, a
"bourgeois gypsy" who seldom lived at home, and so he
was for many years supported by Alice, who worked in the

story department of MGM's New York office all her life. Goodman's erudition rivaled Delmore's, and his "unpublished reputation" was considerable, especially among the members of what came to be known as the Wadsworth Terrace Social, Literary, and Athletic Club. At first, Delmore showed Goodman "the deference one might accord a *cher maître* with an acknowledged *oeuvre* behind him," or as much of an *oeuvre* as any writer in his twenty-third year could be said to have produced. He had acquired a certain worldliness that intimidated Delmore, a knowing manner designed to convey intellectual authority; and while Delmore was rapidly becoming a master at this himself, he found Goodman unassailable, particularly when he was surrounded by his circle.

Out of his relationship with Goodman came one of Delmore's most sustained published works, "The World Is a Wedding," an engaging if rather unfair account of Goodman and his friends, all of whom are readily identifiable. Delmore's gift for recording peculiarities of speech served him well in this story; generally silent when he visited Goodman's home, he came away with a perfect recollection of the pompous tone that attended these gatherings, the bantering, ironic gossip that passed for serious discourse. But he didn't find their manner very amusing at the time. "That he seemed ill at ease in Paul's home is understandable," one member of the circle noted; "the atmosphere was satirical and many of the jokes were almost impolitely private." At Goodman's he was, at least in Alice's view, a "sacrificial lamb." That he was beginning to publish meant little there, since the world outside Goodman's living room was irrelevant to his friends' high purpose: to celebrate their host's unrecognized genius. Delmore's aspirations to worldliness indicated to them only that he was "living beyond his intellectual and artistic means." "The World Is a Wedding" was, in part, an act of revenge for their ill treatment of him on the few occasions when he attended the Saturday evenings at which Goodman's work was read aloud.

On one typical evening, Goodman handed some poems to Delmore, who examined them with a dogged intensity and then began to question the author. Had he been influenced by Auden? Was he imitating Allen Tate? Delmore's questions were reasonable enough, but he missed the sarcastic, insouciant tone practiced among Goodman and his friends. Moreover, Goodman was not a serious student of contemporary poetry, while Delmore followed trends "as intently as a stockbroker watching the ups and downs of the market." As he pursued his line of questioning, a silence fell over the room, until Goodman broke out in mocking laughter quickly taken up by his disciples. Delmore was furious.

But their most serious conflicts often had less to do with literature than with sex. Delmore found Goodman's undifferentiated sexual impulses bewildering and couldn't understand the circle's easy tolerance of anyone's sexual preferences. It was their alleged promiscuity more than their enthusiasm for handball that made Delmore call them the Indoor Athletic Association. They talked of the "heteraceteras" (heterosexuals) and the "ambidextras," those who practiced what Barrett described as "the *juste moyen* between two unnecessary extremes." Goodman espoused a return to the freedom of infantile sexuality, Freud's "polymorph perverse"; any love object was acceptable to him, and this attitude threatened the repressive side of Delmore's nature.

Unnerved by Julian Sawyer's homosexuality, he had eventually broken off their friendship to avoid being identified by the boys in the neighborhood as a sexual fellow traveler. "He might be looked on as peculiar too," Delmore wrote in the course of a cruel portrait of Julian. But a fear of homosexual impulses had begun to trouble Delmore himself; on one occasion, he referred in his notebook to "homosexual images in classrooms." Notably virulent all his life about "faggots"—his favorite term of derogation—Delmore was given to postulating the hidden presence of homosexuality in just about everyone. Parents had children only in order "to prove they were neither impotent nor homosexual," he once observed, and he purported to have found a connection between capitalism and homosexuality: "Puritan morality, partiarchal authority, and middle class property relations" converge to produce Freud's "family romance," which in turn promotes a repression of infantile sexuality. The child, "plunged into the emotional relations between his parents," is required to mediate between them at the expense of his own sexual identity. This was obviously what had happened in Delmore's childhood, and he elaborated his parents' conflicts into an explanation of how unnatural bonds between father and son can be created that resemble homosexual love.

"It would have been easier to be a homosexual," Delmore remarked years later in his journal, implying that women—rather than intimacy itself—were the source of his emotional conflicts; and a Rorschach administered when he was in his mid-thirties tends to confirm his self-appraisal. So "conscious" and deliberate were the homosexual associations in his responses that a later interpreter (who never knew Delmore) conjectured: "It would be surprising if he had not acted out his homosexual impulses, since he communicated that fact at so many different levels." Still, it seems most unlikely that Delmore ever did have any such experiences, given the labor of sublimation that went on for so many years.

In his novels, Delmore depicted himself as puritanical about sex, but insouciant about his conquests; he invariably discovered when it was over that "the whole thing had been nothing much." Puritanical he was, even as an adult; he could never abide four-letter words, and avoided them in one unpublished story about a visit to a prostitute by employing the bizarre idiom "Pluck me! Pluck me!" But he could hardly have been as indifferent as his various personae, for in his later journals he wrote about sex as a pervasive source of guilt. Intimacy seemed to call forth in him a strange malevolence, since it violated his mother's belief that selfish motives dictated all relations between men and women. William Barrett, who knew Delmore's mother, noticed how she "did everything she could to prolong his narcissism, exaggerate his ego with praise, and yet in her clever and poisonous way insinuate in the child, then the boy, and then the young man, that the love and trust of anybody was not to be believed."

Self-conscious and awkward, Delmore could hardly have been considered conventionally handsome; he had a long scar across his forehead—the result of a childhood accident while broad jumping when he was nine—and he suffered from a terrible case of acne until his mid-twenties. His face was florid, his lips full, and he had a slight speech impediment that caused him to lisp and, when he was nervous, to stammer. Still, his features were unusual, even striking: the full, sensuous mouth and contemplative eyes combined with his height—he was over six feet tall—and a certain heavy grace to make him attractive. But he was forced to cultivate a pose of cynical bravado to veil his own sexual inexperience. Sigmund Koch found him "terribly innocent," and suspected he was still a virgin, a conjecture contradicted by Delmore's written accounts and by Barrett's recollection of loitering outside various brothels, too poor to indulge, while Delmore enjoyed himself within. A more typical scenario involved a young woman who "decided that her virginity was something she had to do something about," and approached Delmore as a potential solution. "I have been trying to get your brother to sleep with me," she told Kenneth, but Delmore was "put off by her bogus sense of sophistication."

He found sex less rewarding than the idea of sex; from Wisconsin, he had reported to Julian that Fola was "bestial" because she had given in to him, "much to my disgust." Maurice Zolotow remembered standing beside Delmore at a urinal after an autumn game of tennis and hearing him exclaim: "When you take a piss on a cold day after holding it in, it's better than the best orgasm." When he did embark on quests for sexual adventure, they ended for the most part inconclusively. Accompanied by Koch, he would wander down Broadway, where prostitutes were reputed to be found. Few were sighted, none ever approached, and the act of staring furtively from afar served only to increase his ardor.

·

One afternoon during the winter of 1933 Delmore pointed out to Maurice Zolotow a girl at a neighboring table in the N.Y.U. student cafeteria and announced that he knew her from Mary J. J. Wrinn's Poetry Club at George Washington High School. Her name was Gertrude Buckman, and a number of her poems had appeared beside Delmore's in *The Poet's Pack*. Delmore found her very attractive, "a kind of Dutch beauty," as he wrote later on. "Her face was round, her cheeks were always rosy and her eyes gay, and she looked like the true image of health, amiability, and vivacity."

Gertrude was as literary as Delmore—at N.Y.U. she concentrated in English, fine arts, and French—and she had ambitions as a painter and sculptress besides. Like Delmore, she had grown up in the often-stifling environment of Washington Heights. Her father was a manufacturer of women's clothing, but he was, in her estimate, "a poor and ineffective businessman with very poor judgment of people and business matters, so he was never 'successful.'" Mr. and Mrs. Buckman had "a wretched relationship," so Gertrude was familiar with the scenes of domestic strife Delmore had witnessed in his childhood.

Gertrude was an only child, and Delmore envied the attention her parents paid her; but as far as their daughter was concerned, "it was always of the wrong sort." "Mrs. Fine's disappointment with her husband," Delmore wrote of the parents of Wilhelmina Fine in his story "New Year's Eve," "who was not rich and hence to her mind a failure, united with her hope and disappointment in her daughter." It was perhaps this background that made Gertrude so defiantly unsentimental—"tough and sardonic and hard," a friend recalled. In one of his unpublished novels, Delmore described the "blackness and hopelessness that suddenly arose in Martha"—a character unmistakably based on Gertrude—"and made her turn against herself and everything else." So it was not surprising that she was resistant from the start to Delmore's overtures. His novel provides a revealing account of their courtship in its early days.

After Maxwell had known Martha for a week, he went with her to see a foreign film after school, and as they crossed the street amid traffic, Martha took hold of his hand. Her vivacity and warmth were such that this act made Maxwell think that she wanted him to make love to her, and when they sat in the theatre darkness, he took her hand and squeezed it. But two days after that, when they were looking at the pictures in an art gallery, Maxwell took Martha's hand again and she drew it away roughly, saying that she was the kind of girl who never wanted anyone to make love to her, she was never going to get married, she was going to be an old maid. Maxwell was hurt and he said to her that it seemed foolish to him to go with a girl who did not want love made to her. Martha replied that if that was the way Maxwell felt, then he had better not see her.

Ignoring her lack of encouragement, Delmore pursued Gertrude energetically, and they were soon inseparable. Theirs was an "idealistic" relationship, recalled Sigmund

Koch, conventional and restrained in the manner of the
day. A classmate of Delmore's remembered him striding
about the campus while Gertrude trailed a few steps behind
—a practice corroborated at least in spirit by Gertrude
herself: "I was being the silent one, he the articulate."

Gertrude was reluctant to have Delmore meet her parents, fearing they would disapprove of him; and, inevitably, they did. Mr. Buckman enjoyed having Delmore refute
the commonplace views about politics he gleaned from the
newspaper, but the Buckmans were too conventional to
trust their daughter's nervous, unkempt suitor, whose un-
pressed clothes suggested a disagreeable indigence. And
they were troubled when Delmore, daunted by the long
subway ride from Washington Heights to Brooklyn, failed
to bring Gertrude home after their dates. They wanted
their daughter to find a more respectable companion. Delmore urged Gertrude to remind her parents that he was
soon to inherit a third of a million dollars (a development
he continued to hope for through most of the Depression),
but the Buckmans remained unimpressed.

Delmore was convinced that the Jews of his generation
had been warped by the provincial attitudes of their parents, who had turned marriage into an economic institution
in which the highest priority was given to suitors who
"made a good salary." His own grandmother Hannah was
always urging him to find "a nice Jewish girl," preferably
with lots of money; "the best is none too good for you,"
she would say. And in *The World Is a Wedding*, he told
how his aunt Clara had bargained with her prospective
husband over how much money he would get if they married. This demand for a dowry may well have been a
fiction of Delmore's, but the economic aspects of love were
often stressed in the Schwartz and Buckman households.
The sons suffered because "their lower middle class poverty
kept them from seeking out girls and entertaining the idea
of marriage," Delmore noted, while the fathers were heard
lamenting that they "had lived to see a generation without
shame and without gratitude for the parents who reared
them."

·

The poetry Delmore was writing now owed less to the
stylistic innovations of Modernism than to much earlier
models. At the age of twenty, he had mastered English

prosody and arrived at a characteristic voice, exemplified
in the sonnet sequence he worked on during these years. It
was a voice refined through close reading of Shakespeare's
sonnets, direct echoes of which recur in his own (despite
his use of the Petrarchan form), as well as Milton and
Verlaine. In vigorous, uneven iambic pentameters, he
strove to produce an effect at once declamatory and imitative of American speech.

Some of these sonnets are undistinguished, mere exercises in which he practiced his art; their most conspicuous
flaw, apart from an occasional clumsiness of meter, derives
from Delmore's penchant for diffuse rhetoric. Even so,
they anticipate the passionate, ironic voice he perfected
later on.

> The self is unlike music. They are alike
> In staying air which flows and having sides;
> Walking around the two, nothing abides
> But melts before you see, flake after flake,
> Note after note, of anger, love and pleasure.
> The flute gets spit, the cello's string is bitten
> By flexing finger, and the self is smitten
> By like things: kiss and cough: and in like measure.
> And yet they differ, as Africa and France.
> For music moves to ends that all foresee
> Assured in doubt and known in every chance,
> While the self teeters on a tight-rope, free,
> Step after step, and ignorant of what
> Is safe, blue, right, cold, blind, soft, real and hot.

Delmore was also writing what he called "Songs," ir-
regularly rhymed poems of various lengths numbered, like
the sonnets, in sequence. Where the sonnets often lapsed
into a mannered rhetoric designed to complete their form,
the songs displayed an eloquent force characteristic of his
best work. His themes—city life, the necessity and fear of
love, the invocation of a pure Platonic essence, the use of
great intellectual figures of the past as witnesses—prefigure
the dominant theme of *In Dreams Begin Responsibilities*.

Song VI

> The blueness of the sky is overhead,
> Seen or unseen. The city's burden is

A screen of mountains hiding from the birds
The generous theatre of the lovely will . . .
And if I call your will a waiting bird
As if a natural thing, I mean to show
The hideous balances which wait for it
Flying with anguished breath the cliffs of air.

The bird must fall, the acrobat must fall
Daringly forth with faith to catch his partner,
The animal must tumble and fall down
To learn love's denouement and utter shame . . .

Stretched in the rich confusion of each lapse,
You learn the ground which underlies your will,
The dark nature thick with graves and jewels . . .

The monument, the factory stack, the tree
Blacken against this sunset in which all
All independence, and privacy must fall
Perfectly as the diver straightly downward
Into the dark sea where the first things turn.

And from that dark must rise and fly again,
And fall again, risking the death of the will,
And fall again, to win warm good once more,
For all must rise and fly, all must fulfill
The incontestable game where good is won
And all must lose again and once more fall
Because love bars the anger of the will
And asks the whole surrender of the fall,
But all must fly again, for all must win
From future circumstances the unborn good.
The blueness of the sky is overhead,
Seen or unseen. Love waits beneath,
Known or unknown, ignored or understood.

This ambivalent view of love is startlingly bitter for such a
young man. To fall in love was to plummet toward a "dark
sea," to discover "utter shame," to sacrifice one's "privacy"; it was, in other words, quite literally to fall. Love
was unquestionably the "good," but to attain it required
abandoning freedom's ethereal realm for the more ordinary
world of passion: "Love waits beneath." Delmore at
twenty sounded as grim and philosophical as Donne.

His religious themes were more conventional. One characteristic "Song" began, with a spondee reminiscent of Hopkins, "You, God, your light is my darkness."

Your light is my darkness, my darkness is darkness,
At midnight in the small room reading the black print,
At the two corners between the traffic lights,
At the red light and green light, the choice of two
    avenues,
Cupping my hands to guard the light from dim wind,
Warming my hands to stay the cold wind,
Fitting on gloves, which is my only knowledge,
Suddenly then, as I watch my eyes in the mirror,
Instantly then your light is my darkness
—Tell me now, tell me now! how shall I know you
In the night of light, my terror and darkness?

Derivative as they were—of Yeats's language and Eliot's subject matter—these "Songs" possess what comes to most poets later in their careers, a unique voice and imagery fused with an original sensibility. Sonorous, anxious, longing for a vanished innocence, Delmore had managed to articulate his doubt and passion with a grandiloquence striking in its mature intensity.

Delmore had what Sigmund Koch described as "a sacred obligation, a religiosity of commitment to poetry"; it was "the most sublime thing in the universe" to him, and every morning, before he dressed or had breakfast, he would sit down to read from his favorite English poets. He tortured himself by adopting impossible standards, measuring his own poems against what he read with unsparing self-criticism. Yet this stern apprenticeship was responsible for his having learned the uses of imitation at an early age; and from then on it was simply a question of transforming the conventions he had mastered into an idiom of his own.

·

The Schwartzes moved again during Delmore's junior year at N.Y.U., from the spacious stucco home on a residential street in Brooklyn to an ordinary red-brick apartment building at 2157 Ocean Avenue. Home oppressed him more than ever now that his mother had adopted the habit of entering all their expenses in a ledger so that she could recover Delmore's share once he started to earn a living. Rose resented having to supplement the loan N.Y.U. had given him, and as the debt he owed her mounted up, she began to worry that he would never pay her back. Delmore had wanted an excuse to leave home for a long time; and now, in the summer of 1935, her incessant nagging provoked him to move into a boardinghouse while he completed the few courses necessary for him to graduate in summer school. His mother had been expecting him to take a job, but he announced his decision "with so much sullen-faced determination" that she relented, and he found a rather dismal room at 813 Greenwich Avenue in Manhattan. Vowing to work twelve hours a day to become a great poet, he prepared to undergo a rigorous apprenticeship that included copying out by hand the most famous poems in the language. Virtually the only person he saw that summer was William Barrett, who was living nearby on West Twenty-third Street.

At first, Delmore related in one of his autobiographical novels, he took pleasure in the "grandeur of self-denial" his ascetic life afforded, but it was not long before he was attacked by another sensation, "the vertigo of self-doubt." He was often dismayed by the "weakness and deadness" of his work, and would turn to his school books in order to recover "the sense of power and mastery he had known as a student." For Delmore's persona in his novel, "the obsession which made all else unimportant was his desire to be a great novelist, an obsession and a desire of such intensity that he trembled when he thought of the possibility that he might not have the necessary gifts." There were times when he believed that "the same effort, application, and concentration which he gave to school would be sufficient" and others when his aspirations struck him as fantastic.

Then, one weekend in July, Delmore sat down and wrote a masterpiece. "In Dreams Begin Responsibilities," a phrase taken from the epigraph Yeats chose for his collection entitled *Responsibilities*, was the story of a single afternoon in his parents' courtship, witnessed by their son in a darkened movie theater. "I think it is the year 1909," the story begins, and from there on becomes increasingly vivid and specific as he imagines his parents four years before his own birth. First he sees his father strolling toward the home of his prospective bride, proud of his

recently acquired wealth. But the thought of marriage un-
nerves him, until he recalls "the big men he admires who
are married: William Randolph Hearst and William Howard Taft." As the film unfolds, and his parents depart for
Coney Island, Delmore listens to his father boast "how
much money he has made in the week just past, exaggerat-
ing an amount which need not have been exaggerated,"
and begins to weep, overcome by the futility of Harry's
tragic suspicion that "actualities somehow fall short, no
matter how fine they are." More composed now, he returns
his attention to the screen, where his parents stand on the
boardwalk staring out at the water. Again, their seeming
impassivity distresses him, for he knows, like a spectator in
a Greek tragedy, in what disasters their actions will cul-
minate. Finally, when Harry's proposal of marriage has
been made, Delmore leaps up from his seat and shouts,
"Don't do it! It's not too late to change your minds, both
of you. Nothing good will come of it, only remorse, hatred,
scandal, and two children whose characters are mon-
strous." This outburst, prompted by the inexorable press of
events that had drawn his parents together and culminated
in the long trauma of Delmore's childhood, foreshadowed
the agony from which none of them had ever managed to
escape. In the film, the illusion of innocent courtship is
destroyed by the deeper instincts of irrational fear and
anger that rise up suddenly in his father, impatient in a
photographer's booth, terrified that his life will be spoiled
by his own uncontrollable impulses. And when the usher
comes down the aisle and warns the narrator, "You can't
carry on like this, it is not right, you will find that out soon
enough, everything you do matters too much," he awakens
from his terrible dream to find his premonitions about his
own character undissipated by consciousness: "I woke up
into the bleak winter morning of my twenty-first birthday,
the window-sill shining with its lip of snow, and the morning already begun." Snow, the constant image in Delmore's
work of evanescence, was a sign of both the world's transience and of its impersonal beauty. In his own life, so little
had ever been fixed; always the center of his parents' conflicts, he could look back now and see how their marriage
had been the source of his own uncertainty. Out of this
conflict had come his present misery, but also his masterpiece.

Writing "In Dreams Begin Responsibilities" made him temporarily ecstatic, despite the somber history it related; and when William Barrett came over one afternoon just after he had finished typing it up, Delmore was in a triumphant mood. Barrett, however, had just quarreled with his girlfriend, and was too distracted to fully appreciate the story Delmore thrust into his hands: "Whatever halting words came out of me must have sounded grudging and churlish, and I could see Delmore's face fall." All the same, he was sure he had written a great work. "In Dreams" wouldn't be published for another two years, but when it appeared as the lead piece in the Autumn 1937 issue of the newly revived *Partisan Review*, its impact was to be far greater than Delmore could ever have imagined.

Among the story's most appreciative readers was Vladimir Nabokov, who singled it out as one of his "half a dozen favorites in modern literature." Citing the phrase ". . . the fatal merciless passionate ocean," Nabokov noted: "Although there are several other divine vibrations in this story that so miraculously blends an old cinema film with a personal past, the quoted phrase wins its citation for power and impeccable rhythm." But that was many years later; for the moment, Delmore had a less celebrated though perhaps more crucial reader; on the back of a typescript of "In Dreams Begin Responsibilities," his mother scrawled in pencil:

Dear Delmore

If there is another word besides wonderful I dont know I dont remember telling you all these so accurate. Please save this story and bring it home for me. There are moments in my life, thet I believe all my struggles are worth while.

Mother

4

THE POEM DELMORE conceived not long after his father's death and ostentatiously displayed on the Wisconsin campus was *Having Snow*, which began as a formal exercise in epistemology. Over the years, *Having Snow* metamorphosed into *Genesis*, but not before it had passed through innumerable drafts in both prose and verse. The earliest version survives only in the form of a few notes that appear to date from around 1931, when Delmore was seventeen.

The theme of the poem is the difficulty of knowledge, "as something perceived" in the attempt to know. The existence of objects which do not preserve their identity, for even as we form an idea of what they are they are becoming something else. There are various kinds of objects which change, "grades of permanence," as exemplified by Kenneth, Rhoda, and Bert, who are seen from different "points of view," "perspectives," Wisconsin, Chicago, New York and their places. Various solutions which are emotions, attitudes—Cartesian, idealist, Spinozist, Aristotelian. To the understanding of being finally the utter self-surrender, the phenomenologist, the objectification of the self, defined as the "true way" in the futility of the previous solutions. Seeing each thing as it is, because the barrier of self is passed, which is the beginning of the world.

To know K, R, B is to have snow: the fundamental situation.

Delmore's flights among subtle philosophical propositions always returned to the concrete, for it was here that his genius was most at home. K, R, and B stood for his brother Kenneth, his early love Rhoda, and Bertram Spira, a friend of his from the University of Wisconsin—in other words, for a particular set of relationships that defined his past. "Memory is all we get from existence," he wrote Gertrude when the poem was well along; and he hoped by dwelling on his childhood to discover certain truths about the nature of experience.

Rigorous philosophical speculations proliferated in the poem's early drafts. Delmore had become a proficient logical positivist while still in college, and his notes amount to a sophisticated critique of its limitations. The attempt to confine knowledge to what G. E. Moore described as "sense-data"—that which impinged on our senses alone— was inadequate to Delmore's conception of *Having Snow*, which required a more comprehensive philosophical system. Spinoza's epistemology, with its emphasis on the capacity of the conscious mind to apprehend reality, its concern with the influence of what he called "the passions," and its postulates toward the evidence of God in the phenomenal world, was congenial to Delmore; but phenomenology, then having an early vogue in America, proved to be even more so, since it abandoned the quest for objective certitude in favor of a surrender to subjectivity as the only legitimate mode of knowing. More Husserlian than logical positivist, Delmore's effort to "see each thing as it is" could illuminate his own experience: "I do not think of my brother, whom I love, as sense-impressions. How can I love what I do not know? Do I love only my own sense-impressions, enacting the sin of Narcissus?" To atone for this sin, Delmore sought to ground it in philosophy, as if the torment of excessive self-consciousness could be appeased only through rigorous objective discourse.

The "junior Platonist," as he used to call himself, may have solved in this way the philosophical problem of *Having Snow*, but the very need to examine reality with such obsessive care implied a radical distrust of his own sensations that owed more to his traumatic past experience than to Russell and Moore. Delmore's deepest anguish originated in his blurred self-image; and *Having Snow*, for all its diagrams, metaphysics, and didactic speculations, is essentially a parable of this condition. He used to feel, as he looked back on his family's history, that security was forever eluding them. In Eastern Europe, they had been "a wandering and stiffnecked people," alien to the societies in which they lived; and in America, they found themselves once again denied acceptance in a world that had promised so much from afar. As if the ambiguities of cultural milieu weren't enough of a hazard, he had been forced to contend with his mother's axiom, stressed in these notes, that "you can't trust anyone," and his father's nervous vanity. Too often, the child found himself caught between them in their endless struggles, manipulated and made by each in turn to believe the other was treacherous. So far as Delmore knew, self-interest alone motivated human affairs, and his efforts to comprehend epistemology were made urgent by the sense of isolation such a belief implied. "Conditioned by obsessions in the mother-grandmother half of the family life," as he noted some years later, Delmore studied "the touchstones to motives"; but in his own mind, he was doomed to be "the excluded stranger passing under the lighted window," "an ignorant child in the dark."

To compensate for this "ignorance"—it was one of his favorite words—Delmore invented omniscient deities to preside over his poem. In a somewhat later version, "The Brother Scenario," he introduced what he called a "Monitor," a disembodied presence who draws attention to the narrator's flawed view of the world. Then there was the "Listener," addressed "as if he may be God," and intended to represent "the ego's image of what the world would think (psychologically speaking) of his long confession." Like the ghosts in *Genesis*, this Listener would speak in a formal, even pompous manner, fortified by "relevant quotations from the Bible and à Kempis and Dante and Shakespeare." As for the confession itself, this was to be a testament of "the emotions of the poet as author"; and beside this phrase Delmore wrote: "Uneasiness and self-consciousness before life; jealousy; doubt; fear; insecurity; ecstasy."

Delmore made interminable lists of bizarre episodes for possible inclusion in *Having Snow*, such as being beaten up by a mob of epistemologists or waking to find himself in the role of Charlie Chaplin in *The Gold Rush*; but the poem's real theme can be guessed from a note he scrawled in the margin of these outlines: "Who am I? is the leading

question." It was in the hope of resolving this issue that
Delmore labored over his poem—even though the knowledge he acquired was unwelcome. Finally, he conceived an
episode in which a photographer takes his picture, "but I
do not recognize what I am shown: it is something mon-
strous. I flee from him."

.

Whatever the motives for Delmore's interest in philosophy, he had a great gift for it, and for a time even considered giving up poetry in favor of becoming a "professional
philosopher." It was with this ambition in mind that he
applied to the Harvard Graduate School in philosophy, and
was accepted for the term beginning in September 1935.
His eternal hope of receiving money from his father's
estate had been partially fulfilled the previous January,
when Rose went out to Chicago to investigate her late
husband's financial affairs and managed to wrest a few
thousand dollars from the executors. It wasn't the vast
fortune Delmore had anticipated, but it was enough to
make his mother relent and agree to support his education
for at least another year.

On his arrival in Cambridge, Delmore found lodgings in
a boardinghouse at 9 Story Street. Like the character in
one of his unpublished stories, a young man named Noah
who comes to live in a picturesque New England college
town after having spent his undergraduate years at a city
university, Delmore was awed by the colonial buildings
and elegant residential neighborhoods. But he was lonely at
first, just as he had been at Wisconsin. Less than a month
after his arrival, Delmore was writing to Paul Goodman:
"I am pleased with my courses and with my room but with
little else. An enforced solitude will probably be good, with
all the work I must do, but it is not delightful."

Now that he was a student at Harvard, Delmore could
afford to be imperious with his old friends, who were stig-
matized by having to remain in New York. He broke off
his relationship with Ben Hellman, explaining that Hellman's interests weren't sufficiently philosophical or literary,
and instructed Gertrude to inform Julian Breen that he
would have no more to do with him either. "I'm at Harvard now, those were my N.Y.U. friends," he announced
to a girl who had asked after Hellman and Breen. And he

was just as intemperate with new acquaintances. On first meeting Howard Blake, a poet no less "megalo" than Delmore—he planned to entitle his first book "Prolegomena to Any Future Poetry"—Delmore "matched him presumption for presumption," he reported to Gertrude, "and left him in a state of fine humility by playing the pope as well as ever before."

Delmore was willing to recognize his "papal air"—as he did in a letter to Maurice Zolotow—but reluctant to abandon it. Zolotow, for one, had to be admonished for praising Laforgue over Eliot.

> You're wrong about Laforgue and Eliot. Laforgue writes good lines, as you say, but Eliot writes good poems. Laforgue lacks sustained meanings and rhythms, and Eliot does not. Also I dislike Laforgue's delight in "personality" and cleverness. Ash Wednesday is hardly more "original" than the other poems. The 1st line is directly from Cavalcanti: perch'io no spero tornar mai. But Eliot's purposes are his own, and that is of course all that matters.

And to Gertrude he disseminated what he thought of as "sweet pedagogy," assigning her Diotima's discourse in *The Symposium*, Books VII and VIII of the *Nicomachean Ethics*, St. Paul's Epistle, I Corinthians, and Kant's *Metaphysics of Morals*; "one month is the allotted time," he added.

Popery alternated with "inevitable self-consciousness," Delmore confessed to Paul Goodman, and there were those who found this trait more in evidence than his willful, arrogant side. "He was always uncomfortable with people," recalled the composer Arthur Berger, then a Harvard graduate student; whenever he was introduced to someone, he lisped and spoke in a nearly inaudible voice. A prose fragment entitled "A Day in the Thirties" provides an exhaustive portrait of his reticence and self-absorption.

> On Saturday morning Gottlieb woke up after ten and lay in bed thinking about the previous evening. Wherever I go, he said to himself, I have an important thing to watch, to guard against, to deny. When I go

into a room, a living room, as it is called, and greet
my friends and acquaintances, I begin to watch myself, I think only of whether I am cutting a fine figure
before them. Not to be laughed at, but to be respected, that would be one way of stating my motive.
But it means that I am always intent on myself. I do
not gaze upon the others except to see the effect of my
actions upon them, or to suspect their glance, their
look, their voice, of irony, contempt, or ignorance.
The ego, that is the great beast who stands between
me and a proper view of the world.

The more he contemplated himself, the more Delmore
tended to regard others as potential judges of his conduct
—a consequence of his fear that his own intuitions were
not to be trusted. But it was this very habit of introspection, promoted by a troubling failure of self-confidence,
that made him so eager for approbation and applause,
since "the great beast," his uncertain ego, could not sustain
itself without the esteem of others.

Memoirs of Delmore have tended to emphasize his noble
features, the large imposing head and lumbering dignity of
his gait. In Harry Levin's recollection of Delmore at
twenty-one, when he first came to Harvard, he had "a
laideur sympathique; his face resembled a mottled mask by
Jacob Epstein." To Gerson Brodie, an undergraduate who
got to know him that year, "his eyes and his brow were
indeed (at times) somewhat noble. When he cared to tidy
himself up, he was one you looked at twice in a group
because of his forehead and the crown of his head." These
massive features contributed to his authority. "When he
spoke," Brodie recalled, "everyone listened."

To Goodman, Delmore reported self-doubts that he kept
from his new acquaintances at Harvard. As always, he was
torn between poetry and philosophy, a predicament he described vividly in a letter to Goodman.

That I can make some unity of both is the well-known
pious hope: an abstract project which has but little
fact in my actual habits. Still I do find that the things
I want to think and write about do deserve some kind
of name in philosophy: revery over the essences might
be an adequately dignified title for considering the

tomato sauce on the veal cutlet, and the slice of tomato beside it as both a problem and a moment.

But he was enthusiastic about his professors, in particular Alfred North Whitehead. One of his letters to Goodman is devoted to a comical portrait of the faculty, culminating in a Dantesque account in blank verse of his first
encounter with Whitehead.

My courses are: Cosmologies with Whitehead,
Seminar in the Theory of Knowledge with Perry,
Advanced Ethics with Wild and Comparative Medieval Philosophy with Wolfson. Wolfson seems to be
good; so far he has merely said the things about the
Middle Ages that are no longer news. He has a
terrific accent, which seems almost a parody at times.
Wild is very poor and much too nervous to teach, and
Perry seems quite uninterested, or perhaps tired.
Whitehead, however, is certainly what is called a
character. He is perfectly conscious of his role as a
great man, and it delights him. Indeed he dresses for
the part in a kind of prime-minister's collar and cravat,
and toddles about looking for auditors, speaking of
the autumn of 1880, "when I first went to college"
and announcing that "I am really a muddle-headed
man, you know, liable to speak the most utter nonsense, you know." As he has also said that "Plato was
vewy [lisping] muddle-headed, you know," we now
may feel that muddle-headedness is crowned. His contempt for scholarship and learning is constantly repeated, as in his books, and he speaks continuously
about how inadequate language is, complaining that
the French Academy has just published a dictionary,
thus limiting the possibilities of meaning! No one will
accuse him of being a scholar: "I skip the whole
Middle Ages for two reasons: one, the theological
bias, two, I know nothing of it"; "a . . . a . . . a—what
was the name of that famous essay by Locke." In
today's lecture, commenting on the *Timaeus*, this is
what happened:

"Plato preferred the timeless, you know . . .
An utter mistake . . . absolute nonsense . . ."

And I, when the lecture was over, went up,
   asked Whitehead,
Shy and uneasy: "but I think that Plato
Thought that which is in time moves,
That which moves moves to an end
But that which moves to an end is imperfect.
Therefore the timeless is more perfect,
Therefore Plato preferred it . . ."
"But I can't think of a thing in time
But that it moves." "That's what I mean;
If in time, it moves: but then it is imperfect."
"But . . . a . . . But then he goes off here . . .
In the *Sophist* . . ." Turning the pages,
". . . aaa . . . who are you?" And then my turn
To stammer: "aaa . . . Schwartz . . ." "You've
Given me the proper answer, the proper
Answer. I'll take it up next time.
Remind me."

From then on, a sort of friendship was established between
them, and Delmore was invited to Whitehead's home on
occasion for lunch. Once he read an essay aloud to Whitehead, and was "reproved," he wrote Gertrude, "for a com-
pliment to him in the paper." But when he had finished,
Whitehead told him he had been "very penetrating," and
thanked him for having discovered an "unanalyzed problem" in *Process and Reality*. And on another occasion,
when Whitehead broke off in the midst of advising a student to read the work of the philosopher Alfred Edward
Taylor "with a grain of . . . a grain of . . ." Delmore rushed
to his assistance; "of salt, Professor Whitehead?" "Yes, yes,
I knew it was something mineral!" the relieved professor
exclaimed.

Less formal meetings with his professors occurred at
Bickford's, a cafeteria in Harvard Square, where the
French philosopher Étienne Gilson could be seen "devouring frankfurters and tomato salad as if he had not been
nourished for weeks." Professor Harry Wolfson also took
his meals there, and Delmore often joined him.

Wolfson is so learned [he wrote Zolotow] that he
could drive Sidney Hook into a convent . . . Of the
economic interpretation of philosophy, he says:

Aquinas was a big man—you want to make something of it? This, I hope, suggests his incredible accent
(Whitehead's is incredible, too, at the other pole, e.g.
the jolly bark of the dog, I will bet heavily), and in
Wolfson's class I often feel as if I ought to translate
for the rest of the class.

It impressed him that Wolfson, a Jew from Lithuania, was
a full professor at Harvard, where Delmore was far more
aware of his Jewishness than he had been at Wisconsin.
There were few Jews at Harvard then, and he felt conspicuous in such a Brahmin establishment. On this point,
his ideas were rather vague, as he revealed in a sonnet
composed about this time, "The Ghosts of James and
Peirce in Harvard Yard"; perhaps it was only to achieve a
phonetic effect that he heard in the reverberations of the
Appleton Chapel bell what he thought was Harvard's religious denomination: "Episcopalian! palian! tingled hard!"
Harvard had originally been Congregational, then Uni-
tarian, and later Protestant non-denominational; such dis-
tinctions, however, were lost on Delmore, who thought
only in terms of Jewish or "Other." Convinced that he was,
as Harry Levin characterized it, "in enemy territory," he
found Wolfson's presence on the faculty reassuring, for it
represented the possibility of penetrating behind the lines.
    Delmore established friendships with two other faculty
members, David Prall and F. O. Matthiessen. "Both of
them were bachelors, large-minded and keenly sensitive
men, who gave a great deal of their time and interest to
students," Levin recalled. In Prall's rooms at Leverett
House, Delmore found himself amid an exhilarating circle
of disciples that included Leonard Bernstein and Robert
Motherwell. Prall's "taste and sensitivity" appealed to these
aspiring artists, Arthur Berger observed in the preface to a
posthumous edition of his *Aesthetic Analysis*; like Delmore,
they were eager to establish formal premises on which to
base their work, and they found Prall's approach more
congenial than the logical positivist school then beginning
to dominate the department.
    Since Delmore considered himself an Aristotelian, he
felt particularly isolated from this new trend. Within a few
months of his arrival, he was complaining to Maurice
Zolotow that he was bored by "systems of noting down
logical relations so that they will be entirely free of meta-

physical consequences, and thus—but it does not matter—entirely free of meaning." He also made fun of the "hysterical new German school called Existence" that was coming into vogue. For Delmore, any philosophy that failed to interpret the vast, interrelated design of the world was of little value. He had urgent metaphysical questions to resolve, and the cautious, atomistic bias of logical positivism was no more palatable to him now than it had been when he was plotting the philosophy of *Having Snow* a few years before.

Even so, he found the intellectual atmosphere invigorating, despite his complaint to Zolotow that "the graduate students are haunted—each was a star back home and must work 15 hours a day to maintain his lovely idea of himself." Besides the seminars with Prall and Whitehead, he was taking courses in the philosophy and history of religion, metaphysics with Professor William Ernest Hocking, and C. I. Lewis's seminar on Kant. Delmore established a respectable record of A's and B's, and by the end of the first semester he had acquired a reputation as a very promising graduate student. But he had to force himself to concentrate on his studies; as always, he had to contend with "the pleasures of moving pictures" and other distractions—that year it was the Howard Burlesque Theater downtown and the Boston Table Tennis Triple League.

"I become more and more interested and attracted by Cambridge," Delmore wrote Gertrude just after the New Year. Moved by the snow in Harvard Yard, the ghosts of Emerson and Longfellow, the "eerie calm and power" that descended on him in Widener Library, he aimed at a life of high purpose: "What concerns me all the time, every conscious minute, is the effort to keep up a unity in all the pieces of my activity." He found in the lives of great artists a precedent for his own torments.

> The price of being gifted is being ungifted much of the time and just because the gift is so ravishing, so exhausting. This explains to me why Keats died young, why Beethoveen [*sic*] was ill-tempered, why Dante was vindictive and full of hate. . . .

But he was pleased with his efforts at discipline, celebrating the newly discovered virtues of Emersonian self-reliance in a colloquial, prosaic poem.

now, alone again,
I must take care of my laundry,
apportion my money, be tidy
in all things;
no one will be well-acquainted enough
to tell me what is wrong.

The problems of the hidden heart
must be tended well.
Who would doubt that I can learn
much concerning them
from polishing my shoes myself
and changing to heavy clothes
when it gets colder.

I eat well, when alone;
I get custards and milk, hot rolls and chocolate,
steaks and chops, fresh salads and cheese.
I must take care of myself,
no one else will.

Emersonian as well was Delmore's encompassing religiosity. He was surprisingly fervent in prayer, reserving "prescribed minutes for thoughts about the Deity" before sleep and brooding over "the evil that has darkened me this year especially" with a piety more reminiscent of Cardinal Newman than of a Modernist poet. But his prayers represented a plea to the Muse no less than a desire for salvation. He had made "decisive progress" with *Having Snow*, he reported to Gertrude; "but again I can't tell for sure for my state now is so ecstatic or hysterical that my powers of literary judgment scarcely exist." Vacillating wildly between excessive self-deprecation and lavish self-praise, he waited nervously for the verdicts of the literary journals to which he had lately begun to submit his work. Every day for three months he rushed down to his mailbox, anticipating word from *Southern Review*—and finally received an encouraging letter of rejection inviting him to try again. He had better luck with *Poetry*, which took two sonnets and an intelligent review of Louis MacNeice's new book; and not long afterward, he boarded the night boat from Boston to New York and called on Paul Rosenfeld, who greeted him with the news that a verse play of his had been accepted by the prestigious *New Caravan*, edited by Rosenfeld, Lewis Mumford, and Alfred Kreymborg. A week later, Delmore wrote Zolotow to announce the "widespread reception" of his work; Rosenfeld had called the play "genial," and intimated that, had it not been for a chapter from Thomas Wolfe that he was "forced to print," a short story of Delmore's would have been included as well. This last triumph was more than he could have hoped for, since *New Caravan* represented the older generation, publishing in its pages the work of e. e. cummings, William Carlos Williams, and Sherwood Anderson, among others. Delmore dated his "infatuation with poetry," he told Zolotow, from 1927, when Hart Crane's "Ave Maria" had appeared in the first *New Caravan*.

Both the sonnets accepted by *Poetry* and the verse play *Choosing Company* were characteristic of the vigorous, orotund style Delmore was developing. The precocious obsession with old age, the child's recollection of indeterminate fear, and the self-conscious echoes of Baudelaire that recurred so often in his work: these are the themes of the sonnets, themes that were to be refined in the poems of *In Dreams Begin Responsibilities*.

> Old age is not so serious, and I
> By the window sad and watchful as a cat,
> Build too this poem of old age and of snow,
> And weep: you are my snow man and I know
> I near you, you near him, all of us must die.

Choosing Company displayed another sort of convention, the use of blank verse to dramatize conversational speech. Its plot, suggested to Delmore by a scandal he had read about in the New York newspapers during the summer of 1933, in which an illegal abortion performed by a medical student resulted in a young girl's death, was incidental to the play's rhetoric. Ludicrous speeches imbued with a spurious philosophical urgency alternated with passages of stilted dialogue; he hadn't yet acquired the confidence to make use of the humor that figured so prominently in his extempore monologues among friends. Most of the play was taken up with Delmore's favorite motif, that fate determines character, summed up in Philip the medical student's lament:

> Now I feel the intolerable paralysis
> Of seeing disaster advance, helpless,
> As if I watched the dearest one drowning
> From the vice of distance.

(He might have done better to give more space to the cynical character in the play who remarks, after a particularly abstract speech, "I don't care for your reflections, Philip. Not the least bit, buddy.")

Toward the end of the play, the Radio, disembodied voice that anticipates Beckett, enters on a long harangue. In two pages of hysterical monologue that have nothing to do with the action, Delmore gave way to an unmistakable bitterness and fatigue.

> You must be very tired of me now, feeling that I take things too seriously. And here I become self-conscious once more, but that is good, despite the consequent hesitation and doubt. For hesitation and doubt, shame and remorse, fear and trembling, are the best parts of a human being.

Self-consciousness soon turns to polemic, as the Radio complains, "What sign is there that anyone loves anyone else in the United States of America?" Delmore's aggrieved sense of alienation, which he blamed on America's materialistic values, would deepen as he grew older, but it was even now beginning to affect his work. His attempts to write in a comic vein generally ended up miming what he called the "vaudeville of humiliation," where the artist mocks his own Chaplinesque, pathetic inadequacies. It was not his fault, he implied through the Radio's voice, that he was lonely and self-conscious; it was the fault of American society, which rewarded performers while ignoring poets.

Looked at another way, it could just as easily have seemed that literary talent, far from going unrecognized, was quite a valuable thing, now that *Choosing Company* had been published to considerable acclaim. His professors Prall and Matthiessen had praised it; William Phillips, writing in *New Masses*, applauded its "sensitiveness to the influences of modern literature"; and a notice of the anthology in *The New York Times Book Review* singled out Delmore's "Audenesque drama":

It is in a very modern mode, with a radio as chorus, and an old-fashioned case of abortion as theme, and it is impossible to say whether it is merely a clever piece or a prophetic piece. Probably it is both, and the *Caravan*, as it has done in the past, has given it the publicity it needs to determine its future.

Delmore was achieving recognition in philosophy as well; in the spring of 1936 he won the Bowdoin Prize for the best essay submitted by a graduate student in the humanities. "Poetry and Imitation" is a well-argued, idiosyncratic account of the experience of composition.

> In seeking metaphors, developments, contrasts and extensions of his idea, the poet is doing one thing: he is working out the consequences of his idea, he is finding out what it can amount to, what it results in, what it causes and what is done to it, when it is forced, by the pressure of his artistic act, into the world of his memory, his perceptions, his language and beliefs.

Elsewhere in the essay, he was given to unnecessary displays of erudition and naïve speculations about language and grammar. But his literary insights are cogent, and his casual asides to the "ideal reader" create an effect of confident informality. The confusion he felt in life seldom entered into his work, or at least not until much later on. Behind the intellectual poses and ostentatious literary references was a disinterested pleasure in the satisfactions of pure thought.

That winter the first issue of the *Marxist Quarterly* appeared, edited by James Burnham, Sidney Hook, and Meyer Schapiro, all of whom had been Delmore's teachers at N.Y.U.; and their gifted pupil was invited to reply to Schapiro's essay, "The Nature of Abstract Art," published in the first issue. He began by disputing Schapiro's demonstration of the social basis from which art derives, and set out to prove that art possessed an autonomous expressive value independent of the conditions that give rise to it. Returning to the idea of imitation, the "irreducible element in the artistic act and the artistic product" that had occupied him in his Bowdoin essay, Delmore invoked the

familiar metaphor of the mirror to illustrate how a work of
art reflects the nature of experience by means of what he
called "imitative truth." Here again, his training in philosophy enabled him to make systematic formulations about
aesthetics while providing the artist with a unique purpose:
to discover and reproduce in his own intuitive fashion the
determining features of his private landscape, and to elicit
from these features (perhaps unconsciously) the social,
perhaps even moral character of a particular time.

> Mirror, virtue's feature, criticism, the reality of ex-
> perience and the uncreated conscience: it would seem
> that it is by separating these in discourse and seeing
> them together in the work of art that we can under-
> stand the pleasure and illumination which art affords
> us, as well as its importance in history and society.

In saying all this, Delmore had made a considerable
departure from Schapiro's argument in order to state his
own case against the sort of doctrinaire Marxist literary
criticism that was then in vogue; but he had put aside the
self-conscious mannerisms and contentiousness that flawed
his previous essays in favor of an impressive restraint. This
brief "Note on the Nature of Art" remains among his most
accomplished criticism.

.

Delmore's letters to Gertrude, who still lived at home
and was working for the Federal Emergency Relief Administration, were filled with impassioned declarations of
love. "What an intelligent marriage this is going to be!" he
exulted. "From such critical love will come a symmetry of
moral grandeur, as if the left hand were able to perfect
immediately the imperfections done by the right hand." He
dreamed of the children they would have—"we desire increase—and the thought makes me drunk"—and sent her
poems lamenting that he had "left his heart two hundred
miles away."

And yet, for all their romantic intensity, a peculiar note
of darkness and dread can be heard in these poems. Gertrude was invariably his "warm fate," his "sister," "complex and unclear"; and in an ominous "Song for Gertrude,"
he compared their marriage quite openly to death.

Soon doubled is our mortality,
For one will see the other die;
Soon, marrying, we double deal
The cards of hope and fear, and buy,
For all the friendship of the night,
But night prevails, beyond our job,
A second shadow, sick or well,
And tripled by our unborn boy.

Delmore found Gertrude's "dark side" inaccessible, complaining in his letters of her "bitterness," her "hateful mask," her "sick temper"; but she may well have been put off in turn by his condescension. Nor would she have been pleased when, after an account of some elaborate transactions involving the ordering of books from New York, he remarked: "All of this shows how much I need a wife."

All the same, Delmore's letters to Gertrude were in other ways generous and selfless. Like the Maxwell of still another of his autobiographical novels, Delmore derived a confidence from his recent successes that made him "vigorous and assured. And in his happiness he turned to Martha with an affection which overflowed." There was a restraint, a sort of innocence, to their courtship that was very much of the period. "Most of the boys don't know how to make love," Delmore wrote of the Goodman circle in an unpublished chapter of "The World Is a Wedding," "and they marry the wrong girl because she was the first one or the second to be easy." By his own admission "squeamish" about sex, Delmore preferred to see their relationship in terms of a "thirst after righteousness"; he was "properly scandalized" by the quarrels of a young couple who lived next door until he found out they were married, and accused Julian Breen of being "carnal" because he lived with a girl.

When he was home for vacation, Delmore often slept on a couch in the Washington Heights apartment of his friend Lincoln Reis, an instructor in philosophy at N.Y.U., who was five years older than Delmore and newly married. The younger couple relied on the Reises to mediate their disputes, but it was usually Delmore who presented his grievances, while Gertrude listened in silence. Her doubts were expressed in more subliminal ways; visiting Mary Reis in the hospital, she scrawled the legend "Miserere Me" on a steamed-up window. Delmore, meanwhile, was noting in his journal: "I know at least two girls I would rather marry."

In the fall of 1936, Delmore returned to Harvard in the midst of its tercentenary celebration. More cynical than reverent, he listened to the pompous speeches, observed the grandiose parades festooned with crimson VERITAS banners, and noted the celebrities in attendance: President Roosevelt, John Masefield, C. G. Jung, Arthur Eddington, and Rudolf Carnap, "none of them, it seemed, very much at ease." He took a Dantesque view of the proceedings, remarking, as the classes, beginning with that of 1860, marched by: "One had not known that life had undone so many."

Delmore took up residence that year in a room that rented for only two dollars a month at 94 Prescott Street, down the hall from Arthur Berger and Gerson Brodie. Here he settled into a chaotic existence, the only kind he would ever know: reading all night, his bed strewn with books, he would announce every morning that he hadn't slept at all, and his pale, disheveled appearance supported his claim. He worked hard, hoping to win a fellowship for the following year, since Rose refused to support him any longer. Prall promised to recommend him, but in the end nothing came of it, and in March 1937, Delmore left Harvard in such haste that he neglected even to finish packing or to return the library books he had out. He was now, in William Barrett's words, "a young man in a hurry."

5

———•———

DELMORE LEFT HARVARD without taking a degree because he was "bursting with *the* book he had to get out so that he could then marry *the* girl. And in the optimistic manner of the movies then, this chapter of his life might carry the tag: boy publishes book, boy marries girl." This fanciful account of William Barrett's tells only part of the story, for Delmore had not yet secured any formal proposal from a publisher, although both Clifton Fadiman, then editor in chief of Simon & Schuster, and W. W. Norton had expressed interest in a prospective novel. Fadiman wanted to see ten thousand words before he would commit himself, which Delmore construed to mean that he was eager "to finance an unwritten novel"; in Fadiman's recollection, the work submitted "did not shape up into a book."

As for his marriage to Gertrude, which Delmore had taken to regarding as "inevitable," that too was uncertain; after a violent quarrel in Van Cortlandt Park provoked when he tried to kiss her and was rebuffed, Gertrude said she would never marry him. Writing to Arthur Berger that summer, Delmore offered another reason for the delay; he couldn't afford to get married, since the lawyers in charge of his father's estate refused to turn over what remained of his inheritance until his twenty-fifth birthday.

Whether or not a lack of money was responsible for the postponement of his marriage, it certainly contributed to his decision to leave Harvard. Delmore owed a considerable debt to the bursar, which he would acknowledge only to himself, noting in "The Story of a Heart" his "lies about Harvard"; to others, he stressed that Prall had advised him to renounce the "barren academicism" of the university. "In the end, it would have been possible to return to Harvard," he declared to Arthur Berger, "but only without Gertrude, which made it impossible as far as I was concerned."

In the winter of 1937, Rose Schwartz decided to move back to Washington Heights so she would be closer to her family. Delmore welcomed this return to his old, familiar neighborhood, and was glad to be closer to Gertrude, but he was unhappy living at home, and after another quarrel with his mother when she insisted he read in the kitchen to conserve electricity, he went to live in various boarding-houses or in Woodstock, New York, where he took a room for a while to be near William Barrett. Later on in the summer, he moved to 302 West 109th Street in the Columbia University neighborhood, where he worked in the afternoons before going home to dinner. In a letter to Delmore some years later, William Barrett reminisced:

> The vision of you walking across Broadway through a heavy traffic towards the 8th Avenue subway and home is one of my most vivid, and symbolic memories of the '30's. Skipping through that traffic you certainly looked the lonely 'clerc' (your term) struggling against the world. That day I watched you I felt sorry for you!

He had reason to feel sorry, for Delmore was in a desolate mood that summer. Imprisoned in the "Hell of listlessness," as he described his condition to Gertrude, he was so tormented by insomnia that he went to a doctor, who prescribed the sleeping pills that were to become, over the next three decades, a pernicious addiction. His perpetual exhaustion made any disturbance intolerable, and he fled from one boardinghouse to another in search of quiet, dragging his typewriter and cartons of books all over the city. Once, in Barrett's company, he found a house in the Chelsea district of Manhattan that advertised rooms, but the landlady, "an altogether remarkable blend of Jewish *yenta* and French *concierge*," was suspicious of this "bedraggled pair." Desperately seeking assurances that he would find quiet in her rooms, Delmore "seemed to slip back a generation," Barrett recalled, "and he and the woman might have been haggling across a push-cart." "Sure it's quiet here," the woman said. "What do you want, a tomb?" "I have trouble sleeping," Delmore patiently explained. "Why can't you sleep?" the woman asked; then, pointing to Barrett: "Look at your friend—" "He has his troubles, too," Delmore insisted. "Yeah, but he looks like he sleeps. And look at you—" They finally reached an agreement, but within a week Delmore was out on the street looking for another room. "That woman wouldn't stop talking," he complained.

"In the Naked Bed, in Plato's Cave," one of Delmore's most widely anthologized poems, represents his earliest testament to the torment of insomnia. Originating in Plato's allegory of the cave in the *Republic*, where chained men stare at the shadows on a wall and mistake them for reality, "In the Naked Bed" presents the sleepless Delmore, troubled and awake at dawn:

> In the naked bed, in Plato's cave,
> Reflected headlights slowly slid the wall,
> Carpenters hammered under the shaded window,
> Wind troubled the window curtains all night long,
> A fleet of trucks strained uphill, grinding,
> Their freights covered, as usual.
> The ceiling lightened again, the slanting diagram
> Slid slowly forth.
>   Hearing the milkman's chop,
> His striving up the stair, the bottle's chink,
> I rose from bed, lit a cigarette,
> And walked to the window. The stony street
> Displayed the stillness in which buildings stand,
> The street-lamp's vigil and the horse's patience.
> The winter sky's pure capital
> Turned me back to bed with exhausted eyes.
>
> Strangeness grew in the motionless air. The loose
> Film grayed. Shaking wagons, hooves' waterfalls,
> Sounded far off, increasing, louder and nearer.
> A car coughed, starting. Morning, softly
> Melting the air, lifted the half-covered chair
> From underseas, kindled the looking-glass,
> Distinguished the dresser and the white wall.
> The bird called tentatively, whistled, called,
> Bubbled and whistled, so! Perplexed, still wet
> With sleep, affectionate, hungry and cold. So, so,
> O son of man, the ignorant night, the travail
> Of early morning, the mystery of beginning
> Again and again,
>   while History is unforgiven.

This astonishing poem is the work of an old man, wise with age and the fatigue brought on by contemplating history. "History is a nightmare during which I am trying to get a good night's rest," he once noted in his journal, reversing the famous remark of Joyce's Dedalus. Delmore used to say that he was twice as old as everyone else because he never slept; and the brilliant metaphorical rhetoric of "In the Naked Bed" dwells on the passage of time with a sense of brooding fatality more reminiscent of Hardy in his eighties than of a poet not yet twenty-four.

In his letters, too, Delmore sounded a world-weary note; writing to Arthur Berger, he compared his life to Kafka's *The Trial*. Bitter about the circumstances that had forced him to leave Harvard, he implored his friends there to send him his books and the slippers he had left behind; in one extraordinary letter to Arthur Berger, he even managed to transform his incessant demands into a rebuke.

> I am becoming sick and tired of asking you to do things for me—not that you do not do them, but that I dislike being a nuisance. Nevertheless, there is nothing else I can do but ask you. . . . If you have not yet sent me the slippers, don't mail them but bring them home with you. And if you can, when you are getting stamps, ask about my mail at the post office. I am sure that at least one letter has been mislaid.

In effect, it was Berger's fault that Delmore had to ask him to do so many chores.

Toward the end of the summer, his spirits revived; in "The Story of a Heart" he attributed his improvement to the Giants' pennant drive, but a more substantial cause was literary success. *Poetry* had accepted some poems, and Robert Penn Warren, then editor of *Southern Review*, had encouraged him to submit a short story. He was invited to speak to The Club, a group of young people who met on Surf Avenue on Coney Island to discuss books and ideas, and gave a "charming" talk for which he was paid ten dollars. In July, he submitted some work to James Laughlin, who had founded his publishing house New Directions the previous year, and enclosed a modest note inquiring whether Laughlin "intended to pay any attention to unsolicited contributions." Less timidly, he suggested: "I think the enclosed pieces are the kind of work you want for your anthology." They were, and Laughlin promptly accepted them for the second New Directions anthology.

New Directions had appeared on the scene at an auspicious time. In the late thirties, publishers had still not recovered from the Depression, and Laughlin, scion of a wealthy Pittsburgh steel family, had been encouraged by Ezra Pound to start a publishing house of his own (with Pound as one of his principal authors). In the fall of 1936, back from Pound's home in Rapallo with letters of introduction, he set up an office in Norfolk, Connecticut, from where, not long afterward, the first New Directions book, Montagu O'Reilly's *Pianos of Sympathy*, appeared, followed by William Carlos Williams's novel *White Mule*. By the time Delmore approached him, Laughlin, still a Harvard undergraduate, had become an influential publisher.

The poems of his that appeared in the 1937 anthology, beside the work of Henry Miller, Gertrude Stein, and e. e. cummings, were three slight lyrics typical of the pathos and faint romantic effusion of his lesser verse. But the story was another matter. Although Delmore chose not to include it in *The World Is a Wedding*, "The Commencement Day Address" is a bizarre imaginative tale about a controversial address delivered by the historian Dr. Isaac Duspenser at a college-graduation ceremony. From the beginning, Dr. Duspenser's eccentric and mildly scandalous pronouncements move his audience to nervous laughter; he comes before them as a "travelling salesman," a vaudeville artist whose intent, he tells them, is "to sell you my idea of time." Then, with great vivacity, he begins to lecture to a scandalized audience on the brevity of life and their own mortality. Richard Ellmann has said of Joyce's story "The Dead," written when he was about the same age as Delmore was at this point, that "young writers reach their greatest eloquence in dwelling upon the horrors of middle age and what follows it." Certainly this was true of Delmore, whose most impressive speculative flights were usually reserved for the subject of death. But the other notable feature of this story is the inventiveness of the prose. During a pause in the doctor's speech, "an airplane gnawed overhead, bare, abstract and geometrical in the cloud-flowered sky"; there is "the sizzle of the taxis' tires on the wet avenue"; and, as the audience disperses after the graduation ceremonies, the narrator evokes "the metropolitan city, narrow and tall on all sides, full of traffic, accident, commerce and adultery, of a thousand drugstores, apartment houses and theatres, its belly veined with black subways, its towers and bridges grand, numb, and without meaning."

Other triumphs soon followed. Late that August, he submitted "In Dreams Begin Responsibilities" to *Partisan Review*, which had originally been the official organ of the John Reed Clubs and was now being revived as a literary journal independent of the Communist Party. Philip Rahv, William Phillips, and F. W. Dupee, the founders of the new magazine, were determined to repudiate the doctrinaire Stalinism that dominated the literary magazines of the period in favor of a Marxist-oriented but non-ideological criticism. Earlier, in June, at the Second American Writers' Congress, Phillips and Rahv, joined by Dwight Macdonald and Dupee, had praised Trotsky and spoken in favor of the freedom of writers to pursue their own imaginative vision unhampered by politics, a heresy which promptly caused their expulsion from the Party; not long afterward he joined with Phillips and Dupee to found the new *Partisan Review*.

Where the twenties had seen a resurgence of American literature in the novels of Hemingway, Dos Passos, and Fitzgerald, the editors of *Partisan Review* now turned to Europe in search of a more cosmopolitan intellectual identity; their avowed purpose was to promote what Rahv called the "Europeanization of American literature." In his view, American writers could learn a great deal from Mann, Gide, and "committed" novelists like Silone and Malraux, for whom socialism was a historical force to be taken seriously in their work. As Leslie Fiedler has pointed out, *PR* "was born of a marriage of Greenwich Village and Marxism—or more properly, from the attempt to woo the disaffected, rootless American, who wandered into New York in search of cultural freedom, from bohemianism to radicalism." Among his generation, no one had a more acute sense of these developments than Delmore, for whom exile was both a historical condition and the artist's particular curse. "Art becomes exile too," he claimed in *Shenandoah*; "A secret and a code studied in secret, / Declaring the agony of modern life."

He also had an uncanny gift for anticipating new developments in literary taste, and the editors of *PR*, to whom he had sent "In Dreams Begin Responsibilities" just as they were planning their first issue, "had the sense to recognize it as a masterpiece," in Dwight Macdonald's recollection. They decided at once to place it in the front of their first issue, before contributions from Edmund Wilson, Lionel Trilling, Sidney Hook, James T. Farrell, and even Picasso.

Curious about the possessor of that "unlikely" name, Rahv wrote in September inviting Delmore to lunch. On the day of their meeting, Barrett made sure Delmore was properly dressed, so that he would make a good impression. Rahv, casual, unkempt, more like the "heavy bear" of Delmore's poem than Delmore himself, was not one to stand on ceremony; and when Delmore returned from their date, he reproved Barrett for having worried over such a superficial matter as clothes. "You and your fussing! You should have seen Philip Rahv—He looked like the Paris Commune."

Authoritarian, large and intimidating, Rahv was stubborn about his literary preferences. He cared only for Dostoevsky and the great European realists, with some accommodation for such masters of Modernism as Proust and Mann. Dogmatic about his intellectual heroes, he struck Mary McCarthy as "an intransigent, pontificating young Marxist." But his background and harsh polemical style appealed to Delmore at first. Born in the Ukraine, Rahv had acquired his education on his own, in public libraries, and had more in common with the generation of Delmore's parents than with that of assimilated Jews, a fact which tended to make him less sensitive to the latter's cultural anxieties. To be a genuine immigrant rather than the mere son of immigrants was somehow an advantage; it made for a more authentic identity.

When he first met Delmore, Rahv was impressed by his "extreme precocity"; it was, he recalled many years later, Delmore's "most conspicuous trait." But he was also vain, in Rahv's view, and given to imposing his will on others. While stressing Delmore's "personal charm," Rahv noted "a slight stutter that served only to draw attention to his frequently extravagant speech, whose undercurrent of humor accentuated all the more his exigent sense of being-in-the-world, [but] could seldom obliterate the worried self-concern that possessed him."

Rahv himself was incapable of loyalty, a fact that en-

abled him to give such an unsparing appraisal of his
former friend; nor would Delmore have been surprised by
it, for he was aware of this deficiency in Rahv. "Philip does
have scruples," he used to say, "but he never lets them
stand in his way." And though Delmore was, like everyone
else, overwhelmed at times by the sheer force of Rahv's
personality, he could deflect that force through satire, jok-
ing that Rahv was a "manic-impressive" and referring to
him as "Philip Slav."

Rahv's portrait of Delmore was written late in life, on
the occasion of the publication of Delmore's *Selected
Essays*,* while Delmore's impression of Rahv, recorded in
the forties, is best conveyed by a single manuscript page of
a story called "The Complete Adventuress." The identity of
the couple he describes would have been transparent in any
case, but he removed all ambiguity by writing in the margin, "Mary & Philip (1937)." The Mary in question was
Mary McCarthy, and Delmore portrayed their affair with
comical malice.

When Helena met Stanislaus, a big and powerful
radical politician, she felt for the first time that she
was with one who pleased her whole being. She went
to live with Stanislaus and she took a job which
brought her into touch with radical politics. She soon
found that there was a roughness about Stanislaus and
a rudeness and a habit of being too serious in conversation which she did not like in the least. She tried
to correct his rudeness and roughness, his habit of
getting into taxis before she did, and his brusqueness
in conversing with persons he did not estimate highly.
And she tried to make him cultivate a lightness of
tone in conversation, making him read the sophisticated metropolitan periodicals. Stanislaus was so
pleased with Helena that he tried to improve himself,

* Rahv's attitude toward these essays was extremely contradictory;
when Joseph Epstein, then an editor at Quadrangle Books, wrote to
him after Delmore's death asking whether he thought publication of
a selection of Delmore's essays was warranted, Rahv replied that
such a project would be a waste of time. Then, when the *Selected
Essays* appeared the following year, he reviewed them in *The New
York Review of Books*, and began his review, "This book has been
much too long in the making."

although lightness was foreign to his whole being. More and more, Helena felt an extraordinary admiration as well as affection for Stanislaus. He was superior to her and inferior to her in precisely the way that suited her profoundest need. To their friends who composed a curious circle in which those who were engaged in left-wing politics mixed with those from the theatre and the concert-hall, the infatuation Helena felt and expressed for Stanislaus was such as to make it difficult for one to keep a straight face, for Stanislaus might have remarked merely that the day had been a cold one for early October and Helena then felt compelled to declare that Stanislaus had a consciousness of the external world which disregarded nothing.

Delmore often met Rahv and McCarthy for drinks at the Vanderbilt during the fall of 1937, and McCarthy was fascinated by Delmore's "violet eyes"; he was "beautiful, a mischievous poetic child," she recalled. Delmore was even more fascinated by McCarthy, to the point of obsession, and he devoted many manuscript pages over the years to the vicissitudes of her love life. He was especially fond of a remark Sidney Hook had made to the effect that "people do what they want anyway. She at least admits it." It was this freedom that the unhappily prudish Delmore found so enviable, and he noted the most intimate gossip about her in his journal with a sort of voyeuristic fascination. Later on, as her marriages and affairs multiplied, he perfected for the edification of friends a "day-long epic account" of how Theodore Spencer, a professor at Harvard, had courted her; and he professed to know all about her marriage in the forties to Bowden Broadwater, who wore a coat with a mink collar and was known at Harvard as the "Orchid Boy."

Toward the end of 1937, McCarthy suddenly left Rahv for Edmund Wilson, a development Delmore dwelled on with great exuberance. He liked to put about that Rahv had been so vehement in praise of Wilson's abilities as a critic that the ambitious McCarthy had finally taken him at his word and transferred her allegiance. In a two-page draft of a story labeled "Mary, Philip, Wilson," Delmore further amplified his portrait of "a charming & intelligent"

couple given to "annihilating the pretensions and mocking
the vanity of other human beings," a practice that "gave
them much gratification." (As for Wilson, Delmore observed only that he looked like Herbert Hoover.)

F. W. Dupee, another of the original *Partisan* editors,
received equally unsparing treatment in Delmore's manuscripts and in a published story, "New Year's Eve," where
he appeared under the name of Oliver Jones. Dupee was a
decade older than Delmore, and had worked for the Party
as a political organizer on the New York waterfront. When
Delmore met him, he had just resigned as literary editor of
the *New Masses* to join *PR*. Some weeks after "In Dreams
Begin Responsibilities" was accepted, Delmore submitted
some poems to *PR*, and Dupee took them home to his
furnished room in Chelsea to read. Eager to meet their
author, he took Delmore out to lunch, and came away
with an impression of his "immense charm," the "wonderful flow of remark" that spilled from him spontaneously.
He was "one of the great gossips of all time," Dupee recalled, and despite his "boyish, teasing manner," he could
be devastating in his comments on other people. He
seemed to know all there was to know about the older
generation of writers, their biographies and works, which
he kept track of "like baseball statistics." With his mar-
velous invective, his incredible command of literary information, and "a half-ironic parading of erudition" that reminded Dupee of Auden, Delmore seemed the very type of
the poetic genius.

Dwight Macdonald has also left a vivid impression of
Delmore in the year of his literary debut.

> Delmore was twenty-four that year, but his open,
> ardent manner and his large, dreaming eyes, sensitive
> mouth, and proud good looks as of a newly fledged
> eaglet made him seem younger. . . .
> He was a master of the great American folk art of
> kidding, an impractical joker—words were his me-
> dium—outraging dignity and privacy, present com-
> pany most definitely not excepted, pressing the attack
> until it reached a comic grandeur that had even the
> victim laughing. An intellectual equivalent of the
> Borscht Circuit *tummler*, or stirrer-upper, his wide
> mouth grinning, his speedy raucous New York voice
> running up and down the scale of sarcasm, invective,

desperate rationality, gasping ridicule, his nervous hands clutching his head in despair at the obtuseness of his antagonist or flung wide in triumphant demonstration or stabbing the air with a minatory forefinger. And he could take it as well as dish it out. I can't remember him irritated by the most drastic counterattack; indeed he seemed to welcome direct onslaughts on himself and his ideas like a skilled swordsman who knows he can deflect the thrust. In more placid talk, he was even more impressive, quick on the uptake, bringing to bear on the point a richness of reference and of imagination. He was a conversationalist, not a monologist, his style of discourse being dialectical, depending on the other person, or persons, to stimulate him to his greatest reaches.

This portrait of Delmore as a brilliant talker figures in the recollections of virtually everyone who knew him then, with the exception of the Goodman circle, who found his wit obtrusive; but their allegiance was to Goodman, so that Delmore's ironic manner appeared to them more the defensiveness of an outsider than the gay, lavish vivacity depicted by Macdonald.

Delmore always aspired to write what he described in one of his last notebooks as "contemporary moral and social history," a phrase less grandiose than it sounds if one has in mind Isaac Rosenfeld's definition of gossip as a form of social history; and in one notable story, "New Year's Eve," he managed to raise gossip to the level of literary art. Reading George Eliot and Tolstoy, a character in one of Delmore's unpublished novels despairs of ever writing fiction, "for he was unable to imagine how a man or a woman would act in many different kinds of circumstances." Delmore himself found it difficult to escape from autobiography, but when he did address himself to others, he produced some of the best social history of his time.

"New Year's Eve," inspired by a party at William Phillips's New York apartment at the close of 1937, is written with a fine sardonic eye toward the frailty of Delmore's intellectual friends, all of whom would be readily recognizable even without the key supplied in his notes. Dupee, as Oliver Jones, he depicted as "an interesting and unfortunate human being" provoked by his failure as a novelist into cynical pronouncements on literary history; Macdonald, caricatured in the person of Grant Landis as having "a pathological excess of energy," was shown making endless phone calls to raise money for some jailed labor leaders; the hapless Leon Berg, universally resented "because his chief activity was to explain to all authors that they were without talent," was a malicious version of the critic Lionel Abel; Barrett, the Nicholas O'Neill of the story, "who was unhappy and who suffered from a cold," spent the evening soaking his chilled feet in the bathtub; and Gertrude, as Wilhelmina Fine, was said to have "the sensibility of an only child who for twenty-four years has been adored, tended, and nagged by her parents." Caught up in academic disputes, afflicted by excessive self-consciousness, the guests wore one another down until everyone shared the same condition, "what was soon to be a post-Munich sensibility: complete hopelessness of perception and feeling."

It was for himself, though, in the familiar persona of Shenandoah Fish, that Delmore reserved the most pity. While "in other cages of the room, other human beings were trying without success to get along with each other," he sulked alone, despairing over his inability "not to get into arguments with other human beings, especially those he liked." The promising author of "a satirical dialogue between Freud and Marx" (Delmore's verse play *Coriolanus and His Mother* was such a work), Shenandoah "had for long cherished the belief that if he were an interesting and gifted author, everyone would like him and want to be with him and enjoy conversation with him." Cruel as they seem, Delmore's portraits of his friends are not wholly without sympathy. He considered them as vulnerable as himself, and portrayed this vulnerability as a style of the period. Literature offered a means of acquiring social grace and importance; it gave him an opportunity "to prepare a face to meet the faces that you meet," to conquer the Prufrockian hesitancy he detected in himself and in his friends. So he distributed his fate among them, as if to dilute his private dilemmas by rendering them symptomatic of the "post-Munich sensibility."

•

By late autumn, Delmore's literary career was on its way. Macdonald introduced him at a party as "the new

Hart Crane"; *Southern Review* commissioned an essay
from him on Hemingway; in London, Julian Symons took
a poem for his magazine *New Verse*; and *Poetry* bought
several poems they had turned down for lack of space a
few months before. Laughlin was calling him "the American
Auden" and publishing whatever he submitted to the New
Directions anthology.

As if to conceal his excitement, Delmore tended to adopt
an offhand manner that verged on arrogance. Writing to
Arthur Berger, he declared: "All I ask, so far as literary
fortune goes, is to appear always in the same issue with
[James T.] Farrell—the contrast is wonderful." Modesty
was not one of Delmore's most conspicuous traits, and the
more celebrated he became, the more he reverted to
"megalo"—or, as he now took to calling it, "Machiavellianism." It was an appropriate eponym in view of the
military strategy Delmore had mapped out for his career.
He was convinced that one had to plot and scheme to get
ahead, and once reproached his friend Lincoln Reis for
serving steak when Delmore was the only guest. "You're
throwing this away on me," he said. "It should be saved
for the chairman of the department." In the belief that
"one had to know the right people," he called on Harold
Rosenberg, at the time an aspiring poet in Brooklyn, and
announced that he "would go anywhere to meet a poet."
He was invited to Clifton Fadiman's home, visited Margaret Marshall, the literary editor of *The Nation*, and cultivated the friendship of Dorothy Norman, "friend of
Rosenfeld, Steiglitz, et al.," who was then starting her
magazine *Twice a Year*.

On his twenty-fourth birthday, December 8, Delmore
moved with Kenneth to a boardinghouse just off Washington Square, at 73 Washington Place. Their room, an attic
loft with low rafters above Bertolotti's Italian Restaurant,
could be reached only by climbing a ladder. He soon fell
into a routine of sleeping until noon, working until dinner,
and then walking to Times Square to take in a movie.
Later on, he recalled these months in the preface to a book
on Eliot he wrote but never published.

   After the picture was over and I had left the theatre
with my customary sense of guilt at the waste of an
evening, I returned to the room where I lived with my

brother and for the first time during the whole day enjoyed a genuine human relationship. All that I had done in that respect during the earlier part of the day was to tell the waitress behind the counter what I wanted for lunch and communicate in like terms with the waiter in a restaurant when I had my dinner.

He would come home to find Kenneth eager to talk about what had happened that day in the office where he worked, Pecker Brothers Artificial Flowers. But Delmore was patronizing toward what he thought of as his brother's commonplace existence, and distressed by the differences of temperament that estranged them: "I sighed to think how far apart we were, although we had been in the same house and the same bedroom almost always from the day we were born."

Delmore produced some of the best work of his career during these solitary months. Over three days in November, just before moving to the Village, he composed one of his most impressive stories, a twenty-page tale entitled "Screeno." Why this story was never published during his lifetime,* or even typed up, is hard to understand, for it belongs beside "In Dreams Begin Responsibilities" among his few prose masterpieces. "Screeno" introduces the familiar figure of Delmore, identified by one of the many variants on his name, Cornelius Schmidt, who sits alone in his mother's apartment listening to a Haydn string quartet.

He seated himself by the window and watched the quiet October evening rain soundlessly falling through the bright arc of the streetlight downstairs, four floors below, and pocking and wrinkling the glittering puddles. Automobiles passed with a frying sound which tires make on wet streets. Cornelius took down a volume of poetry of which he was very fond and tried to read it. A poem of his own slipped from the book. He read the first few verses and shuddered, thoroughly disheartened. Drenched by such a tasteless, colorless mood, there was only one refuge, one sanctuary: the movies.

* It has since appeared in *Partisan Review*.

At the theater, he discovers that a lottery is to be held after the newsreel. From there, the story takes a fantastic turn; the houselights come on, the lottery gets under way, and Cornelius realizes that every number the master of ceremonies calls out is on his card. As the numbers continue to come up in his favor, he thinks: "Two more chances to win the big prize, and buy fifty volumes in the Loeb Classical Library." On the last number, he wins, and, declaring his victory in a triumphant voice, strides forward to the stage. The prize, $425, is his. But when the master of ceremonies asks him what he does for a living, Cornelius is too flustered to answer, and the audience roars with laughter at his awkwardness. Defiant now, he takes the microphone and recites a passage from *Gerontion*. "Those verses were written by the best of modern poets," he lectures the audience, "a man named T. S. Eliot, whom all of you ought to read." From here on, the story is full of Kafkaesque incidents; an old man claims that he has also won, and a dispute ensues between him and the management, arbitrated by members of the audience. Cornelius, aware that the old man is being cheated, blurts into the microphone: "Don't be hopelessly middle-class about this. The management is trying to cheat an old man." At once, he is identified as a radical and shouted off the stage. Touched by the old man's lamentations, Cornelius impulsively hands over his own winnings and leaves the theater. On his way home, he meditates on his gracious act:

The problem now, said Cornelius to himself as he walked through the soft-carpeted lobby, is to keep this from my mother, who will consider me Quixotic, as indeed I am. But how small a price for the sense of generosity and dignity which I now have, even though the act was forced upon me by my maudlin sympathy for the old man. Probably I have been foolish, and yet how reasonable I feel at present, and how joyous.

The verses of a fourteenth-century Scottish poet on the transience of worldly goods come to mind, and he recites them happily; upon which, "joyous with a sense of having done proudly what he wanted to do, and with the fog hiding from him most of the street and surrounding his

head, he came back to his house and the room where he
would be once more alone."

His criticism, too, was at its height. In a great burst of
energy, he had revised his brilliant review of Yvor Winters's *Primitivism and Decadence* for *Southern Review*,
written on Pound's latest *Cantos*, and finished a long essay
on Hemingway. For the inaugural issue of *Kenyon Review*,
in 1939, Delmore produced a masterly essay on Auden in
which he proposed that there were really "two Audens,"
the Marxist and the Freudian. He found Auden's espousals
of Marxist ideology unconvincing, and canceled out in any
case by the consequences of the Munich Pact. This aspect
of Auden, the voice of social and contemporary themes, he
labeled the Ego, repository of "the conscious motives of
the poet"; Auden's other, more authentic voice—in Delmore's terminology, the Id—resembled a "sibyl who utters
the telltale symbols in a psychoanalytic trance." It was a
very ingenious model, one that allowed him to show how
too great a reliance on the conscious will and the public
self could serve only to repress the poet's true relationship
to experience, which was to report on his "intuitions of
psychic life." One of Delmore's characteristic stances was
this insistence on the poet as seer, a medium of truths
whose power lay in their independence from the vicissitudes of common reality. His own aspiration was to remain
indifferent to the merely visible, choosing, like Joyce's
Dedalus, to comprehend life "purified in and reprojected
from the human imagination."

Delmore's appraisal of Winters was equally strict, only
here the problem was philosophical. Winters's obsession
with the moral character of poetry amounted to "philos-
ophy-mongering," he complained, a habit for which he rebuked Eliot, Blackmur, Edmund Wilson, and Kenneth
Burke in passing. He was quick to point out the fallacy of
judging an author's belief rather than "the *representation* of
a belief" expressed in a poem: "We have to insist that the
poem is not a mere prolongation of experience upon the
verbal level, but experience grasped, understood, and evalu-
ated." Winters had tried to determine a poem's value from
its meter alone, and the variations on that meter, a method
Delmore refuted by means of a few judicious illustrations
from English poetry—in particular Milton, for whom "the
primary means of expressiveness" was diction; "the fusion

of style and meter, meaning and meter, provides the expressiveness of the poem, and carries its tone and attitude."

It is hard to overestimate the achievement of this essay. Respectful of Winters and modest in registering dissent, Delmore nevertheless presented a systematic critique drawn from the very models Winters had cited in his book. In this, and in the essay on Hemingway, as well as in a long evaluation of Dos Passos published the same year, he was writing major criticism. He himself felt that the composition of these essays had been "forced"; to the reader, no such struggles are evident. Poets have often produced their best work while still in their twenties, but as Rahv noted in his review of the *Selected Essays*, "it is only very rarely that a critic has contributed anything memorable at that age."

These were months of "elation and activity," Delmore recalled in his autobiographical notes, a time of beleaguering magazines for reviews, meeting editors, and writing every day. No sooner had he finished "Screeno," in mid-November, than he composed "The Ballad of the Children of the Czar," one of the best poems in *In Dreams Begin Responsibilities*. His grandfather's desertion from the Russian Army, referred to briefly in this poem, was also the subject of a promising story—unfortunately abandoned after seven pages—that he was working on at the time. "A Letter to a Former Sweetheart" was narrated by one of the young men (in this case, a composer) who had by now become a convention of Delmore's stories, "in love with art, ashamed of the habits and values of his parents, and full of the most serious and childish pretensions." In effect, two stories were told in "A Letter": that of his father's father in the Russo-Turkish War and a poignant account of how his other grandfather was forced out of business in the old country by his competitive brother-in-law, and thus decided to come to America. These largely autobiographical histories were to be further explored in *Genesis*, but he had already begun to make literary use of his family's past. As the narrator's grandmother dictates a letter to her brother's widow in Roumania, Delmore's mastery of the tone of Jewish life approaches perfection.

She wished me to write in the first person and to tell the foreign relatives that her grandson writing the letter attended the best university in America and had already had a concerto performed by a great orchestra. Her brother's children had all been very successful—one daughter had married an army officer—and she wished to show that she too was happy in her children. Meanwhile, in directing me to do this, she emphasized her brother's success and his children's success, her pride in them for my benefit, so that it would be clear on both sides of the Atlantic that she had reason to be pleased.

Far less notable was an incredibly bad verse play, *Venus in the Back Room*, about a familiar existential type named Noah who enters a restaurant and finds himself in the midst of some ominous intrigue promoted by the owner, a Faustian homosexual who threatens to abduct him. After thirty-five pages of portentous nonsense, in which a sinister "Stimme" offers unintentionally comical monologues on the nature of good and evil while the owner's daughter recites bathetic poetry from the kitchen, Noah gambles for his freedom and wins; but as it happens, all is "make believe," and the audience is advised: "Go home, go to sleep, do not give this whole business another thought; it is all very remote and apart from you." Delmore must have sensed the failings of this play, for he has Noah remark in a postlude, "Probably too much has been said that is ridiculous, much that is extremely ugly, much that is merely tedious."

.

Early in January, Laughlin called on Delmore at his boardinghouse and offered to publish a full-length manuscript of poems, with royalties of fifteen cents a copy, and an option on his next five works of prose or verse; not exactly a fortune, but "if you want to serve God and not the devil I can do best for you," Laughlin urged in a follow-up letter. Delmore was jubilant, and accepted the terms without hesitation. A week later, he provided his new publisher with a sketch of his background and opinions:

Your mention of the fruits of sin is piquant, since I have been supported and educated by the fruits of real estate speculation. I am not a "devout leftist"; merely devout would be the word, if I can pretend to so much, and nourishing and being led by a sense of ineluctable evil and the endless bureaucracy involved in existence (Herr Kafka's obsession) and with a profound disgust and hatred of all churches, all parties, which debase always the divine, if only by attempting to give a name and a local habitation to it. When I was an undergraduate I studied for two years with Sidney Hook and James Burnham and thus the best brand of Marxism was pressed upon me, and the only result was a long thesis for Burnham on the relationship of religion and communism which seemed to perplex Burnham exceedingly. It does seem to me, however, that Marxism illuminates very well the inseparable tie-up of social and intellectual elements at any given moment of time, and it is also valuable negatively as a judgement of the present. Only the most naïve actually think that any kind of salvation can come from a political party, and everyone worth speaking to in N.Y. has now seen the moral bankruptcy of Marxism in the Moscow trials. —Now you know what kind of an author you have on your team; you know, at least, as much as he does about it.

Laughlin answered with reports of the praise Delmore's work in New Directions had received from various quarters. But Delmore was beginning to be unnerved by his good fortune.

All these fine reviews and all the rest of the things that I've been getting during the last few months are accumulating to the point where I am going to be terrified [he wrote Laughlin on February 1]. It can't last, I can't be being praised for the right reasons by so many people, it is much too soon, and it is taking my mind away from working. I hope that it does not make you expect me to progress in a straight line; but being a writer, I don't have to be afraid that you will have such expectations. The latest salutation, by the way, is from Wallace Stevens, who sent the Partisan Review a letter, which they're printing, saying that my review of The Man with the Blue Guitar was the "most invigorating review" that he had ever had.

This worried qualification, one of the most poignant passages in all of Delmore's letters, foreshadowed the dread that would haunt him throughout his life; to see his early promise so acclaimed was more a source of terror than of pleasure. Delmore had always feared that his talent might desert him at any moment, or—an even graver fear—that he had less talent than he supposed; but since his precarious identity depended on praise, he could ill afford to become less than a major American poet. And he resisted the gratification of success not only because it threatened to lull him into relaxing his standards but because it meant that his long-imagined fantasies of fame were now to be tested in public. The time had come to deliver on the claims he had made over so many years.

Inundated with opportunities, Delmore soon found himself living out the predictions made to Laughlin. Too many things were happening at once: Sidney Hook had intimated the possibility of a job teaching philosophy at N.Y.U.; in the *Southern Review* he was called upon to reply to a letter from Yvor Winters taking issue with his review of *Primitivism and Decadence*; and he was corresponding with Laughlin about a proposal that he write ballet scenarios for Lincoln Kirstein, who had established his famous School of American Ballet in 1933. He even thought of sending one of his plays to Orson Welles. "I've met a person close to Welles," he informed Laughlin, "who promises to make him read it." In a series of frantic letters to his publisher, Delmore fretted over the photograph for his book and asked incessantly for news of what Pound had said about him.

Laughlin didn't have to act as a messenger for long. By April, Delmore was corresponding with Pound on his own. He began by pointing out a number of errors in the *Cantos*, to which Pound replied: "Suppose you Read some of these writers before telling grandpa he aint been fotografted in his dress suit." Delmore answered with a masterpiece of presumption.

This is only a shot in the dark and a pretty poor one at that. I have read with much care and attention Dante, Homer and Shakespeare, and also, though not as fully, Ovid. One reason, in fact, that I studied Greek was your own translation from the Odyssey—if Homer was like that, I wanted to read all of him. I found out that he was not really like that and as a matter of fact even better. All literary judgment seems to me to be comparative and on this basis it still seems clear to me that the best "frame" for a long poem is narrative. I may be very naïve and literal about it, but when you say that "The Divina Commedia has practically no narration and no plot / it presents a scheme of values / merely a walk upstairs to a balloon landing," I can only keep in mind the literal fact that the poem in question is about a man who was lost in a dark wood where he met various animals and then a great poet's ghost and learned that in order to escape from the wood and the animals, he would have to travel thru Hell, Purgatory, and Heaven. And thus the enormous exaltation of the Cantos toward the end of Purgatorio derives from the character of the story, the narrative that Dante is going to meet the lady with whom he was very much in love for a long time and who has been dead for ten years. I do not expect you to take over broken down values from fat Aquinas nor do I in fact suppose that the absence of narrative in your poem *as a whole* is a simple thing, a pure matter of choice. It seems to me that narrative began to go out of poetry when Coleridge had to write marginal summaries for the "Ancient Mariner" and by the time we get to "Sordello" it has become even harder to tell a story and again there are marginal summaries (at least in some editions) and all this is, I think, a part of a whole complex of both history and literature, partly the increasing quest of certain poetic effects which must of necessity eliminate narrative— could Mallarmé, for example, conceivably have told a story using his style; and partly the development of the novel as a way of getting everything about a character into a medium; and partly the very breakdown of those values which focus interest upon the life and death of the individual soul—thus even the novel now tells almost no story and the leading beliefs on all sides are, as in Marxism, beliefs about classes, not individuals, about history as a whole.

He then went on to compare Pound unfavorably with Dante, Shakespeare, and Homer before entering into the specific instances where Pound was misquoting.

"NEXT / as to the seereeyus and solemp and per-lite / 'A tailor might scratch her where ere she did itch,' 'cul far tombetta.' " It is right after this that you tell me to read some of these writers, so it is only in fairness to the quotations that I point out that you seem to have misquoted both, if you are referring to "ed egli avea cul fatte trombetta" (Inf. XXI, 139) and that song from "The Tempest." But really, you are mistaking me. By serious I do not mean solemn and polite. T. E. Hulme—there was a serious man, and that is what I mean by being serious, and I was trying to say that no matter what you, Ezra Pound, believe, the fact is that very estimable persons have all kinds of beliefs about life and death which you as a poet sometimes (sometimes, I say, not always and who knows what the next 49 Cantos will bring except yourself) sometimes neglect or pass over because you are more interested for the time being in some up-roarious story (they are really uproarious). The mar-velous comedy which takes place at the end of Iliad I, and the comedy in Shakespeare are proportionately less important in the structure of their writing than in yours. But notice this—perhaps I am repeating myself again—this kind of judgment and comparison is made only with the assumption that your poem is good enough to bear such a contrast.

A month later, embroiled in one of Pound's periodic feuds with *Poetry*, Delmore found himself in the role of arbiter, reporting to George Dillon what Pound thought of the magazine and assuring Pound that it wasn't read in any case.

And your unawareness of this fact makes me wish to tell you that you seem to have slowed up—if you will forgive me for presuming to tell you where you stand. What I mean is this: in the old days when you were busy digging up Joyce and Lewis and Eliot, and even ten years ago when you printed those wonderful poems by Yeats *next to* Zukofsky in *Exile*, you were in the middle of everything and knew what was going on with exactitude, and as a result everyone interested in literature was benefitted. Now you seem to have your gaze trained on Jefferson and Social Credit and

Harold Monro, and a phenomenon like Auden—to the author of "Lustra" and "Mauberley," the satirist of the British ought to be an item of some interest— does not seem to exist for you—I mean, as a critic.

And again, it seems to me that you ought to answer some of the critics of the Cantos—especially Black-mur and Wyndham Lewis, who has, you know, been telling stories about you in his recent autobiography. You used to ride the "age"—if not for you, I would certainly have little notion of what it means to be caught up in a period of time, moved by it and at-tempting to move it. Perhaps Jefferson et al. are more important concerns, but certainly, as I said, "we" profited more by your earlier interests. I ought to add, since you ask whether I have lived as near the starva-tion line as my elders, that I am poor and thus acutely sensitive to the economic in its concrete dollar-by-dollar difficulty. Well: what one wishes is that you continue to be our contemporary in the fullest sense.

Pound cannot have been happy to learn that he was al-ready outmoded, but he may well have been pleased by the bellicose independence of his correspondent. No one was more querulous than Pound, who enjoyed and encouraged dissension for its own sake; and while the audacity of Delmore's letters is breathtaking, Pound could at least take comfort in having a disciple conversant with every detail of his life and work.

Distracted by all his other activities, Delmore wrote Laughlin early in March to ask if he could postpone the deadline of July 1 that had been agreed upon for his book, which was now to be called *In Dreams Begin Responsibili-ties*. He was eager to see his book in print, but the pressure of a deadline troubled him. "This is the first year in eigh-teen that I have not been in school (or kindergarten) and in all those years I was tortured by a time-schedule im-posed from without. . . . This year, on the other hand, I have been working as I please and it is not only very enjoyable but it purifies the spirit." Laughlin gave in, and publication was put off a few months.

.

Delmore's uneasy friendship with Paul Goodman came to an abrupt end in June, when Delmore sent off one of those denunciatory letters that often came out of the blue. His letter has not survived, but he read a copy of it aloud to William Barrett, who happened to drop by just after he had mailed it and found him "shaking as if he had just come through an actual scene of violence." It was brief and savage, Barrett recalled, and concluded with something like: "No doubt, you will go on as you have been doing, corrupting young boys and turning them into fags like yourself." From then on, their disputes would be conducted only obliquely, in sporadic attacks on one another's work.

Oddly enough, Goodman had just gotten married a few months before, and Delmore's contempt for his "ambidextrous" practices may well have been fueled by jealousy and apprehension. Over Easter vacation, Delmore had finally prevailed upon Gertrude to marry him, but he was uncertain whether to regard her consent as a victory or a premonition of doom. For years, she had strenuously resisted his advances (in every sense, it appears), and she repeatedly declared her unwillingness to marry Delmore or anyone else. She was so adamant on this point that when her parents, who had never quite reconciled themselves to their potential son-in-law, learned of her engagement, they cried out, "To who?" All the same, they gave their reluctant blessing, and the wedding date was set for June 14.

Delmore's mother reacted to the announcement with even less enthusiasm; she threatened to kill herself. How could her son abandon her in this cruel way? she wailed, working on his guilt. (A few years later, she would greet Kenneth's marriage with the declaration: "He would have been better off in Buchenwald than married to that woman.") But Delmore had doubts of his own; he had vowed long ago not to emulate his father's impulsive marriage ("although I must say that Gertrude is in every way superior as a human being to my mother," he once remarked to John Berryman); and yet he felt—if his novel is to be trusted—"afraid of the terrifying emotion which would overtake him, if he departed." Even so, his letters and the poems he wrote to Gertrude were the works of a young man unambiguously in love, despite the mutual reticence suggested in a letter from Woodstock the previous year: "What enormous tenderness I have for you, but never am able to give you except to refer to it, and it is not even certain that you want it."

But then, as the date approached, Delmore began to experience vomiting and nausea, hardly an auspicious sign. Years later, he recalled the events of the two days just before the wedding.

> The night, no, the Saturday before we were married, she said she wished she were dead. The night before was rainy June, we met unexpectedly in my mother's house, 700 W. 180 St., and my mother said, a friend of yours is here, and we walked to the drugstore and she bought me a comb, and I went back to Washington Place and could not sleep and put on the light when K[enneth] came home and took a third tablet, and slept for the first time well in weeks, the vomiting of my stomach at an end.

On the appointed day, June 14, they were married in the vestry room of the same synagogue where Delmore had been bar mitzvah'd, the Temple of the Covenant on St. Nicholas Avenue, around the corner from his mother's home. Barrett, the only non-family guest present, has given a romanticized account of the wedding: "There were enough touches of a 30's movie about the ceremony to have satisfied any director of the time: a memento of New York as a city of neighborhoods, the celebration of neighborhood pieties and sentimentalities by all the assembled relatives with their small bickering and contented clucking." Unfortunately, a number of minor disasters marred this picturesque scene. Delmore's mother decided she couldn't walk and had to be carried up the stairs of the synagogue by Kenneth and Barrett; the rabbi who performed the ceremony was in a hurry to get to a funeral, and grew impatient over the delay caused by Rose Schwartz's seizure of infirmity; Gertrude was pale, the Buckmans wept.

Afterward, they all went back to the Buckmans' apartment, where a meager banquet of sponge cake and a bottle of brandy awaited the guests. Delmore promptly got drunk on three quick shots, while Mr. Buckman tried to give him some awkward advice. "Go slow," he said, when Gertrude left the room to get her suitcase. "Take care of my tochter," Mrs. Buckman chimed in. Kenneth presented them with a sealed envelope, Delmore's aunt Clara embraced the couple, and his grandmother Baba, aware of his recent bouts of insomnia, called out, "Now you will sleep." As they stepped into a taxi, Gertrude's father kissed him, and they were off to Grand Central—hours early, so eager were they to escape the dismal scene. At the station, they went into a newsreel theater to pass the time, then boarded a train for Albany, where they spent the night at the Hotel Wellington. There, despite his grandmother's prediction, sleep eluded him again. Disturbed by a noisy American Legion convention, he insisted on changing rooms in the middle of the night. The next morning, pleading exhaustion, Delmore hired a taxi to drive them to Bennington, Vermont, forty miles away, where F. W. Dupee had arranged for them to rent a cottage for the summer. Years later, Delmore recalled their wedding journey in a bitter poem that made it seem less a beginning than a sinister omen.

> The river flowed like a holiday,
> Dear was each hope we packed away
> —June fourteenth in Eternity's
> Train trip continues, cannot cease:
> An all night picture, stupid play,
> Or an incurable disease.

6

———•———

"EVERYTHING PROCEEDS VERY WELL with us and the absence of distraction, the very minimum of which is the moving-pictures—is just what I needed," Delmore wrote F. W. Dupee from the picturesque and secluded Overlea Inn, located on a dirt road near the Bennington College campus. The newlyweds played tennis, swam in Lake Paran, and went for rides in a secondhand car they had acquired, a 1931 Ford known as Black Mule (after the William Carlos Williams novel). Delmore was proud that he could drive a car; he thought it displayed the more practical side of his nature, and was eager to show off his battered Ford and his new bride. "Making visits to the intelligentsia in the neighborhood," as he described their journeys to Dupee, they drove up to South Londonderry, Vermont, to see Meyer Schapiro, then called on Laughlin in Norfolk, Connecticut, where they were pleased to find "the old boy," as Delmore referred to William Carlos Williams.

But it wasn't long before a disquieting note could be heard in his correspondence. Lonely for his friends, he sent them all invitations to come up and visit. "The high point of our day is the mail," he confessed to Dupee. And a few days later, he sent a telegram to William Barrett summoning him to Bennington. "On the way up I expected some extraordinary clash or marital hysteria had arisen," Barrett recalled, "but none such was visible when I arrived, and Delmore never gave any reason for this sudden summons. Probably he was just lonely in the country, and he was more used to having me instead of Gertrude at his side to dispel his loneliness." But this explanation was rather too sanguine. Delmore could never get used to having Gertrude "at his side"; haunted by her resistance to their marriage—a resistance she continued to voice during the months in Bennington—and dependent himself on the male companions he had always recruited in lieu of intimate relationships with women, Delmore suddenly found himself in a situation that demanded "the whole surrender of the fall," as he put it in his early poem on the risk of love.

As for Barrett's precipitous intervention, it was a case—in Gertrude's bitter words—of "My lord called and I came." Obedient to his friend's importunate demands, Barrett arrived to find that Delmore expected him to stay the entire summer. Nor was he the first to have been recruited; even before the wedding Delmore had approached Howard Frisch, a member of the Goodman circle, and invited him to accompany the couple on their honeymoon. Now Barrett had been chosen to protect him from the intimacy of marriage, an institution Delmore was already beginning to question. "Why get married unless you must, / Driven by the horses and dragons of lust!" went one of his cynical couplets.

In an unpublished story about the early days of their marriage, Delmore observed of "Martha and Maxwell":

> During the first week of the marriage, they rehearsed the old conflicts between them which had been going on for years. Martha did not like the act of making love and she said that she never would and she was patient with Maxwell, but he was disappointed because he had been sure that once they were married, she would change very quickly.

That this version of matters told rather less than the whole story is suggested by a revision Delmore made in the second sentence, which he altered to read, "Martha did not like Maxwell to make love to her." Whether or not Gertrude was in part responsible for their sexual difficulties, surely Delmore's attitude—expressed to Philip Rahv—that he "would rather write than make love" must have had unpleasant consequences for his marriage. Apart from his desperate requests for visitors, Delmore was almost wholly occupied that summer in revising *In Dreams Begin Responsibilities*, and he revealed his priorities in a laconic journal entry: "One has to get used to a typewriter and a wife."

Delmore devoted his mornings in Bennington to a frenetic correspondence. In a time when the writing of letters had ceased to be one of the significant occupations of a literary life, he found it an exemplary medium for monitoring the defeats and exultations of his career, and in the years when his intellect was at its most vigorous, during the late thirties and forties, a flood of communications issued from his typewriter, often at the rate of six or seven letters a day. Delmore thought of composition as analogous to practicing a musical instrument, a sort of "tuning up"; and his copious letters, like the sonnet "exercises" and blank-verse journals in which he narrated literary history, were often trial efforts at criticism that appeared in a finished form later on.

Of course, they served other purposes as well; many were personal, written out of loneliness or a need to justify himself, while others carried forward the business of his career. In this sense, Delmore was worldly from the start. Letters belonged to the world of "letters," the calling to which he had solemnly apprenticed himself by the time he was seventeen, and his vast correspondence with his elders formed a part of that calling. He liked to be at the center of things, campaigning for himself and his friends, plotting, intervening, debating; and yet his letters are filled with ironic commentaries on the chaotic life he led. As if aware of how revelatory they were, he sought refuge in comedy, a commentator on his own manic excesses. His letters evoke the passion, doubt, and inspiration that alternately overwhelmed him with a vulnerable candor he acknowledged in a journal poem entitled "Old Letters."

> Written last year or ten years old, and bold
> And warm, pretentious as a top hat, and yet
> With the ego's pomp, self-conscious as a stammer
> Self-conscious as a stammer or a whisper
>
> > "These pieces of the self are with my friends
> > They show me as I am, which never ends
> > The word betrays the heart and mind."

Now that he was in demand, and involved with several projects at once, Delmore's letters became more elaborate than ever. Dense with reference and argument, they chronicled his literary opinions and his attitudes toward his contemporaries—usually in the form of vehement denunciations—in a voice at once confiding and minatory. On the other hand, it was important to cultivate the right people; informing Laughlin that Allen Tate had invited him to his home in Cornwall, Connecticut, Delmore noted, "I don't want to do that, but I would like to go over there with you. You can never tell when he might be handy for something, and besides he's a good poet."

And yet Delmore could just as easily be generous when it was a question of writers he admired. While he disparaged Williams's "suspicion of the intelligence" and (echoing a favorite indictment of Rahv's) his "lack of ideas," he claimed that *White Mule* was "the best prose in English since Joyce's *Ulysses*"; "in thirty years, if lucky, I will be able to compete with him." And he was no less enthusiastic about Auden, writing Dupee an elaborate appraisal of Auden's "sensitive mind, which lifts up images of the greatest import and shows them in rugged, crabbed hard language with the kind of 'implicatory' power which is always a sign of mastery."

Delmore loved nothing more than to discourse in this way about books and authors, but he felt oppressed at times by "the waste of spirit in attention to the literary press with all the sense of competition which goes with it." He had published a "great deal" over the past year, he wrote John Crowe Ransom, and it worried him that he would "seem to be anxious, eager, voluble, and in a hurry to state my opinions." And when a New Directions book catalogue arrived with a notice of his book accompanied by the encomiums he had labored so hard to gather, he found the lavish bouquet of praise upsetting: "not angry, disturbed, my sense of position, status, praise, criticism, confronted with stupidity, praise for the inadequate, laurels contesting my laurels."

The postponement of *In Dreams* seemed to have increased rather than appeased the pressure on him; it was as if Delmore couldn't work without creating chaos and a sense of urgency. Now that he had more time, he could afford to be dilatory, ceaselessly revising, altering the poems' order, even composing a new play for the book. Most of the lyric poems had been decided on, and he

planned to include a verse play, *Dr. Bergen's Belief*; the
volume was to begin with the now-celebrated title story.
But he felt that some extended work was called for, a verse
play in the mode of *Having Snow*, yet not autobiographical. One subject he had in mind was the Coriolanus portrayed by Plutarch, a vain, egotistical, yet heroic figure
brought up by a domineering widowed mother. It was a
familiar story, and Delmore set about transforming the
Roman war hero into a modern existential type. From the
moment of their arrival in Bennington, he reported to
Laughlin, he had been working on it "night and day."
Toward the end of the summer, he vowed to continue
revising his play "until the printer cuts my throat," and
Laughlin finally came up on September 1 to collect the
manuscript in person. The next day, after a sleepless night
brought on by the excitement that always preceded travel,
Delmore and Gertrude drove down to New York to look
for an apartment.

·

Delmore was still reluctant to be alone with his new
wife. No sooner had they found an apartment—at 8 West
105th Street, not far from Columbia—than Kenneth
moved in, ostensibly to share the rent. A few months later,
when Kenneth went out to California, he was supplanted
by William Barrett, who began to make almost daily appearances. Delmore wanted Barrett to stay over for dinner
every night, but it was Gertrude who had to cook, and she
would surely have been justified in resenting the arrival of
still another nightly interloper on the heels of Kenneth's
departure. Delmore's excuse was that Barrett—"the Lord
Chesterfield of gluttony"—had to be looked after so he
wouldn't starve; since their meals in the Foltis-Fisher cafeteria during the Depression, he had made Barrett's prodigal
appetite a major anecdotal theme. (Years later, when Barrett and Delmore were dining with the historian Oscar
Handlin in a Boston restaurant, Delmore described their
impending bout of gluttony as "the potato famine of Ire-
land against the famine of the Ukraine.")

In his memoir of Delmore, Barrett described himself as
"the protective mother hen," but Delmore offered protec-
tion in his own way, inviting Barrett over to the house all
the time and acting in the capacity of what he called a

"spiritual brother." So great was his influence that he was able to dissuade Barrett from going to Europe the following summer; if he would wait a year, they could go together. This was Delmore's "trump," as Barrett characterized it, and he agreed to postpone his trip. All the same, he found Delmore's pleadings ominous. "Why just now when he was riding high did he feel this need to bind me closer to himself than ever? Did he have some premonitory fear that he might topple from this perch on which he'd been placed?" And yet, Barrett might well have asked himself whether it was likely that Delmore would ever have gone to Europe. He was married, after all, and had no money; besides, he hated traveling. "How could I go to Europe when I can't even shave at home?" he used to say.

Barrett was away for part of the spring, teaching at the University of Chicago, but when he returned they went off to Harlem in search of girls. Marriage appears not to have prevented Delmore from taking up with prostitutes; "Dinner (twice) with Mexican whores," he confessed in his autobiographical notes. In February, Delmore gave Laughlin a jocular but somewhat ominous account of his relationship with his "justly celebrated wife": "She married me for my money and in order to sleep late, and pays no attention to me. But my devotion is eternal and none too good for her, though she is likely to depart from me any day." A month later, he reported that Gertrude was no longer speaking to him, and this time there was none of the "tiring irony" with which he had signed his previous letter.

Despite the facetious tone of his letter to Laughlin, Delmore's devotion to Gertrude was quite genuine. She had a charm and vivacity captured in one of his novels.

> . . . she turned to her wondrous gaiety, although distractedly and fluttering and breaking off in the midst of it, as she broke off in the middle of a piano piece, tinkling the Mozartian phrase and then rising and dancing by herself the fragment of a minuet while those who looked were left intoxicated by delight and without a gesture to respond, such was the beauty and uniqueness of what she did, such was its character of being out of the world.

But their unpredictable moods unnerved each other, and their uneasiness as a couple was evident to Norman Jacobs, who visited them one evening that fall. Jacobs had just read Léon Blum's *Du mariage*, and was eagerly relating Blum's theory of why couples often suffer on their wedding night from what he euphemistically called "physical disharmony"; it was because men tended to confine their sexual experience to prostitutes before marriage, Jacobs explained, while their wives lacked any sexual experience at all. Delmore and Gertrude became increasingly tense as Jacobs talked on, and when his enthusiastic peroration ended, a terrible silence ensued. Not until that moment did it occur to their well-meaning visitor that he may have been describing a situation all too familiar to his auditors.

The conduct of Delmore and Gertrude on the tennis court was a parable of their marriage. They played together often in Central Park, and Delmore, a good player despite his bearish awkwardness, would pat the ball over the net so that Gertrude could return it. Secretly deriding her for being "lazy, impatient, unskilled" and too easily discouraged, he would struggle to control his temper, and then be so pleased with his "new-found virtue" that he forgot his vigilance; "the next second the suppressed anger gets out and is spoken." This was the usual course of events, with Gertrude's sullen manner provoking Delmore's anger, always so near the surface; but sometimes his virtue had rewards: "On another day, after playing long and well, he tempers the wind to the shorn lamb, he plays pat-pat lightly with her and not only does she enjoy it, but he enjoys it also!" Such shows of patience put him in a self-congratulatory mood: "This is good health, good condition, long practice—he is so successful, she delights in his love for her." The moral of "The Story of the Tennis Ego" or "Tennis Christian," as Delmore variously referred to these notes, was to show how "the right way" could be made to prevail over selfishness and vanity.

.

Marriage, Delmore once confided to John Berryman, had always appeared to him in youth "as a time of seeing friends, a series of 'at homes' "; now that he was married, he could establish his own "salon," and he let it be known that visitors would be welcome on Sunday evenings. Soon their apartment was filled with guests, and not only on Sundays. "This place is getting to be like Parnassus, also a restaurant, but I am willing to go bankrupt in order that my fellow poets may eat," he reported to Laughlin after a particularly hectic week.

Despite a shyness so extreme that he was reluctant even to talk on the telephone, and a contradictory image of himself and Gertrude as "two recluses," Delmore was an animated host. He had a "radiant disposition" when he was relaxed, Norman Jacobs recalled, and he always made sure to have new stories on hand, which he would narrate with elaborate digressions and improvised facts. One characteristic tale of that season concerned a visit to Wallace Stevens at the Hartford Insurance Company. Stevens liked to claim that his associates in the insurance business were entirely unaware of his illustrious reputation. "They don't know anything about my being a poet," he had told Delmore. After leaving Stevens's office, Delmore encountered an acquaintance who worked there, and began telling him what a great poet Stevens was; it was incredible, he expostulated, that no one there knew they had a famous poet in their midst. At this point, his friend interrupted, "Listen, Stevens is the worst insurance lawyer we have in this office; he would have been fired long ago if he weren't a great poet."

Of all his literary heroes, none was the object of a more merciless array of fabricated anecdotes than T. S. Eliot, whose every secret Delmore pretended to know. Eliot's first wife had on occasion been confined to a sanatorium for the treatment of various mental disorders, and from this isolated fact Delmore elaborated stories of a pied-à-terre Eliot kept in London, and insisted that his wife had left him, "after years of mistreatment, for an insane asylum." As for Eliot's poems, they were full of revelatory lore: the refrain "Hurry up, please, it's time," in *The Waste Land* was a concealed reference to orgasm; "Rachel née Rabinovitch" was the name of a Jewish woman who had jilted Eliot and made him anti-Semitic. Delmore's most outrageous stories purported to explain how Eliot had come to marry Vivienne Haigh-Wood in the first place. In one version, attributed to Bertrand Russell, Eliot had kissed her and then proposed in a fit of remorse for having corrupted her innocence. But there was an even more scurrilous variation: when Eliot was a graduate student at Oxford, he and Vivienne were punting on the Cherwell when suddenly Vivienne, wanting to halt at a quiet spot, called out, "Put your pole in, Tom!" Mistaking her words for a sexual invitation, Eliot had responded and then felt the only honorable course was to propose.*

⋅

That fall, Delmore was getting to know writers quite apart from the *Partisan Review* crowd. There were invitations to parties at the Van Dorens' and at Selden Rodman's, where he met William Saroyan, Frederic Prokosch, Horace Gregory, and Louis MacNeice, with whom he spent a bizarre evening in December. Thinking MacNeice would enjoy an authentic tour of New York night life, Delmore dragged him to a nightclub in Harlem, but an overenthusiastic Negro dancing instructor kept coming up to their table and urging the reticent British poet to dance. "Get hot, boy, get hot!" the dancer implored; "you feel better in the morning." MacNeice, stunned into an even more profound silence than was usual for him, could only raise his glass in a bewildered toast.

Delmore had admired Allen Tate ever since reading his introduction to Hart Crane's *White Buildings* in high school. Just before Christmas, they arranged to meet in a Village bar on West Eighth Street, and Delmore was elated when Tate praised his work and offered to propose him for a teaching job at Kenyon College. It was their first meeting, and Delmore was "obviously tense," Tate recalled, no doubt because he was always shy in the company of those he most respected; but he restored his composure in retrospect by telling friends how Tate had appeared unannounced at his door to proclaim him the best poet since

---

* Delmore was in fact astonishingly knowledgeable about Eliot's private life, and at a time when virtually nothing had been written about it. Eliot *did* meet his first wife while punting on the Cherwell, and Cyril Connolly reported that Logan Pearsall Smith had told him Eliot got married because he had "compromised" Miss Haigh-Wood and then felt obliged to propose. Delmore also put about that Eliot had a secret lover in Vermont, and it was true that Eliot went there in the 1940's to visit Emily Hale, who some biographers have suggested was his first love before he left America in 1914. And he contended that Vivienne Haigh-Wood was an ether addict, a claim later made by Aldous Huxley. But how Delmore could have known about any of these matters remains a mystery. Huxley's *Letters*, in which the remark about ether occurs, weren't published until 1969, and other details of Eliot's life have only lately come to light. (See especially *Eliot's Early Years*, by Lyndal Gordon.)

Eliot. It was a characteristic embellishment for someone
who had only recently underscored a passage in Maritain's
Trois Réformateurs where Luther was described by Le
Duc Georges de Saxe as *"le plus froid menteur qu'il ait
jamais connu."*

The final version of *In Dreams Begin Responsibilities*
had been turned over to Laughlin upon his return from
Europe, and publication was now scheduled for early December. As the date drew closer, Delmore's excitement
gave way to anxiety. Too much depended on the book's
success, and the many postponements he had devised over
the last few months were prompted more by a dread of
failure than by a desire for perfection. "Fear of reviews,"
he noted in his journal, ill-tempered and depressed.

Among friends, Delmore was contentious and impatient.
Writing to Arthur Berger in October, he mentioned the
major events of the last few months—his marriage and the
imminent publication of his book—then abruptly broke
off. "I am too displeased with almost everything to be able
to write a decent letter." A month later, he reacted with a
display of unappeasable fury when Selden Rodman, then
editor of the journal *Common Sense*, cut the last sentence
from his review of William Carlos Williams's *Collected
Poems*, in which he had praised Williams as "a great American and a great writer." It was certainly a high-handed
alteration, and Delmore was justified in claiming that "no
editor has the moral right or the legal one to alter what a
reviewer has written." All the same, his blustering threats
exceeded the crime: "I don't know yet what I am going to
do about this, but I am certainly not going to let a thing
like this just happen." Ignoring Rodman's attempts to
placate him, Delmore tried to enlist Laughlin to write a
letter of protest on his behalf. "He will be more useful if he
is afraid," he noted in one of his fiercer moods. Some years
later, moved by a reference William Barrett made in conversation to the passage in Romans IX where Paul speaks
of the potter who shapes some to be vessels of beauty and
others to be "vessels of wrath," Delmore declared, "Yes, I
myself am such a vessel of wrath."

•

In Dreams Begin Responsibilities was officially scheduled for publication on December 12, but a copy arrived in
Delmore's mail on the seventh, just in time for his twenty-

fifth birthday. After spending Christmas with William Barrett and New Year's Eve with the Zolotows, he felt a "lifting of depression" and promptly set about zealously publicizing his book. A flood of directives poured into Laughlin's office: he was to write I. A. Richards, elicit "a generous comment" from Stevens, and send a copy to Dos Passos, who had shown interest in his work. "It might help to get one to Hemingway," he suggested, "if you can reach him before Franco arrives in Barcelona and cuts out his black heart." Auden's copy was to be sent without the jacket, where he was labeled "the American Auden": "he won't be pleased to see that he is the English Schwartz." Auden was not one to commit himself to new writers in print, but Delmore wanted to excerpt from a letter of Auden's to Laughlin the remark "I admire his work; he is very promising," for use as a blurb. (In private, Auden suggested that Delmore's poetry "could use a little more ego and a little less id," borrowing the distinction from Delmore's essay "The Two Audens.") He also sent a copy to Yeats, who—unfortunately for Delmore—had less than a month to live; and in January he reported: "I am holding one last copy until I get Charlie Chaplin's address." (The great comic offered no blurb.)

Just after New Year's, the first extraordinary praise arrived, in the form of a letter from Allen Tate.

> Your book came just as we were leaving for a hectic round of Christmas visiting. We are only now back. I did read the book through, but I am not yet prepared to do it justice. I am writing to James Laughlin a statement that may be useful to you and him, but meanwhile I want to tell you that your poetic style is beyond any doubt the first real innovation that we've had since Eliot and Pound. There's nothing like it, and by comparison Auden and MacNeice are camp followers of easily identified schools. —What you will do with your invention later no one can predict. I imagine the test will come when you try to construct a frame of reference of your own, something different from the rather arbitrary scheme set up by the Coriolanus parallel.

George Marion O'Donnell, the Southern Fugitive poet, wrote: "I shall be glad of the chance to say that I regard you as the foremost writer of our generation," and Mark Van Doren described *In Dreams* as "one of the most valuable and enjoyable books published in its generation." Wallace Stevens, in a quote Delmore lobbied vigorously to have included in all the advertisements, applauded his philosophical gifts, citing a remark of F. H. Bradley's that "what imagination loved as poetry reason might love as philosophy." John Crowe Ransom celebrated "the poetic promise of Delmore Schwartz," while Philip Rahv chimed in, "He is by far the ablest of the younger American poets." Even Delmore's brother, Kenneth, wrote a congratulatory, if disheartening letter from San Francisco reporting that he had "liked the book very much except for the fact that I don't like poetry as I can't understand it. I showed it to a few people and they were very much impressed [and] except for the fact that they didn't have $2.50 they would have bought the book." Twenty years later, a bitter Delmore quoted this letter in a lecture at the Library of Congress as evidence of Americans' lamentable indifference to modern poetry.

Delmore eagerly monitored the praise that poured in, and redoubled his attention to the placement and format of advertisements for the book, anxious to ensure that each quote be printed in full. "Tate's praise is perfect," he crowed; "please try to get in as much as 'originality.' " And a week later: "Am I going to get a full page in ND's annual, quoting ten critics (Stevens, Tate, MacNeice, Blackmur, Ransom, Rahv, Auden, Van Doren, Wheelright, Fitts)?" "Probably all this manoeuvring is not very good for our souls," Delmore worried, but for the moment he was ecstatic. "Some of them are foaming at the mouth and will soon foam in print, and I love it, I eat it up," he exulted. "Every word of praise affords a new kind of pleasure to me, and then I get back to the typewriter and bang out a few more poems."

This stunning burst of acclaim was in advance of the reviews, but Delmore was optimistic, and when they started to come in, he found his optimism justified. Mark Van Doren amplified on the encomiums in his letter of recommendation, writing in *Kenyon Review* that *In Dreams* was "as good as any poetry has been for a long while, say at least a literary generation," and George Marion O'Donnell kept his promise in *Poetry*, heralding the book as "the one genuinely important modification [of the English poetic tradition] to come out of the 1930's in America." Dudley Fitts lauded him in *Saturday Review*; F. W. Dupee claimed in the *New York Sun* that "since Auden's early poems appeared, there has been no verse so alive with contemporary meaning"; and R. P. Blackmur, writing in *Partisan Review*, discovered "an inexhaustible quality in the perception which the associations of image and statement reveal."

Critics unrestrained by friendship, such as Babette Deutsch and Louis MacNeice, were less charitable. The most unfavorable review came from Louise Bogan, in *The Nation*. With irritating condescension, Bogan made fun of what she took to be Delmore's Modernist pose. "Modern talented youth does not think well of itself if it skips one field of modern reference," she chided. In her view, Delmore's allusions to Whitehead and Kafka, Marx and Freud were mere conventions, features of a "literary eclecticism" drawn from incompatible sources. And Bogan was severe on the subject of Delmore's borrowings from the literary myths of the day, "The Kafka-Auden-Isherwood Dog, a monocle and some ice cream from W. Stevens, playing cards from Eliot, and Anglo-Saxon monosyllables from Molly Bloom." Delmore was "a very brilliant young man," Bogan conceded, and she thought the title story a masterpiece. But if Delmore's work were to mature, she concluded, he would have to cultivate the values of "simplicity and directness."

Delmore was livid when he read Bogan's review, and promptly drafted a long reply for Laughlin to send in above his own name. She had misquoted him, made "unwarranted mistakes of fact which indicate the most careless and irresponsible reviewing," and in general been guilty of "incompetence," Delmore complained. Moreover, he confided to Laughlin, Bogan had only written such a damning review to counter what she thought was "a regular conspiracy of praise." Finally a New Directions editor drafted a tepid rebuttal that was published in *The Nation*.

•

What was it about *In Dreams Begin Responsibilites* that created such a dramatic response? Pound had said in "Hugh Selwyn Mauberley"

> The age demanded an image
> Of its accelerated grimace,

and it was Delmore's fate to provide that image for the thirties, just as Pound and Eliot had for an earlier generation. Modernism, the poetic revolution they had initiated in about 1912, emerged from a complex experience of European culture that by the late 1930's had yet to find proper expression in American poetry. Awed and yet brash as the American characters in James's novels, the two expatriates had arrived in England to find European literature in the midst of a renovation of consciousness, and promptly assumed as their province the whole of European culture, as if to prove themselves its legitimate heirs.

William Carlos Williams was the only poet who carried on the work of Modernism at home (except, perhaps, for the spurious avant-garde pose of e. e. cummings). Hart Crane, while Modernist in his themes, was essentially Romantic in diction and cadences, and Wallace Stevens had chosen to appropriate the preciosity of the French Symbolists without transposing their attenuated rhetoric—as Eliot had—to the idioms of his own language. Frost and Edwin Arlington Robinson, eclipsed by innovations that, for the moment at least, had made their poetry seem anachronistic, pursued their solitary courses, while the Fugitives John Crowe Ransom and Allen Tate were determined on a return to the austere and classical meters of the English poetic tradition.

So it devolved upon Eliot to become Delmore's model; he was, after all, the quintessential Modernist, and, what was perhaps more significant, he provided an example of the recognition conferred on those who managed to establish a new poetic idiom. And yet Eliot was, in another sense, the very antithesis of what Delmore thought the poet should be. Authoritarian, dignified, remote, Eliot had achieved a stature that infuriated Delmore even as it filled him with envy; restrained by the limitations of his own background from emulating Eliot's cultivated manner, Delmore could only follow an opposite course, and eventually found more congenial models in those exemplary figures of revolt Rimbaud and Baudelaire. It was Baudelaire who had first conveyed "the deepest feelings of the modern poet," Delmore argued in his essay "The Isolation of Modern Poetry"; since Baudelaire, the sensation of being "a stranger, an alien, an outsider" had dominated the modern poet's sensibility. Eliot may have explored this experience in his poetry, and even known it in his early life, but in Delmore's era he represented the very type of high culture and society; and as such, he had become the enemy, a "cultural dictator," as Delmore later described him.

Delmore's amazing rhetoric, the orotund, passionate expressions of grief and rage recited in varied pentameters, owed as much to what he thought to be the high style of nineteenth-century French poetry as it did to his American elders. He was drawn to Baudelaire's emphatic style of declamation—except that in Delmore's voice defiance was tempered by a note of ineffable sorrow.

> Tired and unhappy, you think of houses
> Soft-carpeted and warm in the December evening,
> While snow's white pieces fall past the window,
> And the orange firelight leaps.
> > A young girl sings
> That song of Gluck where Orpheus pleads with Death;
> Her elders watch, nodding their happiness
> To see time fresh again in her self-conscious eyes:
> The servants bring the coffee, the children retire,
> Elder and younger yawn and go to bed,
> The coals fade and glow, rose and ashen,
> It is time to shake yourself! and break this
> Banal dream, and turn your head
> Where the underground is charged, where the weight
> Of the lean buildings is seen,
> Where close in the subway rush, anonymous
> In the audience, well-dressed or mean,
> So many surround you, ringing your fate,
> Caught in an anger exact as a machine!

Often the most memorable image in a poem was to be found at the very start, as if the effort to begin forced him to concentrate all his inspiration on the first line. "Socrates' ghost must haunt me now"; "Poet and veteran of childhood, look!"; "I am to my own heart merely a serf." It was in these opening measures that his prosody was most original. But he could also produce startling effects by writing in a terse, laconic idiom, as in these stanzas from "Far Rockaway":

> The radiant soda of the seashore fashions
> Fun, foam, and freedom. The sea laves
> The shaven sand. And the light sways forward
> On the self-destroying waves.
>
> The rigor of the weekday is cast aside with shoes,
> With business suits and the traffic's motion;
> The lolling man lies with the passionate sun,
> Or is drunken in the ocean.

And in "The Ballad of the Children of the Czar," Delmore imitated to great effect the Imagist style of T. E. Hulme, but with a charged emotional rhetoric all his own.

> The children of the Czar
> Played with a bouncing ball
>
> In the May morning, in the Czar's garden,
> Tossing it back and forth.
>
> It fell among the flowerbeds
> Or fled to the north gate.
>
> A daylight moon hung up
> In the Western sky, bald white.
>
> Like Papa's face, said Sister,
> Hurling the white ball forth.
>
> II
>
> While I ate a baked potato
> Six thousand miles apart,
>
> In Brooklyn, in 1916,
> Aged two, irrational.
>
> When Franklin D. Roosevelt
> Was an Arrow Collar Ad.
>
> O Nicholas! Alas! Alas!
> My grandfather coughed in your army,

Hid in a wine-stinking barrel,
For three days in Bucharest

Then left for America
To become a king himself.

III

I am my father's father,
You are your children's guilt.

In history's pity and terror
The child is Aeneas again;

Troy is in the nursery,
The rocking horse is on fire.

Child labor! The child must carry
His fathers on his back.

But seeing that so much is past
And that history has no ruth

For the individual,
Who drinks tea, who catches cold,

Let anger be general:
I hate an abstract thing.

Yet his most conspicuous gift was for evoking the disappointment life seemed inevitably to hold, a disappointment so profound that it verged on tragedy. In a contributor's note written the previous year, Delmore had described the subject of his work as "the values by which human beings exist (as distinct from their beliefs and explicit avowals of choice) and the tragic contrast between these values and the tragic environment in which they must be brought to fruition." Resolutely, unrelievedly pessimistic, the poems in *In Dreams Begin Responsibilities* wore Pound's "accelerated grimace" on every page. "The Heavy Bear," perhaps Delmore's greatest poem, was a luminous testament to the struggle between the body's gross, importunate need and the longing for some finer, more spiritual world.

The heavy bear who goes with me,
A manifold honey to smear his face,
Clumsy and lumbering here and there,
The central ton of every place,
The hungry beating brutish one
In love with candy, anger, and sleep,
Crazy factotum, dishevelling all,
Climbs the building, kicks the football,
Boxes his brother in the hate-ridden city.

Breathing at my side, that heavy animal,
That heavy bear who sleeps with me,
Howls in his sleep for a world of sugar,
A sweetness intimate as the water's clasp,
Howls in his sleep because the tight-rope
Trembles and shows the darkness beneath.
—The strutting show-off is terrified,
Dressed in his dress-suit, bulging his pants,
Trembles to think that his quivering meat
Must finally wince to nothing at all.

That inescapable animal walks with me,
Has followed me since the black womb held,
Moves where I move, distorting my gesture,
A caricature, a swollen shadow,
A stupid clown of the spirit's motive,
Perplexes and affronts with his own darkness,
The secret life of belly and bone,
Opaque, too near, my private, yet unknown,
Stretches to embrace the very dear
With whom I would walk without him near,
Touches her grossly, although a word
Would bare my heart and make me clear,
Stumbles, flounders, and strives to be fed
Dragging me with him in his mouthing care,
Amid the hundred million of his kind,
The scrimmage of appetite everywhere.

The failure of life's hopes had become Delmore's obsessive theme before he was twenty-five; his wisdom seemed
that of an old man intoning the loss of innocence, the
tyranny of circumstance, the remorseless passage of time.
On occasion the effect of these grim speeches was unintentionally comic, if only because Delmore's tragic vision

could not always be sustained, and gave way to Angst; but the sheer intensity of his voice saved most of the poems from the bathos of unfocused complaint.

The whole of *In Dreams* was a sort of spiritual confession, but there were many explicit autobiographical references as well. In a note on the title story, Delmore denied that it had any autobiographical elements: "What can a writer reply but that no happening related there has ever occurred?" Apart from the fact that his disavowal was simply untrue, its very vehemence suggests how concerned he was to conceal the literal truth of his revelations. In an unpublished preface to *Shenandoah*, Delmore again belligerently repudiated any connection between his play and actual events, insisting that "the strong appearance of such a connection is false and has only to do with the name which suggested the whole invented play to the author." And in the preface of *Genesis* he was still more adamant: "It is an obvious stupidity and misuse to take any sentences as the truth about any particular human being." It is natural for a writer to demand that his work be judged as literature rather than self-revelation, and Delmore was justified in resisting attempts to read it as autobiography; and yet confession was the medium best suited to his compulsive self-investigations. The ceaseless struggle to locate a fixed identity was often disguised by a Yeatsian preoccupation with masks, but his most moving poems were invariably and unmistakably autobiographical. In the fourth "Fugue," Delmore invoked Eleanor, a childhood girlfriend whose name appears on a list he once made of the girls and women in his life; Bertram Spira, whom he had known at the University of Wisconsin; and his early love Rhoda—three notable participants in what he liked to call "the theodicy of his youth"; they too now belonged to that past.

And in "Prothalamion," he turned to what he regarded as the single most traumatic episode in his early life, the scene between his parents in a roadside restaurant.

> I will forget the speech my mother made
> In a restaurant, trapping my father there
> At dinner with his whore. Her spoken rage
> Struck down the child of seven years
> With shame for all three, with pity for

The helpless harried waiter, with anger for
The diners gazing, avid, and contempt,
And great disgust for every human being.

In "The Ballad of the Children of the Czar" he called to
mind one of his earliest conscious memories, cited in "The
Story of a Heart," of being given a baked potato by his
father when Delmore was "aged two, irrational," and referred in passing to the fabled story of his grandfather's
desertion from the Russian Army; in other poems he recalled his jealousy when Kenneth was born or skating "in
the winter sunset, sorrowful and cold." These were all
momentous scenes in his encompassing memory; they belonged to the mythology he fashioned from his childhood
in order to explain what he had become.

Delmore could not have chosen a better vehicle for this
autobiographical impulse than Coriolanus, on whose life he
based the play that occupies a third of the volume. His
intention had been "to develop a method which would make
it possible to refer, with the least strain and the quickest
transition, to anything from the purely personal to the
international"; and the history of Coriolanus involved the
very forces Delmore identified as having been at work in
the shaping of his own character. Coriolanus' fanatical at-
tachment to the widowed mother who had brought him up
and his desire to please her at all costs mirrored Delmore's
loss of his father at an early age and his subsequent struggle to win his mother's approval of his work. Rose's continued indifference to his literary ambitions was more
frustrating than ever now that he was enjoying success, and
Coriolanus provided a means of elevating his chronic disappointment over this neglect into a conflict of heroic
dimensions. Still, Delmore's Coriolanus was hardly the
grand but flawed character depicted by Plutarch, Shakespeare, and T. S. Eliot. Rather, he was a confirmed narcis-
sist, avid for fame, who stares at himself in a pool of water
only to find there an image of his mother gazing back in
reproach. "His story was my story, he was I," the narrator
cries out in anguish, as Coriolanus, haunted by his mother's imprecations but too proud to relent before the furious
tribunals of the two betrayed cities, lives out the consequences of his egotism.

Delmore drew heavily on Shakespeare's play, following

the same sequence of events and borrowing or distorting phrases more or less arbitrarily. But he made the play his own by introducing an audience of "ghosts"—Freud, Marx, Aristotle, Beethoven (whose *Coriolan* overture is heard at particularly dramatic moments, indicated by a resonant "Bomb! Bomb! Bomb!"), and a fifth, unidentified party.* The ghosts spoke in a sort of burlesque of Elizabethan verse, achieved with elaborate tropes and pompous flourishes, that made for some riotously incongruous effects.

The prose passages that followed each act were less impressive; there Delmore gave expression to the vaudevillian side of his nature, indulging in ostentatious philosophical speculations and raving on about modern consciousness, "Inveterate, gratuitous, too much / Ambiguous," to the point where, the narrator complained, "I tire even myself." Here the strain of confession that motivates the entire play was more openly in evidence. In Delmore's view, his play's hero was "the I, the poet; and what he sees is what is important and constitutes the true action." The result was an excessive reliance on his narrator's self-revelations and the drama of his identification with Coriolanus; more than these repetitive, self-regarding speeches, it is the ghosts' brilliant and entertaining commentaries that distinguish Delmore's play.

On the whole, there were too many conscious echoes of his immediate masters in the other poems; Delmore himself acknowledged that they were "Poems of Experiment and Imitation." As for the play *Dr. Bergen's Belief*, written to fill out the book, the critics hardly mentioned it. Like his earlier play, *Choosing Company*, *Dr. Bergen's Belief* was a piece of portentous nonsense that displayed Delmore's addiction to philosophizing at its worst. Ostensibly a play on the Faustian theme of knowledge as a source of self-destruction rather than salvation, it ended with the mad Dr. Bergen leaping out of a fifteenth-story window, to be followed a moment later by his daughter Martha, while one of his disciples intones: "Knowledge and belief devour the mind of man."

---

* Delmore had also intended to have Kant among his ghostly spectators, but except for a single remark addressed to him by the narrator, no trace remained of the philosopher in later versions of the play. The fifth mysterious ghost apparently signified some unknowable *Ding an sich*.

.

Whatever its particular failings, *In Dreams Begin Responsibilties* articulated the pervasive disillusion of that era in a voice charged with intellectual passion and self-conscious irony. Delmore's poems were dramatic utterances, full of the vivid inflections he had grown up hearing. Irving Howe's description of his prose could apply to his early verse as well: "the sing-song, slightly pompous intonations of Jewish immigrants educated in night-schools, the self-conscious affectionate mockery of that speech by American born sons, its abstraction into the jargon of city intellectuals, and finally the whole body of this language flattened into a prose of uneasiness, and anti-rhetoric." In the stories Delmore was starting to publish, these echoes would be more deliberate than in his poetry, but they were unmistakable all the same. And while "the discussion of the Jewish problem" may have been muted, as he insisted to Laughlin, it was implicit in the poems' very tone. Where Jewish writers like Clifford Odets, Daniel Fuchs, and Henry Roth had confronted their experience directly, Delmore claimed as his imaginative province the cosmopolitan world of letters purveyed in the pages of *Partisan Review*. Faintly Marxist, imbued with a sense of history's fatal flaws in the wake of the Munich Pact and on the verge of World War II, Delmore was, Howe suggests, "the poet of the historical moment quite as Auden was in England." It was as if the self-constituted intelligentsia with which he had allied himself required a spokesman to dramatize its cultural dilemmas.

Delmore had a heroic conception of the poet, and shamelessly identified himself with what he took to be the sensibility of Modernism, calling on those precursors of modern consciousness, Marx and Freud, to guide him in the difficult quest of a "tradition of the new" (to use Harold Rosenberg's fine phrase). Looking back five years later, he recalled:

> A cultivated flatness was my fort [*sic*],
> Being gauche, I sang of poise and certainty /
> Poet, super id and super daemon,
> Byron like Mozart /

and it was no doubt this Byronic element in his character, combined with the subtle tonalities of a wry Jewish ironist, that made his poetry so attractive to a generation whose intellectual style had been appropriated from Europe. When *In Dreams* appeared, Robert Lowell, John Berryman, and Randall Jarrell had not yet published a line. It was Delmore's lot to take up where his predecessors had left off and define the temper of that uncertain era. No one was more surprised than he when his labors were heralded as the flowering of a new generation.

7

"YOU OUGHT TO BE ON BROADWAY!" William Saroyan exclaimed to Delmore at a party not long after the publication of *In Dreams Begin Responsibilities*. Whether he was referring to Delmore's theatrical manner at parties or the success of his book is unclear; perhaps he had in mind some photographs of Delmore that had recently appeared in *Vogue*, which made him look more like an actor than a poet. Romantic and stylized, they showed an ardent young man whose penetrating eyes shone with self-delight.

Delmore was more careful of his appearance in those days than later on, and while he could hardly have been called a fashionable dresser even then, he often wore a conservative coat and tie. His face was animated by a youthful innocence and a nervous, eager tension. Delmore's "immense intellectual devotion" could be discerned even in his features, Alfred Kazin recalled; one was aware of "the fine distraction, the still unconscious sensitivity behind the familiar Jewish-frantic manner." Once Delmore had thought of his stammer as a feature of the poet's utterance, emblematic of a hesitant groping toward truth; now that his self-confidence had begun to increase along with his reputation, his thoughts poured forth in a rush, accompanied by dramatic gestures. Like the Von Humboldt Fleisher of Saul Bellow's fictional portrait, Delmore in 1939 was "slovenly and grand," his ample hair swept back, "His face with widely separated eyes white and tense." Cosmopolitan, radical, at home with Rilke, Trotsky, Pound, he was the very embodiment of the New York intelligentsia. Declaiming in what Kazin described as "gulps of argument," Delmore transformed Greenwich Village in his talk from a province into a cultural capital, importing ideas from the whole European tradition and adapting them to the sprawl and chaos of contemporary America.

Partisan Review had become increasingly influential since its revival two years before as an independent left-wing journal, and that spring Delmore was invited to join its editorial board. He had been writing for the magazine regularly, producing brilliant reviews, an article on Yeats, and "The Statues," a story later collected in *The World Is a Wedding*; but he was reluctant to become an editor because, as he explained to Laughlin, "I would get a Marxist label without being a Marxist." Delmore emulated the reactionary pose of detachment shared by the great Modernists no less than their experiments in literary style, while *Partisan Review* encouraged a type of "Jewish Jesuit" able to "prove anything," he complained; Rahv especially, "heir of a thousand years of Talmudists," had a didactic manner that he shared with critics like Harold Rosenberg and Lionel Abel, whom Delmore classified as *Luftmensch* with "no fictional texture at all, no roots in Jewish or American life." Rather than acknowledge the dangers of this involuntary freedom, they had made of it an intellectual style; and while it was a style Delmore took up with genuine fervor, in his work he refused to ignore the pain caused by the very condition of uprootedness that had enabled him to move with such ease among diverse ideas. Still, he was eager to have his hand in, and put aside his concern about being mistaken for a Marxist to become *Partisan's* poetry editor, a position he was to hold for well over a decade.

Delmore was not a conscientious editor, but he was enterprising enough to publish both established poets and most of those among the younger generation who were eventually to become important. And he was generous toward his friends, doing all he could to get their work in print. But there was often a frantic quality about Delmore's encouragement, and eagerness to show that he wielded power in the literary world. Nearly every day a flurry of letters went out directing his friends to send their manuscripts to one editor or another, with elaborate instructions on how to word their covering letters. In a characteristic letter to Robert Hivnor, a young writer from the Midwest who had submitted a story to *Partisan Review* that Delmore liked, he promised "to insist, if it is necessary, that Laughlin print a part of your book in next year's New Directions anthology," not omitting to remind him that, as poetry editor of *Partisan Review*, he could print "whatever [he] wanted." Delmore's self-acknowledged Machiavellianism served him well as an editor. Writing to Berryman about a poem of his he found "vulgar" but had nevertheless decided to print, he made it clear that he was "acting as editor, not critic."

> Casuistry justifies everything, but what can one do in the case when no one pays attention to a poet unless there is a scandal. Maritain observes that to refuse to use force, as of Gandhi, is to deny the fact that one has a body. The same kind of justification probably works for an editor, who prints insufficient work for the sake of all that is sufficient and is going to be so.

Literary fame and influence were exhilarating, but they provided little income, and Delmore was virtually penniless. His only sure source of money was from literary work, which he figured would amount to no more than three hundred dollars for the whole year. For all the acclaim *In Dreams Begin Responsibilities* had received, sales were slow. "Everything gets better all the time, except that no copies are being bought," he complained in mid-January. Not that he would have prospered even if the whole edition had sold out, since it amounted to only a thousand copies; all the same, it was a question of morale. "In a little while, I am going to feel guilty about the whole thing," he fretted, urging Laughlin to place more ads.

Delmore resented having to write criticism all the time in order to make ends meet, and he hated to borrow from his mother. "My mother has disowned me, demanded the return of her furniture, and I will probably end up on the WPA," he wrote Laughlin in the spring of 1939. And on another occasion, he reported that his mother had accused him of being a failure because he couldn't earn five thousand dollars a year. When Laughlin offered to talk to her, Delmore told him:

> I am afraid it would do no good at all. All the tenacious bourgeois virtues—prudence, a savings account, and a steady job—prevent my mother from seeing any meaning in my supposed profession, and

she seems to think that if she removes her support, I will alter my ways. But we will manage, or God, in fact, will provide.

One solution was to teach, and during the spring several possibilities arose. He had gone to see Theodore Morrison at Breadloaf the previous summer about a job at Harvard, and there was talk of obtaining a position through Mark Van Doren at City College, but nothing came of it; so Delmore pursued another lead, and wrote to John Crowe Ransom.

There is one matter about which I am eager and that is the teaching job, the possibility of one, at Kenyon College. I was supposed, I think, to wait until the proper moment arrived and Allen Tate, who has in a very short time been kind to me in many ways, proposed my name to you. At any rate, although this may be premature, I would welcome an opportunity to teach very much, and I may have certain qualifications, academic ones, I mean, of which you do not know, and I would be grateful indeed if my name was kept in mind.

But no offer was forthcoming from Kenyon either, although Ransom solicited Delmore's work for *Kenyon Review*, proved one of his most loyal sponsors over the years, and credited him with having been responsible for the "ethical-logical" approach Ransom used in his influential book, *New Criticism*.

Early in January, Allen Tate offered to recommend Delmore for a position in the philosophy department at the Women's College in Greensboro, North Carolina, where Tate was in residence. At once, Delmore asked Laughlin for a recommendation, instructing him to "quote as many favorable statements as possible and please inflate me as much as honesty will permit. I need a fulsome *dossier*."

Soon lavish recommendations from Mark Van Doren, Sidney Hook, and Delmore's professor at Harvard, D. W. Prall, were coming into the chairman of the philosophy department at Greensboro. Prall lauded Delmore's technical abilities as a philosopher, and noted that both Professor Wolfson and Professor Perry "thought extremely highly of him too," while Van Doren emphasized his literary accomplishments, praising *In Dreams Begin Responsibilities* as "intellectually brilliant beyond anything of its sort I have seen in years." Hook chose to concentrate on Delmore's potential as a teacher, his "fine presence, a gift for persuasive exposition, a readiness to understand difficulties," and a remarkable command of philosophy. But Hook reserved his most elaborate praise for Delmore's visionary genius: "A creative artist in his own right, his dramatic and imaginative power makes it possible for him to recapture the great visions of the past, and to make them relevant to certain phases of contemporary experience." All in all, it was a dazzling array of recommendations; but, once again, no appointment was offered.

"I have begun to take desperate measures to avoid landing in the poorhouse with little Gertrude," he wrote Laughlin in March, and immediately began casting about for other possibilities. One alternative was to work for New Directions, either in Cambridge or at Laughlin's home in Norfolk. At first, when he still thought he would be offered the post at Greensboro, Delmore had volunteered the services of Gertrude; this way, he explained to Laughlin, he would "really be getting the services of two brilliant minds." If Delmore found that he wasn't happy teaching in North Carolina, he could "look forward to freedom in Massachusetts on my wife's labors." When this odd arrangement was deemed impractical, he put forth the Norfolk plan, but this too proved untenable when Laughlin's aunt objected to *In Dreams* (the word "fuck" had appeared in it twice); she considered Delmore "a mixture of sex-fiend and Communist," he complained to Robert Hivnor. Years later, recalling the struggles of this period, he noted bitterly: "It took me five years to get used to the idea that I was not what a relative termed a rich heir and the idea that the Depression was not just an interval before a new period of prosperity."

With the approach of summer Delmore and Gertrude didn't even have enough money to leave town. Delmore had applied to Yaddo, the writer's colony in Saratoga Springs, but he was discouraged by a rule that "the creative husband must come without the non-creative wife," he reported to Mark Van Doren (forgetting that Gertrude also had literary aspirations). "It is obscene, the desire to separate whom God hath joined," he complained to Laughlin, but qualified it with another of the strained ironies that seemed to attend any reference to their marriage: ". . . since Gertrude has been planning to leave me since we were married, I think I had better stick around while she is still able to endure me." Apart from a weekend with James Agee and his wife, Alma, in Flemington, New Jersey, he was in the city until August, writing articles and negotiating with Yaddo. Berryman was living in the country that summer, and Delmore envied his rural life, "one of the most pleasant of life's false simplicities."

The administrators at Yaddo were finally persuaded to accommodate Gertrude, and in mid-August the Schwartzes took the train to Saratoga Springs, where they planned to stay "until asked to depart." Since they couldn't afford to maintain their apartment in New York, all their belongings had to be packed up and taken with them. "The desire for a home has become, in me, the desire for a place to rest my books," he said in a poignant note to Laughlin; "they have traveled thousands of miles in the last few years."

Yaddo, founded at the turn of the century by a wealthy philanthropic family from upstate New York, was a grand, sprawling estate set among five hundred acres of pine woods and lakes and dominated by a huge gray-stone Victorian mansion. Artists in residence lived in the main house or in the farmhouses and studios scattered about the estate. Delmore and Gertrude were assigned to North Farm, which they were to share with the composer David Diamond. There were conflicts from the beginning, for Diamond was an urbane and worldly homosexual who had lived in Paris for several years, while Delmore had only a rudimentary knowledge of music and was struggling to finish a translation of Rimbaud's *Une Saison en enfer* equipped with what he admitted was a "high school" proficiency in French. Even so, he didn't welcome Diamond's criticism, and was openly contemptuous of his homosexuality. When Diamond boasted of having met Gide, Delmore dismissed the great novelist as "just another faggot."

The "post-Munich sensibility"—Delmore's term for the malaise that had settled over his contemporaries as events in Europe approached a crisis—was inescapable even at Yaddo, now that war had broken out. In his journal, Delmore offered a concise interpretation of its causes.

When the Depression came two roads were left,
War or Socialism: knowing the populace,
Can we be surprised at war's selection?

Always apolitical, he viewed the war as a farcical drama
in which "two raging giants," Germany and Russia, were
certain to destroy each other and, eventually, the world.
While the editors of *Partisan Review* debated over what
line to take in the cause of socialism, Delmore worried
about the more general threat to life and letters. The widening of the war meant "a null period for immortal poetry," and he reminded Laughlin that nothing could be
more important in such a time than to continue publishing
books, in order "to make possible the life of the spirit,
which is the only thing which makes a human being
human." He predicted that America would enter the war
within two years. "Every goddamned lie will be used to
make everyone think that something will be accomplished
by any side's victory or defeat, and those Russian bastards
have made the whole thing worse."

Four years later, in a review of Saul Bellow's first novel,
Dangling Man, Delmore summed up the experience of his
generation, which he liked to refer to as the class of 1930.
For those who came to maturity during the Depression,
followed by "the sanguine period" of the New Deal, the
days of the Popular Front, and the Munich Pact, "the
slow, loud ticking imminence of a new war" signaled the
end of their faith in history. Disillusion with Marxism had
marked only the first stage in their unwilling confrontation
with events beyond their control.

With the advent of war, every conceivable temptation not to be honest, not to look directly at experience, not to remember the essential vows of allegiance
to the intelligence and to human possibility and
dignity—every conceivable temptation and every plea
of convenience, safety and casuistry has presented itself.

All the same, the drama of war was at times exhilarating; "When it began," he recalled a year later, "I felt we
were back in 1914 once more, I was thrilled for the moment; it would be foolish to deny it." He read the news-

papers every day, and sent Laughlin detailed interpretations of events from a Marxist point of view (which he resorted to only when corresponding with his ruling-class publisher). Laughlin himself was in part responsible for this war, Delmore insisted: "Captialismus corrupts you who are rich as it corrupts me who am not, too much and too little always being forms of disease." While artists starved and suffered, "tormented all life long by economic need in this economic system," the idle rich, "brutish oafs," mercilessly exploited them.

Delmore and Gertrude were so poor that the directors of Yaddo invited them to stay on through the autumn, along with a few other guests. As the fall wore on and the summer residents departed, Delmore felt abandoned in the little farmhouse with winter approaching and no certain prospects for the coming year. Brooding over the war's ominous escalation, he took comfort in the sturdy simplicity of Mark Van Doren's "A Winter Diary"; it evoked, he wrote the author,

a way of life in Nature or rather next to Nature which is going to last as long as men have to get food from the land, no matter what else is wiped out.

What made me take up the poem this time was that we had decided to stay here at Yaddo during the coming winter in the old farmhouse we were given when we arrived. This will be the first time that we have lived apart from the city, for a long span not a vacation, in our lives, and since both Gertrude and myself are both irreducibly the products of metropolitan childhoods, I expect a certain unrest at times, when the possibility of a dozen different activities which exists in the city is removed. But I have said so many times that I was a recluse by temperament that it is about time I proved it. That is, if we are lucky, I'll have a chance to prove it. The prospect of America's entry into the war by next spring comes from the best Marxist source, Trotsky himself, and he's been right too often before this.

Our summer in Yaddo has been a mixture of many new impressions of the literary life. A generalization about writers drawn from the writers who have been here this summer is probably not a fair sample, since so many seem to have little more than a talent for journalism; but so far as that generalization goes, it makes me sick with the idea of how, as a class, writers are self-indulgent, full of self-pity, forever seeking reassurance, constantly occupied with what they consider the proper conditions of work, and the next thing to invalids in their demands upon life.

By mid-autumn, Delmore had quarreled with virtually everyone at Yaddo. Trying to be ironic, he reported to Dupee:

By this time, no one, of the five remaining guests (as they are called) is speaking to the other four, with the exception of Gertrude except that is when she is not speaking to me. There are all kinds of curious combinations of silence and anger; and it would remind me of explorers on Arctic expeditions but for the fact that the lack of harmony comes not from enforced isolation but from the contempt of one kind of writer for another.

Delmore was himself one of the most active promoters of this contempt. "Never before had he been among so many intellectuals," he recalled in the notes for a novel about Yaddo; and he had arrived there with great expectations, only to find that "*being-left-out* was one of the chief experiences at Boileau."

The months at Yaddo were a time of "slumber, anger, & loneliness." Delmore sat by the stove in the little farmhouse day after day, reading through Edith Wharton's novels and a recently acquired edition of the *Encyclopaedia Britannica*, one of his favorite works. It was from this avocation that he collected the compendious store of historical and anthropological facts which later found their way into *Genesis*. ("I might have lived my life out without ever knowing that tadpoles are not affected by light," he wrote his friend Arthur Mizener later on that year.) He often drove alone to Saratoga Springs in search of "the passive enjoyment of the silver screen," a practice which confirmed his later assertion that he "spent his first marriage at the movies."

Delmore was still haunted by his father's death, and over the winter he produced a series of "Exercises" that obliquely rehearsed that traumatic event by transposing it to a story about a young man's refusal to attend "the funeral of the man who had been his father's best friend." Convinced that he had never properly mourned his father, Delmore imagined—in the person of "M——," or "Mee," a spelling derived from Milton by which he proposed to represent himself in his autobiographical writings—that he had purchased a plot beside his father's grave in order to atone for his supposed indifference to his father's death. Rose, too, was imagined to be dying in one of these "Exercises," then to have died, which he learned "with an emotion of great fear."

Another scenario written one morning just after he had received a letter from his mother occurred to him while he was in the bathroom shaving; Gertrude called out to him and his failure to respond promptly

suggested a story in which a young man is in the bathroom and when he is called, he does not answer, permits them to think something has happened to him, until the whole family is greatly disturbed, the door is broken down by the police or the janitor, young man and family mutually denounce each other.

It was, in its own way, a commonplace fantasy of retribution, in which the child resorts to dramatic and punitive means to gain the attention of his family; but in this instance it had a special meaning. It was as if Delmore had to repress his urge to "denounce" his father for dying and his mother for her selfish conduct by means of these parables; and that impulse was in turn converted to guilt.

As Delmore implied in his letter to Dupee, there were conflicts with Gertrude; in his journal, he confessed to being "angry and ugly" with her when she interrupted him while he was working, and noted how her mood changed when he referred to the delicate issue of their "not to be born child." Delmore was always mourning their "unborn Shenandoah," while Gertrude was opposed to having a child because—if one is to trust Delmore's fictional account of their differences—"she was an only child and she was childlike herself and as she had told her husband, she would be jealous of any child to whom she gave her being." But she must have also had doubts about what sort of father Delmore would have made. He was all too eager to cast Gertrude in the role of housewife, while he pursued his career. And his reasons for wanting a child were not always the soundest; he often declared that what he really desired was "to be a grandfather," and Gertrude—at least in Delmore's novel—insisted he was interested only in "an expansion of [his] ego." But he delighted in the births of his friends' children, and when he heard, a few years later, that he had become an uncle, Delmore was ecstatic. Childbirth implied "joy of generation and joy of newness, continuous dynasty and more," he proclaimed in his journal.

•

Delmore spent a good part of the fall putting the finishing touches to his translation to Rimbaud's *Une Saison en enfer* begun five years before, which Laughlin had encouraged him to revise for publication. Convinced that Rimbaud had prophesied a crisis drawing closer each day, Delmore was in a hurry to get the book out as soon as possible: "Now is just about the time for the sticks of dynamite which the later Rimbaud was throwing at the disorder and conflict and disease of Western civilization, while by next year another war may be so brutal that verbal brutality will seem without relevance." And there were other, more practical motives as well; if the book was well reviewed, he hoped to obtain work as a translator of French novels, while Laughlin calculated that it would offer a means of recovering at least a part of his investment in Delmore's career.

What Laughlin hadn't counted on was Delmore's poor command of the language, a failing no amount of diligence could disguise. He had studied French in high school, taken a rigorous course in seventeenth-century French drama at Wisconsin, and read most of the major Symbolist poets. But the level of sophistication demanded in these courses was another matter; writing to Julian Sawyer from Wisconsin, Delmore once gave a sample of what transpired in class: "We listen to French, and must answer in French —no English—'*Andromaque*, c'est très bien; mais, mesdemoiselles et messieurs, je préfère *Phèdre*; quelle grande passion,' said the young teacher." It was not the sort of dialogue designed to increase her pupils' fluency; but Delmore was less interested in *Une Saison en enfer* as a literary document than in what it represented, and threw himself into researching the history of the Commune and the Franco-Prussian War, which in his view formed the "background" of the poem.

Another assignment that occupied him that fall was a retrospective essay for *Kenyon Review* on T. S. Eliot's journal, *Criterion*, which had ceased publication in 1939. Delmore had been a regular reader of *Criterion* almost from the beginning, and had gone through every issue in the library at the University of Wisconsin, collecting voluminous notes along the way. Now, spurred on by a prodding letter from Ransom, he managed to produce a masterly—and by no means entirely laudatory—résumé of *Criterion*'s history, taking issue with Eliot's political views, his editorial choices, and the inconsistent ideas put forth in his commentaries. It was courageous of Delmore to criticize Eliot's occasional fatuity, the naïve, pontificating manner that seemed to overcome him whenever he touched on non-literary matters; but the tone of his critique was moderate, and it was obvious that he had read every word Eliot had ever written with fanatical attention. The dominant "criterion" of Eliot's journal, he concluded, was simply the "intelligence," a term Delmore meant to be understood in "the most flattering way possible."

Early in November, a letter arrived from Eliot thanking Delmore for his article. "I feel the less diffidence in writing," Eliot wrote, "because your article was not *altogether* commendatory, and I was struck by the justice of the strictures both on my own contributions and on the faults of 'The Criterion' as a whole." Eliot was impressed by the care with which Delmore had read through back numbers of the magazine, and agreed with his contention that few British critics were equal to Blackmur, Tate, and Edmund Wilson. "You are certainly a critic," Eliot concluded, "but I want to see more poetry from you: I was much impressed by *In Dreams Begin Responsibilities*." No single event in Delmore's literary career was more significant to him than this letter; he never tired of talking about it, and endowed it with a sort of talismanic value. It was as if Kafka's K had finally gotten through to the authorities high up in the Castle.

•

Early in December, the Schwartzes drove over to Bennington to visit drama professor Francis Fergusson, whom they had met on their honeymoon. On the way there, Delmore was "too concerned about the car to gaze with sentiment and memory at the old sites, our white house of the summer of 1938 and the small factory town in the country." Once at the Fergussons', he worried that he was talking too much, and had made "too many remarks of deliberate malice." Holding forth on the causes of war, he was overcome by "the old feeling of being unsure of [his] auditor's frame of mind"; and on the way home, driving through waves of thick white fog in the darkness, he felt exhausted by the strain of visiting and being taken from his work. When they got back to Yaddo, he described the visit in his journal, and summed up, "Great wits to madness are near allied."

This journal was a new project of Delmore's. He had started it earlier in the week, on December 8, his twenty-sixth birthday, "a neat occasion for the commencement (I have always looked for such schedules and occasions, perhaps because of a feeling for form)." He shared with Joyce a superstitious regard for birthdays, but in Delmore's case they were always occasions for dread: "My birthday has brought me the usual sentiments of time wasted and work which is not good enough, because I hurry, am impatient, turn to too many interests."

The approach of old age, while hardly imminent, dejected him as it did on every birthday. Consulting the actuarial tables of the life-insurance companies, he was consoled to learn that he could hope to live another thirty-eight years. Even so, he felt compelled to qualify his relief; that he would live that long "reason or at least mathematics promises; but not to me as an individual, not to my immortal soul; only to one unit of the class of citizens who are twenty-six years of age." Despite such dour caution, he was optimistic enough to conceive of the journal as a project "intended for the pleasure and insight of an old man."

All his life, Delmore kept journals, on scraps of paper, in ledgers, on the typewriter, sometimes just a line or two and sometimes many pages for each day; but what distinguished this particular journal was the meticulous effort he made "to turn more frequently to objective observation." It was not sufficient simply to review events or their motives. "Self-analysis is easy and has been accomplished often enough." Nor was Delmore entirely unjustified in claiming to be "objective"; his difficulties were caused less by a lack of self-knowledge than by the unpredictability of his moods, which had vacillated wildly between elation and extreme depression for as long as he could remember. These journals document what had come to be an almost continuous struggle to master his own temperament. Exhorting himself to be patient, not to hurry or "permit excitement to keep time from disappearing wholly"; striving to contain the "sickening excitement" that overcame him in moments of inspiration: each day was a trial in which the same anxieties arose and had to be conquered. By annotating his feelings daily, he hoped to discover a pattern in them, and in this way manage to subvert their tyranny.

Within a week, the journal gave way—at least for the time being—to more momentous events. Delmore had been invited to address the Modern Language Association in New Orleans over Christmas, and on the fourteenth he left with Gertrude for New York, where they were to meet James Laughlin and drive down together. "Always the emotion of excitement which goes with any decision to travel," he noted in his journal, "for all imperfect things must move." When they arrived in New York, Gertrude went home to her parents in Washington Heights, while Delmore stayed at the Macdonalds', sleeping on a couch in their living room. The next few days were occupied in a round of visits from William Phillips, Clement Greenberg, F. W. Dupee, and John Berryman. Amid all this activity, he was seeing very little of Gertrude; on the twentieth he had "another minor brush" with her as they were driving back to her parents' apartment. After a lonely period at Yaddo, Delmore was unwilling to share his friends' attention, and cruelly banished his wife to Washington Heights while he carried on a frenetic social life downtown.

Later that week, Robert Hivnor called to say that Auden was eager to meet Delmore, and the next afternoon they took the subway to Brooklyn, where Auden had recently moved into a house on Montague Street. Auden was very gracious and affable that day; he talked animatedly about America, still a very new experience for him, and wanted to know if loneliness was characteristic of American life; most of the Americans he had met seemed to have few intimate friends. So far, Auden had found them reserved, accessible only up to a certain point, after which they retreated into a sort of inviolate privacy. The greatest value in America, Auden contended, was "personality"; success came more easily to "extroverts," and yet the American poets he knew all struck him as "introverts" intent on cultivating their own sensibilities. There was a lively discussion about Eliot, who, both Delmore and Auden agreed, was a better poet and editor than critic, especially when it came to religion or politics. They talked for several hours, and Delmore left "feeling high" even though disappointed that Auden had made no mention of his article "The Two Audens."

From Auden's, he rushed off to Manhattan, two hours late, to meet Gertrude and John Berryman at the Museum of Modern Art. When Berryman learned that Delmore had just been to see Auden, he promptly fainted "in front of the pity and terror of one of Picasso's blues," as Delmore related the incident to Mark Van Doren. Berryman was notorious for his fanatical jealousy, and Delmore was convinced he had "staged a faint."

Just before Christmas, Delmore, Gertrude, and Laughlin drove down to New Orleans, where two opposing literary schools had gathered: the "eastern seaboard liberals" (as Arthur Mizener designated them) and the Fugitives*; of the latter, Ransom, Tate, and Robert Penn Warren were the principal figures. The "liberals" thought of the Fugitives as "Protofascists," while the Fugitives considered the "liberals" Communists. Delmore, of course, admired the Fugitives, and had learned a great deal from the stern academic criticism of Austin Warren and Cleanth Brooks. Nor was he unsympathetic to the reactionary politics of the Fugitives, since they valued the artist's autonomous creation over what they regarded as the transient crises of the modern world. But he naturally conceived of himself as a member of the opposition, given his associations with

---

* *The Fugitive* was the name of a journal published in the South between 1922 and 1925 to which Ransom and Tate, among others, contributed some of their earliest work. Later on, when their particular ideology of regionalism, traditionalism, and classicism came to be defined in a collection of essays entitled *I'll Take My Stand*, the label of Agrarian replaced that of Fugitive, and Ransom and Tate eventually came to be known as New Critics; Fugitivism was an earlier version of the polemical, aristocratic bias manifest in their criticism.

Partisan Review. The two groups, initially so suspicious of each other, recognized "with almost ludicrous rapidity," Mizener recalled, "that they were very close together indeed in literary matters and felt alike on an astonishing number of social issues."

Delmore, delighted as he was to be among so many literary elders, treated everyone with his customary irreverence, in particular Ransom, whom he attacked one day at lunch for having published in *Kenyon Review* a poem Delmore pronounced "commonplace." He spent a long evening with Norman Holmes Pearson and Robert Penn Warren, who had been encouraging him from the start of his career, and ended up going to a gambling hall with Albert Erskine, a young instructor of English at Louisiana State University who also happened to be married to Katherine Anne Porter. Drinking in hotel rooms, staying up late, carousing in nightclubs, and going down to the marketplace by the wharfs for café au lait at all hours of the night, Delmore was exhausted when the time arrived for him to give his talk. Rosemary Mizener's first impression of Delmore suggests the state he was in that week: "His complexion was greenish-muddy and he had poor teeth. We knew he had severe insomnia problems, and these seemed to account for his pallor and the dark smudges under his eyes." But she was taken with Delmore's gaiety and the "richly ramified" anecdotes he told with such unself-conscious ardor.

On the day of his speech, Delmore was so nervous that he rehearsed it in his hotel room. He was not a forceful public speaker, tending to mumble and rush his words out of shyness, and by the time his turn came to read he was overcome with impatience; but his arguments were sound, his presentation confident and informal—even if he did find it a "sickening experience" when some people got up to leave while he was speaking. His subject was "The Isolation of Modern Poetry," a condition he traced to the mid-nineteenth century, when a conflict arose between "the sensibility of the poet, the very images which he viewed as the world, and the evolving and blank and empty universe of nineteenth century science." In part, the poet's isolation originated in these immense developments, which had caused him to retreat inward; culture, Delmore argued in a bold critique of the whole enterprise of Modernism, "has fed upon itself increasingly and has created its own autonomous satisfactions, removing itself further all the time from any essential part in the organic life of society." Surprisingly, he found much to deplore in the "cultivation of his own sensibility" that had become the poet's fate; rather than belligerently decry the philistinism of the public, as Randall Jarrell was to do some years later in an essay, "The Obscurity of the Poet," Delmore suggested that the poet had lost touch with "the common language of daily life, its syntax, habitual sequences, and processes of association." Not, perhaps, through any fault of his own, given the estrangement of culture from society characteristic of modern life; all the same, isolation was a condition to be resisted, and to encourage this resistance, Delmore proposed a restoration of what he called the "human," storytelling element to poetry.*

The next day Gertrude and Delmore left for Baton Rouge, where they stayed with Albert Erskine and Katherine Anne Porter. They had a memorable dinner on New Year's Eve, featuring roast suckling pig and the exchange of "eloquent compliments" between Delmore and the famous writer. "The most impressive thing," he wrote Mark Van Doren some weeks later, "was Katherine Anne Porter trying to stay up all night with her husband and your sleepless correspondent and talking all the time of being 20 years older than either of us."

After an obligatory glance at the Mississippi ("effort to be adequate," Delmore noted later), they set off on the long trip north accompanied by the Mizeners. Laughlin had decided to stay behind, but subsidized the Schwartzes' return trip anyway, since as usual they had no money; so they lived lavishly during those few days, staying in hotels and dining out while Delmore amused the Mizeners with his endless monologues. His vivacity contrasted sharply with Gertrude's reticence; she seemed "very self-conscious about herself," Rosemary Mizener recalled, while Delmore, stim-

---

* Years later, recalling this speech in his journal, Delmore felt he had been "self-deceived in histrionic posture and opera."

> Thus and thus,
>   in the late adolescence of youthful arrogance
>   and self-arrogance
>   I damned modern civilization
>   or donned the mantle of the critic and prophet
>   mocking the madness of modern life

ulated by travel and the sympathetic companionship of new friends, was at the height of his inventive powers.

After stopping off at the Tates' in Princeton for a night, they went on to New York, where they retrieved their own car and drove up to Saratoga Springs, arriving completely frozen because the heater had broken down. Furious with Laughlin for having abandoned them in the South, with Macdonald for having attacked his Rimbaud translation during their visit to New York, and with his mother for the usual reasons, Delmore wrote them all angry letters, then decided not to mail them. To make matters worse, the directors of Yaddo could offer no further assistance, since their funds had diminished "as a result of the decline of dividends in some Mexican silver mines because of the Cardenas regime," Delmore explained to F. W. Dupee (a circumstance he found emblematic of "the far-flung character of modern life" and a paradigm of his own). It was hard to settle down to work with the future so uncertain, and a week later he wrote to Laughlin begging him to give Gertrude a secretarial job at New Directions. "We want the job and, as you know, we need it badly. I will spare your delicate sensibilities a picture of this our exile at Yaddo; the main thing is this business of living at the edge of being penniless all the time; *it interferes with the functioning of the creative artist.*" Laughlin's plan was to move the New Directions office to Cambridge, and Delmore, still hoping for a teaching job at Harvard, promised that Gertrude would work for at least a year, even if he happened to be hired elsewhere. "We can bear the separation for a time much more than we can bear our present economic status." Besides, Laughlin owed him a favor, Delmore suggested; not only had he turned down an offer from Louisiana State University Press to publish a collection of his essays, but Random House had lately expressed interest in his work. "I wish I had Random House's letter to send you right now," Delmore went on, but he had sent it to his mother instead, to show her that he wasn't a "failure." At once abject and threatening, he called himself Laughlin's "serf" while reciting how much money in advances from other publishers he had turned down over the last two years.

Delmore was justified in stressing his loyalty to Laughlin, whose terms were not always the most generous; the royalties for *In Dreams Begin Responsibilities* had been

only 6 percent. But his books were published in small
editions, and the "steelmaster scion," as Delmore liked to
call him, had already advanced considerable sums while
having to deal with "the well-known Schwartz delay"; his
eagerness to be in print was always at war with a fanatical
scrupulosity about his work and a fear of criticism, so that
his books were invariably late, and on several occasions
were never completed at all.

Toward the end of January, Delmore's prospects improved; he had heard there was a good chance he would
win a Guggenheim grant, Laughlin had agreed to hire
Gertrude, and he could report to Berryman that he was
being considered for teaching posts at both Harvard and
Kenyon. "This has excited me immensely but also presented the possibility of an embarrassingly rich choice
some time soon."

8

ON FEBRUARY 1, 1940, Delmore and Gertrude arrived in Cambridge to look for an apartment, and within a few days they were installed at 41 Bowdoin Street, near the Radcliffe campus. Delmore was still not certain of a job at Harvard, but within a month he learned that he had been given a one-year appointment as a Briggs-Copeland instructor. Ambivalent about teaching, he wrote Mark Van Doren, "Our return to Cambridge has been a matter of mixed emotions"; and perhaps he had in mind as well the antipathy to Jews that persisted in the English Departments of Ivy League universities well into the forties. Jews were considered "exotic" at Harvard in those days; and while Harry Levin insists that " 'indifference' was a liberating watchword and *laissez-faire* was a social principle" when he was starting out there, Delmore never saw it that way. To the very end of his life, he continued to recall how much he had "suffered in being a Jew at Harvard," and in his last months filled one spiral notebook after another with a virtually illegible novel about Harvard in the forties that rehearsed the sense of estrangement he had known there.

At first, Delmore tried to be satirical about his Jewishness, reporting to Laughlin that he had become "what Harry Levin would refer to as a Pet Jew," and claiming with genuine pride that he "dined only with the Murdocks, and spoke only to the Conants"; but it was evident from the start that he had entered a world in which he would never feel at home. To be a Jew was to bear the impress of his people's history, heir to "the passion which yet roves in us." Like Abraham departing from his father's house, Delmore noted in one of his "exercise" poems, he had gone forth to Harvard only to find himself in exile. And while he made jokes about sharing an office with Harry Levin, which he called the "Golden Ghetto," he was secretly unnerved to discover that his Jewishness was an ineradicable trait. When he looked in a mirror, he could see "Judaea" in his face, mingled with an Asian, Mongol lineage. He consoled himself with the conviction that "Anti-semitism ever / Sharpens Jews to be more clever," but he was far from reconciled to his ancestral fate.

Delmore was particularly troubled by expressions of anti-Semitism in literature, though he was fond of stressing that his great intellectual heroes, Freud and Marx, were Jews, along with characters in some of the century's most celebrated novels: Proust's Swann, Mann's Naphta in *The Magic Mountain*, and, of course, Joyce's Bloom. On the other hand, "Eliot, James and Adams did not really know the Jews," he complained. "They knew only the storekeepers and the social climbers," types of Jews from whom he was careful to dissociate himself. Delmore was troubled by Edith Wharton's portrait in *The House of Mirth* of Rosedale, the Jew who aspired to marry the "Gentile" Lily Bart; and he was offended by James's condescending description of New York Jews in *The American Scene*. "My mother and father both lived at just that time in the part of New York James was looking at," he objected to R. P. Blackmur. The overt anti-Semitism of Pound and Eliot disturbed him even more than the oblique disdain of James and Wharton. In his journal, he copied out Eliot's observation in *After Strange Gods*: "In the good society reason and religion combine to say that free-thinking Jews in large numbers would be an anomalous and undesirable element" and substituted "Anglo-Catholics" for "Jews."

Delmore felt personally slighted whenever his literary heroes expressed distaste for Jews, for it fed his self-hatred and cast doubt on his self-chosen identity as their cultural heir. After reading Pound's *Guide to Kulchur*, he was so infuriated by Pound's references to Jews and the "Semitic race" that he dashed off a letter announcing his refusal to serve any longer as one of his disciples.

Dear Mr. Pound:

I have been reading your last book, "Culture." Here I find numerous remarks about the Semite or Jewish race, all of them damning, although in the course of the book, you say:

"Race prejudice is red herring. The tool of man

> defeated intellectually, and of the cheap poli-
> tician."

which is a simple logical contradiction of your remarks about the Jewish people, and also a curious
omen of a state of mind—one which can support both
views, race-prejudice and such a judgment of race-
prejudice, at the same time, or in the same book.

A race cannot commit a moral act. Only an individual can be moral or immoral. No generalization
from a sum of particulars is possible, which will
render a moral judgment. In a court of law, the crim-
inal is always one individual, and when he is condemned, his whole family is not, qua family, condemned. This is not to deny, however, that there are
such entities as races. Furthermore, this view of individual responsibility is implicit in the poetry for which
you are justly famous.

But I do not doubt that this is a question which you
have no desire to discuss with anyone who does not
agree with you, and even less with one who will be
suspected of an interested view. Without ceasing to
distinguish between past activity and present irrationality, I should like you to consider this letter as a
resignation: I want to resign as one of your most
studious and faithful admirers.

Sincerely yrs,
Delmore Schwartz

It was a brave and admirable gesture, considering Delmore's reverence for Pound's work, and the purity of his
rage was to be further established by his continued willingness to write favorably on the *Cantos* as they appeared.
Only a year later, in a note designed to serve as a promo-
tional pamphlet for *Cantos* LII–LXXI, Delmore claimed
that Pound's versification constituted "a new basis for the
writing of poetry, which, when it has been dissociated from
Pound's particular vision, should have an immense influence on the poetry of the next hundred years."

The very real manifestations of anti-Semitism Delmore
encountered in literature and, far more subtly, at Harvard,
were no doubt magnified by his pervasive insecurity, as he
acknowledged in a 1944 symposium on "American Literature and the Younger Generation of American Jews." As a

child, he recalled, he had been unaware of what it meant to be a Jew, and his "ignorance" had not been dispelled until he went off to the University of Wisconsin.

> There too, however, my ignorance of the character of anti-Semitism was increased, in a way, by a personal weakness, namely, the weakness of supposing that when anyone did not like me, the reason was my personal character and behavior. . . . If one is regarded as *peculiar* and if one is *left out* of the social life only by Christian boys and girls, then one is tempted to be impersonal and to be sure that each time it is the consequence of being a Jew.

Even so, most of Delmore's friends, both at Wisconsin and at N.Y.U., had been Jews, and he was unprepared for the few direct expressions of anti-Semitism he encountered later on.

The most dramatic instance occurred in the early 1940's, when Delmore and William Phillips were standing on the deck of the Staten Island ferry smoking, which provoked a woman to a half-hour tirade about "refugees" and "dirty Jews." But there were other painfuul injustices in what Delmore referred to as the "Cambridge ghetto." Landlords, even Jewish ones, were anti-Semitic, he complained; and the Navy students who had come to Harvard as part of the officers' training program were openly racist. One student had even sent him an anonymous note with the message "Fuck the Jews!" In the story "A Bitter Farce" (collected in *The World Is a Wedding*), Delmore recounted his efforts to argue them out of their anti-Semitism; he has Shenandoah Fish remark:

> My ancestors, in whom I take pride, but not personal pride, were scholars, poets, prophets and students of God when most of Europe worshipped sticks and stones: not that I hold that against any of you, for it is not your fault if your forebears were barbarians grovelling and groping about for peat or something.

Delmore shared to some degree the mandarin literary attitudes that prompted Lionel Trilling to write his book on

Arnold, and Philip Rahv to sponsor a Henry James revival; but he was determined to fashion from his Jewishness "a central symbol of alienation, bias, point of view." If he was to be discriminated against by the very writers he most admired, then he would have to display his identity as a shibboleth—or, as he put it in a more abject declaration to Dwight Macdonald, to exploit "the alienation which only a Jew can suffer, and use, as a cripple uses his weakness in order to beg."

Delmore felt he suffered an additional liability at Harvard in being a poet as well as a Jew. "I never thought about anti-Semitism," he once told Harold Rosenberg, "because everyone was against me as a poet." He thought of himself as "peculiar, not typical, a strange ornament in which the university indulged itself because [his] book made a big splash." But this was hardly the case, since Delmore was one of the earliest beneficiaries of a policy—one that continues to this day—of hiring writers to teach English composition. In the 1940's, Theodore Morrison was gathering at Harvard a remarkable group of men just starting out on their literary careers, among them John Berryman; Mark Schorer, later to become the biographer of Sinclair Lewis; the novelist Wallace Stegner; and the poet Howard Baker. Far from being persecuted as a poet, Delmore thrived on his identity; Laurette Murdock, the wife of a Harvard dean, said he resembled one of Blake's angels.

Then there was John Wheelwright—once described by Matthew Josephson as "a dandy, a bachelor of convivial habits, an Anglo-Catholic in religion, and a socialist in politics"—who had a literary salon of sorts in his mother's house on Beacon Street in Boston. An "improper Bostonian" who published his curious, talkative poems in private editions and took his politics into the street, Wheelwright was nevertheless a Puritan descended from an old Pilgrim line; in the somber parlor of his house Delmore noted the dignified portraits of his ancestors. Until Wheelwright's tragic death later that year at the hands of a drunken driver, Delmore attended several of his dinner parties, where he met Conrad Aiken, a son of William James, and, on one occasion, V. F. Calverton, the voluble, energetic editor of the socialist *Modern Monthly*.

Apart from his many new acquaintances, Delmore was seeing a good deal of his former professors, Wolfson, Prall, and Matthiessen. With Prall, who had long been frail and tubercular, he had a rather harrowing interview that spring which later made its way into *The World Is a Wedding*. On Delmore's first visit, Prall announced that he was dying. Unnerved, Delmore tried to evade the issue. "We are all dying," he blurted. But Prall, unwilling to release him so easily, insisted, "No, I am dying faster than other men." "I think it would be boring to live forever," Delmore lamely rejoined, but when Prall died soon afterward, he was haunted by remorse.

There was also an unpleasant scene with Matthiessen that spring, when Delmore invited him over to have a drink with Macdonald, Barrett, and Dupee. Matthiessen had remained a fellow-traveler, and Macdonald, a confirmed anti-Communist, began taunting him about his politics. Matthiessen left early, and before he had even gone out the door, they all started attacking him, only to see him appear in the doorway with a hurt look on his face. A guilty silence hung over the room as Matthiessen retreated slowly down the hall.

By April, Delmore was weary of Cambridge. "The people I see here are pleasant and kindly, but all sleepwalkers who have hardly heard of history except as a course in the catalogue." he complained to Dupee. He missed the political infighting at *Partisan Review*, the fast pace and literary intrigue he thrived on in New York. In *The Education of Henry Adams* he found a passage that corroborated his feelings: "Several score of the best educated, most agreeable, and personally the most sociable people in America united in Cambridge to make a social desert which would have starved a polar bear. . . . Society was a faculty-meeting without business."

Late in March, Delmore learned that he had been awarded a Guggenheim Fellowship. He had long suspected that Malcolm Cowley, one of the judges that year, was opposed to his candidacy,* and knew that awards were rarely given to those under thirty, so he felt a special triumph in his success. Delmore and Gertrude were now

---

* The year before, Delmore had published a letter in *The New Republic* attacking Cowley's interpretation of Yeats's politics in a review of his *Autobiographies*—not without some justification, since Cowley, at the time an orthodox Communist, had placed rather too much emphasis on Yeats's sporadic expressions of populist fervor.

better off than they had ever been, and he could turn to his long poem without having to worry about money. In April, he wrote cautiously to Dupee:

> As you probably have heard, my luck is holding out for the most part. By now I know it is luck and very little else, and when I say that I've had a great deal more than I deserve, I express a sincere, though rather recent sentiment.

Superstitious of success, Delmore thought of modesty as a sort of talismanic charm empowered to ward off misfortune.

This notable event had little impact on the desolate mood that had afflicted him since his arrival in Cambridge. "The result of so much moving about and so many changes of circumstances during the past three months has been the numbness and lack of energy which makes me even unable to read," he reported to Arthur Mizener. For most of his life, Delmore complained of a mysterious illness that beset him in February and March, although he never specified its symptoms; and insomnia, that other chronic affliction, was now beginning to assert itself once more. At times, he could be satirical about his malady; a news item about a man in India who hadn't slept for two years fascinated him, and he once annotated a definition of Buddha as "The Awakened One" by writing in above it, "Not the Sleepless One." But his condition frightened him, and he transcribed in his notebook a passage from a book by Wilhelm Stekel: "Ungratified wishes and psychological conflicts (anxiety for the future, fear of legal procedures, or of moral and social disaster) prevent neurotics from sleeping."

One substantial cause of anxiety was the fate of his ill-advised Rimbaud translation, which New Directions had just published. By February, the reviews were starting to come in, and they were more than negative. Justin O'Brien, writing in *Kenyon Review*, thought it was "something like a sacrilege," and Philip Blair Rice, an editor of *Kenyon* who had always been appreciative of Delmore's work, accused him in *Poetry* of having "unfortunately neglected to acquire the rudiments of the French language," and went so far as to demand that it be withdrawn from circulation. Paul Rosenfeld, reviewing Delmore's translation beside

Lionel Abel's version of *Some Poems of Rimbaud* in the *Saturday Review*, pointed out a few of the more glaring errors,* and objected to Delmore's attack on previous translations in his acknowledgments, where he had complained of their "ignorant unwillingness to distinguish between translation and continuous paraphrase." In Rosenfeld's view, Delmore was "living in a glass house and throwing stones." The critic Mary Colum, wife of the Irish poet Padraic Colum and a friend of Joyce, was even more unsparing. She was astonished to find that *je rêvais*—the cardinal verb in Rimbaud's poem—had been translated as "I review." Delmore had not only succeeded in "evolving Rimbaud from his inner consciousness" but had "also evolved the grammar and vocabulary of the French language"; in other words, he had invented his own version of *Une Saison en enfer*, only out of ignorance rather than imagination. His translation, Colum concluded, presented Rimbaud "in the English of a schoolboy tackling a 'sight' translation and with an elementary knowledge of the French language."

Delmore would have been consoled to know what two of his mentors thought of the tranlation. Eliot told Laughlin it was "fairly good," while Wallace Stevens defended Delmore against Rice's criticism in a letter to Leonard Van Geyzel. "Schwartz's translation is considered to be sophomoric," he warned, but "it might be sophomoric from the point of view of translating from one language into another and yet contain things that matter." In print, however, only Herbert Gorman had anything good to say about the translation; Delmore had come "surprisingly close to the original," he claimed.†

That Delmore's translation was in many ways a disaster is undeniable; he himself admitted begrudgingly to friends that he had a poor command of French, and had only done it to have an "adequate pony" for his own "edifica-

---

* The most comical was the rendition of *troupeaux* (herds or flocks) as "trumpets"; but there were others just as embarrassing. Moreover, entire phrases and sentences were simply omitted, and some negatives were construed as their opposite.

† A year after Delmore's death, Roger Shattuck, one of the most eminent critics of French literature in America, judged Delmore's *A Season in Hell* the best modern version (although he wondered if his verdict wasn't "sheer perverseness").

tion." "What happened was that I took so much time with my criticism, editing, and other wastes of time that I did not go over the translation, though it had been done five years before," he wrote Berryman, forgetting the time he had spent on it at Yaddo. Even so, he was reluctant to take full responsibility for his own carelessness. "If I had not been at Yaddo because of poverty, I would have shown it to someone at Columbia," he explained to Laughlin. Twelve years later, still troubled by the experience, he came up with new excuses; the translation had been full of errors because "I trusted and overestimated Will Barrett's knowledge of French and my first wife's ability to look up words in a dictionary."

Barrett did in fact assist Delmore in preparing a complete revision of *A Season in Hell* for a new edition, the first having sold out its 850 handsomely printed copies by March. Published toward the end of 1940, the revised translation showed a considerable improvement over the "pony" of 1934. The many howlers pointed out by reviewers (Delmore had at first insisted there were only ten) had been corrected, and a new introduction supplied. This translation was not without its virtues; Delmore had always been attracted to the sonorous, rhetorical qualities of the French language as he imperfectly understood it, and so managed to convey at least some of the passion and fervor of Rimbaud's prose poem. He may have misconstrued a few words, but he had an intuitive sense of Rimbaud's style, combined with a fine ingenuity that in part redeemed his literal misreadings. As for the new introduction, it was rather more prosaic than the earlier one, where Delmore had concentrated on the extravagance of Rimbaud's rebellion against "the whole of bourgeois culture," his hatred of Christianity, and his renewal of the Romantics' quest for a new vision of experience.

The history of poetry since Blake, from this important perspective [the Romantics' turn away from Christianity and the world they saw developing under capitalism], is the history of men who found the social order into which they were born increasingly inadequate in every *human* respect and wholly deficient in satisfying the inevitable human need of a whole view of life.

A Season in Hell, Delmore noted in the second introduction, was a testament to "the last extreme of Romanticism," and it was obvious that he felt a profound affinity with Rimbaud's fate; Delmore, too, had long been convinced of his estrangement from any "community," a condition he was determined to resolve, like Rimbaud, "by himself and by his poetry."

.

Delmore was disappointed when T. S. Eliot turned down his Rimbaud translation for Faber. "I should in better times be much more interested in his original work," Eliot wrote Laughlin, but the war had forced them to curtail their overseas commitments. "Maybe the Old Possum will change his mind," Delmore wrote wistfully in the margin of Eliot's letter.

He was discontented with things in general, a mood that showed up vividly in his correspondence, which was "like coming into a bathroom full of steaming air from another's bath"—a metaphor he thought so felicitous that he used it several times. Forever gossiping, explaining, defending himself, Delmore wondered if his letters seemed "tiresome or feminine or Jewish," a triad of undesirable identities. In truth, they were more ill-tempered than anything else. Dwight Macdonald in particular came in for a good deal of bantering abuse; polite and restrained with those he knew only casually, Delmore reserved his more intemperate remarks for intimate friends. Affectionately addressing Macdonald as "Master Mind" and praising his "brilliant originality," Delmore nevertheless managed to insinuate that his correspondent's legendary combativeness was "neurotic." Macdonald, in turn, was hard on Delmore, disparaging both his criticism and his poetry with relentless candor. Their correspondence was impassioned, rude, impulsive—and mutually delighting, for they shared a polemical ardor sharpened by the habit of denunciation.

Delmore's fiercest insults were for the moment confined to other contributors to *Partisan Review*. An article by Lionel Trilling was pronounced "very good . . . except that I wish he would not make the most obvious remarks in the tone of one who has just discovered a cure for cancer"; a contribution of Lionel Abel's was said to have been inspired "by Stewart's Cafeteria coffee and some bedraggled girl's outcry that he is a genius"; Clement Greenberg, while praised on one occasion, was derided on another as "Sir Clement Greenberg O.M., Ph.D., D.Litt., W.C. (Oxon.), PMLA." The most vituperative abuse, however, was directed at Paul Goodman, whom Delmore reviled for pages at a time. He had not forgotten their quarrel of a few years before, and the mere mention of Goodman's name was enough to provoke a diatribe on his "systematic misinformation" about everything. It was a disturbingly vicious assault, even allowing for Goodman's peremptory treatment of Delmore during the 1930's and the petulant, high-minded tone for which his criticism could be faulted. (One of the few to escape Delmore's denunciations, it should be noted for historical purposes, was a young unknown he referred to as Bellows, whose work he found "very interesting.")

It was characteristic of Delmore to malign his friends behind their backs while making strenuous and selfless efforts to advance their careers. He worked very hard to get John Berryman a teaching appointment at Harvard and to find a publisher for his poetry, while observing to William Barrett that Berryman embodied an "ontological contradiction" in that he was "stupid" but still managed to write good poems. Writing to Laughlin, he made fun of an unpublished novel by Robert Hivnor, proposing satirical titles for it—"Power and Light in Ohio" or "Pity and Terror in the Middle West"—but at the same time instructed Hivnor how to get invited to Yaddo, how to deal with Laughlin, and how to improve his style. Delmore's splenetic outbursts were, at least in those days, less an expression of deliberate malice than a way of exorcising rage.

Delmore was bitter over William Barrett's part in what he came to regard as the "Rimbaud disaster." Barrett had "mocked" at the reviews, he complained to Berryman, intimating that "their friendship was at an end." All the same, Barrett made another of his familiar appearances that summer, coming up from Brown, where he taught philosophy, to rent a room across the street from Delmore and Gertrude. All during July and August, he was over nearly every night for dinner, until Gertrude finally objected. But Barrett seemed so hurt that she soon relented, according to a story Delmore wrote about this episode: "Then Louise felt extreme compunction and she often asked Arthur to come to dinner, for Arthur came every night after he had eaten alone in a shabby inexpensive restaurant." Even so, she was more impatient than ever with Barrett's intrusions, which had long since become an established feature in their lives. In Delmore's interpretation, "Louise was not omitted from their conversation, nor was she without some learning herself. But the bond between the two young men was such that she resented it at the same time as she accepted it." If so, it was only because she had no choice. They were "like Loeb and Leopold," she said.

In the fall, Delmore took up his Harvard appointment, which required him to teach only one course of freshman composition a week. Teaching appealed to him at first, and within a month he was writing proudly to Mark Van Doren that he had become "an expert on their whole generation." Scandalized by his students' ignorance, he made epic tales of their lapses, in particular the girl who had read aloud a line from Eliot's "The Love Song of J. Alfred Prufrock" as "Shall I part my bare behind?" Early in the term, there was a memorable exchange with a student who handed in a 200-word theme where 1,500 words had been assigned. When Delmore rebuked him, the student disdainfully retorted: "The Sermon on the Mount was less than two hundred words, sir." "If you'll come down to the Charles and walk on the water for me, I'll give you an A for this theme," Delmore said. "I'll wait until it freezes over," the student replied.

Delmore was not a distinguished teacher; he was too self-absorbed to be effective in the classroom. Moreover, teaching distracted him from writing, and his resentment tended to convey itself in a desultory attitude toward his students. But he found it edifying as well. "How much he learned by teaching composition!" he exclaimed in his journal, "about himself & about language & about an audience." The only drawback—apart from the fact that it was time-consuming—was the self-consciousness and "stage-fright" he suffered. "What a grotesque I am before my class!" he confessed, comparing himself to a burlesque queen and a "polka clown"; but a verse portrait of himself as a teacher reveals a prouder view. "Examination of Profession," as Delmore entitled his poem, incorporated his favorite examples of grammatical errors his students had made and put forth his own principles of composition:

How fluency is dear, against the class
—Ten years and a great city is the gulf
Between the students and myself
—I trot out jokes and stories to amuse them,
Enigma is a little animal,
Swimming is one boy's chief abstraction, one
Writes of a slightly ugly neighborhood
Keep Thinking All The Time, I cry to them,
This is the motto which must rule the class!
Nothing is more important than our tongue!
I warm when their attention glows, I fade
At silence and the lack of lolling laughter,
Nevertheless I teach them of precision,
To visualize the Word; to verbalize the Thing;
To Seek the Generality and Yet to Find
The Just Example which convinces all,
To Take an Attitude, To Criticize,
To argue pro and con, to look beneath
The face for insight's gold, to seek and find
The order natural to the subject-matter
And from that order grow expressive order
—To seek the metaphor as an example,
—To draw together many distant things,
—To seek the theme which every story shows,
—To seek significance one with detail:
This is the way I teach my rhetoric.

Despite this fulsome self-appraisal, Delmore was haunted
by the fear that his students "disliked or disregarded him,"
Wallace Stegner recalled. He was, in fact, a popular
teacher, and students were drawn to him by his reputation;
but he was often less vivacious in class than his pedagogi-
cal self-portrait would indicate. Nervous and shy, he
tended to mumble inaudibly, and when he was too exhausted to teach, he would simply read aloud.

   Genesis, the poem that had begun almost a decade before as *Having Snow* and had been through innumerable
transformations since, was considerably advanced by now.
Brandishing the talisman of irony, Delmore reported to
Hivnor that he was "in the middle of what will probably be
the longest and worst poem in American literature." For
years, he had vacillated between an exuberant conviction
of its greatness, when reading it over "made [his] hair

stand on end," and fear that it was destined to be a grandiose failure. "Sometimes it just looks peculiar and full of private obsessions," he confided to Arthur Mizener.

Long convinced of the epic drama his own life could be made to yield, Delmore had not yet hit upon a strategy that would enable him "to get the actuality and the transcendence into the structure and texture" of his poem; and so he practiced with other versified experiments in autobiography. It was a sign of Delmore's vitality that the terrible traumas of his early life diminished in importance before the pleasures of recollection.

> How many years I have lived
> And how many souls I have seen!
> Anger and love were my gifts
> And all that I had to give,
> But that which makes me a mind,
> Infinite curiosity
> As an avid appetite.

For all his insistence on the artist's difference from others, a conviction expressed in his lecture "The Isolation of Modern Poetry" and in his introduction to Rimbaud, Delmore's interpretation of his past was informed "By the presumption / That all are like myself / And that I am *like* all." The great virtue of art was in the exercise of an observing faculty able to confer on commonplace experience a universal value and thus restore significance to the life of the individual. Echoing Henry James's famous definition of the novelist's craft, Delmore celebrated "All the discriminations / In which *nothing is lost*," and allied himself with Dostoevsky, whose themes were "freedom and money and living." Delmore's memory was both the emblem of his genius and the source of his malady, for the same events he was writing about now with such amazing clarity were to haunt him later on with obessional force.

"The Story of a Heart," that compendious source book for any biographer of Delmore, was also written in March. Intended to be the "subject of the story," this extraordinary outline began with "Grandfather S." in 1878–80—the years of the Russo-Turkish War—whose adventures would be related in *Genesis*, then chronicled "the years of the helpless infant," whose memories of snow, "hiding behind piano after wetting," and other crucial scenes signaled the birth of "the ego's existence" and its dissociation from what Delmore called "prehistory," those events and forces which had converged to form the child. During this period, "the divinities are virtually absolute," he noted, meaning that the child was subject to the rule of "contingency," his fate determined by the laws of history.

Once the stage had been set for the nascent ego's appearance in the world, Delmore went on to explore the child's consciousness from 1918 to 1926; here the four-year-old Delmore awakened to a litany of sensations: "Night and the wish not to sleep [a wish he would rue later on] but to live more and more. . . ." From random images —"baseball and the waking dream; the newspaper and the library; the traffic and fear of the dead"—he moved toward those larger features of history that governed his childhood: "America as geography and as history, America as finance-capitalism, America in the newspaper, the newspaper as objective mind."

In the pages that followed, Delmore noted every significant moment in his life: "The father's departure and the mother's effort to keep the house"; "Bet with Billy, pennant races, value of betting in the family, fear of mother"; "beginnings of self-abuse." For some forty pages of single-spaced typed and closely handwritten pages, this remarkable exercise in what could be called, reversing Proust, *mémoire volontaire*, continued through to the very moment of its composition, twenty-six years of lived experience in which it appeared that *nothing had been lost*. Such a project may have seemed enormously egotistical, but Delmore had more in mind than autobiography. "The Story of a Heart" was to form the basis of *Genesis* in its final, published form.

.

It is a paradox of Delmore's career that lyric poetry entirely determined his conception of himself, and yet in his most productive years he wrote so little of it. So grand was his vision and the ambition made to serve it that he could no longer confine himself to that compact form; only longer, more sustained works would do. His verse plays and the vast poem *Genesis*, which occupied him for so many years, constituted virtually the only poetry he wrote during the 1940's. But he had by now discovered a characteristic voice that could provide an effective vehicle for his self-dramatizing imagination. This was a sonorous, faintly archaic, uneven blank verse, and during his first year in Cambridge Delmore wrote two of his best verse plays in that form.

The most famous, *Shenandoah*, concerned that crucial theme in his life, the naming of the child. Over the years, Delmore had conceived a passionate resentment of his name; and while he could be satirical about it in company, in his stories he deliberated endlessly over the Gentile/Jewish names of his personae, substituting one for another and inventing ever more incongruous variations: Marquis Fane, Richmond Rose, Bertholde Cannon, Maximilian Rinehart, Cornelius Schmidt—and of course Hershey Green. The Jewish tradition of the bris, in which the male child is circumcised and formally given a name, was for Delmore the symbolic moment when his false identity had been established through his mother's emulation of the "Gentile world"; and it was this conflict that he returned to in the story of the haplessly named Shenandoah Fish, who stands in the wings, now twenty-five, observing his mother choose the name he bears from the society column of a newspaper while he comments on the metaphoric value of each scene. When Mrs. Fish suggests to her husband that he telephone his non-Jewish lawyer for advice on how to resolve the dispute, Shenandoah remarks sardonically:

> What a suggestion! fearful and unsure,
> She seeks the Gentile World, the Gentile voice!
> The ancient wisdom is far from enough,
> Far from enough her husband's cleverness—

And when the doctor's proposals are brushed aside, Shenandoah notes how "The war between / Divine and secular authority / Is old as man in Nature!" Oppressed by his parents' ingratiating manner, he sees how their abdication of pride in their own origins has made him "an alien and a freak." Only by comparing his fate with that of other exiles —Joyce in Trieste, Rilke dwelling in "empty castles," Kafka in his Prague insurance office—is Shenandoah consoled. Art will triumph where life betrays, by giving purpose and value to experience.

All over Europe these exiles find in art
What exile is: art becomes exile too,
A secret and a code studied in secret,
Declaring the agony of modern life:
This child will learn of life from these great men,
He will participate in their solitude,
And maybe in the end, on such a night
As this, return to the starting-point, his name,
Showing himself as such among his friends—

From 1914 to the present, Delmore detected a pattern of
history that prophesied only ruin; writing just before America entered World War II, having been born as World
War I was beginning, he invoked the moment of his birth
in the deliberately inflated rhetoric that had become a feature of his verse.

—Now in the great city, mid-winter holds,
The dirty rags of snow freeze at the curb,
Pneumonia sucks at breath, the turning globe
Brings to the bitter air and grey sky
The long illness of time and history,
And in the wide world Woodrow Wilson does
What he can do.

Shenandoah was both Narcissus and Romeo, "bound /
By the sick pity and the faithful love / The ego bears
itself." But where did this oppressive narcissism come
from? From the Jewish habit of reposing hope in one's
children, who had always been regarded as if they were
"the Magi, seeking Zion's promise." In this way, the individual's character, presided over by culture and history,
was formed by events beyond his control. Once again,
Freud's family romance and Marx's historical determinism
were made to converge in a brilliant self-investigation.

Shenandoah was "a rite of naturalization in America,"
Delmore noted in his journal, "as well as a defense against
a joke by telling the joke oneself, an old habit." In the
same way, Paris and Helen, written later that year, was a
very sophisticated "joke" about his attitude toward "the
wincing wound of wounds / Sex, guaranteed to hold the
interest / Of men condemned to death." In Delmore's version of the familiar story from the Iliad, the voluble author

featured in all his work is forced to contend with a philistine Hollywood producer who has little patience for his orotund philosophical discussions of sex. "Why must it be a play in verse? What good / Is that? Get to the point, I always say," the producer argues, to which the dramatist retorts:

> The function of the meter is to heighten
> Attention to the words as such,
> The function of the meter is to strengthen
> The power of the words so that they flow
> Into each other and create fresh sense,
> Or hang like robes, fluent about the body,
> Letting the meaning have its varied way—

In the dramatist's unorthodox version of events—interrupted by philosophical digressions on love and history—Paris is a pitiful coward who seduces Helen by appealing to her vanity and convinces Hector that he would have done the same if the opportunity had presented itself. Delmore was always at his best in these long-winded discourses, as Rahv noted in a review of the play; by depicting Paris as "coward and pleasure-grabber, as average man," he had managed to "bring him forward into a familiar perspective without contradicting the traditional view of him." For all his love of heroes, Delmore was more interested in their failings than in what had made them great. He had what could be called a democratic imagination, in that it reduced all men to the same condition of anxiety and nameless discontent.

.

These early years at Harvard were among the most productive Delmore ever had. He wrote some of his best and most characteristic stories, his most incisive criticism, and worked at *Genesis* with a singular dedication. "Tuning up," he wrote steadily every day, despite incessant complaints of depression and lassitude. Notes, journals, and "exercises" proliferated, all devoted to recording the vicissitudes of mood that swept over him so unpredictably. There were prose accounts of his childhood, sonnets, and long passages of blank verse in which he "tuned up" for the composition of *Genesis*. In some characteristic pages entitled "Idiom,"

Delmore discoursed with brilliant ease on writers, ideas, world history, exercising his immense curiosity on the typewriter and striving for naturalness of cadence and idiom.

> —I think maybe an artist's faculties
> Can function at their best only if caught,
> Caught like a forest in a blazing fire,
> Only if drawn into the age itself,
> Like a witty fellow present at a party
> Who cannot be himself, cannot be happy,
> Cannot be witty and enthrall the guests
> Unless he feels *at home, at ease,* marked out
> By sympathy, expectancy, and joy . . .

During the summer of 1940, Delmore began writing a different sort of "Exercise" called "Present Moments." In casual free-verse lines, he set about exploring the rhythms of his thought, intent on discovering significance in life's most ordinary moments. On July 4, he defined the purpose of his new enterprise.

> I will observe present moments, he said, perhaps they
> will give me a little happiness / . . .
> He always looked toward the particular fact, seeking
> to generalize from it. . . . This is another reason
> why he turned from the world as seen, though delighting
> in it.
> But delighted much more when he could say:
>   this is an instance of Dignity or of Pleasure or
>   of Existence.

Delmore took pleasure in his supple mind; he loved to note its associative leaps, convinced that the "*Freedom of the Will* is in the present moment," where reflection could be liberated from self-consciousness. It was a procedure that led to some comic observations, as when he noted Hegel's definition of tragedy as "the conflict between Right and Right" and commented, "(Never thought of conflict between Wrong and Wrong!)." "Present Moments" was more than a simple exercise, though; it was a trial for the poem that lay ahead, and a means of learning to control his inspiration. "It is important to keep calm," he reminded himself, "not to get excited / By the mere fact of thoughts and observations; / To work slowly; to compose from line to line." Citing Pound's description of *vers libre* as verse "just running down the road," Delmore worried that these exercises were too casual; but he sensed that in emancipating him from rules they promoted a rhetorical ease that would be valuable later on.

Always avid to discover new means of refining his perceptions, Delmore produced his most bizarre "Exercise" during a single day in November, when he typed out some twenty pages of stream of consciousness at what appears to have been a single sitting. Monitoring his thoughts with uncanny virtuosity, he meditated on history, the cosmos, and his own past, fixed in his imagination by memory, "a resourceful, relentless prosecutor, proving to him who and where he was." In his more exalted moments, Delmore possessed a sure conviction of his genius, and the manner in which that genius operated in the world was one of the motifs of "Hallmarks"—as he titled this exercise:

> Genius as an extreme variant—a new form of being; breathing changes the air into something, changes the air into a spiritual thing, the emotion, the sign, the Agh of disgust—a new relatedness of body and thought and the times and the city—foliation of the trees, girls cutting across the lawn. Institutions for the normal and the merely gifted. The plight of one in six million. Hyper-sensitivity, instability of structure, energy of mind; at odds with society—partial break-up of instinctual life, duplication of renewal—*mutatis mutandis*—of the heroic episodes in the planet (like child in womb—great creative aptitude amid chaos; habits and instincts as institutions of the body. Language and laws and manners keep the egoist dancing from very pride in disinterested patterns. We lie on the epicenter of some great creative violence.

"Hallmarks" was a remarkable display of what the Surrealists had known as "automatic writing." Joyous in his fluency, Delmore exulted: "I do not care, I sometimes say to myself, I have enough to do in enjoying knowledge and perception and permitting my sense to become drunk in the sunlight or with *Gemütlichkeit*." He wanted "to become wholly a typewriter with a definite metre"; and "Hall-marks" provides an exact record of the weird associative leaps, the very cadences of thought he labored to call forth from his unconscious.

For the moment, Delmore was confident about his progress. "I have arrived, in style, at a greater degree of concreteness in my symbols; a greater declarativeness and organization and composition in versification," he noted early in the year. When he was writing fluently and well, he derived an almost childish pleasure from his work. "Joy in description, something new for me, / And a new view of rhymes, hearing more of them," he declared in May. Like Joyce's epiphanies, the spontaneous insights Delmore recorded in his journals were designed to capture and record moments of heightened insight: "To praise the fresh new morning sounds, milkman, starting car, brush and breeze of the passing car in the Avenue, / Is to praise the act of perception moving through modern life." "Never mind fame," he exhorted himself; "observation is / The human life divine."

But these were the peaks of his "manic-depressive roller-coaster"; just as often, he felt uninspired. April, despite occasional bursts of composition, was "a month without progress, except for here and there revision, and that not systematic nor persistent." To counter such moods, he would lecture himself tirelessly about the need for discipline.

> A page a day! no day without a page!
> So must I pay attention to myself
> Until my being's sources are as clear
> As my quick gifted hands. And just as near.

In a particularly striking image, Delmore evoked the vicissitudes of feeling that swept over him so abruptly: "I went through the day as a train passes through a brief tunnel— back in the sunlight again, the darkness forgotten." There were "dead days" characterized by "emptiness of thought, emptiness of paper," and days when he could write: "I fear disaster soon / From exultation's brink." So familiar was he with these sudden shifts of mood that he could anticipate and prepare for them; on the last day of May, for example, he wrote in his journal:

> I feel the growth of powers day by day,
> Perception, narrative, analysis,
> And all in a rhythm like a running boat /

Whatever his mood, its every calibration had to be recorded, for only writing certified experience. If someone told an interesting story, Delmore would exclaim, "But you should write that down." It was inconceivable to him that any experience should be squandered in mere talk, even though his own talk was so legendary. What he read, what was said about him, what he happened to hear: all went into Delmore's journals. One night, deliberating whether to attend a party or stay home and read, he explored the latter option in very approximative blank verse.

> Shall I go there tonight, not Dickens read
> Who is so large, says [Edmund] Wilson, almost Avon's
> Great height (desiring this man's gift, and that
> Man's scope and hope) who might teach much,
> And give much joy. (He also had bad taste,
> Was maudlin and, says Wilson, "pretty bad"
> Are the short stories shoved in "Pickwick Papers")

Unlike many of his poems, Delmore's journals were natural exercises of wit and inspiration; in ceaselessly recording the temper of his life, he could give it narrative form and articulate the myth it had become in his imagination.

Delmore identified with the great authors of the past, eager to discover affinities between their lives and his own. It was characteristic of him to wonder, as his twenty-eighth birthday approached, "Where was Tolstoy and where was Shakespeare and Dante just before their 28th birthday?" He was always comparing his life to those of the great writers who had lived before him, striving to see them as ordinary men with conflicts like his own. Did Hawthorne masturbate? Did Keats "abuse himself with his eyes shut / And vividing the face of Fanny Brawne?" In establishing literary antecedents for his conduct and his work, he could feel that he belonged to the great tradition of the past, and in identifying his own conflicts with theirs, he made neurotic suffering seem a curse that all artists had to endure.

Echoing Eliot's celebrated remark about Henry James, that "he had in mind so fine no idea could violate it,"

Delmore once wrote Blackmur, "I have a sensibility that
can be violated by *any* idea"; and it was this very receptiv-
ity that made the verse journals so vivid. Always in search
of causes, Delmore looked to the literary past for illumination of the myths by which he lived. But he was aware of
the dangers of contemplating that past with uncritical
reverence. Heir to the Romantic legend of the poet as the
very embodiment of imaginative powers, he could still regard its legacy with irony.

> We all grew up with Romance in our heads.
> The Romance that the secret of success
> Was genius, blazing gifts lighting the world,
> Genius, the noble individual
> Long-haired, peculiar, and long suffering,
> A kind of Christ, in fact, or Fisher-King . . .

For many fluent pages at a time, Delmore converted
literary history into loose blank verse. On reading that
Arnold Bennett used to count the number of words he had
written at the end of every year, he wondered:

>   did industry
> Corrupt his heart or not? This is the way
> Each heart becomes a capitalist, this is the way
> Capitalismus manages to live /

His interpretations of the lives of Tolstoy, Wordsworth,
and Emerson were exemplary biographies in miniature.

> When Tolstoy rode upon his green estate
> & knew the goodness of the family life,
> —Agrarian, manorial, and yet,
> Withal, haunted by the Enlightenment,
> —Judgment & Praise—until he dragged himself
> In the cold night to flight from his old wife,
> —Sad that the modern Homer died that way
> —Detested Shakespeare and hated music's charm.

> Wordsworth in Calais knew a pretty girl,
> And in tranquillity remembered it,
> The Revolution howled on every coast,
> And a new day seemed, that a lucid state

Might like a classic temple reign, serene
—But when the rage and terror turned to stone,
He sought in childhood's wood goodness profound,
Turned from the city, Rousseau in the mind,
Harked to the Mariner who talked all night
Of the true world composed by consciousness
And found in Nature the experience
Of innocence. And thought it was the Good.

. . . Emerson gazes on his soul, serene:
With that serenity, he blesses all
—Pressing the frontier now, the pioneer
Is self-reliant in his solitude
—The Indian scout hears, in the wilderness
Crouched, decrees of silence and of good;
They move through Emerson as fabulous
—His brothers die and his wife dies, too young
In the sick blaze, consumption: yet he exclaims
Life is pure good! goodness consumes all things!

Interspersed with these ingenious commentaries were observations on himself.

This is the way
My mind runs. From peak to peak, I read
The purple passages of prose and verse,
Having only the stumbling stamina
Of one who comes back after each defeat—

Delmore's natural genius for metaphor and paraphrase was never more evident than in these exhilarated passages, where whatever occurred to him could be transformed into poetry; it was the principle of his earlier "Hallmarks" put into blank verse. The idea was to animate life, imbue it with significance, observe the general in the particular.

I see the Sunday winter street. I know
As girls come back from church, as fiancés
Dressed best, stroll on, seeking themselves,
As an old man patiently follows his dog,
And as the light winds on through afternoon
(O ancient Fury, sister of all that is!)
That this is it! Is Actuality

> Brimming, a chaos, full of characters
> I do not know, thick with what secret
> Stories to make my mind grow quick and strong

The one course of salvation available to Delmore was his writing; only in the act of composition did he ever seem to experience genuine pleasure. He worshipped the Muse, "an old courtesan who has received many young men," but he hated her when she rejected him; once, in a despondent mood, he apostrophized, "Poetry, my stern step-mother, perhaps I will depart from your house." Delmore believed in the Romantics' concept of poetry as divine, just as he believed in the concept of good and evil; and the two beliefs fused in his fervent prayers to God for inspiration: "Our Father who art in heaven, make use of me / For knowledge, Love, Love's Truth & Poetry," he pleaded in his journal. Poetry was Delmore's sacrament, the emblem of his true purpose in life: "Give me this day my daily bread & wine, / The poetry which makes each thing a sign."

When he was writing well, nothing else mattered, not even worldly success; for all his limitless ambition, Delmore had—at times—a pure imagination that thrived on symbol-making, and with no thought of self-aggrandizement. "Fecundity, activity, responding applause: these are good things," he noted; and in the order he gave them, these were the three conditions on which his own happiness depended.

.

Delmore could have acquired a distinguished reputation as a literary critic no less than as a poet had he chosen to think of himself in that way. Because he gave himself to poetry with an almost mystical fervor, he "put no particular emphasis on his critical work," as Philip Rahv has pointed out. But it was this very casualness, the absence of methodology and an open avowal that he possessed "a Washington Heights view of our time and our country," that made Delmore's critical essays so vivid. By the end of 1941, when he published his essay on Faulkner—years in advance of Malcolm Cowley's influential Viking *Portable Faulkner*, the book generally thought to have first gained him recognition—Delmore had amassed a body of criticism that would surely have justified a book. Why this failed to come about until well after his death is hard to understand; Laughlin had announced the book as early as 1940, but Delmore continued to procrastinate until the project was finally abandoned. A book on Eliot—which he actually completed but failed to revise for publication—met the same fate, as did a biography of F. Scott Fitzgerald said for many years to be "in preparation" for the American Men of Letters series edited by Joseph Wood Krutch, Mark Van Doren, and Lionel Trilling. (The Fitzgerald book was never even begun.)

Long projects overwhelmed him, but he excelled in evaluating an author's whole achievement in the space of twenty pages or so; and while *Partisan Review* was largely concerning itself with European authors, Delmore was producing some of the most important criticism of American novelists to appear in his time. His essays on Dos Passos, Hemingway, and Faulkner can only be called definitive. Delmore could question Faulkner's fascination with the lurid, illustrate the limitations of naturalism in Dos Passos, and see through Hemingway's posturings while generously stressing their power and originality. There was a confidence, a natural voice, in his criticism that often seemed to desert him in his poetry.

Two other important essays, on Allen Tate and Thomas Hardy, appeared in *Southern Review* that year. Both revealed a characteristic preoccupation with an author's beliefs and ideas as they revealed themselves in his poetry. Delmore may have abandoned the systematic study of philosophy, but he still relied on it to inform his judgment of literature. It was no simple matter to extrapolate Tate's agrarian view of history from his poems, or to determine the nature of his Christian faith, but Delmore managed both with impressive ease. The premise of all his criticism is conveniently stated in this essay: "The poet brings into his poem a sensibility dominated not by particular characters, events, scenes, or landscapes, but dominated by general ideas about the basic metaphors which are involved in all the scenes and events of our lives." Tate's reactionary effort to restore a social and literary tradition threatened by the modern industrial world could be seen to conform in some respects to the quite opposite ideology of Marxism, or at least to an awareness that "values have their necessary roots in the whole social complex"; surprisingly, Delmore

The poet's parents, Rose and Harry Schwartz, in Brooklyn, 1910-11

Mr. and Mrs. Schwartz, circa 1914

Left, Delmore with his father at Rockaway Beach, 1915-16. *Right,* with his mother, 1914-15. *Below,* Harry Schwartz in Lakewood, New Jersey, 1915-16.

Delmore, *right,* with his younger brother, Kenneth, circa 1920

Below, the brothers with their mother, circa 1921-2

In Lakewood with their mother, circa 1923-4

Below. Delmore at Camp Pocono, 1926

Photo by Mrs. Forbes Johnson-Storey

Two portrait studies of Delmore in 1938, shortly after the publication of his first book

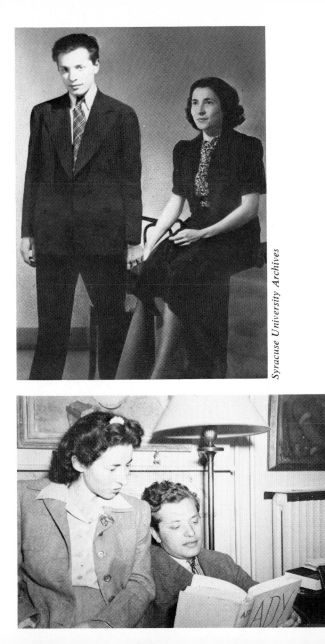

Photo by Helen Levitt

Left, at top, Gertrude Buckman and Delmore shortly after their marriage in 1938. *Bottom,* in Cambridge about five years later. *Above,* James Agee and Delmore at the former's house in New Jersey, around 1939

Above, Delmore on Ellery Street, Cambridge, Mass., in the forties. *Right,* Delmore with a group of poets and writers at Kenyon College in 1950. Standing: from left, Arthur Mizener, Robert Lowell, Kenneth Burke, Delmore Schwartz. Front row: Philip Blair Rice, William Empson, John Crowe Ransom, L. C. Knights, Charles M. Coffin

Elizabeth Pollet in 1949, at the time of her marriage to Delmore.
Right, a photo of Delmore taken about the same time

In 1948 the poets gather at the Gotham Book Mart to honor Sir Osbert and Dame Edith Sitwell, seated in the center. In front row, left to right: William Rose Benét, Charles Henri Ford, Delmore Schwartz, and Randall Jarrell. Behind them, at right: Marianne Moore (seated), Elizabeth Bishop, and W. H. Auden (atop the ladder in rear). Behind the Sitwells, left to right: Marya Zaturenska, Horace Gregory, Stephen Spender, Tennessee Williams, Richard Eberhart, Gore Vidal, and José Garcia Villa

Courtesy of Frances Steloff

A portrait of Delmore painted by Nela Walcott.

One of the last photographs of Delmore in 1961 at Washington Square Park

insisted that Marxism was the "background of the age," and it was against this background that Tate's achievement had to be measured. In resorting to an abstract critique of history, he argued, Tate was guilty of "a certain obliqueness, narrowness, and overconcentration"; but he applauded Tate's adamant defense of the values of the past.

Delmore's essay on Hardy was no less masterly. Demonstrating once again a sophisticated competence in the history of ideas, he contrasted Hardy's problematic assent to the new scientific views that had surfaced in the late nineteenth century with his conviction that nature remained the shaping force in human destiny. "The inside of the human psyche" rather than the cosmology of nineteenth-century science dominated the landscape of Hardy's poems, Delmore claimed. "The subject of poetry is experience, not truth, even when the poet is writing about ideas." It was Hardy's attention to the "concreteness" of experience that distinguished his poetry—a trait that was to become one of the most significant features of Delmore's own work. In *Genesis*, he would acknowledge the considerable influence of Hardy's long poem, *The Dynasts*, with its deities and fatalistic view of history.

.

The summer of 1941 offered a pleasant interlude from teaching. There were visits to Maine, where R. P. Blackmur, F. O. Matthiessen, and Philip Horton—Hart Crane's first biographer and a friend from Delmore's graduate school days—all had summer homes; and toward the end of August, Delmore went alone to the Cummington School of the Arts in Cummington, Massachusetts, where he had been invited to spend a week in residence. He was expected to read the work of younger writers and give them advice, but he seems to have devoted most of his attention to the pursuit of girls—if the accounts he gave Laughlin of what he called the "Playhouse in the Hills" are to be trusted. In his "Cummington memoirs" (as Laughlin referred to these letters), Delmore hinted at a great many sexual conquests, but he was reluctant to say more out of fear that his letters would fall into other, unspecified hands. Promising to abandon his "unnatural reticence" if only Laughlin would promise to return them, Delmore confined himself to innuendo.

I saw the new generation, recognized that I was no longer young, enjoyed the sight of young ladies paying $40 a week to be there and also waiting on tables, drying dishes, and making beds. As to this new generation, they appear to regard sex as a form of violent exercise a little less serious than tennis.

Then, as if embarrassed by such revelations, he reverted to a characteristic rectitude, claiming to have told the aspiring writers that "chastity was good for the poet since coitus was such a drain on the spirit as well as the body . . . this shocked them; many felt that they knew now why they had written so little since coming to Cummington, so to speak." This decorous pronouncement was confirmed by Milton Klonsky, a young writer of eighteen in residence at Cummington that summer, who thought Delmore less a Don Juan than a "moralistic rabbinical type" when it came to sex.

The more he read Freud, the more Delmore subjected himself to complicated psychoanalyses. "Sublimation must be distinguished from the cessation of object-love in narcissism," he once noted, aware of his condition but unable to reverse it except by contribing a myth of Platonic love, the ideal that inevitably eluded him. One of the most poignant expressions of this ideal is to be found in a little verse entered in Delmore's journal.

To love is, in the end, to stand
Looking down from a height, from an infinite distance
Upon the promised land.

Love was unattainable, and yet to be valued above all; in its absence, Delmore could only write verses about "Love the Dark Victor Whom No One Evades"—but never really possesses. In a comic monologue entitled "A Testimonial Dinner to God," he once confessed: "I preferred that girl who did not love me to some who did love. This made me conclude that I was not an egotist, for if I had been, then would I not have preferred to be loved?" But it was precisely Delmore's egotism—demonic, ambition-dominated, "a gross balloon," as he once depicted it—that made the pursuit of love so difficult. The demands of self-contemplation conspired with a fatalistic view of his childhood to

blot out any hope of escaping the relentless narcissism
bequeathed him by his mother. "Your mother rises up in
you / (You rotting Jew!)" went one exasperated couplet.

None of this was auspicious for his marriage, and by
1941 there were evident signs of strain. In his more affectionate moods, Delmore thought of Gertrude as an "actress
of childhood who plays the child with no false note," while
he was an "ignorant Joseph," solemn and ungainly. But
there were times, he complained, when "the sick old maid
in you places her sword / Between you and all nature"; and
in a later notebook, he even compared her to Beethoven,
"domineering, inconsiderate." Militantly unsentimental,
Gertrude was capable of cruelly thwarting Delmore's awkward expressions of feeling. Once, when he offered to buy
her a fur coat, she was "utterly disgusted" by his proposal,
and thought it maudlin. But she had reason to be bitter;
while she did the secretarial work for New Directions (at a
salary of sixty cents an hour), Delmore received all the
attention. And in public, it was always Delmore who dominated the conversation. "Everyone seems to be successful
but little Gertrude," he noted in his journal.

For some time, there had been sardonic intimations in
Delmore's letters to Laughlin that Gertrude was threatening to leave him, but in August he announced that they
had rented a house on Memorial Drive, adding, without a
trace of irony: "She has promised not to abandon me for
at least a year; but if she does, I will of course bear whatever cost the upset occasions you." Albert Erskine, who
had come up from New Orleans to be the managing editor
of New Directions, was leaving for New York, and Laughlin agreed to locate the office in the Schwartzes' new home,
one of a row of four wooden mansard houses on the
Charles River. (They have since been torn down.) On
September 10, Delmore wrote Laughlin: "Gertrude and I
moved on Saturday, the office moved yesterday, and there
certainly has not been so much disorder since the Jews left
Egypt."

9

———•———

WITH SO MANY PROMISING writers around, all just beginning their careers, Harvard was an intensely competitive place in the early 1940's. Feuds and rivalries dominated everyone's conversation. "The English department seems like a snake-pit to me now," Delmore complained to Laughlin that autumn. "I have never seen so many friends hate each other with such intensity." Early on, he himself had conceived a passionate loathing for certain of the faculty, in particular Theodore Spencer and Robert Hillyer, who he was convinced had made a deliberate practice of isolating him from visiting writers; and he resented even more their power over him, since his appointments were generally renewed on a yearly basis.

"The small intricacies of academic social life in Cambridge interested and amused him for a while," William Barrett recalled, but they also caused him considerable unhappiness. Whenever he heard about a party to which he hadn't been invited, he suffered a by now familiar sense of persecution. Delmore had made some remark critical of Matthiessen to Harry Levin, and Levin had reported it to Matthiessen, he complained to R. P. Blackmur, imagining the whole episode; as a result, he had not been invited over to Matthiessen's for months, "not even to the Christmas punch when all are asked." And when he thought the Schorers had excluded him from one of their parties—another imaginary betrayal—he was reminded of a slight some twenty years before, when a Washington Heights neighbor, Mrs. Berkowitz, had failed to invite Rose Schwartz and her children to an open house on New Year's Day.

Delmore's most famous epigram, that "even paranoids have real enemies," could well have served to characterize Harvard's intellectual climate, for he was hardly alone in being competitive, high-strung, and temperamental, and had only to elaborate and refine real instances of rudeness in order to arrive at the conspiracies he found so dramatically satisfying. Some of the teaching fellows "ran with the Breadloaf people, the Morrisons and Frost and Bernard De Voto," as Wallace Stegner put it, and Bowden Broadwater refused to invite the Schwartzes to his parties because "they are always imagining that people are talking about them, and they glower from corners." In his journal, Delmore exercised this proclivity for suspicion: "How often snubbed in the Square"; "Did Bernard De Voto see me in the Dinner Bell?" Encountering Robert Hillyer in the Yard early one morning, he went home and examined their seemingly innocent exchange for signs of some deeper portent, concluding darkly: "No crime of which the imagination is not capable."

All the same, Delmore was himself a specialist in this sort of literary animosity, and his obsession with Harry Levin, then just beginning his brilliant career as a scholar, culminated in one of the most notorious incidents of the academic season. Levin and his wife lived next door to Delmore and Gertrude on Memorial Drive, and for a time the two couples were quite amicable. They often had dinner and drinks together, after which Delmore and Levin would sit on the front steps, "talking pessimistic," as Levin's wife, Elena, described their conversation. Delmore was "gentle and temperate," Levin recalled, "albeit prone to sadness and sometimes bitterness. His face was an expressive tragic mask."

When the Levins' daughter Marina was born that year, Delmore composed a commemorative verse (to the tune of "Frankie and Johnnie") inspired by Elena Levin's practice of calling her "Goodka" or "Badka."

> Goodka and Badka were sisters,
>   The daughters of Mrs. Levin.
> Goodka she was a good little girl,
>   But Badka was bad as sin.

The second stanza was about Delmore himself.

> Next door there lived a poet.
>   His name was Mr. Black.

> He sent his verse to the editors,
> And the editors sent it back.

By this time, no editor would have thought of sending back Delmore's verse, but he could indeed be "Mr. Black," and within a few months he had conceived a merciless antagonism toward Levin. "Mortimer was handsome in the style of a matinée idol of a foreign art theatre (it was observed that he resembled Joseph Schildkraut)," he wrote in the inevitable story about the Levins, entitled "Modern Romance" and conveniently labeled "Harry & Elena" in case there was any doubt about the identities of his subjects. "He was proud, arrogant, pretentious, stiff in manner, precious, and eminently proper in dress. And to many he seemed to be learned and brilliant, an impression he worked very hard to give." Unsparing as it is, this portrait of Levin was not entirely inaccurate, nor is the story without traces of affection. However fantastic, Delmore's account of Levin compulsively returning to his shelves a book his wife had left out on the table because it violated his sense of "orderliness," and his contrast of Elena's charming vivacity with Levin's reserved, meticulous nature were prompted less by malice than by a profound fascination with their characters. Delmore was "mesmerized" by Levin, Mary McCarthy recalled, discerning in his rival everything that he himself was not. Where Delmore suffered from his abrasive relationships with members of the faculty, Levin was generally gracious and polite; where Delmore had to worry over his uncertain status as a writer at Harvard, Levin held the more secure position of a faculty instructor; and where Levin made little of being Jewish, Delmore brandished his identity with defiance and shame.

But it was, above all, Levin's increasing reputation as a literary critic—and in just those areas most precious to Delmore—that he found so unbearable. Levin's brilliant early commentary on *Finnegans Wake* in the 1937 New Directions anthology had resulted in praise from Joyce himself* and a commission from Laughlin to write a book

---

* In a letter to James Laughlin, Joyce lauded Levin's essay as "the most striking one that has appeared so far," an opinion he echoed in several other letters to friends.

on Joyce. To compound this triumph, he had published an article in Eliot's *Criterion* while still an undergraduate, then been invited to call on the great man while in London on a traveling fellowship. This was too much for Delmore, and years later he was still bitter enough about Levin's successes to satirize them in "The World Is a Wedding," in the character of "a youthful teacher and critic, Mortimer London, who was reputed to be brilliant." London, so the story went, had paid a visit to T. S. Eliot and been given a letter of introduction to Joyce. Confronted with "a cruel choice, whether to use the letter and converse with the author of *Ulysses* or to keep the letter in which a great author commends him to a great author," London decided to keep the letter. Delmore's version of these events was untrue, since Levin had sent on Eliot's introduction to Joyce, who was too ill to see him; but in Delmore's view— spoken by Rudyard Bell—Mortimer London was "insane" and flawed by pride.

Delmore's jealousy was one indirect cause of his break with Levin; another may have been Levin's unfavorable reaction to a story Delmore was about to publish in *Kenyon Review*. But there was a more crucial transgression for which Delmore could never forgive Levin, involving Cornelia Walcott, a painter and heiress who lived in one of the row houses on Memorial Drive. Nela smoked and drank a good deal, and late one night set her mattress on fire, having fallen asleep with a cigarette in her hand. Gertrude rushed over to help, and the two women dragged the smoldering mattress out of the house, where it burned through the night. When the mattress was removed the following day, it left an indentation in the snow that Levin jovially referred to as Delmore's grave. Delmore was convinced that Levin's remark was really a veiled reference to his translation of Rimbaud and, consequently, his literary reputation. From that moment on, he never spoke to Levin again, and began attacking him in letters to Laughlin and in his journals. "H.L. warms up slowly, like a radio," he once noted; and on another occasion, wounded by what he took to be condescension on Levin's part, Delmore complained that he was "moralistic" and had an "insincere smile." In a letter to Blackmur, Delmore compared Levin to the cold and ruthless Gilbert Osmond in James's *Portrait of a Lady*, or—more charitably—Tolstoy's Karenin. Fabricated stories about his rival were soon added to Delmore's comic repertoire: how Levin rehearsed his lectures in front of his wife before class; how Levin had called him up and insisted upon reading a book review over the phone at eight o'clock in the morning, until Delmore passed out cold. By 1942, Levin had joined Paul Goodman in the camp of those who could never be forgiven.

It was a difficult autumn for Delmore. Grading endless themes, upset by delays in the publication of *Shenandoah*, he moped about the house, insomniac at night and sleeping in the afternoon until the postman arrived. The mail was a major event in Delmore's day—he would stare out the window at "the hunched letter-box, proving news and love" —and was invariably depressed when there was nothing for him. Emily Sweetser, a recent Bennington graduate who worked in the basement office, would hear him pacing up and down on the floor above; occasionally he would come down to count how many of his books had been sold, but otherwise he hardly did any work at all for New Directions. Ill-tempered and melancholy, he refused to speak to Gertrude or Emily for weeks at a time. By October, the situation had become so unpleasant that Emily quit her job and went off to New York. When *Shenandoah* failed to appear week after week, Delmore complained to Laughlin that "Mrs. Conant and Mrs. Munn have both written angry letters asking for it," and boasted of a letter from Francis Fergusson "certifying" the play.

When *Shenandoah* finally came out in November, the reviews were mixed. Mary Colum atoned for her devastating attack on Delmore's translation of Rimbaud the year before by praising the play's "considerable profundity" in *The New York Times Book Review*, and other favorable reviews—by Oscar Williams and David McDowell, among others—followed later in the year. But once again Delmore had to face the disapproval of Louise Bogan and a number of other critics; Babette Deutsch found the writing "undistinguished," and the reviewer in the New York *Herald Tribune*, in a spiteful and unfair notice, called it "adolescent, pretentious and humorless."

Ignoring these unfavorable verdicts, Delmore reported to Laughlin that *Shenandoah* had been "received with much delight and enthusiasm by [Howard] Baker, Levin (Holier-than-thou) and T—(There'll always be an England) S—[Theodore Spencer]. The last, though not uncritical, declares the verse to be very moving, the play full of 'great possibilities.'" Most gratifying of all, Alfred Kreymborg had decided to include *Shenandoah* in his anthology *Poetic Drama*, and it appeared late that year in an immense volume of verse plays "From the Ancient Greek to the Modern American." In his preface to *Shenandoah*, Kreymborg proclaimed the author "an original poet and dramatist with a daring imagination," heir to the tradition of Eliot and Auden but unique in his view of history. In Kreymborg's estimate, Delmore had written a play that belonged among the classics of verse drama.

December 8 was Delmore's twenty-eighth birthday, an event that called forth the usual feelings of anxiety. He was discouraged to find that he no longer experienced the years as "separate entities," he complained to Robert Hivnor. "I was very depressed about all that concerns me," he noted after seeing a film about "adolescent youth" which upset him "because it viewed adolescence from a comic perspective"; this was one theme that could be treated only with the utmost solemnity. The death of James Joyce a month later increased his desolation, and he summoned William Barrett from Providence to come up and "keen for our dead brother." From then on, Delmore always referred to Joyce as "our poor dead king," echoing Mr. Casey's lament for Parnell in *A Portrait of the Artist*.

One ominous trend apparent in the journals of 1942 was a reliance on wine, which had become a crucial source of inspiration. Until now, Delmore had been a moderate drinker; "Jews don't drink," he used to say. As a freshman at Wisconsin, he had confided to Julian Sawyer some minor episodes of drunkenness, and there had been others at N.Y.U.; but only in 1942, when he found that it helped him to write by increasing his perception, did alcohol really enter into his life.

> Wine brings all things closer—vivider,
> I see the Harvard houses, neo-Georgian,
> just like Petersburg, as Harry [Levin] said/

> A city of canals, bridges, rivers, gov-
> ernment buildings, white trim on the red brick
> & neo-Georgian style/—the cure is wine/
> Wine is my inspiration, exaltation,
> Magic, Pegasus, and peerless peaks & heights/

Wine blunted other temptations, such as the movies; and it also made him a more charitable person.

> With wine do I forgive my enemies,
> Forget my hatred: is this bestial then,
> —I am a proper Christian when with wine,
> Where shall we get the virtues which Christ sang?

> Our beliefs, even such a belief as wine, create with
> the world, and in humility and guilt I do not hate or
> see as hateful those whom sober I detest;

He had been abstemious earlier in life, Delmore confessed, only because alcohol had made him ill. Now that he had discovered its pleasures, he began to drink unsparingly, happily celebrating the virtues of wine: "The Kingdom of Heaven is within you, this was my waking thought, as I poured myself a glass of wine." Of course, he knew that his drinking had other motives than sheer pleasure, as he acknowledged later in the year: "I am an exaltation-drinker; perhaps a sleep drinker or escape drinker too."

Delmore's increasing dependence on alcohol was compounded by his continued recourse to Nembutal, and the combination was disastrous. Often he would take a sleeping pill, then drink enough sherry "to put himself out"; and since he had been using barbiturates regularly since his early twenties, he was gradually coming to require a larger dose. It was a habit that would have fatal consequences.

.

"I am going through Boston womanhood from A to Z," Delmore boasted to Laughlin early in 1942, and there was some truth to his claim, for it was no secret that while Gertrude sat at home moodily playing the piano, he was more or less openly spending a good deal of time with his neighbor Nela Walcott, whose husband, John, was overseas in the Army. And to John Berryman he gave a long report of an affair with June Cannan, a young woman he had met at Cummington the previous summer. June delighted in Delmore's reputation—perhaps too much, for she once announced, to his dismay, "The only reason I slept with you was because I wanted to see what it would be like with a man who might be a great poet." Gertrude, on the other hand, was indifferent to his accomplishments, he claimed; when people asked her if she was proud of her husband, she would reply, "No, why should I be?" "She has threatened to leave me hundreds of times . . . and I beg her not to," Delmore confided to Berryman.

In his journals, Delmore tirelessly reproached himself for his infidelities. "How far can I go in evil, how far," he wondered—"since the aesthesis of goodness has so great an appeal for me?" At times, he felt that he was close to achieving grace. "I have always wanted to be good and became evil because I expected too much of other human beings and tried to force them to behave as I thought they should." But he was conscious of the Manicheanism that divided him, a division he believed to be visible in his face; the left side radiated good, the right side evil, and he would hold his hand over one or the other to illustrate their difference. He seemed almost to delight in his malignant impulses. "I am a scoundrel," he would gloat, quoting Ivan Karamazov, and he made up a comical variation of Joyce Kilmer's line: "Poems are made by ghouls like me." Delmore's piety was in some ways strangely conventional; it was a vindictive Old Testament God whose judgment he invoked in his confessions, a God who witnessed his "long struggle with body and Pleasure-Principle" but disclosed Himself only in the form of a pervasive guilt.

One of the more unfortunate consequences of this tenacious guilt may have been impotence, as Delmore intimated in his journal, where he recorded several conversations with a doctor whom he had begun to see in 1942. Dr. Benjamin Sieve, who operated out of opulent offices on Commonwealth Avenue, was a well-respected if eccentric —and some said fraudulent—physician who went about in a chauffeur-driven limousine, wore tailored Bond Street suits, and believed in the rather dubious practice of giving his patients endocrine injections. It was from Dr. Sieve (who committed suicide some years later) that Delmore learned to think of his malady as "glandular," a vague term he adopted from then on to describe virtually any ailment. In his journal, he complained of "the immense pressure of the defeated or held down libido," which Dr. Sieve hoped to "restore" by "supplying missing substances." On several occasions Delmore referred obliquely to "failure," remarking in his journal: "Another drink and two things would have happened: he wd. have lost his scruples, but also his potency." But there are many accounts in the journals of sexual experiences that would seem to belie this interpretation, apart from other evidence of his numerous affairs; in any event, he still experienced his sexuality as a torment and a stubborn source of guilt, with consequences that affected both his life and his work. "As I am kept from giving myself in love & in friendship," he confided in his journal, "so with the reading of books to the end—and teaching and editing and devotion to literary forms."

Delmore himself was skeptical of Dr. Sieve, whom he admitted was given to "experiment for its own sake." But these consultations did have the practical effect of securing him a deferment from the Army. As the war went on, he was on the verge of being called up on several occasions, a prospect he dreaded no end. He had curvature of the spine, and in 1943 developed a mysterious skin condition that led him to sign his letters "brown-spotted"; but by then the Army was taking virtually everyone.

It was the threat of induction that kept Delmore at Harvard, confined to "the prison-house of English A." Had he been found eligible in respect of his health, he would most likely have been able to obtain a deferment through Harvard, provided he taught a rather heavy schedule of Navy classes. Most undergraduates were overseas, and he was appalled by the ignorance of the students in the officer-training program. Given the choice between teaching or possible induction, Delmore reluctantly chose the former, but he found it a chore to teach grammar and composition to these unsophisticated men, and felt intimidated by them, "for they had seen death at close quarters, while he on the other hand had led a sheltered existence, so called, and he had been regarded as a privileged character."

By early 1942, the war had come to dominate his thoughts. He seemed to know every detail of the campaign in Europe, and read the newspapers avidly. All the same, he was a vociferous opponent of the war. In a notebook entry of 1942 entitled "This Obscene War," he protested against the way "hundreds are rushing to wrap themselves in the flag." It oppressed him to see intellectuals refusing to speak out against the war. "Why is Edmund Wilson silent? And why does Tate apply for a commission to defend finance-capitalism, the order he has so often attacked?" A month after Pearl Harbor, he wrote Laughlin:

> Now we will have a war until every Chinaman has to buy Gillette blades or lose his self-respect. I don't know why I make a point of speaking of this, except that it is depressing to think of five years perhaps of War, when it is not necessary. Needless to say, my feelings ought not to be broadcast, should the occasion arise.

This desire not to have his views "broadcast" precipitated an acrimonious dispute with Dwight Macdonald, who had broken with *Partisan Review* over the war issue. Macdonald had been opposed to the war from the beginning, and, knowing that Delmore agreed with his views, had sought to enlist him on his side. But Delmore's assumption was that "no political position is possible for intellectuals at present." Since they perceived themselves as a class "just like the Elks and the Free Masons," and had "a vested interest in truth," it was incumbent upon them "to proceed to a detailed and constant criticism of the War"—but only as an "abstraction"; in other words, with a judicious detachment that obviated committing themselves to any position.

Macdonald was annoyed by this casuistical argument, and accused Delmore of "trimming [his] sails to prevailing winds by keeping silent on any hot, controversial issues." Delmore supplied another, still more practical excuse. "My draft questionnaire is packed with lies," he confided to Berryman, and he was reluctant to draw attention to himself by making public his opposition to the war. Still, he was willing to state his opinions when it was a matter of defending his own "class," and when William Carlos Williams published a loud harangue in *Partisan* attacking intellectuals for their ambivalent stand on the war, Delmore was so incensed that he drafted a stern reply. He found Williams's accusation that intellectuals were unpatriotic insulting, and said so in a letter that resembles in tone and spirit his earlier "resignation" as a disciple of Pound. It was a historical irony of those years that the Trotskyist radicals of *Partisan Review*, disillusioned by the Moscow show trials, had become hostile to the Soviet Union, while the reactionaries defended it, calling for an alliance that would assure military unity. But Delmore was personally wounded by Williams's virulent anti-intellectualism, and defended his position as an academic in a second letter that followed a week later: "You have as much notion of what the academy is like now as I have of the care of infants," he said, insisting that it was an "honorable calling" to teach English composition. He saw himself as "a kind of dentist," whose only concern was to instruct his students in the proper use of the English language, and offered as an example of the sort of problems he encountered a Radcliffe student who had written that "a liberal arts education makes a girl broader."

But he soon retreated to a more deferential tone: "If I am half as good as you at fifty, I will be a lot more pleased with myself than I am now." It was typical of Delmore to be at once outspoken and overly polite in corresponding with writers he admired, ransoming his dignity as the price of his convictions. "I've never won any argument with anyone and being in the middle of my twenty-ninth eternity, I don't have the energy of old to nourish often defeated hopes," he concluded in his most confiding, self-deprecatory voice—and then went on to compare Williams with Alfred Noyes, a once-popular British poet who had accused Proust of being responsible for the fall of France.

·

Delmore and Gertrude had been thinking of moving again, since Laughlin wanted to relocate the New Directions office in Norfolk, Connecticut. As it happened, the Hortons were leaving town, so the Schwartzes decided to take up the lease of their house on Ellery Street.

I get free of this summer school [Delmore wrote Laughlin], which is nothing less than the Black Hole of Calcutta, on the 16th of September and there are twelve full days before I must again mark freshman themes: perhaps I will be able to get through during that period, if the process of moving to 20 Ellery Street, the old Horton homestead (where the rent is twenty-seven dollars less a month), does not upset everything.

While "the Chinese Wall of the War gets higher and higher," he added, he was correcting forty freshmen themes a week and cultivating a "post-War soul." A week later, he went off by himself to the Cummington School, where he found that he had "no energy during the day to be fluent or sensitive enough to teach anyone." Still, his visit had not been without its pleasures. "I was drunken every night of my stay," he wrote R. P. Blackmur, "and feel that few things can equal drinking in the open air in summer."

Delmore was pleased with their new home, a handsome gray Victorian house inhabited by many "ghosts" from his past. It was at 20 Ellery Street that he had seen John Wheelwright "for the last time in this difficult and beautiful life," he reminisced to Blackmur. And it was there that Nela Walcott had fallen down the stairs and Winfield Townley Scott had been "drunker than anyone I've ever seen"; the Hortons' gay dinner parties had been "Roman" in their prodigality. It was "the only place to be comfortable and have social joy in Cambridge."

For all his complaints about Cambridge, Delmore was proud of its history. He liked to go for walks in the old neighborhoods, pointing out the houses where e. e. cummings, the James family, and the Nortons had lived, and he appreciated Harvard's neo-Georgian architecture. Always in search of literary antecedents, he could imagine Howells and James "strolling to Fresh Pond, discussing form amid the murmurous trees." Whenever friends visited from out of town, a pilgrimage to the graves of Henry and William James in Cambridge Cemetery was obligatory, and Delmore's accounts of how various friends had responded to these outings became one of his "set pieces," Macdonald recalled, "as detailed as a Dutch genre painting."

Delmore enjoyed "that gratification of the snob and historical sense" Cambridge provided, and it pleased him to know so many relatives of famous men: T. S. Eliot's brother, Henry Ware Eliot; Melville's granddaughter; the grandson of John Singer Sargent; descendants of Aaron

Burr and Edgar Allan Poe,* the latter with "haunted rolling beautiful blue eyes." He was particularly delighted by his acquaintance with a son of William James, for he thought of William and Henry as "the best brothers" in America, and was beginning to feel that Henry James was the greatest of American novelists, even better than Edith Wharton. *The Portrait of a Lady* in particular appealed to him as an illustration of "the great theme of freedom and necessity."

Delmore, never one to be solemn in his literary enthusiasms, liked to amuse his friends by noting the sexual associations he was convinced were to be found in the names of James's characters: Fanny Assingham in *The Golden Bowl*, Caspar Goodwood in *The Portrait of a Lady*, Mrs. Cundrip† in *The Wings of the Dove*. For a time he entertained the idea of a rather morbid satire in which Henry and William James—"William all lucidity, Henry all indirection"—try to elicit from Henry Adams the reasons for his wife's suicide. The Jamesian moment would occur with the appearance of Marian Adams's ghost, and the play was to end in "a terrific and complete ambiguity."

Delmore was now "in the easy upland, the shining plateau of success, of his life," in William Barrett's view, "and it seemed to stretch so evenly and uneventfully before him that he didn't have to worry about tumbling down from it." A rather too sanguine estimate, given Delmore's chronic lapses into depression that lasted for months at a time; but when he was inspired, his enthusiasm knew no limits. "I've hit the top again and now expect to begin going down soon, but feel like yelling, Eureka! The Indias! America! The glory, the power, the illumination of form!" he cried out in a letter to Hivnor that he considered so revelatory he demanded its return. It was, indeed, an astonishing display of enthusiasm; but he cautioned:

> I've felt this way before this many times, only to find out that sometimes I was wholly deceived, I was mistaking the excitement of writing for the excitement which should have come *from* the writing, objective on the page.

---

* Since Poe was childless, one wonders who this "descendant" could have been.

† This was Delmore's version; in the novel it was Mrs. Condrip.

The trouble, for me, in this up and down is that, knowing it won't last, I rush to get as much done as I can while I can, and the rush and the excitement destroys my powers of discrimination, such as they are where my own writing is concerned. . . . Great works may be in the making, but I think it would be best if one tried not to think of greatness; it becomes less likely then, for obviously the mind is diverted somewhat by its sense of glory.

Delmore's promise shone forth in those years. One of John Berryman's impassioned Dream Songs affords a glimpse of him in 1942.

> You said 'My head's on fire'
> meaning inspired O
>
> meeting on the walk down to Warren House
> so long ago we were almost anonymous
> waiting for fame to descend
> with a scarlet mantle & tell us who we were.

No one was more given to adulation than Berryman. "His taste for what he despised was infallible," Robert Lowell recalled, "but he could outrageously hero worship living and dead." His poems are crammed with celebrations of his contemporaries' genius, and he recognized in Delmore —his elder by only a year but even then imbued with an image of mature achievement—the very embodiment of his own Romantic myths.

With his literary impresario's eye for talent, Delmore had been laboring on Berryman's behalf ever since Mark Van Doren had introduced the two poets in the summer of 1938. Within a month of his arrival in Cambridge, Delmore was proposing a "complicated and unscrupulous scheme" by which Berryman could obtain a Briggs-Copeland lectureship. Together they ran a tireless campaign, and that autumn Berryman had joined him at Harvard. But they were too high-strung, too blunt, too grandiose for that world of scholarship and sensibility. Delmore used to joke that they would come to be known as the "Sleepless School of Poetry"—a vivid epithet, given the vulnerability that plunged them both into what Berryman described as "Machiavellian chaos." They devoted interminable hours to plotting their careers, berating the merciless editors who thwarted them, and reading aloud Delmore's mail—which invariably brought news of fresh betrayals and perfidy: how Mark Schorer had borrowed ideas from Delmore's conversation for a book review in the *Boston Globe;* Harry Levin's "treachery over the PR review of Matthiessen's latest book"; James Laughlin's "newest triumph of duplicity"; or William Phillips's malicious observation that Dwight Macdonald was "looking for a disciple who will tell him what to think." Berryman professed to be shocked when Delmore showed him a "fantastically topical and libellous story called *New Year's Eve* in which he & Gertrude figure with Mary McCarthy and Wilson & the whole P.R. crowd." There was so little truth to these rumors and stories that perhaps only the gullible Berryman could have believed them; but he found Delmore's reckless irreverence bracing, for it represented a pose of defiance that he was in those days too timorous to cultivate himself. "I have Machiavelli's grandson, Delmore, for a model," he confided in his journal.

Suspicious, prone to grievance, avid for approval, Delmore and Berryman formed a peculiar alliance. "Thrustingly vehement in liking"—to borrow Lowell's arresting image—Berryman depended on his vociferous admiration for those he respected (Delmore in the forties, Lowell and Bellow later on) to bind them closer to him, as if his pride in their accomplishments could alone produce a sort of conspiratorial intimacy. "Let's join forces, large and small," he wrote Bellow toward the end of his life, reviving memories of Princeton in 1953, "with the Bradstreet blazing and Augie fleecing away. We're promising!" In Delmore, this image of promise was incandescent; Berryman drew sustenance from its glamour, while Delmore bestowed on his friend confidences and confessions that heightened his own sense of drama.

Berryman was awed by Delmore's dignity and formidable powers of fabulation, which seemed never to desert him. "His mind—" Berryman noted in his eccentric prose, "insensitive as it is now to Shakespeare, to logic, dubious, intermittent—yet roves." He was so intimidated by Delmore that he became "inarticulate" in his presence, and he relied on Delmore's advice in literary matters to the point of endowing him with the highest authority of all; having completed a manuscript of poems, he decided "to let God (i.e., Delmore) look at it" before submitting it to Laughlin.

The homage Berryman paid in a Dream Song to Delmore's "electrical insight as the young man / his wit & passion, gift, the whole young man / alive with surplus love," is nowhere more evident than in his journals, where he recorded Delmore's every word: endlessly ramified chronicles of his childhood; his thoughts on Shakespeare and Dante ("His notion that Shakespeare not only *was betrayed* before the frightful period of Hamlet & M[easure] for M[easure], but *betrayed*. This is a real insight"); tales of his graduate years at Harvard ("No story of such length and complexity was ever told so well"); his calculation and bravado ("You know me, John,—I'm an opportunist;—I say anything I can get away with"). And he studied Delmore's appearance with a novelist's eye: his unmatched socks; "hair standing out in all directions"; the "short quick steps when he walks." Berryman's Boswellian zeal complemented Delmore's Johnsonian wit.

But he was more than a slavish amanuensis to his subject. Delmore was "scarcely sensible in talk about 1 Henry IV," he noted after one of their talks; and on another occasion, when Delmore had poured out some tale of academic malfeasance, Berryman observed: "His control of his faculties [was] very imperfect." Moreover, Berryman's earliest verse homage to Delmore—the eleventh stanza of "At Chinese Checkers," written in 1939—was rather more ambivalent than the reverential Songs:

> Deep in the unfriendly city Delmore lies
> And cannot sleep, and cannot bring his mind
> And cannot bring those marvellous faculties
> To bear upon the day sunk down behind,
> The unsteady night, or the time to come.
> Slack the large frame, he sprawls upon his bed
> Useless, the eloquent mouth relaxed and dumb,
> Trouble and mist in the apathetic head.

Delmore professed to be "flattered" by this portrait, subtly disparaging though it was, and even cruel in its reference to the insomnia that tormented him all his life; but the truth of it could not have escaped him. Berryman had a shrewd sense of Delmore's uneven qualities and a natural jealousy that conspired to produce this vindictive poem.

The two poets were inevitably competitive. Berryman's possessiveness irritated Delmore—and proved irresistible to his taste for malice. Berryman was the sort of person you were fond of, "but you liked him to live in another city," he once told Lowell; and he was fond of comparing Berryman to Don Quixote or Henry James's unworldly Roderick Hudson. But Delmore admired Berryman's poetry and did everything he could to promote his reputation; he compared him favorably to Wallace Stevens, claimed he was "ten times better than Jarrell," and lobbied in vain with Laughlin to include him in *Five Young American Poets.* Delmore loved nothing more than to work behind the scenes, a military strategist in the service of literature, while Berryman monitored in his journal their victories and defeats. Once, when Delmore's praise was even more emphatic than usual, Berryman noted tersely: "I felt like weeping." And when Laughlin turned down a later manuscript of Berryman's, Delmore submitted it for him to Frank Morley at Harcourt, Brace.*

In the autumn of 1941, Berryman moved to Boston, which only increased his isolation from Harvard. "Living alone as he does, in Boston not Cambridge, and seeing no one at all for days at a time, he is not well off," Delmore reported to Van Doren; "and being improvident, he sometimes spends all his money and then tries to feed himself on chocolate bars until the 1st of the month." Berryman considered his conversations with Delmore in the Faculty Club or the Statler Bar "my way of getting from one day to the next." Delmore was solicitous about Berryman's condition, which he described to Van Doren in the spring of 1942:

My own impression, whatever it is worth, is that the only thing wrong with John is some kind of hysteria. The fainting fits he has occur when he is spoken to sternly or contradicted; I don't think they're sheer

* Morley rejected Berryman's manuscript, and Robert Giroux, who was then at Harcourt, Brace, later became his publisher.

frauds, but if they spring from his secret disease, the disease is an open secret, and besides the fainting, there is no sign of anything wrong with him.

This was a bewilderingly optimistic appraisal, since Delmore had on one occasion to dissuade Berryman from leaping off the Weeks Bridge. It is hard to know how serious he was, since the river it spans is so shallow that he may well have found himself wading ignominiously ashore. Berryman was not yet the desperate suicide of some three decades later, plunging from a high bridge in Minneapolis; but his threat was an eerie foreshadowing of his eventual fate.

.

As the pressures on Delmore increased—to finish *Genesis* and teach at the same time—he became more and more irascible. "Suspicion is a form of imagination," he observed in his journal, and it certainly required a great deal of imagination to conceive of some of the wrongs he conjured up. When Alfred Kazin's *On Native Grounds* came out that year, Delmore begrudgingly conceded the book's merits, but assured Laughlin that Kazin had been "dishonest in a dozen important ways" and had stolen ideas from other critics without admitting it—and Delmore himself had been among Kazin's victims. If only his own book of criticism had been published before *On Native Grounds!* "Now when it appears, Kazin will undoubtedly accuse me of borrowing from him sans acknowledgment," he complained. Delmore's hostility toward Kazin was all the more bewildering in that he himself had been awarded special praise in the book as one of the most promising critics to come out of the 1930's.

Too much rested on the success or failure of Delmore's poem, as he suspected even then. It was "our successes, not our defeats" that posed "the greatest danger," he wrote Laughlin, but in truth the possibility that *Genesis* would fail haunted him more than ever. What if he was deluded about the magnificence of his poem? What if he suffered the fate of Melville, who "went to the grave thinking that *Moby Dick* was a failure" because the "stupid critics" had condemned it? To counter this increasing dread, he resorted to some notably unrestrained flights of self-praise. "I read some more of *Genesis*," he reported, "and now fear that it is so good that no one will believe that I, mere I, am author, but rather a team of inspired poets." To quiet any doubts, he urged Laughlin to "read the giant work then, and see how with the right handling it will bring in kudos and O above all dollars." It was a work that "will last as long as the Pyramids," a work over which he had exhausted his "youth and joy." But it was worth any sacrifice, because *Genesis* was destined to be the most significant poem of the age.

> In days to come—mark you!—this poetic style will be seen as the beginning of Post-Symbolism, as Cézanne was the beginning of Post-Impressionism. As he gave to Impressionism the solidity of the museums, so I with like usages of style give to the Symbolism that has reigned from Baudelaire to Eliot the solidity and the lucidity of the classics and the narrative ground of the epic.

What was it about this project that provoked Delmore to such exorbitant claims? Long convinced that his own life could be made to yield an epic drama, he was now confident he had found a form that could accommodate the whole of his experience. By means of what he called "Biblical prose" interspersed with the blank-verse passages employed in his plays, the story of his protagonist could be transformed from mere confession into a sort of allegorical drama in the mode of Hardy's *The Dynasts*. The commentaries of Hardy's chorus of Spirits, mediating between abstract rhetoric and ordinary speech, provided a perfect dramatic model for Delmore's poem. Once he had found a form appropriate to his subject, he could turn to the subject itself.

"Freud was a disaster for Delmore," William Barrett observed; and it was true that when he began to read Freud in earnest—during the 1940's—Delmore increasingly came to see his struggle with the "Furies of the Family Life" as one he could never win, since one's character and fate were determined in childhood. But it was also true that he found in Freud the explanation he craved for the strenuous conflicts in his life. His notebooks for the spring of 1942 are filled with quotations from Freud, for the most part related to the question of the "family romance"; and it was largely from these investigations that he derived a point of view suitable for *Genesis*. He celebrated his new discoveries in a Keatsian verse journal that April.

> The poetry of wine will never end,
> But as for me, I have—this is, I think,
> The source of the successes, if, in fact,
> It was not luck!?—a different light
> And more important light, Psychologizing!
> Better than texture! and imagination
> Seen in the act of making forms for itself—

The poem had advanced through many different stages by the time Delmore noted on April 4 that he was revising Book I, "changing references and hurrying." At first, he had thought of writing the story of a typical Jewish family in 1920, but by now *Genesis* had become a vast chronicle of the past of his new persona, Hershey Green. In his eagerness to learn about the history of his people and their migration to America, he tried to enlist his old friend Benjamin Nelson, a medieval historian, to research the genealogy of the Schwartzes and the Nathansons. When Nelson visited him in Cambridge, Delmore could talk of nothing else, and spent most of his time sitting up in bed combing through his cherished volumes of the *Encyclopaedia Britannica* for any information that might conceivably bear on his family's origins. Then, early in January 1942, a disaster occurred: the manuscript was lost.

Delmore had sent his only copy to Laughlin in Utah, where he had gone to ski, and it had apparently been lost on the way. For weeks he flooded the offices of Railway Express with inquiries, but to no avail; and by March he was resigned to its loss. After two months of anguish, he wrote Van Doren, "The whole business is beginning to seem like a blessing in disguise." Now he could start all over again, correct the defects of the original version, and adopt a more deliberate pace.

> I have begun to get the habit of trying to write all day and walking up and down the room between the lines; instead of rushing along as I always have, before the intuitions wore off. It makes me feel like a

professional for the first time and no longer at the mercy of periods of inspiration and and drought.

No sooner had he arrived at this reconciliation, however, than the manuscript turned up under the floorboards of Laughlin's station wagon, just as Delmore was about to collect $150 insurance; "thus were four months of my life destroyed," he wrote Blackmur in April.

Laughlin had reservations about *Genesis* from the start; the sprawl and chaos of the poem discouraged him, and during 1942 he began to voice doubts which only provoked Delmore to noisier protestations. Signing his letters "annoyed" and "justly aggrieved," he pressed for an earlier publication date and a larger advance. "You'll be sorry if this book is not an immediate success because you won't meet the offers I've gotten and can get from other more well-to-do publishers," he threatened. Now cajoling and pleading, now importunate, Delmore began to boast of a novel he claimed to have in progress: "When you see what pages of fiction I have just written, you will be willing to do the only thing that can hold me, make me a powerful editor." And as for *Genesis*, Laughlin was only concerned about his own "fame and glory," not his author's; why didn't he do more to promote what was sure to be Delmore's most enduring work? The proofs were wrong, the contract was wrong, the photograph was wrong. "We must get another picture," he insisted; "I am nervous and sensitive, and don't want to be kidded."

Eager to convince Laughlin of the value of *Genesis*, Delmore reported that Berryman had said it was brilliant, that Matthiessen was preparing to lecture on it, and that Van Doren, Blackmur, Conrad Aiken, and James Agee had praised it. But in the same letter he suddenly became self-protective: "I doubt very much that my reputation stands or falls on this book." The proposed edition of three thousand copies seemed too large, and he suggested that a thousand would be more realistic: "If this is the flop you think it will be, then I want the rest of the paper for a new book just like *In Dreams Begin Responsibilities*."

It must have been disheartening to have to deal with his own publisher's lack of enthusiasm, which Laughlin made no effort to hide. But he had always been patient with Delmore, giving him substantial advances and encouraging him in his work. Until now, Delmore had been grateful, and he still professed "an irrational devotion" for Laughlin that went beyond their publishing relationship. They were like Cellini and his patron Medici, Haydn and Esterhazy, Beethoven and Napoleon, he declared with feeling, if not always with historical accuracy.

A less flattering analogy was the comparison of himself to Pétain and Laughlin to Hitler; and it was thus that Delmore gradually came to view Laughlin's role in his life. He had always wanted to play a significant part in the affairs of New Directions; proposing authors, reading manuscripts, pushing friends, Delmore had come to feel that his "whole fortunes were bound up with ND." Now he wanted to become an associate editor, and when Laughlin ignored his suggestion, he began to sign his letters by that coveted title and demanded a symbolic fee of a dollar a month for reading manuscripts. Nor was it a symbol to be taken lightly: "The schizophrenic separation of my mind from self which I often celebrate in my immortal verse makes my mind say to you: is it not unwise to refuse such minor demands, precious only to the soul of a poet?"

Delmore stepped up his demands as publication day approached. He wanted the book to be vigorously promoted and he wanted a larger advance. After all, other publishers would pay thousands for a chance to take on the genius so many had acclaimed.

I long ago earned more than five thousand dollars in terms of intangible prestige. No author you published—not Pound, Williams, Thomas, Fitts, McAlmon—made anything like the splash I've made *for you*. I don't deceive myself that this shows that I am really good. It shows that in some way or other I have the vulgar but very important gift of attracting much attention. . . . I am the best advertisement you ever had, and since all you want is success, you ought to act accordingly.

Laughlin's most unforgivable transgression was to intimate that Delmore was neurotic and drank too much. "To be neurotic is to suffer from a state of mind," Delmore retorted, "of whose real causes you are not conscious, which prevents normal behavior." Such unwarranted accusations were typical of their relationship, he complained, citing a list of grievances that dated back to 1939. Laughlin had insulted him in Baton Rouge, had opened a letter addressed to him "in violation of the laws about the mail," had once called him a "crook"; the megalomania of Delmore's high-school days had returned in force.

Delmore worried that too many laudatory quotations on the book jacket would provoke "resentment." "It is fine for a first book," he explained, "but here I have kept going for five years and those who resent their own failure looking at me will only suppose that they had better shut up and not add any more to a growing fame." When his rivals saw how many stories, poems, essays, and reviews he was publishing, "the wrath of jealousy will rise again."

His fears were misplaced, for not long afterward he received some crushing advice from two preliminary readers of the manuscript, Mary Colum and W. H. Auden. Both urged Delmore to postpone publication. Mary Colum found much to praise in the poem, but thought he was still too young to have really understood and assimilated his experience, while Auden, in an eloquent six-page letter, questioned the poem's theology. As a devout Episcopalian, he took seriously (perhaps more seriously than Delmore had intended) the issue of faith explored in *Genesis*:

26.8.42   As from c/o Mr James Stern
                                     207 E. 52.
                                     N.Y.C.

Dear Delmore Schwartz,

I have taken an unconscionable time with your mss, I fear, but I had to go off to the Middle West for a bit, and then because it raises questions of great importance which are very difficult for me to express without misunderstanding, I have been trying to get clear in my mind just how to explain to myself and you why I feel you would be wise not to publish a poem on which you have spent so much time and thought.

To state my opinion in a sentence, I feel that you have advanced along the road of consciousness until you have now approached the frontier where the question of religious faith is inescapable (p. 190.* "All my

---

* Auden's page references are to the manuscript of *Genesis*.

life / I felt my self's lack of necessity"), the point at
which you have become aware that ahead of you lies
either faith *or* despair, but that you are still confused
about what faith is: because the road that has led to
this point has been that of aesthetic and ethical consciousness, you still cling to the hope that it crosses
the frontier—but it doesn't; it stops on a precipice and
you have to jump, ie [*sic*] you have written this
poem, I think, with the hope that in the process you
would find your answer given you, when as a matter
of fact, the poem could only be written *after* you had
first taken the decisive jump.

You say (p. 196) that Augustine and Rousseau
'had to blurt out all, being oppressed / by what they
lived like nausea'. This may be true of Rousseau, but
it is completely false as regards Augustine.

Augustine isnt [*sic*] oppressed, nor does he try to
tell all. He has a perfectly definite purpose in mind in
writing his confessions, which governs his selection of
memories. Believing that he has been led by the grace
of God from error to truth, what he tells about himself is what in the light of this truth he finds significant; he is not, (as I think Rousseau is) trying to be
'interesting'.

The aesthetic success of any work of art in which
the subject matter is personal recollection depends on
the memories being viewed in the light of a decision
already taken. e.g. *Une Saison en Enfer* presupposes
Rimbaud's rejection of Poetry as Religion, *La
Recherche du Temps Perdu* presupposes Proust's decision that to exist is to despair, hence (if one does not
take the same deduction) his extremely one-sided picture of love. *The Prelude* presupposes Wordsworth's
conviction, the opposite of Rimbaud's, that the poetic
imagination and the religious revelation are one (in
my opinion a false conviction which brought its appropriate punishment in the drying-up of his imaginative faculty).

When I ask myself why *Genesis* doesn't seem to
come off aesthetically while *The Prelude* does, I think
it is because Wordsworth really manages to believe
this, while you are trying to, but are too advanced to
succeed. To begin with you have an insight that

Wordsworth lacked, and which to me is essential, into
the significance of suffering. (p. 135. "A Jew, born to
the long habit of pain / and alienation, of the people
chosen for pain"). The use of the word *chosen* im-
plies a great many things that I think you run away
from. What I think you know, has been succinctly put
by Kierkegaard.

> "One must never desire suffering. No, you have
> only to remain in the condition of praying for
> happiness on earth. If a man desire suffering, then
> it is as though he were able by himself to solve
> this terror:—that suffering is the characteristic
> of God's love. And that is precisely what he
> cannot do; it is 'the spirit' which witnesses with
> him that it is so; and consequently he must not
> himself have desired suffering."

What the 'neurotic' individual compared with the
'normal' individual, or the Jews collectively compared
with the 'Aryans' collectively, see clearly is that suffering has value. For this reason qua neurotic and qua
Jew they are tempted to desire suffering; —hence the
tenacity with which the neurotic clings to his neurosis
and the Jew to his race-consciousness (the aesthetic
temptation).

On the other hand what people in the modern 'scientific' age in general compared with earlier ages, and
in America in particular compared with other countries, see clearly is that one must not desire suffering,
but strive for happiness on earth. For this reason qua
modern and qua american [*sic*], they are tempted to
be ashamed of suffering as something disgraceful and
vulgar. Hence Freudianism, Marxism, Positivism etc
as *religious* (instead of techniques of unmasking).
(The ethical temptation)

You seem to me to be torn between these two insights and not yet to have fully realized the paradox.

Citing passages in which Delmore had spoken of the pride,
guilt, and sin of his protagonist, Auden insisted these were
"religious concepts" unrelated to the "Freudian mythology"
Delmore had in mind, while the God invoked in *Genesis*

was only "a convenient aesthetic or metaphysical meta-phor."

> It isn't that I think Psychoanalysis or Metaphysical speculation are without value, but that their use pre-supposes a religious faith, and that they become de-structive when they presuppose nothing but them-selves, ie human consciousness.
> The value of the Freudian technique is as a weapon against Greek and Eastern Dualism, against the pride which makes finiteness the source of evil. (cf the Judaic-Christian view that the source of evil is the human pride that refuses to accept its finiteness). eg. It infers, for instance, that going to the toilet is a religious act, and that the earliest expression of human pride that a baby can make is constipation.
> But when, as they usually do, Freudians deny such an attitude, their dialectic is destroyed and freezes into a monism, which in practice means that the ultimate arbiter of values is the collective Super-Ego of the community at any given moment. (See Freud's iden-tification of ontology and teleology in his treatment of art.)
> Similarly metaphysics is important as a work of clarification once it can presuppose a faith to clarify; but in so far as it attempts to remove the necessity for faith by proving the existence of God as a logical necessity, it deserves the attack made on it by the Positivists, for it can only produce an As-If-God, about whom one can argue after dinner but on whom one's eternal happiness could not possibly depend.

Auden also objected to Delmore's preface, where he la-mented the absence of any "beliefs and values" by which to live in the modern world; only the authors of the Gospels, "who perhaps had only to look up or remember," could be said to have found their world harmonious with their be-liefs, Delmore had argued. In Auden's view, it was this attitude that finally vitiated *Genesis*.

> The central fault in your poem is, in my opinion, just this false hope that if you only look up and re-member enough, significance and value and belief will

appear of themselves. To look up and remember is good because it brings one in time to despair, and it is only when that point is reached that it is possible to submit to something that one cannot find for oneself by scientific experiments or writing poetry or ferret out of books, parents, churches, the past or what-have-you; ie the wish to be able to say *I done it* has first to be annihilated.

After such stern criticism, Auden's concluding remarks were generous and well-intended: "This is a muddled and priggish letter I fear, but I really am both interested and hopeful and anxious about your future development, as you have obviously been given great gifts which, like us all, you are turning against yourself." Delmore must have been disheartened by Auden's advice not to publish the poem until these questions had been resolved (he ignored it in any case), but the close attention Auden paid to his manuscript was a remarkable tribute all the same.

Auden's reservations about *Genesis* were, it must be said, idiosyncratic; ignoring the poem's thematic weaknesses and obsessive self-investigation, he preferred to read it in theological terms. Delmore was devout in his own way, but his God was a mystical deity beyond the reach of Auden's orthodox conception, and he may well have been bewildered by Auden's literal reading of what was essentially a poetic device.

.

As Delmore awaited the publication of *Genesis*, now delayed until the spring of 1943, he grew increasingly morbid, filled with forebodings of death. "Genesis—all eggs / one basket," he noted tersely in his journal; his whole life seemed to depend on the fate of this poem. He was tormented by dreams of deaths in the family, and would awake in the middle of the night close to tears, imagining the dissolution of his own body: "At night, when the hair grows on your face, and your body grows longer, and dinner is changed to blood, and your nails grow longer, you ought to remember, however empty your sleep, how much is untouched by the conscious mind."

Haunted by the war—which he continued to denounce bitterly in his letters—by teaching, and by what he called an "inevitable mid-winter staleness," Delmore found himself amid two crises in the spring of 1943. On March 2, he learned that a committee had been formed to decide on whether to offer him a five-year appointment as a faculty instructor, and they proposed to visit one of his classes. Delmore, "in a frozen slump" at the time, objected strenuously to what he thought of as an unprecedented procedure, and decided to refuse their request—"on principle," he told Berryman. At once defiant and unnerved, he worked out an elaborate argument by which he hoped to win Morrison's support before presenting his position to the committee: "With enough benzedrine and coffee, in half an hour I can win them over."

"I feel like a tragic hero . . . of a sort," Delmore announced to Gertrude and Berryman on the night of his "fatal interview"; and with that timid valedictory set off to confront Morrison, convinced that his protest was foredoomed to failure and that his "enemies" on the faculty were trying to force him out. An hour later, he returned with the news that Morrison had "surprised" him with a letter from the Dean indicating that President Conant had just required all five-year appointments to be investigated in a like manner; moreover, Morrison had emphasized their friendship, and implied that he would be "embarrassed" if Delmore objected to the committee's visit. "As always, Harvard is too much for us," Berryman noted ruefully in his journal.

That night, Berryman reported, Delmore was "savage and unhappy, both of us felt crushed, but gradually we drank more and talked about Shakespeare and verse and in the end we were as happy—in the context of despair & humiliation—as I ever expect to be." But the ordeal lay still before him, and he was disturbed about the committee's composition, in particular Robert Hillyer and another English professor, Howard Mumford Jones; the only one for whom he felt any affinity at all was Dean Leighton, and that only because his first name was Delmar. On the fateful day of their visit, he was infuriated when Dean Cross sent his secretary in lieu of attending himself, and went in tears to Morrison, who demanded an apology from Cross and promptly removed him from the committee. A week later, Delmore wrote Mark Van Doren that his teaching had been "praised in the most superlative terms by the committee" and his contract renewed.

Throughout these harrowing weeks, the tension between

Delmore and Gertrude had become "ferocious," Berryman observed. Once, when Gertrude showed Delmore a book review she was writing for *Partisan Review*, he pointed out the number of words beginning with "ex-" and remarked, "Freud could make something of that." "You don't need Freud. You can make enough out of it yourself," she retorted harshly. "Why, Gertrude, I only meant that 'ex-' means *out of, away from*," Delmore replied; then (turning to Berryman) "her characteristic course." Almost every exchange seemed to call forth cruelty and insolence on both their parts. What he found most difficult to forgive was her insulting challenge, "What girl would want you?" —a rebuke he brooded over in his journal for years.

But of course Delmore was hardly an innocent party in their disputes. "My gross need for affection makes me cut off one by one those who come near me and violate it," he wrote her a few months later, conceding that the "lava flow of [his] towering vanity" had made her life unbearable. Delmore demanded more praise and allegiance than anyone could possibly give, while Gertrude was willfully undemonstrative. Years later, he noted in his journal, "Wife did not like me enough"; and he admitted to her that "to try to force a human being to love one is like trying to make a child a musician because of a love of music." Gertrude had been apprehensive about their marriage from the start, and Delmore had a fatalistic view of poets' marriages in general, as he indicated in a little poem written a few months before his own broke up.

> All poet's wives have rotten lives,
> Their husbands look at them like knives
>   (Poor Gertrude! Poor Eileen!
>   No longer seventeen!)
> Exactitude their livelihood
> And rhyme their only gratitude,
> Knife-throwers all, in vaudeville,
> They use their wives to prove their will—

Late in March, they decided to separate, and Gertrude went off to New York, leaving Delmore alone in the house on Ellery Street.

10

———•———

"I MUST THINK of the house on Ellery Street where I lived alone, drank until I was a problem drinker, fell in love foolishly and vainly, and wasted the years when I should have been at the height of my powers." So Delmore in 1959 recalled the forties. Now that Gertrude was gone, he felt more bereft than ever in Cambridge, "that sad & used suburb of the heart." Not that he had ever felt comfortable at Harvard, where he thought he made a poor impression "as a Modernist poet, editor of a radical magazine, and Jew"—and he had now acquired yet another stigma in the form of domestic strife. Fearing that if Gertrude's departure became known his job would somehow be in peril, he suppressed the news for as long as he could, and instructed her to do the same. If she encountered any of their friends on the street (a likely event, since she was living near the office of *Partisan Review*), she was to say only that she had come to New York to be with her mother, who was dying of cancer. "It might be best for you to pay a state or official visit to the Macdonalds and Phillipses," he added, "to maintain the deception."

When, months later, Delmore reluctantly began to disclose their separation, he tried to make light of it. The breakup had been "amicable," he reported nonchalantly to Blackmur, and to Berryman he intimated that Gertrude had implored him to take her back, on the assumption that "they might as well be unhappy together." But the many letters he wrote to her in the months that followed were among the most moving and sorrowful he ever wrote. With genuine humility, he traced the downfall of their marriage, denouncing his conduct and pleading with her to forgive him. "If you had married some bon vivant of the heart, your charm and beauty might have been like a new school of lyric poetry," he declared. "And the more I think of it, the more I see my wrongness, for no one may *ask* from anyone, what I wanted, and asked for." Addressing her as "Dear dear dear belle and belle" and signing his letters "very much," "too much," or, less enigmatically, "with helpless inept devotion," he told Gertrude she was "beautiful" and hoped that she would be able to write to him "with some kind of pleasure or satisfaction." He put up her photograph in his study, mourned when the movers carried away her piano, and on New Year's Eve, when "Auld Lang Sync" came over the radio, "I looked at the floor, I thought only of you, & I wondered who kissed you then."

Apart from the pain of Gertrude's absence, the failure of his marriage represented to Delmore the failure of that ideal love he had always celebrated. "In the first few years of marriage, hopes, the truly great hopes, fade and become unreal," he observed in "The Eden Party," a story begun about this time. "For do we not turn away from love as from an unpleasant or disgusting thing?" Like his hopes of literary success, Delmore's longing for a happy marriage had been thwarted in part by his own unrealistic expectations. It was this experience that led him to propose "abandoning the ideas of success and failure," ideas responsible for the destruction of love, since they conspired to produce disappointment and competition. Had he not been so driven to succeed in his literary career, Delmore postulated, perhaps the ideal Platonic love he so desired would have come to him. Confining his bitterness to the stories he was writing, Delmore defended his wife in a letter to Laughlin.

> Child Gertrude left not for the sake of a man, or a woman I must add, knowing your mind; but because she felt guilt about the strain and difficulty she made for me. I don't think you understand or saw her real goodness, despite inadequacies she was unable to do anything about. After all, book-keeping is not the only trial of character.

Given the burden of self-hatred and remorse that had been accumulating for so many years, it was natural for Delmore to conceive of his failed marriage as still another vindication of his mother's oracular pronouncements about his future. "I pity the girl that marries you," she had once said when he failed to hang up his coat; and it had been Rose who condemned her son to believe that he was only "*disjecta membra*"—in his own terrible words—the issue of a plot to retain her husband's affections. Delmore had a melodramatic theory about what he called the "French guilt," the story of how his mother had unexpectedly received a French war bond and then decided to have an operation that would enable her to conceive; as a consequence of this transaction, his very existence seemed to him a trespass against fate.

The day after Gertrude had left, Delmore received a telegram from his mother announcing her imminent arrival in Boston. He refused to meet her at the station, and when she appeared on his doorstep, he explained that Gertrude was away for the weekend and that he himself was leaving the next morning for Cape Cod.

> The evening passed in the most degrading recriminations [he reported to Gertrude]. I learned that my suit was three sizes too big for me; that Kenneth regarded me as a crackpot and remarked how in last September's photograph I still wore one of his ties of 73 Washington Place; that I was miserly, the house unpleasing, and cold, for the fire had gone out, and the dining-room table disgraceful.

Rose had come, apparently, to report on her recent visit with Kenneth, who had married a "shiksa" out in California and now had three children. "Everything is bought on the installment plan," she complained, and Kenneth's wife dominated the household; "he gets two cents for gum." Mortified by this display of "grossness and gall," Delmore persuaded her to leave the following day, but only by promising to resume sending her twenty dollars a month. "How appropriate that she should come the day after your departure," he remarked to Gertrude; "how often Life has a literary design."

A month later, Delmore was still despondent. He refused to see one of his former students who had come back to Cambridge, explaining that he was "inept and silent before any visitor." Alone in the house on Ellery Street, he wrote plaintively to Gertrude: "The house is full of your style and idiom"; and in his journal, he wondered, "Does she

still miss me?" Eventually he acquired a cat and filled his
letters with news of its activities. A calamity occurred one
night when he was driving with Oscar Handlin to visit
William Barrett in Gloucester and the cat jumped out the
window. Delmore embarked on a frantic search, ringing
doorbells and leaving notes with people in the area to call
him if the cat turned up. "First Gertrude, and now this!"
he cried.

Despite his loneliness, Delmore admitted to himself that
Gertrude's departure had "liberated bound forces in the
unconscious." They continued to see one another on occasion, but such visits served only to remind them of why
they had separated. When Delmore announced that he had
reviewed a collection of Edna St. Vincent Millay's poems
for *The Nation*, Gertrude looked downcast. "This was the
jealousy she had admitted as her dislike's root," he remarked in his journal. And after she had gone, he noted,
"Gertrude's visit spoiled two days."

.

"When I get scared, I get devious," Delmore confided to
R. P. Blackmur as *Genesis* was about to appear; and considering the measures he took to ensure its success, he must
have been scared indeed. From his headquarters on Ellery
Street, the Machiavellian embarked on what must have
been one of the most unremitting campaigns in literary
history. A "cabal of enemies" was ready to destroy his
reputation, and only Laughlin's intervention could save the
book from such a fate; he was to visit editors, "send out
free copies to the right people all over *before* the review
copies go out," collect blurbs, and advertise everywhere.
Meanwhile, Delmore was preparing his own campaign; in
New York, he had seen James Agee and Philip Rahv, he
reported to Laughlin. "The former might help with the
Time review. . . . But for Christ's sake," he cautioned,
"don't do anything that will reveal to Agee and Rahv that I
had such ideas in mind when I visited them for the first
time in years."

He was ashamed of these "non-noble strategies," Delmore conceded, but on the other hand,

I do not intend to forget that we are living in this
world, where dog eats dog, and books of noble poetry.

> The main thing, obviously, is to be perfectly aware that one is not being noble; it is only when one begins to deceive oneself about the character of one's manoeuvres that one is really lost and damned forever.

Laughlin's defection from the cause of *Genesis* left Delmore no choice but to protect his work himself from the world's indifference to poetry. It was important to remember that America was in the midst of a war, and "if publication coincides with a great military campaign, not much attention will be paid by anyone."

The height of Delmore's own campaign was a letter of some thousand words describing in minute detail just how Laughlin was to organize the promotion of *Genesis*. Apparently, random suggestions had not sufficed, and it was necessary to come up with a separate strategy for every magazine, to be carried out with a precision and subtlety that would have astonished Admiral Darlan, Delmore's favorite commander in the war. Laughlin should call on Margaret Marshall at *The Nation* and "remark upon extraordinary character of book"; write Caroline Ford at *View*, an avant-garde journal of the day, "and say that Schwartz has been converted to Surrealism"; and remind editors that "other poets are apt to be competitive and ungenerous." On the subject of *The New York Times*, he was even more specific.

> Write to Adams,* explain unusual character of the book, and author's distinction as an instructor at Harvard and Guggenheim. Remark upon fact that IDBR, hailed on all sides, was not even reviewed in the Times. Warn against usual run of reviewers, Colum, E. L. Walton. Suggest Herbert Gorman, Louis Untermeyer, Alfred Kreymborg.

But no amount of calculation could prevent critics from saying what they really thought, and when the reviews started to come in, they were inevitably disappointing, given Delmore's inordinate expectations. Still, some re-

---

* J. Donald Adams was a well-known critic in those days, and editor of *The New York Times Book Review*.

viewers were quite enthusiastic. Richard Eberhart, writing in *The New Republic*, called *Genesis* "a harmonious work of art"; Dudley Fitts noted "a compelling honesty that seeks the core of things"; Frank Jones, in *The Nation*, echoed Eliot's description of Pound's "Hugh Selwyn Mauberley" in praising it as "a positive document of sensibility"; and Northrop Frye wrote, in *Canadian Forum*: "The whole scheme is worked out with considerable intelligence and power, the writing is competent and much of what the chorus says is strikingly acute and profound." But there were others who had nothing good to say about it; William Rose Benét and Horace Gregory were among the harshest, and even the more approving reviewers thought *Genesis* too long. Alarmed by the announcement on the book jacket that two more volumes were to follow, the reviewer in *The New York Times* observed that "when completed, the dour chronicle will bulk up to the size of a Thomas Wolfe novel."

Two reviews pleased Delmore—Blackmur's notice in *Kenyon Review* and Matthiessen's in *Partisan*—but he had expected them, and late in May he wrote Dwight Macdonald (ignoring the most vehement dismissals): "Apart from you and Goodman, everyone seems to like at least some of it very much, although so far as being noticed in the wide world goes, it has been like a big boulder dropped in mid-ocean." Macdonald had never approved of *Genesis*, finding it "unreadable, flaccid, monotonous, the whole effect pompous and verbose." Delmore should give up trying to be the "Eliot of the Thirties," Macdonald counseled, and exploit his talent for "satiric, humorous, intimate, realistic description and commentary." (It wasn't bad advice, even if rather too emphatically imparted.)

Delmore was demoralized by Macdonald's criticism, but defended his poem energetically, insisting that an "inner necessity" had prompted him to write with such rhetorical urgency: "such a life had been lived and then had been thought about many times, differently from year to year." Paul Goodman's review in *The New Leader* was a far more serious matter. "It is difficult to review this combination of ineptitude and earnestness," he began, and from there went on to denounce the "calamitous lack of language, inaccurate learning," and other failings to be found in *Genesis*. It was a vindictive review, motivated by jealousy—as Delmore well knew—but Goodman was an able literary critic, and some of his objections were just, in particular a description of the poem's narrator as "a young man illequipped and over-equipped struggling with a self-analysis when all his data are nothing but what his repressions and ambitions allow him to remember; nowhere able to tap a spontaneous impulse, and relapsing into gloom." Delmore claimed that Goodman had sent copies of his review to every member of the Harvard English Department.

But it was Matthiessen who noted the real problem with *Genesis*, when he recalled how, five years earlier, *In Dreams Begin Responsibilities* had received "more critical acclaim than has come to any other American poet of his generation." Such early praise had placed Delmore "in the hardest position for a young writer to sustain in a spotlighted age, a beginning poet with a reputation to live up to." *Genesis* was to have been the work that finally established his reputation, and yet Delmore himself had eerily prophesied the fate of his poem in "Poetry and Imitation," written when he was twenty-three

A poet who sits down at his table to write a long poem in which he intends to "express" the "Spirit of America" will probably write a poem which does not in the least reflect the spirit of America, whatever that spirit may be. But because the nature of poetry is essentially reflective, the poet will turn out a poem which shows just what it is like to be A-Poet-Who-Would-Like-To-Write-A-Poem-About-The-Spirit-Of-America, that is, a poet with no sense of proportion who is deluded about his own gifts and who would like to be famous as an epic poet: the ideas he uses, and the cadences, phrases, vocabulary and metaphors will all reveal his mind in a way which nothing else and no one could, not philosophy, not the psychologist and not the daily newspaper.

But this prophecy was too harsh, for *Genesis* did express —and with considerable vividness—the drama of the Jewish immigration which Delmore used to proclaim as his great theme. Moreover, his own mind was sufficiently interesting to be the subject of a long narrative poem, and it would be unfair to say that he was "deluded about his own gifts"; it was only that he sometimes chose to cultivate others in which he was less richly endowed. When he strove for grandeur and significance, *Genesis* became ponderous, overly solemn, freighted with didactic argumentation; when he gave expression to the fantastic wit and irony that characterized his conversation, and exercised his genius for detecting the forces of history in the particular incidents of a life, the poem worked.

For twelve years Delmore had labored over the design of *Genesis*, until he was convinced that "it made a *real* poet and it gave me / Two methods which can paint the living world." These methods were blank verse and what he called Biblical prose, long declarative sentences that carried the burden of the story. The blank-verse passages were spoken by ghosts identical to those in *Coriolanus and His Mother*; only here Freud and Marx had been replaced by nostalgic old men given to soliloquizing.

In a defensive and querulous preface which he himself admitted was "pretentious," Delmore argued that since he was unfortunate enough to live in a time when "no author can assume a community of ideas and values between himself and his audience," it was imperative for the poet to "bring in his ideas and values openly and clearly." This was to be accomplished by the ghosts, whose long-winded speeches interrupt the plot in Delmore's version of Aristotle's *peripeteia*, "a shift from ignorance to awareness." For some two hundred pages, eloquence alternates with vaudeville, that raucous, deflating humor so congenial to Delmore. Eager to demolish cultural myths, one ghost observes:

> Verdi at eighty-seven kneeled beneath
> The bed to find a collar stud,
> And apoplexy struck him down. Alas!
> 'Twas this he left out of his operas,
> —Of actuality, the ragged richness!

Others invoke Henry James, "fat, profound, and ponderous," or disparage the "foolishness, / Self-pity, sentimentality, weak tears" of Rousseau. Literary anecdotes, religion, world history, popular culture, philosophy: all of Delmore's favorite themes were explored by these ghosts,

> Each tireless as the Ancient Mariner,
> Learned and sick as Hamlet Coleridge,
> And like him full of generalities—

"Should my verse prove attractive to posterity," Delmore once told John Berryman, "I would like it to be known as 'Delmorean' "; and nothing could have been more Delmorean than these ghosts. For all their high seriousness, they were essentially kibitzers, hiding their wisdom behind a screen of cynical banter.

But these blank-verse passages, however vivid and interesting, were ornamental; the true subject of the poem was Delmore. "Hershey Green, c'est moi!" he exulted, echoing Flaubert's famous declaration about Madame Bovary; "the psychology of *Genesis* is all my own."

> "Giant, phenomenal, and purposeless,
> How the divinities, America,
> Europe, Capitalismus, others too,
> move through the life of this Atlantic Jew!"

It was this ever-intrusive theme that Delmore labored to depict and that dominates the Biblical prose, where the story of his family's life in Eastern Europe and their immigration to America sets the stage for the author's own appearance.

> The family moved to a nearby town, a town by a river which flowed to the Black Sea, a town of many churches, and an ancient university,
> Here during the next ten years four more children were born to Noah Green and his wife, all of them engendered by the sudden end of the Russo-Turkish War. . . .

Once Hershey Green was introduced, the familiar tale of the French war bond that resulted in Delmore's birth having been rehearsed once more, *Genesis* became a sort of *Bildungsroman*. The drama of kindergarten, a "Congress of thirty Ids" (and here Freud arrived to relieve Marx of the burden of interpretation); of learning to read in first grade and being promoted to an advanced class; of incurring a D in conduct: these events, all drawn from Delmore's autobiographical outline, "The Story of a Heart," prefigured the strenuous ambition shared by so many intellectuals of his generation. To achieve success in life was a compulsion passed on from immigrant fathers to their sons. "It was not for myself that I was expected to shine," wrote Alfred Kazin, "but for them—to redeem the constant anxiety of their existence. I was the first American child, their offering to the strange new God; I was to be the monument of their liberation from the shame of being— what they were."

In Delmore's view, the child's Jewish identity was only one of the many elements that converged to form the competitive personality. As he noted in a shrewd if rather oversimplified review of two books by the psychologist Abram Kardiner, the Oedipus complex, "involved as it is with a repressed hatred of the father, brings about the tendency toward extreme aggressiveness, competitiveness, and hostility, the consequence of which is the systematic anxiety and insecurity which also have always characterized Western society." Capitalism, Delmore argued—echoing Max Weber—further served to transform the personality thus created by its emphasis on obtaining "self-esteem and success" through self-denial.

Delmore's close reading of Freud had some unfortunate consequences for *Genesis*, which at times resembles a clinical case study more than a poem. Hershey's sexual encounters with little girls, the crisis when he wets his pants in class ("he knew the sex in the event, / The letting go of need and of feeling, / When inhibition failed"), and other traumas associated with infantile sexuality are explored in lurid detail. The relationships examined abstractly in his journals of the period became the subject of *Genesis*, where the child, "plunged into the emotional relations between his parents," is precociously forced to mediate between them. In this way, the love that should be reserved for him is squandered by his parents in their conflicts with each other, leaving the child bereft of affection. "Anguish and shame, anger and guilt enact / The in-ness of your being-in-the-world—" a ghost remarks after the violent confrontation between Hershey's parents that ends the book; and it was Delmore's fate as well to be haunted by this scene, the most significant and oppressive memory of his childhood.

The tireless inventory of desolation, malice, and treachery catalogued in *Genesis* was perhaps its most damaging feature; but there were also flights of brave, exhilarated rhetoric that vivified the poem. And where the verse flagged, the story's intrinsic interest carried it forward. It was a difficult enterprise, and Delmore was aware of the difficulties involved; but he was confident of its virtues, and capable of persuasively defending them.

> It may seem for a while [he wrote Laughlin] that the alternation of Biblical prose and blank verse is too predictable, but it will, I think, be felt as an acceptable *formal* device, like the refrain in a ballad or like rhyme or like a tragic chorus. If the dead as a chorus seem bizarre, remember that Dante wrote the best poem ever written *by using the dead as voices*. If the fusion of narrative and commentary seems strange, remember that, as I intend to point out in a short preface, this event-succeeded-by-commentary is one of the profoundest most deeply-rooted and most accepted experiences of modern life: the newspaper story-editorial, the play-and-review-of-the-play, the travel-film-with-voice as commentator and newsreel with commentator are all primordial examples of what is going to be an inevitable literary form (inevitable because the life we live forces it upon us).

The most salient objection that can be made to *Genesis* is that it belabors private themes which lack even the semblance of universality needed to give them dramatic interest. For many pages at a time, Delmore managed this imposing leap from the banal crises of childhood to metaphysical discourse; but what finally flaws the poem is the trait he called "megalomania," the voluble celebration of self: "No matter where he was, what he felt, what event, he was to himself / The center of the turning world."

Had further volumes of *Genesis* appeared, and had they continued to dwell so remorselessly on every crucial episode in Delmore's life, it would have become perhaps the longest poem in the English language. By the close of Book I, some two hundred pages, Hershey Green was only seven years old. Delmore did persist for several hundred pages more, and those pages contain some of the most brilliant

passages he ever wrote, surpassing in their eloquence and
brio anything in Book I. Meditating on the crowd of
images that throng his memory, one ghost cries out:

"O Atalanta, the apple of the eye!
O Eve before the tree which is this world!
O bird, O beast, O flower everywhere,
All the *richesse* of being through the year,
For the earth turns like a carousel on which
All sensibilities ride horses, grasp for rings . . ."

Another ghost exults in the boy "who'd painted his father's
life / On the long walls of his mind," spilling forth interpretations in a gay voice resonant with rhetorical enthusiasm.

What wins
In Hershey's heart, triumphs over his mother,
Over his shock, his shame, and his *tabu?*
—Marriage and Money, both the Polity's
Sheer values, shining chandeliers!

On and on went this inspired tale, but it was too diffuse,
too long, too improbable, and eventually Delmore con-
signed it to the growing corpus of his unfinished works.
Years later, when someone at a party asked him when
Book II would appear, he replied, "Posthumously."

.

"No reputation is more than snowfall," Delmore remarked to John Berryman, drawing on his favorite metaphor; "it vanishes—it exists from book to book." Disillusioned by his experience with *Genesis*, he was eager to take
up new projects, in particular a novel he had been writing
during the past year. "It will be up to you to pay for it in
advance," he warned Laughlin. "The short novel will give
you an opportunity to decide whether or not you want to;
there are them that do, without any preliminaries." Once
again, Delmore's hopes of success on a grand scale soared;
he wanted a contract arranged for English publication, and
even dreamed of a deal with Hollywood. Laughlin had
promised him a stipend of six hundred dollars a year if
Genesis proved a success, Delmore claimed; "which, so far

as I am concerned, it was." He threatened to give his novel to a commercial publisher if Laughlin failed to provide a generous contract, but was furious when Laughlin offered to release him from their agreement, which had called for New Directions to publish Delmore's first five books. To punish Laughlin for his apostasy, Delmore began intimating to friends that his publisher was stealing from him, furtively issuing new editions and making off with the profits. The royalty statements were "sheer impressionism," and "the whole of New Directions was based upon a complicated evasion of the income tax."

Teaching every day but Sunday, "day of rest, that is to say, collapse," Delmore found his academic responsibilities exhausting. While he professed to find teaching "a great seduction, too easy and too pleasant," and was gratified when one of his classes applauded on the last day, more often his letters expressed impatience, boredom, and a wish to devote more time to his own writing. He had a martyred view of his profession. "When asked by my grandchild the classic question, What did you do in the war to make the world safe for the lesser evil?" he wrote Auden in November, "I will be able to say, I was in the Navy, defending the English language." Now that he was an associate professor, Delmore no longer enjoyed the privileges of a Briggs-Copeland lecturer, which allowed one to teach part-time, and he was responsible for eighty-seven students and the grading of 257 themes a week. (He was always very exact about such matters.)

"What did Henry [James] do with himself," Delmore wondered, "since he had no friends? No intimate friends?" To be sure, Delmore knew many people in the Cambridge community (more than James had known in his day). There was his friend George Palmer, who had published a few poems in *Partisan Review* under the name George Anthony; William Van Keuren, who had inherited some money that he wanted to invest in the new literary journal Delmore often contemplated; and a number of Radcliffe students with whom he carried on desultory affairs. (Once, after giving a poetry reading, he announced to Berryman, "There were five women there I had slept with.") He often had visitors from New York, among them James Agee, Clement Greenberg, and Auden, who spent several weekends at Ellery Street, "with scenes of comedy hardly to be equalled," Delmore wrote Laughlin, "the two of us composing verse in parallel rooms and becoming irritable about who was to have the only eraser in the house."

For the most part, though, he was lonely. "Everyone is gone into the world of light," he wrote Blackmur in midsummer, "& I sit alone lingering here with memories of Ellery Street parties." He often thought of returning to New York, where there were "old relationships like banked fires." "I mean to return to Brooklyn, where my dark body began," he wrote Gertrude, with a poetic flourish, "and to stay on the treeshaded street with the brownstone house, backyard, English breakfast room, and period quality." Estranged from Cambridge, he considered it emblematic of his life that he had gone to the barber shop on a local holiday and found it closed: "Even to this fact, some significance can be attached; for my life & awareness so places me in the community that I do not know what is closed on Patriots' Day."

Delmore's longing for a family had been one of the crucial issues in his marriage, for it was through the institution of the family that he hoped to recover from his own damaged childhood. "The neurotic technique is only the attempt of the isolated individual to get back into the family," he noted in his journal, and his poignant relationships with his friends' children were perhaps an expression of that impulse. He was always writing dedicatory poems to them, the most notable being inspired by the birth of Dwight Macdonald's son.

> When Mike, Macdonald's scion,
> Utters his first *mot*
> If it happens to be: "Stalin,"
> *Out the window he will go.*
>
> But if Macdonald's scion,
> The cunning consummate calf
> Shouts out "Lev Davidovitch!" [Trotsky]
> *They will make him a member of the editorial staff!*

Delmore was particularly fond of the young son of his friends Wallace and Rose Dickson, to whom he consecrated several poems and many chapters of an unpublished novel about these years, *A Child's Universal History*. He was pleased that Jeremy Dickson had such affectionate feelings toward him, and flattered by the child's habit of announcing, "I am Delmore Schwartz." Delmore even talked to his classes about his new five-year-old friend, proclaiming him "our next Socialist king"; and he was especially gratified by Jeremy's love of trolleys, the symbol of Delmore's awakening to poetry.

Later on that summer, Delmore fell in love with a graduate student in English, Aileen Ward (she was eventually to write a distinguished biography of Keats), whom he met at a going-away party for Richard Ellmann. Aileen possessed a legendary beauty, and another professor, the equally legendary Perry Miller, had already fallen in love with her before going off to war. For Delmore, it was "love in the grand style"; but Aileen, while honored by his attentions, was still in love with Miller, and a painful courtship ensued. Charmed by his company and "Coleridge-like" talk, Aileen was at first unwilling to recognize the depth of Delmore's infatuation, which can be inferred from feelings attributed to Maxwell, his persona in an unpublished story about their relationship: "He had always wanted or thought he wanted modern love and supposed that romantic love was an unnecessary illusion." Now that he had encountered it himself, Delmore was agitated by his ardor, which "had reached the point of intensity where his whole being felt a dark undertow which dragged it far from the shore and [made him feel] helpless and without control."

Delmore's desperate attempts to master his emotions, the struggle to declare his love—a love he was always examining in his journals but could only with great difficulty bring himself to reveal—occupied him through most of 1943 and the following year. He was deeply wounded by Aileen's formality. "She looked very beautiful," he noted after a cocktail party she gave that summer, "but there was in her manner something official, social, and of polite emptiness." In his novel, he recorded the suspense with which he waited for her to reciprocate the feelings he himself could only intimate.

Eventually Delmore began to raise the question of marriage, but only "in an indirect way." Aileen insisted she would not marry anyone else, but she was far from committing herself to Delmore either. When he learned that the "anyone else" in question, Perry Miller, had been writing her from London, he was furious, and denounced Miller in the most vehement terms. After that, Delmore and Aileen saw less of each other, but he never forgave Miller, and when his rival returned to Harvard they once came close to blows.

One hot summer night, as Delmore sat by his window, he glimpsed a couple making love in the house next door. "Why go away for the summer," he wondered half ironically, "since these spectacles & performances will increase with the heat & opened windows?" It was a measure of his own distance from love that such a scene could awaken in him all the sadness of his thwarted longings—longings he found depicted in the futile love of Swann for Odette in Proust's *A la recherche du temps perdu.*

.

Delmore had never regarded his birthdays with equanimity, but this December 8 was more ominous than ever, for he was turning thirty "and deceived by inspiration and losing hope & hope's lies." Writing to Berryman that morning, he tried to be lighthearted.

> Today is my thirtieth birthday, and I had thought of a Gold Rush birthday for myself in the dining-room, plates with melting ice cream, all flavors, even tutti-frutti, for friends absent, dead, misunderstood, offended (this list will take too long)—but then I corrected myself, enough of this self-pity, I said to myself, you have no kick coming, and don't forget, there are too many unwashed dishes as it is.

But later in the day, encountering Aileen in the Yard, he spoke of "thirty dead years, thirty thousand dead imaginations of what this day was to be"; and in his journal he remarked: "On this birthday too M* walked about in the same grave, not different." But this was only the beginning of a series of commentaries that continued for several months. Contrasting what he had been at twenty-two—"a

* During 1944, Delmore often reverted in his journals to the "M" of "Hallmarks," the stream-of-consciousness "Exercise" composed in 1941. By writing in the third person, he could achieve some distance from the relentless "I" of his earlier journals. "M" appears to have stood for "Me."

gross & naïve though self-conscious egoist; yet not without a growing intelligence"—with what he had become, Delmore lamented: "No wife, no child, no mastery." Reading Thomas Mann on Wagner, he noted another of those literary parallels that so appealed to his imagination: ". . . melancholy, sleepless, generally tormented, this man is at 30 in such a state that he will often sit down to weep an hour without end. He cannot believe that he will live to see *Tannhäuser* completed—" To the beloved Muse who had abandoned him, Delmore addressed a despairing plea: "Thirty years of madness have I known / Because you come and go." Another poem of Yeatsian defiance began: "Now thirty years are passed: well! what of that?"

What was it about this admittedly unnerving birthday that awoke such panic in Delmore? Three months later he noted in his journal: "Thirty years, the idea which made me feel, too late! too late! so much not known, not mastered—" It was the cry of one to whom the world had once seemed to promise a brilliant future, and who had come to expect life to be "all exaltation, all pleasure, all joy." Like so many American writers, Delmore had succumbed to the pressure to distinguish himself by an immortal work, and as a consequence had pushed into realms beyond even the reach of his prodigious genius, striving to rival Wordsworth and Milton instead of exploiting his gift for lyric poetry. His demands upon an intractable world that offered only marginal success to poets were perhaps unreasonable, but those demands formed a significant aspect of his character, and had arisen from circumstances not entirely of his own choosing. "For two thousand years the main energies of Jewish communities in various parts of the world have gone into the mass production of intellectuals," Harold Rosenberg once observed. For Delmore, to become a great American writer was to claim his portion of that history, and to fail was to relinquish the hopes on which his whole identity depended.

It was not only poetic inspiration that Delmore missed; the sheer enthusiasm for life celebrated in *Genesis* and in his journals, the pleasures of memory and observation, seemed to have deserted him as well. Depressed and alone, living like a "clochard"—as John Berryman's wife Eileen once described him—"heavy and gray like his overcoat" (in his own self-portrait), Delmore dreamed of the luxurious existence depicted in Renoir's *Luncheon of the Boating Party*, where elegant young men and women enjoy themselves on a sun-splashed terrace. Renoir's painting represented the life to which he had always aspired, he told Aileen Ward, the life of the *rentier*.

The New Year brought no improvement in Delmore's mood. "I almost wept into my Hungarian goulash," he wrote dolefully in his journal. More unhappy than ever with teaching, miserable about Aileen and other women, he was distressed to find that "the idea of a social circle, and a full life in Cambridge, had vanished with the summer excitement." As for himself, he felt "like a new man," but with a significant qualification:

> The new man like the suit which has just been dry-cleaned; someone says, "It looks as good as new." And it does, from a distance; closely examined, the nap has worn off or the texture of the cloth is thin; and it looks stale, not fresh and new.

He was unable to write or concentrate, and took solace in recording his daily life with clinical exactitude. Visits to Dr. Sieve, conversations with Aileen, the struggle with alcohol, the hope of a term off: these are the themes of Delmore's journals in the spring of 1944. An entry in mid-January is typical.

> My years have rifted from me. One to thirty. How do I know how many more, and where will I be and when will I die and will I be sorry that I am I. Yes? Guess!
> Married and parted, published and punished, unfinished, praised and appeased, and envied and hardly understood. So much over and so much rejected, so much desired and tossed and untouched.

It was "an old kind of depression" that often overcame him, "childhood's depression." Staring with "distaste" at an old photograph of himself, Delmore recalled the encomium bestowed on his first book and lamented: "That photo too will fade, America's Auden / Quickly faded."

And yet Delmore was inclined to "distortion and melodrama," as he himself acknowledged, and his journals tend to exaggerate—at least in these years—his predicament. He was in demand as a critic; every new anthology contained a selection of his poems ("From Beowulf to Schwartz," he boasted); *Partisan Review* now featured him on the masthead as an associate editor. There were times when he could celebrate a "return of sensibility" and a renewed enthusiasm, as when he looked back over the previous year.

> Last year in April at this time, or a month after, how little I imagined the year to come, the heights and the depths, excited classes, poems, Van Keuren, Phoebe [one of his Radcliffe girlfriends], Aileen, the reception of "Genesis," the eight o'clock class, failure before my classes.
>
> What is in the year to come now? Perhaps a new excitation, even, perhaps, Aileen.

" 'It has all been very interesting,' although full of passive suffering," he concluded, quoting one of his favorite phrases, the last words of Lady Mary Wortley Montagu. Even the most disconsolate entries in Delmore's journal enlist a sort of grim humor. "I played poker with a dogmatic belief in my good fortune," he writes, or "I lie on the sofa like a horse with a broken leg, waiting to be shot." Moreover, his recurrent complaints of "silence, blankness, apathy" and inability to work were belied by the reviews he was writing for *The Nation* and *The New York Times Book Review*, which invariably combined a fine polemical edge with a casual erudition.

The book on Eliot was another matter. Delmore had been writing incisive criticism of Eliot since college, and his mature essays on the man he referred to in the 1940's as an "International Hero" and later on as a "Cultural Dictator" were widely anthologized. Despite his reverence for Eliot, Delmore was aware that his importance was symbolic as well as literary, and he was a shrewd observer of the contradictions inherent in Eliot's many roles. There was no sarcasm in his labeling Eliot a hero, however, for Delmore considered Eliot the prophet of modern life, a visionary wise enough to have articulated its "literary, philosophical, cosmopolitan and expatriated" character before anyone else.

While Delmore's published writings on Eliot were gracious and even deferential, in private he would picture Eliot as a self-promoter engaged in shameless literary politics. Eliot's career was "the paradigmatic instance of the success he craved," remarked Philip Rahv—and the more oracular Eliot became, the more Delmore resented him. But he also aspired to a personal relationship with Eliot, and was distressed by the distant tone of Eliot's replies to the letters he wrote about various literary matters in connection with *Partisan Review*. "Letter from Eliot, feared, and dismayed by the withdrawn politeness, for M expected too much," he wrote in his journal late in 1943. But when Eliot came to Harvard to give a lecture during the 1940's, Delmore was unwilling to meet him. "He's a great poet, but a dead poet," he told Oscar Handlin. To resolve this impasse, he found a surrogate in Eliot's brother, who terrified him almost as much as Eliot himself; Delmore saw Henry Ware Eliot socially on several occasions, and ascribed a symbolic significance to their encounters, as if Eliot's brother were a medium between himself and the remote arbiter of taste. More than a decade later, in another of his polite letters to Delmore, Eliot regretted that their paths had never crossed, but it was Delmore who avoided Eliot, rather than the reverse.

Given these complicated feelings, he found it difficult to write on Eliot, and his difficulties are painfully apparent in the critical book he completed but abandoned without revising in the late 1940's. Ponderous, overly cautious, and banal, Delmore's prose style here has none of the incisiveness of his published criticism. He wrote with a deliberate naïveté, as if innocence could protect him from the ambivalence he really felt. In one draft after another, he labored over the syntax of his simple, declarative sentences. "T. S. Eliot is a great poet and a great critic," one version begins, but no sooner has he said that than he feels compelled to qualify his terms. Some of his axioms recall the earnest philosophical investigations of his college days. "The actual is that which exists"; "It is a human necessity to 'put things into words' "; and so on. It is evident from the style alone that he mistrusted his intuitions and had lost confidence in his ability to formulate critical judgments. His book was thorough and not lacking in intelligence—the one gift Delmore never really relinquished—

but only the chapter on Eliot's anti-Semitism, a model of tact and critical self-effacement, had any real force. Comparing Eliot's beliefs to those of Henry James and Henry Adams, he noted how Eliot's vision of European civilization "at a particular moment in time when social strata were being broken down and entered by outsiders" had contributed decisively to his prejudice. In saying this, Delmore provided no apology; rather, he opposed Eliot's cruel bias as an "abomination." It is a pity that he felt obliged to write with such artificial constraint in this book, for Delmore understood Eliot as well as any critic of his day.

·

Since leaving Delmore, Gertrude had been working at various jobs in New York. She was a secretary to Kurt Wolff at Pantheon for a time, worked for the Bollingen Foundation, and later became a fiction editor of *Collier's* magazine. Now that she and Delmore were apart, he encouraged her more than he had when they were married, as if to atone for the many years when he had been so self-absorbed. He was always urging Gertrude to keep after editors for assignments, and it wasn't long before she was reviewing for *The New York Times Book Review, Partisan Review, The New Republic*, and *The Nation*; and they were good reviews. She could write about Nelson Algren, Katherine Anne Porter, Christopher Isherwood, or a translation of Rilke's *Rodin* with informed ease, and was acerbic about new books by now-forgotten novelists; one of her fiction chronicles for *PR* was titled "A Meagre Crop."

In February, Delmore and Gertrude agreed to file for a divorce, not without some hesitation on both sides. The proceedings turned out to be a farce, since New York State laws required proof of adultery to establish sufficient grounds for divorce and Delmore was either unwilling or unable to supply such evidence. So they decided to stage their own findings of what he called "specious adultery," and rented a hotel room in New York, then summoned their friends Maurice and Charlotte Zolotow to witness the scene. The Zolotows were to enter the hotel room just in time to see a woman disappearing into the bathroom while Delmore lounged on the bed in a guilty attitude. Since no woman could be found to play the part of the adulteress, however, Gertrude herself stood in. "This was one time when he wasn't with another woman," she remarked to William Barrett.

Delmore feared that word of adultery would get back to Harvard and jeopardize his career. To protect their anonymity, he suggested they file as D. Schwartz and G. Schwartz so that *Time* wouldn't report it "and titillate some Radcliffe girls." Moreover, it was important to describe Zolotow as a witness against Delmore, "for it was he who spurred me on when I saw you again in the distance, at a table" (in the N.Y.U. cafeteria where they had met a decade before). These elaborate tactics proved unnecessary when the divorce was routinely granted. Afterward, the two conspiring couples went off together for a melancholy drink.

That weekend Delmore gave a reading with Mark Van Doren and R. P. Blackmur at Cooper Union. Public readings were always an ordeal for him, and he recited his poems inaudibly, "as if contemptuous of life," murmuring in a low monotone to conceal the terror evident in his stark white face. The audience was "polite enough," Berryman recalled, "but dull, bored, silent, inert." It was a "painful occasion," made even worse when Delmore's mother suddenly materialized from behind a post and rushed up to embrace him. "You have no way of knowing how horrifying this was and for what reasons," he wrote Helen Blackmur two years later, the traumatic event still fresh in his mind.

After the reading, Delmore went down to Princeton, where he spent an evening at Edmund Wilson's house. Delmore had great respect for Wilson, whom he thought of as the czar of American literature, but he was far from reverential. In a letter to R. P. Blackmur, he compared Wilson to Henrietta Stackpole, the brash American newspaper correspondent in *The Portrait of a Lady*, and in his journal noted: "He thought he travelled to the Finland Station / But it was Stamford in Connecticut!" Delmore had just published a devastating review of Wilson's anthology of American literary criticism, *The Shock of Recognition*, and, a year before, a shrewd appraisal of Wilson's accomplishments and limitations as a critic. That evening, Wilson reprimanded him at great length, addressing him with increasing familiarity as one drink followed another: first as Mr. Schwartz, then Schwartz, then Delmore

Schwartz, and finally, Delmore. "If I'd stayed longer as urged," Delmore told Berryman, "he would have been nastily saying, 'Hey, you!' "

On returning to Cambridge, Delmore wrote Gertrude a disconsolate letter in which he intimated the possibility of a reconciliation.

> The only pleasant thing about my trip was our own accord or concord, and I've been haunted, as by the idea of falling from a brink, by the idea of How it-all-might-begin-again. The mind has its reasons which the heart can never understand, to invert Pascal, and I try to remember exactly what you said on Tuesday night: "How awful it must be to be in love." Was that what you said? Whatever the exact words, it was what I did not remember and should have remembered: your own distance from love for ten years: for only love can make everything acceptable and accepted.

But the letter's signature—"Your only brother"—seemed to discourage any hopes of a renewal of their relationship on the old terms. It was as if, now that the divorce was final, Delmore could imagine a reconciliation without having to act upon it.

Throughout 1944, Delmore continued to regret the end of their marriage in letters which Gertrude, remembering his conduct while they were together, found "too kind, too forbearing, too loving and forgiving." Alone in the house "where many a party rose with the wine and the laughter," recalling "what a *good* boy, with all my shortcomings, I was *then*"—in the early days of their courtship—"how full of the desire to be good, generous, friendly," he dreamed that Gertrude was having their child while he sat in the kitchen; but he was "afraid," and when the child was born, it turned out to be "a big girl of five" who resembled Gertrude and whom he "did not like because she was so big." For all his interest in psychoanalysis, Delmore was obviously not one to reflect on the implications of his dreams, or on what they would reveal to Gertrude. His self-absorption further displayed itself when Gertrude's mother died that summer and he failed to attend her funeral, since "the consequent exhaustion would not have been any help."

Delmore was disenchanted with himself and his friends,

who seemed "too unhappy or dead to bear." One party in
Cambridge, "whose scenario must have been written by
Dostoevsky," ended with drunken recriminations and a fist
fight between R. P. Blackmur and another guest. A few
weeks later, in New York,

> there was a foolish party at William's [Phillips] and
> Diana Trilling asked me if I thought I looked like her?
> to which I said after a stunned silence, It is very kind
> of you to ask me. . . . I felt immense depression to see
> everyone paralyzed, unable to go forward with their
> work, not different or better than in 1938, and having
> nothing to say or foolish things to say. . . .

He brooded over "the growth of anxiety" that interrupted
his own work, and confessed to "outbreaks of anger and
accusation." Once, on a visit to Cambridge, Gertrude discovered that he had chopped out the lock in the bedroom
door in a fit of impatience when he had trouble opening it
one day.

.

Still intent on taking a leave of absence from Harvard,
Delmore appealed the following autumn to Theodore
Morrison, who examined his record and discovered that he
had taught more consecutive terms than anyone else on the
faculty; so he was granted a year's sabbatical, to begin at
once. Faced with the uneasiness of true freedom, he left
for New York in January 1945, and moved into lodgings at
91 Bedford Street. In his journal, Delmore described his
arrival in New York: "Ego-dominated in his walk, he
pushes ahead—slow like a weight—an acute sense of the
external world—the way he disposes of his luggage and
secures a boarding house."

PART TWO
1945-1957

———•———

Whence, if ever, shall come the actuality
Of a voice speaking the mind's knowing,
The sunlight bright on the green windowshade,
And the self articulate, affectionate, and flowing,
Ease, warmth, light, the utter showing,
When in the white bed all things are made.

11

·

ONE NIGHT NOT LONG after his arrival in New York, as
Delmore sat in a bar off Washington Square crowded with
friends, he suddenly turned to William Barrett and shouted
exultantly, "1919!" Post-World War II New York was to
be his twenties, the literary dream since mythologized beyond recognition; and—for a brief moment at least—he
thought he had found the community so long desired.
Happy in the polemical ambience of *Partisan Review*, he
knew the "delights of conversation" he had missed in
Cambridge. The editors of *PR*, discouraged by the difficulty of reconciling orthodox Marxism with their true
sympathies—the plight of the intellectual—had long since
given up on radical politics. They still paid homage to the
idea of revolution, but ever since their mentor, Trotsky,
had reprimanded them for taking refuge in such abstractions as "freedom" and "independence," Rahv and Phillips
had more or less acknowledged that revolution meant less
to them than "individual integrity"—as Rahv had avowed
back in 1939. By the mid-1940's, their brief flirtation with
the working class was a distant memory; the failed dreams
of their "Marxist decade" (which had never been strictly
Marxist in any case) had given way to Modernism in its
newest form: Ortega y Gasset, Alberto Moravia, Karl Jas-
pers, and Albert Camus. European authors were the vogue,
and their political sympathies mattered less than their value
as interpreters of the human condition in the postwar
world. The intellectual climate was favorable to Delmore
in these years, when New York became once again the
cosmopolitan city Saul Bellow evoked in *Humboldt's Gift*.
"It was a case," Bellow wrote, echoing Lionel Abel, "of a
metropolis that yearned to belong to another country."

Bellow himself was not the least of the city's new intellectual attractions. *Dangling Man* had appeared the year

before to considerable acclaim, and he was now publishing regularly in *Partisan Review*. Delmore began to see a good deal of him and of Bellow's friend Isaac Rosenfeld, another promising writer from Chicago. Until now, the second generation of American Jews, who were to dominate the "New York intellectuals" of the 1940's, had—with the exception of Delmore—hardly made their collective presence felt. Emerging from the thirties with their ambitions if not their political hopes intact, they had yet to prove themselves as writers. Their radicalism, "anxious, problematic, and beginning to decay at the very moment it was adopted" —in Irving Howe's words—would no longer serve them, and they turned their critical energies toward literature and social commentary.

Delmore often talked of writing a novel about the *Partisan Review* circle, as did Philip Rahv, who wanted to title his *The Truants*—an epithet intended to reflect the peculiar sense of freedom brought on by the war's end. But "it wasn't in the cards," to echo Rahv's concise summation of those years; and Delmore's hopes were among the first to be crushed. When Barrett returned from the war, he found his friend "a changed man." Apart from the two crises Barrett noted—the unenthusiastic reception of *Genesis* and the failure of his marriage—Delmore's anxiety was evident in his drinking, a habit sharply in contrast to the summer evenings spent over ice-cream sodas in Harvard Square of a few years before. Now, four summers later, they resumed their old practice of dining together every night; but Delmore was no longer the clamorous, eager youth of the thirties. His talk had a frenetic edge to it that the euphoria of the postwar era failed to conceal.

Delmore was not the only one disposed to an embattled, intense, occasionally malicious social style. The character of the *Partisan Review* crowd derived in part from their polemical clashes, which everyone took very seriously in the 1940's. Heirs of the Depression, the New York intellectuals engaged in political and literary argument with a fervor generated by their need to establish themselves as a genuine force in American life. "Bring a number of talented people together in a close area, and the neurotic tremors begin vibrating," Barrett observed. There was no place for civility in the feverish, urgent talk of Delmore's friends; as Barrett shrewdly noted, "Americans, who have

less of a tradition of the salon or literary circle, fling themselves at the business with greater innocence—and violence. It was not exactly an atmosphere to bring Delmore
further peace."

                              •

"Maxwell decided that perhaps he might free himself of
his obsession with Patricia if he lived in New York City for
a year and before long he had secured a year's leave of
absence from teaching"; so Delmore wrote in one of his
unpublished autobiographical novels. Still desperately in
love with Aileen, he had come to New York not only
because it was home to him but to escape a relationship
that had become a torment; and to facilitate his escape, he
soon found himself in the midst of two other affairs.
"When a man seeks different girls, he affirms his belief in
the existence of the external world," he noted.

One of the two women was Elizabeth Pollet, a young
writer Delmore had met in the spring of 1944, and the
other was Eleanor Goff, a dancer to whom Delmore's
friend Milton Klonsky had introduced him during an earlier visit to New York. Eleanor was twenty-two that year,
and had come to New York from Mills College in California to work with Merce Cunningham's dance company.
Delmore was enchanted by her grace and elegance. She
had a spiritual approach to dance, a reverence for art and
poetry as fervent as Delmore's; or, in Klonsky's less idealized view, she was an "intellectual's chorus girl." But she
was devoted to her work, and during the forties and fifties
acquired a considerable reputation in New York as a per-
former and teacher of dance.

Elizabeth, the daughter of a well-known painter, Joseph
Pollet, had gone to Black Mountain College for a year
before transferring to the University of Chicago in 1939.
After graduation, she moved to New York, where she
began to write fiction, supporting herself through various
jobs: at the Guggenheim Museum, Western Electric, as the
editor of a trade journal. When Delmore met her, she was
living in a cold-water flat on Hudson Street in Greenwich
Village—later evoked in a story she published in a 1953
issue of *New World Writing*: "There was a large tower of a
hot water heater, a sink, a tub, and a gas stove. The ceiling
had a band of ornamented woodwork, and there were huge

sliding doors at the end. The room seemed empty, filled with space."

In a preface to "Cold Water Flat" intended as "an introduction to the author," Elizabeth described herself as "awkward and self-conscious." Like Delmore, she "felt undefined," and believed "writing is living." Her fiction was hesitant and introspective—like her personality. Her shyness appealed to Delmore, who found her at once demure and glamorous; with her blond hair and delicate blue eyes, "she looked like an airline stewardess," a friend recalled. Delmore worshipped her beauty, "that great tyrant," but he was no less pleased by her charm and talent than by her looks. And he was convinced that he was attractive to her for the same reason; when a friend once asked how they had met, Delmore replied: "In the pages of Oscar Williams," implying that his reputation had drawn Elizabeth to him.

Delmore continued to see both Eleanor and Elizabeth for several months, until one day they showed up simultaneously at 91 Bedford Street. Delmore fled in panic to Barrett's apartment, but he was philosophical about this inevitable denouement: "Well, I got away with it for six months." After that, he saw more of Elizabeth and thought less about Aileen Ward.

•

"Maxwell's being was such that no matter what his conscious resolve, he became intimate with any girl he saw often," Delmore wrote in one of his autobiographical novels; yet he also knew that "he was unable to give himself to another human being." So great was his fear of intimacy that he could rarely bring himself to spend the entire night with a woman, and would often depart in haste after making love, eager to be alone. In the margin of a letter from Elizabeth, he once scrawled, "Nobility vs. nubility vs. mobility," three conditions to which he aspired and yet found contradictory. For the moment, the most insistent problem was solitude, which implied the choice of "nubility." "When will he be in the married state—able to eat dinner not alone?" he wondered.

In his journals, Delmore speculated about his difficulties with a psychoanalytic zeal acquired from his reading of Freud's *Collected Papers*. He relished the vocabulary of psychoanalysis; libido cathexis, narcissism, ego ideal: this was now the language of Delmore's tireless self-interrogations. But his theoretical grasp of Freud obtruded on his therapy. Once, after a session with his last psychiatrist, Dr. Max Gruenthal, he announced that he had just emerged victorious from an hour-long debate on some point of interpretation about his childhood. "Delmore is crazy," William Phillips said later; "he pays money to teach the analyst his business." Suspicious of the notion of "adjustment," he was convinced that American therapists had no understanding of alienation, and so were unsympathetic to the particular problems of the writer in society. "You do not know what that is, a poet?" asked Rilke in *The Notebooks of Malte Laurids Brigge*. "No: not many have ever known," Delmore rejoined in the margin of his copy.

Delmore was given to excoriating himself in his journals while in his conversation he excoriated everyone else.

> He invariably presented himself as a person perpetually harassed but exempt of all blame . . . [wrote Philip Rahv]. Saturnine by temperament, he took an exceedingly comfortless view of the conduct of human beings, of whose motives he was chronically distrustful; and his habit was to denounce endlessly what he saw as their moral lapses even while taking care to exculpate himself.

Rahv's friendship with Delmore had deteriorated by the mid-1940's, and his contention that Delmore lacked the conversational wit ascribed to him by Dwight Macdonald was perhaps provoked by the recollection of having been himself a victim of that wit. And he was annoyed by Delmore's casual attitude toward *Partisan Review*, where, despite having been made an editor, he seldom did much work. Delmore was a diligent poetry editor (although he tended to lose manuscripts or fail to return them), and took an active part in editorial decisions, the preparation of symposia, and the acquisition of essays, but he was hopeless as an administrator. He rarely showed up at the *Partisan* office on Astor Place—perhaps in part because his mother was always calling there and complaining to whoever answered that her son had deserted her—and when he did, his own work occupied him more than editorial mat-

ters. Moreover, Delmore liked to make fun of Rahv's
portentous, heavy-handed prose. "You've got to remember
that English is still a foreign language for Philip," he used
to say; and whenever possible, he tried to write *Partisan's*
editorials himself. Rahv was also jealous of Delmore's purported success with women; "Poets get all the girls," he
complained.

Delmore was democratic in his satire. Theodore Spencer
"looked more and more like a depraved Roman senator,"
Alfred Kazin was a "psalm-singing peasant," and Allen
Tate, he wrote Lowell, "exhausts his friends and starts
running himself down, and then accuses himself of lack of
charity, forbearance, and imaginative sympathy." Even
Meyer Schapiro, whom Delmore revered, was not exempt.
"He is so passionate a monologist that he thinks anyone
who listens to him is brilliant," he once noted in his journal. Visiting Robert Lowell and his wife Jean Stafford in
Maine that summer, Delmore sat around their kitchen
table drinking vodka and milk and retailing "in a croaking
voice" his newest anecdotes about Eliot. "Everything had a
motive," but his talk was "a revelation," Lowell recalled.
Delmore's conversation possessed a natural associative ease
combined with erudition: "If he met T. S. Eliot [which he
never did] his impressions of Eliot would be mixed up with
his impressions of Freud and what he'd read about Eliot;
all these things flowed back and forth in him."

Delmore liked to draw others into his view of the world's
conspiratorial character, and had a habit of reporting gossip that would have been better left unsaid. When he heard
Manny Farber, a film reviewer for *The New Republic*,
complaining that Clement Greenberg had plagiarized one
of his ideas, Delmore at once told Greenberg what Farber
had said, thus precipitating a notorious fist fight. And when
Rahv announced to Delmore that William Barrett "had no
ideas," this information too was promptly reported to its
victim. He was a "loyal but thoughtless friend," in Greenberg's view.

In November, Delmore attended a series of lectures on
Impressionism given by Meyer Schapiro at the New School.
Years later, he would record the profound influence they
had on him in his astonishing poem "Seurat's Sunday
Afternoon along the Seine," which owed a great deal to
Schapiro's remarks on *La Grande Jatte*. He took extensive

notes, and was particularly struck by Schapiro's observation that, for Cézanne, painting had acted as "a means of escaping from his aggressiveness." Delmore's own aggressive manner troubled him, and he made it a theme of his self-analysis after hearing Schapiro's lecture: "The superego punishes him after anxiety and sensitivity have led to acts of aggression—a prosperous period renews his narcissistic & megalomaniac hopes, leading to anxiety (sexual over-activity as an effort to compensate for other frustrations of the ego)." This, in brief, was the cycle of Delmore's moods, from exaltation to the despair brought on by dread of failure. There were still moments of elation, when he felt his condition had improved, "though painfully, slowly, in an eccentric way, as one who learns a language not by lessons in grammar and vocabulary, but by reading parallel texts of the Bible." But his predominant mood that fall was expressed in a Wildean aside made in reviewing Mark Van Doren's new edition of Whitman's poems: "The idea of experience is to actual experience as a slick travel folder is to the trip itself."

Delmore was not alone in his estimate of his decline; Allen Tate, in *Sixty American Poets*, concluded that he had not "lived up to his early promise," and Horace Gregory, in his *History of American Poetry*, claimed his "promise was more in evidence than [his] achievement." Delmore could deal with self-generated disapproval, but when it came from others, he was deeply wounded. "If I say my work is a failure, I enjoy the discussion," he noted, "[but] if M[acdonald] says it, I become depressed or even angry." He was now the young man of a story begun that year who had "put away his hopes as if they were old love letters: tied, in order, in the closed drawer."

.

It was one of the many paradoxes of Delmore's career that the beginning of his worst depression—from which he never entirely recovered—and the subsequent decline of his work coincided with the moment when (despite Tate's stern rebuke) his importance as an American man of letters became firmly established. By 1947, he was the most widely anthologized poet of his generation, as well as its "ablest critic of modern poetry," wrote John Berryman some years later. He was an editor of *Partisan Review*, the most respected journal of his time; the short stories that had been appearing in various reviews during the 1940's brought him generous praise; and he was an influential critic and reviewer, writing in *The Nation* on Whitman, Aldous Huxley, Virginia Woolf, and Joyce, among others. A shrewd critique of Van Wyck Brooks's *The World of Washington Irving* also appeared that year, in which he demonstrated the false optimism of Brooks's version of American literary history. "His books represent a triumph of style, which is not astonishing in the least," Delmore observed, "since his method of composition is confessedly that of anthologizing the golden passages of his authors, who are sometimes great masters of expression." He had attacked Brooks before, in reviewing his popular *New England: Indian Summer*, where Eliot's *The Waste Land* was so crudely dismissed; and now he castigated him for ignoring the darker side of American literature and history in favor of a resolute cheerfulness. Delmore's own view was considerably darker.

> What a beautiful world! What a beautiful culture! And if the quality of life has seemed otherwise, if, to some, neither systematic optimism nor pessimism seem adequate, if the literary life from the time of Irving until the time of Brooks seems full of difficulty, conflict, unhappiness, frustration, misunderstanding, false recognition and false disparagement, sectarian struggle, national tragedy, personal tragedy and mighty poets in their misery dead—if these things seem representative, perhaps it is the fault of one's point of view. Certainly it would be wonderful if Brooks's view were true. But it is untrue.

The literary life Delmore had in mind here was undoubtedly his own. He "believed in nothing so much as the virtue and reason of poetry," Alfred Kazin remarked, but his obsession with the politics of his career conflicted with his exalted sense of the poet's calling; and the more influential he became, the more he decried the lot of the writer in America.

.

Not long after Gertrude had left him, Delmore encountered in the Talmud an enigmatic phrase: "The world is a wedding." For months he had thought about the meaning of this line, expounding it in letters and offering such bitter variants as "The world is a divorce." Now, in the fall of 1945, it occurred to him that this phrase could stand for the complicated, intimate, emotional relationships of his friends, wedded to one another by sympathies that bound them into a loving and quarrelsome family. Struggling to find the proper narrative form for the story he wanted to write, he began with a fictional portrait of F. W. Dupee in 1938 (if there was ever any doubt about these characters' identities in life, Delmore obviated it by putting the initials of their models at the top of the page), then turned once again to Mary McCarthy, describing her estrangement from "a famous and domineering husband"—Edmund Wilson. What was it that made this woman go from one marriage to another? "Dinah [as Delmore named her] wants to get married again so that she can once again have someone to whom to be unfaithful," one character remarked. (Delmore's peculiar fascination with McCarthy may well have been exacerbated by a failed attempt at seduction, which he conveniently reversed, making her the aggressor, in reporting the episode to friends.)

These were promising sketches, and it is a pity that he abandoned them after a page or two to write about himself. "The Jewish writer suffers from the unavailability of a sufficient variety of observed experience," Clement Greenberg once noted, recalling his own experience as a second-generation Jew. "He is forced to write, if he is serious, the way the pelican feeds its young, striking his own breast to draw the blood of his theme." This ingenious metaphor—drawn from Catholic imagery—surely applied to Delmore, who found in his own life the illustration of every significant literary idea. "He sat among his possibilities, unconsolable, turning in his mind the phrase, like a knife at uncut pages, 'the true illness is the loss of insight into one's real situation,'" began one version of "The World Is a Wedding," a sad meditation on Delmore's own lost possibilities. He had taken to reading *Genesis* over, on occasion finding himself impressed by it, but more often alarmed by its weaknesses. In the story, he recalled how, "when he had written it, he had felt the madness of joy. . . ." Since then, however, he had come to believe "the book was worthless"; his only consolation was an awareness of "the passage of deception and illusion," and even this insight had to be qualified: "He might be deceived in thinking that his gift was a real one, or it might be that he overestimated very much the nature of this gift."

Another version of "The World Is a Wedding" began as a Faustian fable in which Satan appears before the author and announces: "You have written the matchless works you desired so much. You need no longer say to yourself, 'What else is there to do? What better thing?' Here, enjoy these works as if you lounged in the sunlight, and take pleasure in their goodness and their splendor." All that Satan asked was for the author to "forget about [his] desires to compose any more such works." But Delmore knew that hope was essential to his survival as a writer, and he resisted any such pacts, creating from these unpromising fragments the fine story that "The World Is a Wedding" was eventually to become.

•

As the end of his year in New York drew closer, Delmore once again began casting about for some alternative to Harvard. "If you can't make John [Berryman] your assistant," he wrote Blackmur in Princeton, "you might do worse than importing one of the children of Israel from Cambridge, Massachusetts, an importation you once mentioned frequently and then ceased to mention." He was depressed by the thought of Cambridge, teaching seemed an unpleasant chore, and he knew he would miss the excitement of New York: the lunches with Matthew Josephson and parties with Camus, the constant activity around the *Partisan Review* office, the dinners with Barrett, Macdonald, William Phillips, and his many other friends.

But when Delmore returned to Cambridge in mid-January, he found himself "pleased to be back and glowing with triumph" despite his apprehensions, and immediately began a flurry of correspondence, sometimes writing seven or eight long letters a day. One to Elizabeth Pollet was typical.

20 Ellery St.
Cambridge, Mass.
January 19, 1946

Dear Elizabeth,
    As you may have seen in the newspaper, I narrowly

averted death by returning to Cambridge last Saturday
instead of yesterday.* I am back in my own house
and tomorrow I intend to make my own breakfast,
which means that existence is as normal again as it
has ever been for me. But what a week [it] has been:
I drove my tenants from the house, for they had
painted the dining room an extraordinary aluminum
silver, and the floor of the bedroom an obscene red,
for they were newlyweds. And I accused the landlady's husband of treason because he objected to drink
in general and my drinking especially when everyone
knows I never touch the stuff and the Volstead Act
has been repealed. The day after my return Bill [Van
Keuren] and Jeremy [Dickson] both went to bed
with the flu, but not before I had had interesting
conferences with both and begun the Odyssey in a
free paraphrase as the story of a boy who was looking
for his father. But to return to my labors which gave
me a feeling of self-reliance proper to New England, I
summoned the locksmith, I secured coal from an unwilling dealer, I started the well-known furnace, I
bought wood and paint, the well-known Chem-Tone
for to take that vulgar silver from the dining room
walls. I carried books, on which my tenants had spat-
tered paint, I bought soap, eggs, coffee, crackers,
toothpowder, oranges, and milk. I visited the sick,
greeted the well, and inspected Jeremy's cats. Simplex,
named because it was for a time supposed that he was
simple, is an ageing tom-cat, quite affable, not very
clean, and addicted to lost weekends from which he
returns wounded and exhausted. Carrie is quite young
and a girl, but Simplex is not interested in her, perhaps because of her extreme youth. Both are likable,
but needless to say not in the same class as Riverrun,
in whom Jeremiah has expressed no little interest.
Simplex has one trait which made me think of poor
Pushkin, dead in early youth. He is not interested in
the fish in his dish as long as he thinks he has a
chance at a handout from the dinner-table.

* When a plane from New York to Boston crashed a week
after Delmore had flown back, he took to congratulating himself on
a narrow escape.

It turns out that the university is still running on a war-time schedule for the educational reason that thus it makes more money. This appears to mean that I will have to teach next summer, but not during the fall term, so that I can again come to New York's cold-water flats for four months. Bill has an excellent apartment which he never uses and to which I now have a key, and I would say that it is only an hour and ten minutes from New York to here except that after yesterday's accident, I don't want anyone to visit me by plane, although I intend to come to New York by plane so that it can be said that I left this life in the cause of literature, hurrying to argue with William and Philip.

Will you tell Will to send my mail and my copies of *Time* here, so that I can keep up with the current falsehoods? And will you take possession of my big orange squeezer, my coffee-pot, my electric stove, and my broken turn-table, especially the latter, since you can't get a phonograph in Cambridge? Now that you are at leisure, you ought to write me a long letter.

As ever,
Delmore

When he was overstimulated, Delmore liked to foment excitement, and his letters were filled with urgent, complicated directives: to collect his laundry, to send up an electric heater he had left behind, to return his books, to recommend him for a grant. Gossip, flights of literary criticism, reports of Jeremy Dickson's latest adventures, and chronicles of his daily life poured forth unremittingly. Even when he was lamenting that Cambridge was "dirty, cold, snowed down and worn out," or that his landlady distrusted him because he drank, Delmore managed to turn his difficulties into high comedy.

·

In mid-January, Robert Lowell and Jean Stafford came to stay with Delmore at Ellery Street. "One might think that this was not a household but a literary movement," he wrote Helen Blackmur, "when each morning in three rooms three authors compose literary works and two typewriters move from left to right." Only Lowell did not type, "for he is even more than I a manual lunatic and cannot

even play the phonograph. . . ." Lowell's famous poem in
Life Studies offers a vivid, if fantastic glimpse of Delmore
in the spring of 1946.

To Delmore Schwartz
(Cambridge 1946)

We couldn't even keep the furnace lit!
Even when we had disconnected it,
the antiquated
refrigerator gurgled mustard gas
through your mustard-yellow house,
and spoiled our long maneuvred visit
from T. S. Eliot's brother, Henry Ware. . . .

Your stuffed duck craned toward Harvard from my trunk:
its bill was a black whistle, and its brow
was high and thinner than a baby's thumb;
its webs were tough as toenails on its bough.
It was your first kill; you had rushed it home,
pickled in a tin wastebasket of rum—
it looked through us, as if it'd died dead drunk.
You must have propped its eyelids with a nail,
and yet it lived with us and met our stare,
Rabelaisian, lubricious, drugged. And there,
perched on my trunk and typing-table,
it cooled our universal
Angst a moment, Delmore. We drank and eyed
the chicken-hearted shadows of the world.
Underseas fellows, nobly mad,
we talked away our friends. "Let Joyce and Freud,
the Masters of Joy,
be our guests here," you said. The room was filled
with cigarette smoke circling the paranoid,
inert gaze of Coleridge, back
from Malta—his eyes lost in flesh, lips baked and black.
Your tiger kitten, *Oranges*,
cartwheeled for joy in a ball of snarls.
You said:
"We poets in our youth begin in sadness;
thereof in the end come despondency and madness;
Stalin has had two cerebral hemorrhages!"
The Charles
River was turning silver. In the ebb-

light of morning, we stuck
the duck
-'s web-
foot, like a candle, in a quart of gin we'd killed.

The stuffed duck wasn't Delmore's—"I've never shot anything but pool," he told Lowell—but his friend William
Van Keuren's, and Lowell revised Delmore's variation on
Wordsworth, which went: "We poets in our youth begin in
sadness / But thereof come, for some, exaltation, ascendancy & gladness." The "long maneuvred visit" from
Henry Ware Eliot was to have formed part of an elaborate
strategy to obtain for Lowell a Briggs-Copeland lectureship, which Delmore insisted was essential to any literary
career. But he could be satirical about such marginal characters as T. S. Eliot's brother, who was at one remove from
fame; once, after an evening with some people of that
dubious classification, he remarked: "We got nothing but
skimmed milk."

Life at Ellery Street was chaotic. The stove was likely to
blow up at any moment; the refrigerator had a perpetual
leak; Delmore prowled around in the middle of the night
knocking over furniture. He liked to display the immense
closet on the second floor where he had been disposing of
bottles over the last three years; it was filled nearly to
capacity. But the Lowells were themselves chaotic, and
their visit was unmarred by conflict—for a time.

Delmore was envious of Lowell's Brahmin background,
and his envy sharpened after Lowell took him to dinner at
his parents' house on Marlborough Street. They weren't
"that grand," Jean Stafford recalled, but Delmore was intimidated by the servants, heirlooms, and a certain reserve
on the part of the Lowells. The elder Lowell's attitude
toward Delmore can be guessed from his habit of telling
his literary son that he "talked like a Jew." Delmore resented the way Robert Lowell kept bringing up a Jewish
relative remote in time, Mordecai Meyers, the grandfather
of Lowell's grandmother. Lowell insisted that he himself
was $\frac{1}{8}$ Jewish, and made much of a portrait of Meyers
that hung in the drawing room on Marlborough Street.

Things were never the same after that evening. Delmore
baited Lowell mercilessly, made fun of his parents' home,
and tried to destroy his marriage by circulating malicious

rumors. Finally Lowell swung at Delmore, Jean Stafford had to separate them, and soon afterward the Lowells left for Maine.

　　　　　　　　　　·

"Never send an angry letter at night—only in the morning," Delmore used to admonish himself—a necessary precaution, since he was increasingly given to sending the notorious poison-pen letters that ended so many of his friendships. In the spring of 1946, William Barrett was the recipient of one of these furious epistles, and he was astonished when Delmore arrived on his doorstep a day later without even referring to the letter, which had announced the end of their friendship.

Barrett was often called upon to intervene in Delmore's life that spring. The first time, Delmore summoned him by telegram when the furnace broke down, but after that no further excuses were offered. Delmore was again depending on Barrett in every crisis, a responsibility to which Barrett always capitulated. But even he noticed that Delmore's erratic conduct "had now reached a new stage: it was no longer sequential." Lonely in Cambridge, he would rush down to New York, where the pace of life and others' demands would hasten his return. But Delmore continued to hope that he could find a way to live permanently in New York. "I doubt that I will be groping about this abyss for more than two years," he wrote Berryman in April, "since as you know I want to die in Brooklyn which is abysmal too, but a less foreign abyss."

In his disenchantment with Cambridge, Delmore had taken to showing open contempt for its ways. Once, at a party for Richard Eberhart attended by Robert Frost and Oscar Williams, among others, he arrived with some boisterous friends, appropriated a few bottles of beer from the dining-room table, and made an early and furtive departure. Later on that spring, when I. A. Richards was giving a lecture in Leverett House, Delmore walked in late looking drunk and disheveled, and flung himself onto a couch behind the speaker, where he promptly fell asleep— Richard Wilbur recalled—"with a fearful visibility and audibility."

Now that he was on his own and away from New York, Delmore was less certain about Elizabeth. "I've been making myself marriage-forestalling or contra-espousal meals, nothing but the best in cans," he reported to Barrett. And in his journal, he composed a revealing little poem on the subject.

> Till death do us part?
> O fearful long thought
> To the bitter, curved heart!
> That all must be sought
> Within another's heart

Moreover, he was still writing rather feverish letters to Eleanor Goff, inviting her to come up to Cambridge and claiming that he was now far more domestic than he had been in his cold-water flat on Bedford Street. In March, when Elizabeth accepted too readily what Delmore thought had been only a vague proposal that she come live near Boston for the summer, he replied in alarm: "I see that you have decided about the summer without waiting for me to decide anything." All the same, he was willing to test her expressions of loyalty in a businesslike way: "If it is not mere rhetoric and you really mean what you say when you say, 'I will do anything you want me to do,' then let us have a real though minor trial: will you learn shorthand as soon as possible?"

Desiring only "a home and family with many literary companions," Delmore found himself instead in pursuit of that elusive, ideal love celebrated in his journals, a pursuit which excused him from the emotional commitments of love as one ordinarily finds it in the world. "I have a theory that one becomes unhappy because one sleeps with too many girls," he confided to Laughlin. He suspected he was in love with Elizabeth, despite the "groping & fumbling & self-torturing speculation" he had to endure in reaching that conclusion, but he was terrified of marriage, and vacillated until Elizabeth found someone else. When he learned of this development, he appeared at her apartment in a rage, wild-eyed and threatening, and she had to flee by climbing down the fire escape. Elizabeth summoned Barrett, who rushed over and managed to put Delmore on a plane back to Boston. "Love exists only when it is unrequited," he had written in the margin of Rilke's *Duino Elegies*.

·

In March, Delmore learned he had been made an assistant professor, an accomplishment he felt called upon to disclaim by calling it—in at least four letters—"a meaningless ascent all connotation, like Swinburne" (whose phrase it was). Since it was still not a tenured position, Delmore suspected his promotion was only a means of enticing him to remain there to teach freshman composition. (Another possible motive was "to give Harry Levin a few more stomach ulcers.") In his journal, Delmore was less insouciant about the implications of the "vainglorious title" bestowed on him: "I shall get tenure in the grave." Nevertheless, he was elated by the news, and only his usual superstition of success made him treat it with caution. Delmore was more worried than ever now about his conduct, and warned Elizabeth that henceforth she would have to stay with friends or in a hotel when she visited him in Cambridge.

That summer, Delmore taught a fiction-writing course, but was too depressed to make more than a minimal effort. Standing before the class "green-faced, toad-like, and dishevelled"—as one student saw him—in the faded green corduroy jacket he never changed, he appeared morbidly shy, and never directly addressed the class, speaking always toward one corner. Even so, he managed to give an impression of significance and dignity; Delmore still embodied "the image of a real poet," his student Kenneth Koch recalled. His intense devotion to the poetry of Yeats and Stevens, Wordsworth and Milton, invariably conveyed itself in his teaching, which concentrated on appreciation more than scholarship. And he could still become animated when he read aloud "Sweeney Agonistes" or talked about one of his favorite ideas, "The Irreversible Track of Discrimination," by which one came to appreciate certain authors who in turn spoiled one's appreciation of other, lesser authors. He was devoted to a few masterpieces— among them *The Possessed*, *The Cossacks*, *Fathers and Sons*, *Light in August*, *The Last Tycoon*, and all of Edith Wharton—which he insisted were required reading for anyone seriously interested in becoming a writer. Fear of failure was the dominant force in American life, he told the class, convinced his own life embodied it. By autumn, he was hardly attending any classes at all.

In October, Delmore wrote to Mark Van Doren about the possibility of teaching at Columbia, and the English Department invited him down to give a lecture. Arriving in New York several days early, he checked into a hotel in Greenwich Village and began to prepare his talk, assisted by Barrett, who brought in a typewriter and took down his dictation. The fluent argument that distinguished his earlier criticism was noticeably absent, and he had to struggle with every thought, pacing back and forth in his room while his amanuensis sat poised before the typewriter. "My God, I'm forgetting simple words. Am I losing my mind?" he cried, quoting Chekhov's Uncle Vanya.

On the day of the lecture, Delmore's spirits improved. During a long afternoon of drinking with Milton Klonsky and a friend of his, George Schloss, he was lively and intense. Then, as they were riding uptown to Columbia in a taxi after dinner, he suddenly grew apprehensive, began talking incessantly, and insisted on stopping at a liquor store to buy a pint of gin. At the lecture hall, Delmore filled a tumber beside the lectern with gin, and it stood empty by the time he had finished his talk.

Whatever agony Delmore suffered in preparing his lecture, no trace of it appears in the published version, "The Literary Dictatorship of T. S. Eliot," a brilliant account of the contradictions in Eliot's criticism and the imperious manner in which he reconciled them. Noting Eliot's penchant for ranking English poets, Delmore attempted to "make systematic" random pronouncements that had been so influential but haphazard. In so doing, he managed to show how Eliot's development as a poet had coincided with his various estimations of the English tradition, and ventured to predict—on the evidence of *Four Quartets*—that Eliot would soon reverse himself on Milton, whom he had long condemned. It was a notable instance of Delmore's attentive, even prescient monitoring of every vicissitude in Eliot's career, for just a month before (unknown to Delmore) Eliot had repudiated his earlier view of Milton in a lecture before the British Academy.

Whether it was due to Delmore's erratic performance at Columbia, or to the wariness of Lionel Trilling, who had heard unsettling reports of his conduct at Harvard, the matter of a job was quietly dropped. Delmore dreamed intermittently of his lost chance, dreams "which reached the point of 'it is not true' 'it is true'—I wanted it after all"; but he consoled himself with the thought that such an appointment would have meant "not being able to write as I want."

As the year wore on, Delmore became more and more indifferent to his classes. Visiting Leslie Fiedler, then a graduate student at Harvard, he was "melancholy and unavailable," carried a hip flask in his pocket, and showed little enthusiasm for any subject except the movies. Even the lavish praise of the publisher Salman Schocken failed to move him. "He thinks you're the only creative Jewish writer in this country and would very much like to get you to do something for his house, no matter what," Elliot Cohen, the editor of *Commentary*, wrote in February; but what Delmore found most significant about this offer was the question of "a permanent connection," a phrase he underscored.

Delmore spent a good deal of time that year at a rooming house on Kirkland Street where some of his friends were living, among them William Van Keuren and the owner of the house, John McCormick, whom Delmore had helped to get a teaching post at Harvard. During the winter, Delmore himself lived there for a while with a Bennington undergraduate on leave for a term. But he reserved his deepest affections for his cat, Riverrun—the first word in *Finnegans Wake*—with whom he carried on an elaborate relationship, feeding her expensive Portuguese sardines, worrying like a parent when she failed to come home, and coaxing her to sleep in his bed.

Suddenly, in the spring of 1947, Delmore left Cambridge and returned to New York, failing even to notify Harvard of his plans.

12

———•———

EXHILARATED BY THE DECISIVENESS with which he had abandoned Harvard, but unnerved by the prospect of freedom, Delmore spent his first afternoon in New York drinking in Chumley's Bar on Bedford Street with John Malcolm Brinnin and William Barrett. Rosetta Reitz, owner of the Four Seasons Bookshop on Greenwich Avenue, found him an apartment on West Fourth Street, and a week later he was writing Dupee to ask about a job at Bard College in Annandale-on-Hudson, New York: "Everything is undecided at the moment except that I am not going back to Cambridge if I can possibly manage not to."

Like the Ellery Brown of a story begun that summer, who had come to New York "resolved once again to find out if he could be helped, perhaps even liberated from the recurrent sieges of acute melancholy which overtook him every few months and lasted most of the time," Delmore was in a desperate mood. He seldom left his apartment, and when he did, it was usually to wander about Washington Square Park, morose and alone. "He felt each day"— Delmore wrote of Ellery Brown—"as if the entire day had been spent seated in a car before a railway crossing, the white gates down, waiting to begin to move again as he watched an endless succession of nondescript faded grey box cars pass before him."

Elizabeth had by this time married Delmore's rival, who had pressed his suit from California with a series of cajoling letters, and eventually persuaded her to give up Delmore—which she did perhaps only to escape the Dostoevskian scenes he was staging at every opportunity. "Delmore had become the play-actor of his own neurosis," William Barrett observed. "He had begun to melodramatize his own evil." Barrett's efforts to placate Delmore only provoked him to louder fulminations. "We live in the world of Hitler and Stalin, and you want me to be gentle!" he cried out one afternoon as they sat on a bench in Washington Square.

Delmore consoled himself with other women, among them Aileen Ward; but she found his behavior unpredictable. He once took her to see a production of *Antony and Cleopatra*, and brought along a pint of gin which he swigged during the play. As the liquor took effect, Delmore began to laugh uproariously at inappropriate moments and created a disturbance by claiming in a loud voice that one of the actors looked like FDR and that the play was an allegory of the Yalta Conference.

·

It was in 1946 that Delmore "formulated fiction as reality-testing," a principle suggested to him by Turgenev's *First Love*. Of course, his poems and stories had always been drawn almost exclusively from his own experience, but only now did he resolve to compose a work of sustained autobiographical prose. The particular "reality-testing" he had in mind involved the same subject examined in *Genesis:* his family, his childhood, and the lessons of the Jewish immigration. In a sardonic little notebook poem written during the summer of 1947, he meditated on that vanished past.

> Ellis first shadowed me, Brooklyn was where
> My body began before the First World War
>
> Drugstore, cigarstore, haberdashery
> The bread and wine turned to commodity
>
> I need that like I need—O what a trope—
> A hole in the head! My forebears like that spoke
>
> A generation sad & used at last!
> Dwindling with hopes they do not know are lost
> I read their obits in the New York Times
> And understand—too late—an age's themes.

"America! America!," a charming story about the fortunes of a typical immigrant family early in the century, was Delmore's testament to that generation. Based on his mother's involved tales of the Salomon family, who had lived next door to the Schwartzes in Washington Heights, his chronicle of the Baumanns reproduced with an exact fidelity the attitudes and habits of language that defined them. In a symposium, "On American Literature and the Younger Generation of American Jews," Delmore gave an account of how he had acquired such a sensitive ear for their speech.

> To be the child of immigrants from East Europe is in itself a special kind of experience; and an important one to an author. He has heard two languages through childhood, the one spoken with ease in the streets and at school, but spoken poorly at home. Students of speech have explained certain kinds of mispronunciation in terms of this double experience of language. To an author, and especially to a poet, it may give a heightened sensitivity to language, a sense of idiom, and a sense of how much expresses itself through colloquialism. But it also produces in some a fear of mispronunciation; a hesitation in speech; and a sharpened focus upon the characters of the parents.

For the Baumanns, as for Delmore's parents, America was a source of wonder, "a subject much loved by all the foreign-born." As their own fortunes declined, and their children failed to become "millionaires, rabbis, or philosophers like Bergson," they were left to their dreams of a future prosperity announced in the newspapers read aloud at the dining-room table. Drinking tea from a tall glass, Mr. Baumann was the very type of the Jewish immigrant businessman, garrulous, enthusiastic, at once provincial and shrewd. Shenandoah, impressed by his mother's inexhaustible commentaries and disturbed by the "self-contempt and ignorance" that compel him to repudiate his past, ends up lamenting his own lack of irony. In the familiar cadence that closed so many of his stories, Delmore echoed the bitter wisdom of the young man, "a creature driven and derided by vanity," in Joyce's "Araby": "No one truly exists in the real world because no one knows all that he is to other human beings, all that they say behind his back, and all the foolishness which the future will bring him." It was as if his self-consciousness had come to seem a betrayal of the authentic cultural identity of his parents, innocent of a world from which they would always live apart.

It was this milieu that had produced his own generation —"the class of 1930," as he called it—and Delmore discerned in the Goodman circle the characteristic features of those years. Throughout the mid-1940's, he worked on a full-length novel about Goodman and his friends, and about his own life in the thirties—in particular his courtship with Gertrude. This novel ran to some four hundred pages before it was finally abandoned; the story published under the title "The World Is a Wedding" forms only a chapter of it.

The World Is a Wedding, like all of Delmore's books, appeared only after considerable delays. Originally promised for 1945, it had gone through many drafts by the time it appeared three years later; the title story itself wasn't begun until after he returned to New York. Considering the confused state of Delmore's manuscripts and the many stories he was writing at once, it is remarkable that the book appeared at all. Even more remarkable is how impressive a book it was, given his conviction that he had dissipated his talent.

Where in *Genesis* Delmore had written entirely from a limited, even narcissistic point of view, depending on a remote and artificial narrative voice to chronicle the minute details of his own family's past, in the stories that made up *The World Is a Wedding* he provided a history of a whole milieu—and in doing so, produced what R. W. Flint, writing in *Commentary*, called "the definitive portrait of the Jewish middle class in New York during the Depression." Adapting the "deliberate flatness" of *Genesis* to suggest a tone of cautious, self-deprecating irony tinged with the wry inflections of Jewish immigrant speech, he depicted the doggedly intellectual, brutally contemptuous mannerisms of Paul Goodman and his friends; the self-important, unhappy *Partisan Review* crowd (in the story "New Year's Eve"), and the vain, ambitious, unworldly Baumann family of "America! America!" And when Delmore wrote of his own family, in the novella-length "The Child Is the Meaning of This Life," he brought to the subject a dispassionate, laconic style that saved him from the shrill confessions of *Genesis*.

The World Is a Wedding really constituted a portrait of

two generations: Delmore's parents and those second-generation Jews known as the New York intellectuals (many of whom could recognize themselves in these stories). And it was a brilliant self-portrait as well, for in the grotesque yearnings of the Baumanns and the cruel "family romance" enacted in "The Child Is the Meaning of This Life" Delmore could observe how "the life he breathed in was full of these lives and the age in which they had acted and suffered." His sense of the frailty of people—whom he liked to refer to as "human beings" in order to imbue them with both ordinariness and universality—is forgiving but unsparingly satirical. The fatuous remarks of Rudyard's friends, the feeble cleverness and malice indulged in at the New Year's party, and the pieties of the Baumanns tellingly reveal their flawed, self-deluded natures in portraits that confirm the "comfortless view" of human conduct Philip Rahv ascribed to Delmore.

Seymour Hart, the central figure in "The Child Is the Meaning of This Life," is a very different sort of person from the troubled intellectuals Delmore usually wrote about (which probably contributes to the story's effectiveness). A childish, limited, irresponsible idler who spends most of his time lolling about at home and fails at everything he attempts, Seymour bears a striking resemblance to Delmore's uncle Irving. Delmore never got along with his uncle, as the uncomplimentary portrait of him in this story reveals, but he had already told the story of his own life in *Genesis* and Uncle Irving supplied a convenient vehicle for examining his family from a less obviously autobiographical vantage. Besides, Irving was in his own way a victim of the same cloistered world of experience from which Delmore had fled to poetry.

It was this world that Delmore studied so resourcefully in "The Child Is the Meaning of This Life." Many of the stories related there—of the promising uncle who died young; the clashes between Seymour's sister and her husband (Delmore's parents); his other sister's marriage later in life—had been told before in *Genesis*. But in the plain, direct prose he had learned from Turgenev, Delmore could accomplish a more evocative portrait of the milieu in which he had grown up—the cramped New York apartments where his family, beset by selfishness and vanity, carried on their bitter disputes. All the same, it was not a vindictive story—except perhaps in the portrait of Delmore's mother as a hostile, grasping woman. Delmore had long ago resigned himself with sadness rather than cynicism to the spiritual and actual poverty of his family's surroundings, their lack of warmth or generosity. Shenandoah Fish dreamed of "some other world, some world of goodness; some other life; some life where the nobility we admire is lived." For Delmore, there had been only deceit and disappointment. The story of the Hart family's faded expectations—set against the background of the Depression years—was, sadly, the story of Delmore's own life. It was the capacity to write about that past with such forgiveness and grace that raised his stories from disguised confession to art.

Impressive praise adorned the jacket of *The World Is a Wedding* when it appeared in the summer of 1948. Featured were John Crowe Ransom, Mark Van Doren, Wallace Stevens, William Carlos Williams, and Hannah Arendt; Lionel Trilling had also sent in a few congratulatory sentences to New Directions which for some reason were never used. The reviewers were naturally less effusive than those who provided blurbs, but far more enthusiastic than they had been about *Genesis*. Not a single notice was hostile, and most singled out Delmore's unusual style for praise.* *Time* went so far as to compare him with Stendhal and Chekhov, acclaiming him as "among the dozen or so most accomplished young U.S. writers."

The review in *Time* raised hopes of a commercial success, and Delmore immediately began elaborate calculations: even if only 10 percent of *Time*'s three million readers read the review, and only 10 percent of those purchased

---

* It is strange that among those who have written about Delmore since his death, the harshest critics of *The World Is a Wedding* have been his former friends William Barrett and the late Philip Rahv. Barrett unfairly suggests that in all but one or two stories, Delmore "falls off into the self-complacency of the raconteur retailing anecdotes." The title story he considers "dull, unless you happen to know the people." Rahv, while judging four of the stories "superior," found "The World Is a Wedding" "excessively, even compulsively 'literary' in the pejorative sense of that term." How account for these inadequate verdicts except to speculate that the familiarity of Delmore's style obscured for them, writing a quarter of a century later, its original impact on a generation who saw in the stories the reflection of its own experience.

the book, he would sell 30,000 copies. A mere 3,500 copies had been printed—and this was double the figure for *Genesis* or *In Dreams Begin Responsibilities*; but two years later less than half the edition had been sold.

The photograph that accompanied *Time*'s review dated from the feature in *Vogue* twelve years before about America's most celebrated young poet. It was a photograph "handsome as I have never been," Delmore insisted; but when *Time* called up to arrange for a new photograph, he refused and went off to the Polo Grounds instead to watch a double-header. He was "remorseful about not having a new photograph taken which would destroy the delusions created and sustained by the old ones," but far more remorseful about the shocking metamorphosis he had suffered in just over a decade, from a somber and radiant young man to one whose face was "coarsened by drinking" —as Eileen Simpson observed him that year—and whose "gait had become more awkward with added weight."

Later on that year, a party for Dame Edith Sitwell and her brother Osbert was held at the Gotham Book Mart, and Delmore was among those in attendance. A famous group photograph published in *Life*—featuring Stephen Spender, Tennessee Williams, Gore Vidal, W. H. Auden, Randall Jarrell, Marianne Moore, and Elizabeth Bishop, among others—memorialized the event. In the photograph, Delmore sat beside Jarrell, with whom he had just been having some literary argument; and this accounted for what Delmore took to be a rather "gleeful" expression of triumph on his face. "Anyone who sees that picture may think that I am a very cheery person and wonder about the great sorrow which is one of the leading themes of my work."

One Sunday afternoon not long after *The World Is a Wedding* appeared, Delmore was sitting in the Minetta Tavern on Mac Dougal Street, alone at the end of the bar. George Schloss, who had met him the year before in the company of Milton Klonsky, stopped in for a beer and, having just read Delmore's new book with great admiration, went over to congratulate him. Delmore started to cry quietly. Schloss put his arms around him to comfort him; but Delmore, sobbing uncontrollably, was beyond any consolation. "If I could accept defeat," he had written in his journal a few years before, "then I might once more be able to *see*. If I can be patient: humility is the way and patience is the way—none other; or will I die broken-hearted, or is this the way to failure, such as most endure who had lofty hopes?"

•

Unhappy in her marriage, Elizabeth left her husband within a year, and by the summer of 1948 she and Delmore were reconciled. They lived together in a book-lined apartment with high ceilings at 75 Charles Street during the spring of 1949, while Delmore was giving a series of lectures at the New School. He had by now decided that he wanted to marry Elizabeth, and she made it clear that she had been in love with him from the start; but she was frightened by the "emotional violence" he practiced, and hesitated for months, explaining that she was "confused about her feelings." Her diffidence supplied still another source of anxiety: "I felt panicky again at the idea of E's not marrying me," Delmore noted in May. A month later, on June 10, 1949, they were married. "I got married the second time," Delmore recalled years later, "in the way that, when a murder is committed, crackpots turn up at the police station to confess the crime."

13

IN JULY, Delmore and Elizabeth drove up to Woodstock in his old beat-up Buick—which he called the "wreck of the Hesperus"—to spend the summer on the Pollet family farm with Elizabeth's father. It wasn't long before he felt the "old-new love of the country returning," and experienced "some deep change": he was able to sleep, he suffered "no nervousness & eagerness to drink after dinner," and he was no longer "so passionate to impress people." Every morning after breakfast, he would sit out on a bench in front of the farmhouse for hours with his typewriter, books, and papers. But his enthusiasm for the country distracted him from writing. "The truth is that I was not feeling very productive and could hardly have convinced myself that I was doing much work," he recalled in a story entitled "An Author's Brother-in-Law" written some years later, one of the many "reality-testing" fictions Delmore worked on during the 1950's.

Nine-year-old Sylvester, the brother-in-law in question, occupied a significant place in Delmore's life that summer. He reminded Delmore of his younger brother, Kenneth, whom he had not seen in many years, and he liked to drive Sylvester into town after dinner for sodas. Sylvester was curious about what Delmore did all day, and wanted to know how he made his living. When Delmore described himself as "self-unemployed," Sylvester suggested he might earn a respectable wage as a caddy at the local country club. "Just sitting in a beach chair in the meadow all day, and doing nothing more than reading a book, turning the pages of a magazine, and writing for a few minutes seemed so strange to Claude [Sylvester]," Delmore wrote in "An Author's Brother-in-Law"; and when a new Oscar Williams anthology arrived in the mail one day with a selection of his poems accompanied by a familiar photograph from the

Vogue era, he felt vindicated, and showed the book triumphantly to Sylvester.

But Delmore was still bitter about the commercial failure of *The World Is a Wedding*, which, like all his books, was a *succès d'estime* that didn't sell. "I had long since grown accustomed to being told by most people that they did not understand modern poetry," he explained in "An Author's Brother-in-Law," and their incomprehension was the cause of his neglect. The same conviction informed a brief essay published in *Partisan Review* that year, "Views of a Second Violinist," in which he examined the supposed "difficulty" of modern poetry. "Every modern poet would like to be direct, lucid, and immediately intelligible," he noted, but "every modern poet would also like to be successful, popular, famous, rich, cheered on Broadway, sought by Hollywood, recited on the radio, and admired by Mr. J. Donald Adams." It was the fault of Modernism, which had encouraged writers to reflect the fragmented consciousness of the twentieth century, that poetry had become obscure. These formulations were supposed to be droll and ironic, but Delmore disclosed what he really thought of his predicament when he characterized the response of contemporary poets to their situation as "one of panic, a panic which leads to false moves and desperate over-simplifications."

Some of the pieces he was writing for *Partisan Review* in the late 1940's were themselves rather oversimplified, jocular commentaries on American culture. The more defensive he became about the public's neglect of his work and his inability to earn a living, the more Delmore retreated in his critical prose to banter and whimsy. Writing in 1948 on the question "Does existentialism still exist?" he paraphrased Heidegger's formulation that we must die our own deaths as "Existentialism means that no one else can take a bath for you." And in "Views of a Second Violinist," he invented a dialogue in which the Greek poet Agathon complains of Orpheus' abstruse poetry, "This is not what the public wants."

No matter how disconsolate he was about his own prospects, Delmore's interest in baseball—"the most lucid product of American life"—never flagged. There was no trace of pose or condescension in his worship of the Giants; it was a genuinely consuming passion. When the

team was away, he would sit in his apartment listening to
games on the radio while he worked. "Now, at almost 4,
working mood & mood of contentment spoiled because
Cubs scored 5 against Giants in 7th to lead 6–2," he noted
disconsolately one afternoon. On another occasion, when
his radio broke down during a crucial game, he called up
Milton Klonsky in a panic to demand that he turn on his
radio and put it beside the telephone. "Why don't I feel the
same intensity about the writing of poems as I do when I
root for the Giants against the Dodgers?" he wondered.

.

Partisan Review, which had long since considered itself
the most accurate reflection of how America's intellectuals
saw their country and themselves, sponsored a symposium
in 1952, "Our Country and Our Culture," intended to
monitor their altered self-conception since the 1930's. In
their introductory remarks, the editors cited expressions of
earlier disenchantment by Dos Passos, Pound, and Van
Wyck Brooks, contrasting them with Edmund Wilson's
post-war encomium to the United States in *Europe Without Baedeker*. "For better or worse, most writers no longer
accept alienation as the artist's fate in America," the editors declared; "on the contrary, they want very much to be
a part of American life." It was a poignant expression of
their longing to seek accommodation, but Delmore was
hardly as sanguine as the authors of this statement.
Whether or not they "accepted" alienation, it was still a
significant concept for him, as he indicated in his reply,
which called for intellectuals to revive the "critical noncon-
formism" that had always characterized their relations with
society. Whatever changes had occurred since the thirties,
Delmore insisted, intellectuals were still a minority.

> As things are and as they are likely to be in any near
> future, the highest values of art, thought and the spirit
> are not only not supported by the majority of human
> beings nor by the dominant ways of modern society,
> but they are attacked, denied or ignored by society as
> a mass.

This conclusion had by now become so compelling to him
that he could feel none of the awakened optimism shared
by many of his contemporaries. Nevertheless, he too threw

himself into the bureaucratic work of disseminating high culture. His name was on the masthead of the Committee for Cultural Freedom, the Ford Foundation's magazine, *Perspectives*—edited by James Laughlin—and *Diogenes*, a journal published in four languages by the International Council for Philosophy and Humanistic Studies. Only in his poetry could the darker themes of the thirties still be heard.

Most of the poems Delmore produced in these years were sonnets, and not very good ones; but they revealed a great deal about his mood. Sentenced to "the nervous doubt which thought and art assure, / Causeless despair, or causeless joy alone," he could still invoke that sacred ardor which had impressed his friends when he was twenty.

> Yet from the sadness of what has not been,
> Look how there is, above unhappiness,
> A certain thing which is not meaningless;
> Phoenix affection rises again and again,
> Beyond the harm and loss wincing in us:
> A bird still chants and is magnanimous.

There was a terrible note of desolation in these poems, evocations of the "dull dim suffering, / Through ignorance and darkened hope, and hope / Risen again, and clouded over again, and dead despair." His search for "the true, the good, and the beautiful" had taught him that in America poetry "wins silence like a wall." This was the burden of Delmore's complaint, that his long apprenticeship and early success had not been properly rewarded. But no amount of esteem from others could have assuaged his discontent. "I glowed disgusted with my heart," he wrote in the late 1940's. That he had not done more, that he had squandered his talent, was the one unforgivable transgression.

Elizabeth, meanwhile, had finished a novel, *A Family Romance*, which New Directions published in 1950. It was an impressive book, simply written and yet full of vivid incidents, depicting—as the Freudian title suggests—the complicated relationships within a single family: Carl Lucas, a quick-tempered, troubled composer; his invalid wife; and their three children, Marjorie, Sally, and a young boy, Paul. The novel was in some ways autobiographical; Elizabeth also had a sister and a younger brother, and the composer may have owed some of his traits to her father, a painter who had separated from her mother when Elizabeth was six. But the experiences of Marjorie—her sexual panic, her boyfriends, the traumas of her first year away at college—form only part of the story, which is far more than a disguised memoir of adolescent Angst. The most dramatic conflict in the novel involves her father, whose incestuous passion for her older sister Sally moves toward a powerful scene of confrontation. *A Family Romance* was widely reviewed and, for the most part, well received. *Time* thought Elizabeth had achieved "a rare, fresh tone of youthful warmth and wonder," and the *Saturday Review* praised her "delicacy and perception." Only *The New Yorker*, in its "Briefly Noted" column, was dismissive.

When the summer was over, Delmore and Elizabeth returned to their apartment on Charles Street. Delmore sensed—whether justifiably or not—that the "élan of the honeymoon" had vanished; and his doubts provoked him to irrational recriminations. He liked to boast of how he had given up drinking over the summer, but now his journals were filled with exhortations about the "big project"— to control his drinking. The moments of well-being he had enjoyed in the country vanished within a few weeks of their return, leaving him more depressed than ever. "He thought of time, of the passing of time, of the years he had lived—as one might hear the news of an incurable disease."

Loitering through the afternoons, Delmore would drop in at Stewart's Cafeteria—a vestigial occupation from the thirties—where he could usually find such Village friends as Isaac Rosenfeld or Saul Bellow. He taught a course in aesthetics at N.Y.U., and for a time gave poetry lessons to a millionaire by the name of Hy Sobiloff, taking over the job from Anatole Broyard. Sobiloff had less talent than money, and Delmore felt some remorse about being paid to encourage him. When Broyard argued that Sobiloff was better than some other poets, Delmore replied: "It's like being paid by a fat woman to tell her that she is not fat and getting others to write letters to her affirming that other women are fatter than she is." But he needed the money, and once a week Sobiloff would drive down to the

Village, parking his limousine around the corner in order not to offend his tutor with ostentatious displays of wealth.

Delmore had trouble working, and squandered his days reading old magazines, attending editorial meetings at the *Partisan Review* offices, copying out long passages from books, and writing in his journal. He had taken to looking through his notebooks of the 1940's and was surprised to find them "full of interesting phrases, almost entirely free of false notes." He regretted that he had not always kept such exhaustive journals, for they enabled him to gauge his moods; moreover, given his obsession with the past, it was important that he possess a record of every significant incident in his life. "If I had kept this kind of record in 1935 & 1940, how much more material (and habitual observation) I would have at hand," he lamented. "False pride prevented me, each time I tried—and, under it, the intense ambition and doubt."

The calculations about the conduct of others that he entered so meticulously in his journals formed a part of this legacy. "HL / [Harry Levin] must have encouraged FOM / [F. O. Matthiessen] to write his book on James because RPB [Blackmur] is writing one," he noted in a characteristically intricate passage; "thus he encouraged me to write about Wilson & Brooks because he thought I would attack them." The Trillings fascinated him on account of their alleged "mannerisms" and the arrogance he felt they displayed in public; but he believed Trilling was "honest," since at least he was "aware of his motives"— even if, "like all of us, he talks too much about them." All the same, he was astonished when Trilling announced at a party that he "hated literature, and felt great hostility toward books." How could he hate literature? Delmore asked. "Because I was meant to write books, not to read them," Trilling replied.

Delmore was often withdrawn at these literary parties; distracted and self-absorbed, he tended to hold forth less than he had in the 1940's. At a cocktail party for Christopher Isherwood attended by Djuna Barnes and Auden, among others, he suffered from "nervousness and numbness"; returning from dinner with James Agee or Theodore Roethke, a party in an Eighth Street loft for Dylan Thomas, or an evening at William Phillips's house where he met the phenomenologist Maurice Merleau-Ponty,

Delmore would brood over his peculiar conduct. "Evening at Margaret Marshall's," he noted late in 1949: "the tremors increase, as predicted—terrifying nervousness and inability to listen to what was said to me by S[tephen] Spender." Literary parties seemed to him, he wrote Randall Jarrell, like "a traffic jam of the lost waiting for the ferry across the Styx."

Delmore was particularly troubled by his relationships with famous men, who "destroyed [his] literary illusions and social poise." Where he avoided meeting Eliot, he cultivated the friendship of Wallace Stevens, who had always admired his work. Replying to a warm congratulatory note from Stevens on the occasion of his marriage, Delmore urged him to visit them in New York, and they saw one another several times during the early 1950's. But Delmore worried that he had not been "brought up very well," as he confessed in a whimsical memoir about his encounters with celebrated poets; he suffered from "hero-worship" and felt awkward in their presence. Some of his embarrassment may have been exaggerated and self-punitive, for he was still capable of capturing an audience with a burst of anecdotes; but his self-consciousness was aggravated in company, especially the company of those whose approval he desired. "How many false words have I used!" he confessed in his journal, "how many false attitudes struck, pounding my chest; and then, at other times, preserving an expressionless or unmoved face; or deceptive, saying the opposite of what was expected of me because I knew it was expected."

Once Delmore actually met the poets he revered, his fear of them diminished; but toward Eliot he continued to feel a hopeless awe. During the 1950's, he dreamed about Eliot incessantly, dreams in which Eliot "made displeasing remarks," or evinced disapproval of Delmore. The more obsessed with Eliot he became, the more he circulated scandalous stories about the older poet's sex life; he was particularly suspicious of Eliot's observation, in *Thoughts after Lambeth*, that sex was "the most imperious of human desires." One excuse Delmore offered for his failure to complete the book on Eliot was that it contained revelations too scandalous to publish during the poet's lifetime, a statement which came back to haunt him in a dream where Eliot rejected a manuscript of his. This dream was involved with another about a peep show, which Delmore associated with the phrase "peeping Tom" and the supposed gossip contained in his book: "hence rejection & guilt."

"Running up and down the hills and dirt roads of sensibility," Delmore still enjoyed moments of elation and relief. Reading over *Finnegans Wake*, he found Joyce "alive as it has not been for months"; it satisfied "some deep need—beyond love of language & rhythm," and he devoted long hours to it. In a manic mood, he read back issues of *The New Yorker* which had seemed to him "dull" before. "A new period is beginning, has begun," he noted hopefully; "renunication—concentration—silence & a new kind of assimilation." Even when he was despondent, Delmore evinced a sort of laconic wit. "I feel I am being born again," he once remarked, then qualified it, "But being born is no great pleasure." "Why are most human beings living?" he wondered. "Because they're alive and have not yet died." Methodically, he disposed of other possible motives for survival.

> Fame?—most of them won't become famous
> Money?—most of them won't become rich
> Pleasure?—most of them don't have much of that!
> > Yet they're afraid to die!
> They are living because they like living and they hope, beyond ever-mounting evidence, tomorrow will be a transformation, next year will be marvellous—all evasions of the emptiness and the frustration they face at every turn.

Delmore had by no means given up hope of illuminating his past in a novel, and toward this end he produced countless drafts of stories which he could never bring to any satisfactory conclusion. As it was, he accumulated endless pages of notes, and many titles, among them a comic list of possibilities for a play he had in mind about "a colony for sexual happiness": *Violated in the Vatican, Shamed in Chicago, A Pass in El Paso*. "Dear Pope," a long poem composed in couplets, was another bizarre project that occupied him for a time. Like the earlier blank-verse "Exercises," "Dear Pope" addressed various intellectual and literary heroes, in particular Freud; but this too was abandoned after several pages (perhaps because, as Delmore himself conceded, "O Spiritual Father, Holy Pope, / I speak of matters not within my scope").

In the fall of 1949, Delmore was invited to give a series of lectures under the auspices of the prestigious Christian Gauss seminars. He spoke on Eliot, and it was obvious from the start that he was insufficiently prepared. His talk was full of abstractions about the medium of poetry that recalled the evasive tone of his book on Eliot. The format of the Gauss seminars called for discussion after a paper was read, but the audience was too perplexed to respond, and attendance fell off as the series continued.

Delmore was increasingly obsessed by Eliot's anti-Semitism, which he made a prominent subject of his lectures. Defensive about the plausibility of his contentions, he labored over his evidence, intent on proving the fantastic theories he had collected over the years. Those who challenged him were invariably told, "You couldn't know what I'm talking about because you're not a Jew." And if his interlocutor happened to be Jewish, he would insist, "You're not the right kind of Jew." As he grew more uncertain and suspicious, Delmore began to feel more

> Conscious of being a Jew
> criticized from the start
> about the motives of the heart

Judaism had always been for Delmore a significant emblem of his identity, and one he had made symbolic use of in his work, conjoining the artist and the Jew, both of whom occupied a unique, anomalous place in society. But by the 1950's the great excitement of the two previous decades, when the Jews of Delmore's generation had first acquired intellectual prominence, was fading before the complacencies of the Eisenhower era. The Trotskyites of the thirties were now professors, and "notes from underground are not customarily issued from high places," as one commentator on that period shrewdly put it. Delmore's own grievances and disappointments had their source in his stalled career, but he had depended—perhaps more than anyone else of that generation—on the radical climate of the Depression to provide the symbol of his difference. Lately, that difference had become a burden unredeemed by the ideologies of an earlier, more fervent era, when to be a Jew was to have special access to the condition of the artist in America. Now it was simply another sign of his foreign origins. He dreamed of William Empson noting a passage in *Romeo and Juliet* that "proved some character was Jewish by the way he talked."

"Conscious villainy is really rare, and this is one of the errors of paranoia, and paranoid systems, such as Orthodox Marxism," Delmore noted in his journal that spring. It was a striking observation, given his increasing tendency to detect "conscious villainy" everywhere. He complained that irate poets whose work he had rejected as poetry editor of *Partisan Review* were calling him up in the middle of the night, and got an unlisted phone number. He quarreled with Philip Rahv over editorial decisions, and early in the summer provoked a final break with William Barrett. "Dostoevsky unspoken but in the air, and madness lurking in ambush," Delmore goaded Barrett to the point where no reconciliation was possible. "I remember his eyes, always so expressive, gloating now in self-recrimination for his own evil," Barrett recalled. Delmore added Barrett to the lengthening column of "injuries and negligences," but confided in his journal: "I did the injuries first!"

．

During the summer of 1950, Delmore was invited to teach at the prestigious Kenyon College School of Letters, founded two years before by Trilling, Ransom, and Matthiessen. Under their direction, the School of Letters consistently attracted the most prominent scholars and writers in America, and that summer Delmore was joined by William Empson, Robert Lowell, Kenneth Burke, and Allen Tate, among others. Early in June, Delmore and Elizabeth prepared to leave for Ohio, only to discover at the last moment that they didn't have enough suitcases for all their belongings; in great haste, they threw their books and manuscripts into twelve cartons and rushed off to the train.

Delmore felt excluded from the rather Anglophile ambience of Kenyon, with such eminent British scholars as Empson and L. C. Knights setting the predominant intellectual tone. Where Arthur Mizener, "with his big convertible and striped polo shirts looked like an ad for the best Scotch whiskey"—recalled the novelist George Lanning, who was in residence that summer—Delmore was "shambling, sweaty, untidy." His wrinkled suits and urban pallor contrasted oddly with the physical beauty of rural Ohio; "Gambier [where Kenyon was situated] might have been an idealized village in Barsetshire," and Delmore's bohemian dishevelment struck a discordant, though not exotic note in this Trollopian setting.

Delmore taught a seminar in the short story and a lecture course on Yeats and Eliot, but spent most of his time poring over a battered copy of *Finnegans Wake*. He never prepared for class, preferring to talk randomly about baseball or the relationship between Joyce and Pogo. Informal to the point of incoherence, rising to occasional moments of eloquence, he would stand before the class nervously rolling up his sleeves, which soon unraveled as he gestured; it was part of Delmore's general dishevelment that he often wore shirts with French cuffs but never owned any cufflinks.

Delmore's suspicions about his friends were by now verging on paranoia. When the Schwartzes gave a cocktail party that summer, he unleashed a furious attack on Allen Tate for his part in awarding the 1949 Bollingen Prize to Pound. (Among the other judges were Eliot, Auden, Robert Penn Warren, and Robert Lowell.) It was a controversial issue, and Delmore would perhaps have been justified in objecting—as Irving Howe and others did in *Commentary* and *Partisan Review*—had he confined himself to the matter of Pound's politics or anti-Semitism. But he was certain that an intricate conspiracy implicating Eliot and other, more shadowy figures had cleverly manipulated the committee into giving the award to a Fascist. Lowell was at the party and tried to placate Delmore, which only fueled his agitation. When William Empson, just back from China and sporting a Mao suit, volunteered that giving the Bollingen Prize to Pound was the best thing America had ever done, Delmore turned on him and accused him of being a traitor to England because he was a Communist. The Mizeners, who lived next door, heard Delmore shouting long after the last guests had gone home.

•

Late that summer, New Directions published *Vaudeville for a Princess*, Delmore's first new collection of poetry since *In Dreams Begin Responsibilities* twelve years before. Interspersed with the poems and separated by black pages designed to suggest theatrical blackouts between acts,

Vaudeville was, with the exception of a few poems that possessed the power of his earlier work, a slight achievement. Childishly simple rhymes and awkward diction spoiled too many of the poems, while others suffered from an excess of rhetoric. The long sequence of forty sonnets that took up the last third of the book showed little, if any, advance over the sonnets Delmore had written in college. There was a certain undeniable fluency to these poems that masked their lack of substance, but Delmore's talent for eloquent abstractions lapsed at times into mere verbosity.

> Evergreen, heart forever! The head afire
> Flowing and flowering in a fountain's death
> Declares all turns and burns and yet returns,
> The breast arises from the falls of breath,
> After the burst and lapsing of desire,
> Light! Light like the deathless past remains.

And he tended to pad his iambic pentameter, which had once filled out with such apparent ease. The weary intensity Delmore had once borrowed from *Les Fleurs du mal* to such notable effect now seemed artificial.

There were, to be sure, moments of inspiration reminiscent of the passionate, eager voice heard in *In Dreams Begin Responsibilities*, poems that resonated with Delmore's invocations to the masters of world literature. In "The Masters of the Heart Touched the Unknown," he celebrated the lives of his favorite authors and, in the manner of his verse journals, "rehearsed their passions' history"; and in the much-anthologized "Starlight Like Intuition Pierced the Twelve," Delmore's most accomplished poem since the work collected in *In Dreams*, he recovered the balance between rhetorical flourishes and idiomatic speech that distinguished his verse plays. The testimonies of Christ's twelve disciples, disillusioned with themselves and intimidated by the "unspeakable unnatural goodness" of their master, lament their own failings in the melancholy voices of the ghosts in *Genesis*. "My attitudes have been misunderstood / If seen as aught but a wish for what is good," Delmore once wrote in his journal; and "Starlight Like Intuition Pierced the Twelve" embodies this same conviction, as well as its impossibility. Like the disciples faced with the example of Christ, Delmore longed to embrace the good with an urgency that resembled prayer; but always before him loomed the irrevocable evidence of his frailty. The poem's culminating lines, with their evocations of guilt and vanished hope, express—perhaps more pointedly than anything else he ever wrote—the tragedy of Delmore's life.

> Forgiveness, love, and hope possess the pit,
> And bring our endless guilt, like shadow's bars:
> No matter what we do, he stares at it!
> What pity then deny? What debt defer?
> We know he looks at us like all the stars,
> And we shall never be as once we were,
> This life will never be what once it was!

Whatever its failings, *Vaudeville* displayed Delmore's gift for inventing vivid titles. "I Wish I Had Great Knowledge or Great Art"; "How Strange to Others, Natural to Me"; "The Self Unsatisfied Runs Everywhere": in these sonnets, Delmore's characteristic gift for hitting on memorable phrases was still intact, even if too often they came to nothing.

The brief prose pieces included in the book were another matter. Vaguely imitative of Ring Lardner, they revealed how little confidence Delmore had in his own authentic voice. The self-deprecating tone of these pieces was uncongenial to his sensibility, which showed to best advantage in the grandiose, mock-epic comedy of his verse plays and the sardonic character portraits in *The World Is a Wedding*. In "The Ego Is Always at the Wheel," an account of the various cars Delmore had owned, and "The Difficulty of Divorce"—both autobiographical, although in the latter he disguised the scenario of his divorce from Gertrude by attributing the events related there to a "friend"—Delmore strove to be natural, garrulous, digressive, gay; but the special feature of his humor, a grand, incongruous, elevated diction played off against idiomatic speech, had vanished. Delmore's interpretations of *Hamlet, Othello*, and the Don Giovanni of Mozart's opera were contrived. *Hamlet* could be understood only "if we suppose that everyone is roaring drunk from the beginning to the end of the play"; Don Giovanni is said to be "a Lesbian, that is to say, someone who likes to sleep with girls"; Coleridge was "an expert on German philosophy, indecision, and laudanum"; and so on. It was a sorry departure from the calculated ironies of his early prose.

Still, Delmore was a famous man in 1950, and most reviewers were surprisingly respectful. The stern Louise Bogan, who rarely passed up an opportunity to write condescendingly about Delmore, faulted *Vaudeville* for its "banality"; but Richard Eberhart, Dudley Fitts, and other reviewers in the literary quarterlies found much to praise. Even the British critic David Daiches, who was later to publish a gratuitously brutal attack on Delmore in *English Literature* (1964), wrote a very favorable review proclaiming that he had achieved in *Vaudeville* "the extreme sophistication of the decadent music-hall."

But Delmore was beyond consolation by reviewers who had in mind his distinguished reputation, or even by the loyal Wallace Stevens, who wrote in October:

Dear Delmore:

I read your VAUDEVILLE yesterday. At first reading one gets only the interest of it and its Jean-Paul Richterishness. This morning before breakfast I read some of the poems in the last section a second time. I mean to know these better because I prefer the tone of the last half of the book to that of the first. However, to say that only the peasant desires happiness and that the evil man does evil as the dog barks overlooks the idea that the Drang nach den Gut is really not much different from the Drang nach the opposite. You are fascinated by evil. I cannot see that this fascination has anything on the fascination by good. A bird singing in the sun is the same thing as a dog barking in the dark. Again, your antithesis between evil on the one hand and thought and art on the other involves quite other ideas.

It is always true in everything you write that the way you say what you say takes hold of one as much as what you say does. I don't mean turns like November, ember, a dido that occurs, and a very agreeable dido, but the whole succession of details. The book is a collection of the values of your particular mind and of your extremely keen hand and I am happy to have it.

Sincerely yours,
Wallace Stevens

This enigmatic judgment, polite though it was, could hardly have dispelled Delmore's dissatisfaction. In the past, he had always persuasively defended his work; about *Vaudeville*, he was strangely silent. Only once, in a reply to Stevens, did he even mention it. "I'm not particularly pleased with it myself," he wrote diffidently, "now that I see it in print." He gave a copy to Anatole Broyard and pressed him for his opinion; then, as if dreading what he would say, never asked about it again.

A year later, after Delmore had once more mastered the disappointment that always followed publication, an ominous letter arrived from Karl Shapiro, the editor of *Poetry*. "We are printing an unfavorable review of *Vaudeville* in our October issue," Shapiro wrote apologetically. "I like the book very much and tried for a long time to get a favorable review; it turned out that the people I asked declined on the ground of friendship for you." Since friendship had never deterred Delmore's friends from reviewing his books in the past, it must have been obvious to him that their refusal was prompted less by a show of impartiality than by a fear of what they would have had to say.

Shapiro eventually managed to commission a review from Hugh Kenner, which he held back for months and published only at Kenner's insistence. It was a cruel piece by a critic known for arrogance and ill-tempered polemics. "The unbelievable badness of these poems is irrelevant to any criteria of technique," his review began inauspiciously, and still more vehement objurgations followed: "maudlin self-abnegation"; "Laforguian or Eliotic exacerbations without a trace of the appropriate irony"; "beery self-distrust"; "incredible banalities the poet has maneuvered himself into thinking publishable." The prose interludes read "half like scripts for a Borscht-circuit monologuist and half like high-school imitations of Thurber." "The poet feels terribly *inadequate*, that is his burden," Kenner concluded. It was a just, if destructive, estimate.

The Kenyon School of Letters reconvened in Bloomington, Indiana, during the summer of 1951, and Delmore was again invited to teach. He drove out to Indiana in June with Elizabeth and Philip Rahv, whose driving was so

hazardous that when they arrived Delmore went around
telling everyone, "Rahv drove until I was exhausted, and
then I drove." He was in a disturbed mood that summer;
he suffered from insomnia, drank Coca-Colas for breakfast, and appeared haggard before his eight o'clock class in
seventeenth-century literature. He was more indifferent
than ever to teaching, despite having such promising pupils
as Richard Howard, John Hollander, and Hilton Kramer,
and spent most of his time playing tennis or rehearsing
Eliot's "Fragment of an Agon" with Irving Howe for a
recitation that never came off. "Bored, restless, impatient,
and disorganized," as Howe recalled him that summer,
Delmore was rarely animated, although the gaiety of his
earlier years still burst forth on occasion—as it did one
night when he attended a party at the home of the re-
nowned sex researcher Alfred Kinsey, who was then living
in Bloomington. Stimulated by the various erotic treasures
on display in Kinsey's living room, Delmore went skipping
through flower beds on the way home shouting "Pistils and
stamens!"

At the end of the summer, Delmore and Elizabeth returned to New York and entered into negotiations to purchase a farmhouse they had found in rural New Jersey.
"After much careful study of the financial situation, I
came to the tentative conclusion that this is the time to
borrow money," he wrote Laughlin, "since inflation is
likely to continue and when you have to pay the money
back it will be worth less than it is now." They had raised
all but a thousand dollars of the $4,500 necessary to buy
the farmhouse, which boasted six acres of land, three bed-
rooms, a barn, "a Bartlett's pear tree, two peach trees, a
vegetable garden, a wonderful rooster," and a bathtub, "for
which I have yearned these last four years since leaving
Cambridge." He persuaded Laughlin to advance them the
remaining amount, and they gave up their apartment on
Charles Street and moved out to New Jersey early in December. It had always been Delmore's peculiar fate to feel
alien in his surroundings, but of all his many residences,
the ramshackle farmhouse in rural New Jersey to which he
was about to exile himself would come to seem the most
anomalous of all.

14

———•———

SITUATED ON A DIRT ROAD a few miles from the village of
Baptistown, New Jersey, the Schwartzes' farmhouse looked
out on a vista of fallow cornfields and chicken farms. Saul
Bellow's description of the rural New Jersey farmhouse
inhabited by Von Humboldt Fleisher offers a striking resemblance to the Schwartzes' dilapidated home: "Burdocks, thistles, dwarf oaks, cottonweed, chalky holes, and
whitish puddles everywhere. It was all pauperized. The
very bushes might have been on welfare." As for the in-
terior, it was "Greenwich Village in the fields": a random
collection of furniture acquired over the transient years or
donated by Elizabeth's mother, shelves crammed with
books, a new couch bought as a wedding present, a kerosene space heater. Confused by this unfamiliar milieu,
Delmore couldn't decide whether they were "landed gentry
or poor white trash."

No one was more incapable of leading a placid rural life
than Delmore, and once they had settled in, he became as
harried as ever. They bought another used car, a 1949
Buick, "after extorting a loan from a friend," and promptly
received a ticket for speeding. A day later, Delmore was
given a second ticket for parking on the wrong side of the
street in Manhattan, and the day after that one of the back
tires fell off as they were driving home from Princeton.

My life at present [he wrote Laughlin] consists of
an imitation of all the difficulties encountered by
Laurel & Hardy, Abbott & Costello, Hercules, John
Berryman, and anyone who was ever drafted into the
army. I must rise at 5:30, drive 33 miles with Elizabeth to Princeton's Art Museum where she is employed, waste my diminishing life and day gassing

away with the literati all day while my wife works for
our food, gasoline, and kerosene, lunch lavishly at
Princeton's most expensive restaurant at my own or
my wife's expense since the installed literati won't eat
anywhere else and think it rude of me not to go with
them, etc. At 5, I drive Elizabeth back to our country
estate and when we get home after driving over unfamiliar country roads in the dark I am so enervated
and exasperated and exacerbated by all that has occurred that I get good and drunk which makes me feel
untroubled by the fact that the pump has broken
down every other day, the windshield wiper on the car
does not work, there is no heater in the car, and I am
not in all truth a native country boy.

But when Elizabeth learned how to drive, Delmore was
lonely staying home by himself all day on the farm. "I am
going to conclude as a drunken widower," he complained,
"or I will throw myself into [Elizabeth's] grave, bearing
two bound volumes of *Partisan Review* under each arm."

Delmore's letters were more effusive than ever now that
he was so isolated. Apart from a torrent of letters to
Laughlin, he was feverishly corresponding with friends and
editors. When he learned from John Crowe Ransom that
Van Wyck Brooks had objected to his review of *New England: Indian Summer*—reprinted that year in a selection
of essays from *Kenyon Review*—he sent off a long, disturbed letter to Brooks.

> RD 1, Box 230
> Pittstown, New Jersey
> February 8, 1952

Dear Mr. Brooks:

John Crowe Ransom forwarded to me, the other
day, the note you wrote him about the error in your
[*sic*] piece about "New England: Indian Summer,"
which was reprinted in *The Kenyon Critics*. I am
sorry about the error ("sky parlors"), but glad to get
the note, since I had been thinking of writing you for
several reasons, one of them being that I had been
reading your new book, "The Confident Years," in
December, and though I had to read my borrowed

copy rapidly, I felt very strongly that I had to re-examine what I had said and written about your books.

I hesitated because I had no way of knowing if you felt any interest in any change of mind on my part. The piece to which you refer was written in 1940 and I wrote another of the same kind in *Partisan Review* (of "The World of Washington Irving") in 1944. Both pieces were written under personal circumstances which induced a bias of which I hope I am now at least in part free. And I did not know that the piece in *The Kenyon Review* was going to be reprinted, since I was ill when Mr. Ransom asked for permission and my wife was taking care of my correspondence. I have thought, however, of reprinting both pieces in a collection of criticism, but not without adding a third part in which I stated what I thought was wrong with the bias and the point of view from which the previous expressions of opinion had been written. To try to be brief as possible about what my change of mind is and some of the reasons for it: I was unaware, although I should not have been, of the extent to which Henry James and T. S. Eliot were hideous snobs in their work. I would have [been] less unaware, had I not been living in Cambridge, Massachusetts, and struggling with the unfortunate consequences of an unfortunate marriage. Since that time, I've returned to New York, moved to the country, and gotten married again, all of which has had the effect of making me see with some clarity how one-sided and distorted my own view of literature (and in particular, of the relationship of literature to life in America) had been in certain important respects. I still think that James and Eliot are great authors, but I feel now that the leading social attitudes in their work is [*sic*] vicious and destructive too often. I do not think the same is true of Joyce, however, for he seems to me to be fundamentally affirmative in a way that neither James and Eliot are. If you happened to have seen any of the criticism I've published during the past four years—particularly, my review of "Four Quartets" (the only unfavorable review) and "The Literary Dictatorship of T. S. Eliot" (in *Partisan Review* in 1949)—the nature of the change of mind will be clear to you. What I think now, in short, is that although one cannot condemn a literary work because some of its elements are reactionary and despairing, one must nevertheless recognize and evaluate the effect of those elements upon the reader, no matter how eloquent and powerful the work may be. I did not recognize that this was one of the most important things you were doing until I read "The Confident Years" and perceived how much more fruitful as a creative writer I might have been, had I not suffered from too uncritical an admiration of Eliot in particular. For personal reasons which will be obvious to you as well as for principled ones, I think, no authors more than James and Eliot would be likely to create so many feelings of self-distrust and conflict of mind in a person existing in my own social and literary situation.

I hope that I have not been too personal in making this explanation, nor too involved. Someone quoted Metternich's advice recently: "Never explain, never excuse" as [an] example of the European mentality in comparison with the American, which explained and excused all the time. So if I've explained too much, I think I can claim that it is a habit induced by environment, although I know there are other reasons.

Yours sincerely,
Delmore Schwartz

Not the least alarming feature of this weird, even mad letter was Delmore's confession that Eliot and James had induced in him "feelings of self-distrust and conflict of mind." In the past, he had always managed to scrupulously —perhaps too scrupulously—separate the political and social ideas of these two "hideous snobs" from their work. Only now did he reveal, nakedly and without immediate provocation, the depth of his bitterness about the "social and literary situation" which had made him feel as if he were a despised alien.

Van Wyck Brooks was an irrational choice of ally in Delmore's revision of his formerly tolerant attitudes. Himself the victim of a nervous breakdown during the later 1920's which had prompted him to reverse his earlier condemnation of the insularity of American literature, Brooks had by the 1950's become a proponent of the "neo-Americanism" once condemned by the editors of *Partisan Review*. Years later, in conversation with a colleague at Syracuse, Delmore recalled his correspondence with Brooks in derogatory terms: "By then he was a spook." But his ingratiating letter, with its embarrassingly personal revelations about his marriage and his mood, revealed a forlorn desire to please his elders largely absent from the letters of his youth. In a polite, reserved reply, Brooks declared his respect for Delmore's "intellectual honesty"; but Delmore's letter was less an atonement for his own "too uncritical" admiration of Eliot than a wild polemic against certain dimly perceived social forces which he was convinced had conspired to destroy him. Not long afterward, he regretted the "stupidity of letter to Brooks, written at height of mania when anxiety was intense."

Delmore's bitterness about the fate of being a poet and a Jew had, like so many of his complaints, some justification in actual experience. The Harvard faculty of the 1940's and the Princeton English professors whom Irving Howe once described as "buckshoe humanists" echoed, however faintly, the mandarin haughtiness of Eliot and James. To this sense of exclusion had been added Delmore's poverty through the years, the constant struggle to earn a living as a writer—which in fact he managed with more success than many. But the promise of affluence held out to him in youth and then denied only served to exacerbate a condition that might otherwise have been accepted as simply the unhappy lot of most American writers. Delmore's grandiose—and, it should be said, typically American—vision of success could no longer be achieved through literature alone; his "Thirty Years' War with the Almighty Dollar" waged on one front what his poetry waged on another: the wish to establish a secure identity in a society which failed to recognize the importance of poetry. "Delmore and Humboldt," Anatole Broyard wrote in a review of Bellow's novel, "spent their lives searching for a philosopher's stone which would magically make their 'madness' pay off in celebrity and hard cash." The "hard cash" was a later object of Delmore's ambition, which began as a desire to serve poetry alone; only when he could no longer write did he adulterate his dream, turning from the Muse he had courted with such ardor to the more common pursuit of capital and academic respectability.

It was not in Delmore's nature to be subdued or docile, and as late as 1951, in an essay entitled "The Vocation of the Poet in the Modern World," he was still proclaiming the heroic character of the poet's role in rejecting "the seductions of mass culture and middle-brow culture." Joyce, as always, was his model for the artist in the modern world. Why had Joyce chosen Bloom, an Irish Jew, to be the protagonist of *Ulysses*? Because the Jew "is an exile from his own country and an exile even from himself," Delmore claimed, "yet he survives the annihilating fury of history." In a ringing declaration that could serve as the slogan of Modernism, he concluded:

In the unpredictable and fearful future that awaits civilization, the poet must be prepared to be alienated and indestructible. He must dedicate himself to poetry, although no one else seems likely to read what he writes; and he must be indestructible as a poet until he is destroyed as a human being. In the modern world, poetry is alienated; it will remain indestructible as long as the faith and love of each poet in his vocation survives.

Unlike Eliot's celebrated call for the "extinction of personality," Delmore's far more ominous injunction that the poet would have to be "destroyed as a human being" in the service of his art was the disastrous culmination of an idea that could be said to have originated with his early hero Rimbaud: that poetry was at once the sole agent of truth and the means by which the poet sacrificed himself in its pursuit. In the later suicides of his contemporaries John Berryman and Randall Jarrell—as well as those of Anne Sexton and Sylvia Plath—the power of this idea is manifest. One myth widely credited in A. Alvarez's book on suicide and literature, *The Savage God*, in *Humboldt's Gift*, and in Berryman's *Dream Songs* has been that the indifference of America is to be held accountable for these poets' deaths; it is a myth that has given Delmore's tragic life a spurious symbolic value for which he was himself in part responsible. But that he also knew the waste and futility of that myth is evident from the consolation he took in his art. Writing was therapeutic, "a way of working off anxiety." "The way to solve one's emotional problems is to sit at the typewriter and solve them," he once wrote in his journal. And it was more; poetry animated the past, imbued it with form and a new, higher reality. For Delmore, the religion of art differed from the more orthodox variants espoused by Baudelaire, Rimbaud, and the neo-Thomists who had such a considerable influence over him in one crucial respect: where for them art promised escape from the world, for Delmore it promised salvation in this world —the world as it was, and as he wrote about it. His aspiration was to transmute the ordinary into something luminous and enduring, and only when he could no longer write did he begin the long descent into madness that culminated in his death.

•

Delmore had just turned thirty-eight when he moved to New Jersey, but he looked a good deal older. Still a handsome, commanding figure, he was also heavier and more unkempt. Fatigue had formed pools of shadow under his eyes. For fifteen years now, his body had suffered the assault of barbiturates and amphetamines, as well as massive doses of alcohol. His dependence on Nembutal and Seconal was so great that when he learned Dr. Gruenthal was leaving for Europe, he wrote in a panic requesting prescriptions to tide him over during the doctor's absence.

Delmore's intake of Dexedrine, which he resorted to when he was depressed or to countermand the effect of sleeping pills, was even more alarming. By the 1950's, his incessant recourse to amphetamines had produced a tolerance that called for ever larger doses, and there were days when he took as many as twenty Dexedrine pills, swallowing them like candy. Since prolonged abuse of Dexedrine tends to cause depression and fatigue—while, in Delmore's case, exacerbating insomnia—he found it more and more difficult to extricate himself from the cycle of moods which had afflicted him since childhood. And his manic periods were intensified by this immense consumption of amphetamines; hyperactivity and compulsive talking were not simply character traits, as Delmore's memoirists have supposed, but symptoms at least in part induced by his depen-

dence on Dexedrine. Moreover, the notorious paranoia
that dominated his last years was aggravated—and could
even have been induced—by amphetamines. His violent
rages and suspiciousness conform to the pattern of what is
known as amphetamine psychosis, which leads naturally to
the supposition that his madness may well have been less
divine or poetic than pharmacological. In any event, he
was aware of his self-devastation: "How many years have I
shortened my life / By barbiturates and alcohol?"

Despite this somber prognosis, Delmore eagerly awaited
the moments of release from his depression, anticipating
the manic phase that was sure to follow. Then, in February, only a few weeks after the move to New Jersey, he
received a letter from Laughlin inviting him to serve as a
"confidential literary consultant" to *Perspectives*, a guest
editor of some future issue—with a budget of $2,500—and
a reader of manuscripts for New Directions at a salary of
one hundred dollars a month. Delmore lost no time in
exploiting these options. At last he could exercise his en-
trepreneurial genius. Long advisory letters flowed from his
typewriter, interrupted by extensive commentaries on his
struggles with broken plumbing and the kerosene space
heater. Why not a piece by Meyer Schapiro on Van Gogh?
he urged. "Van Gogh is a best seller in department stores,
so maybe even the Ford Trustees will have heard of him."
Edmund Wilson, Sartre, Cyril Connolly, and the German
critic E. R. Curtius were other possibilities. Delmore loved
to engage in this sort of speculation on the literary stock
market, trading in reputations and ideas. After all, if the
famous educator Robert Hutchins—whom Delmore called
"the wonder boy emeritus"—could use "the whole of
American culture as a farm system of minor league clubs,"
why shouldn't Delmore be in on the act? But it was important not to become overexcited by their success, he
warned, invoking Napoleon: "It was when he was most
victorious that he made the errors which brought him in the
end to Waterloo."

One of Delmore's responsibilities was to provide syn-
opses of important articles published in the literary journals. It was not very rewarding work, and he knew that
Laughlin had accepted his proposal of this thankless chore
only out of charity; but he threw himself into the project
with enthusiasm, summarizing hundreds of articles in brief

paragraphs. In a manic letter, he supplied some comical samples.

> *Hudson Review*—Fall 1949:
> Yvor Winters asserts that Howard Baker's "Ode Against Indolence" and J. V. Cunningham's "Stanzas Written in a Time of Avid Adultery and Constant Copulation" are the greatest lyrics in English since Milton's "Lycidas," qualifying his claim, however, by saying that if anyone other than Mr. Baker and Mr. Cunningham agreed with him, he would have to reconsider his opinion.

For all their energetic wit, there was a suggestion of near-hysteria in these letters, as if the fluent discourses on baseball and the many crises that beset him in the countryside were embarrassing even to their author. "If I sound a trifle frantic in tone and wild and far-fetched in making associations," one of his letters ended, "it's partly because I read too much in *Finnegans Wake* last year." Alarmed by the desperation his letters revealed, he promised, "I will calm down as soon as I don't have to move around so much."

.

"Really, apart from a few months in 1949, I have not been a practicing poet," Delmore admitted in the summer of 1952. He had become an impresario of journals and committees, and now received a salary of $550 a month from Intercultural Publications and a further $200 for serving as a consultant to *Diogenes*. Even so, he was by no means well off, and complained to the publisher Roger Straus, "What perplexes me most of all about trying to do these things is how it happens that I am asked to do so many things and paid so little"; he wondered if he represented "some sort of bargain rate." What perplexed him even more was how he had managed to so entangle himself in worldly affairs at the expense of his work. He had a reputation, an advance of long standing for Schocken for a novel, sincere expressions of interest in whatever he wrote from Roger Straus—who had recently founded his own publishing house—and opportunities to publish everywhere. But he now found himself in a position where he no longer had time to write, and couldn't even bring himself to produce a legible typescript for John Crowe Ransom, who had accepted a short story of his for publication in *Kenyon*. Straus was baffled by the incoherent mass of pages Delmore submitted from his novel, *A Child's Universal History*. "I was neither surprised nor discouraged to hear that my manuscript left you bewildered," Delmore replied, offering as an excuse that his filing cabinet had not yet been put in order.

One day a week he drove into New York and rushed about to various offices, performing his editorial chores ineffectively and in great haste. From *Partisan Review*, he would hurry to the Pierre Hotel, where *Perspectives* had its office, but he never felt comfortable in those elegant surroundings. "The elevator boys seem to think that I am an agent of the Mafia, bringing opium to the real patrons." More often than not, he would leave after an hour in the company of Hayden Carruth, who was also working for *Perspectives*, and go off to some dark, lavish, empty bar on Madison Avenue.

> He still looked rather boyish [Carruth recalled] like that old photograph in the Oscar Williams' anthologies, but his features were somehow softened, hazy, blurred, and his voice was so quiet that I had to bend my head to hear him. I had the impression of great sadness and sweetness. It was as if he was lost and knew he was lost, and had given up caring about it. The exhilarated spirit his older friends remember was never apparent to me, but rather a quietness and a desire to cling to little things—little actions and objects—as if from a simple attachment to littleness for its own sake. He looked and spoke like a defeated shipping-house clerk.

Between his harried visits to New York, Delmore tried unsuccessfully to work at his fiction or watched television at the local tavern. "The dramas on TV have an effect hitherto unknown in any literature or art," he wrote Laughlin. "Their representation of existence makes existence appear to be so awful, banal, vulgar, and pointless that the 'viewer' returns to his own life with a feeling of escape." But he found his own life just as intolerable. Tortured by self-doubt, he recalled how "very promising" his first book had been, and acknowledged to himself that many people thought "In Dreams Begin Responsibilities" his only masterpiece. What had happened?

> *Either* it is true that I am not good—not first rate *or* I am unread because of having turned to the theme of the Jew after my first book
> or read and not liked because the fashion has been different or / and / having alienated the poet / critics —Tate—Winters?—Blackmur?—Auden & alienated J. Laughlin?—and been abused by Philip Rahv—or have left too much time between books

As he sat among the clutter of books and papers in his room far from New York, tallying up favorable and unfavorable reviews and recalling his friends' opinions of his various books—Delmore had an infallible memory for this sort of information—he thought longingly of his early fame, and how little it had come to. "This is the heart (or something important) of my mind," he noted; "the fascination with what the past was (the perception, looking back) the pathos of 'Had I but known.' "

·

Delmore had not seen his brother since 1938, when Kenneth left for California, and had completely lost touch with him over the last few years. In the summer of 1952, Kenneth came East to take a temporary job as an engineer in Trenton, and brought his three children with him. They stayed at the farm all summer, while Delmore sat up in his room typing day and night. When Kenneth came over from Trenton, he and Delmore would sit out on the porch drinking martinis and reminiscing. On the first night of their reunion, they stayed up all night talking about their mother, and Kenneth described how she had come out to California and tried to break up his marriage by criticizing his wife and children. She complained tirelessly about her poverty and arthritis, and was convinced she had some fatal disease. Delmore was relieved to find that Kenneth shared his hostility toward their mother, and as the two brothers compared their grievances, he began to sense the justice of his hatred. It was an "electrifying moment."

That summer Delmore's beloved grandmother Hannah

died at the age of eighty-eight. Born "in the same decade as Whitehead and Yeats," Delmore noted with his unusual enthusiasm for literary parallels, Hannah had "a better heart and a superior mind."

> In my most euphoric moments (which become more and more infrequent) [he wrote Laughlin] I suffer from the delusion that if I live long enough I may be half as good as she was at 50. She was the only woman I ever loved (don't repeat this) except for Elizabeth who is probably largely a disguise or substitute for her.

He was so remote from his family that he only learned of her death four days after the funeral.

In the fall of 1952, Delmore took over the creative-writing program at Princeton while Blackmur was away in the Middle East as a Fulbright lecturer. It was a position he had long coveted, and he was glad to have the salary of $4,500, but teaching now had to be added to his burden of obligations. Besides, Princeton was even more uncongenial to Delmore's temperament than Harvard had been. He felt ill at ease among the academics who set the tone there, and suspected them of regarding him with a mistrust reserved for bohemians, while he in turn felt both envy and contempt for their staid lives and tenured professorships.

Delmore exaggerated the degree of his estrangement from the Princeton community, for it was to the 1950's what Harvard had been to the 1940's, a place where eminent American writers gathered. Edmund Wilson, Ralph Ellison, R. W. B. Lewis, John Berryman, and Randall Jarrell were in residence there, along with Saul Bellow, whom Delmore had brought in to serve as his assistant during Blackmur's absence. It was a "real society," recalled Monroe Engel, then a graduate student at Princeton, "not without its real sillinesses and its troubles, but offering a lot of amiable talking, drinking, and other amusements, and occasionally some pretty aggressive moments of education." Delmore was himself practiced in this sort of aggression, and found the hard-drinking Princeton crowd not so very different from the *Partisan Review* crowd of a decade earlier. Blackmur in particular was a contentious debater who could hold his own in argument with Delmore—except on

one occasion, when Delmore ended a loud discussion
about the merits of socialism by pushing him into the
fireplace. On another evening, Delmore greeted the composer Edward T. Cone at a party by threatening to "knock
his block off"; and after a Gauss lecture by Paul Tillich in
which he mentioned Aristotle, Delmore went up to him
and belligerently announced, "Listen, I've been studying
Aristotle since I was a child—nobody can tell me anything
about Aristotle."

Bellow was Delmore's closest friend at Princeton, and
perhaps the only one of his contemporaries for whom
Delmore had unequivocal respect. He wrote an effusive
review of *The Adventures of Augie March*, ranking it
above *The Adventures of Huckleberry Finn* and *U.S.A.*;
and in warm letters to Bellow he reiterated his praise, both
of that book and of *Seize the Day*—which he referred to as
Caesar's Day. Princeton was "a sanctuary, a zoo, a spa"—
as Bellow described it in *Humboldt's Gift*—where "drinking, boredom, small talk, and ass-kissing" were the only
activities that mattered. In this dreary landscape, Delmore
saw himself and Bellow as "blood brothers," intellectuals,
writers, Jews, banded together in academic exile.

A significant topic in the fall of 1952 was the candidacy
of Adlai Stevenson, whose urbane intelligence appealed to
many writers and academics. Delmore was convinced that
Stevenson's election would pave the way to power for intellectuals, and that he himself would be among the first to
benefit. Responding to the question "What groups might be
interested in knowing about your book?" on a New Directions questionnaire, Delmore noted: "I was told that Adlai
Stevenson said to a reporter during the campaign that he
was particularly interested in my work as a poet, story-
teller, and critic." He took to signing all his letters "Long
Live Adlai!" and produced improbable commentaries on
American politics.

> . . . it does seem as if we may be living through the
> last days of the Great Republic [he wrote Laughlin]
> for if Eisenhower is the megalomaniac some say he is,
> it will be Julius Caesar all over again, and even if
> Thomas E. Dewey plays Brutus and assassinates him,
> and tries to take power himself, one of Eisenhower's
> nephews, Octavius Augustus Eisenhower (now a stu-

dent of Blackmur's at Princeton) will win out after Dewey falls madly in love with Lana (Cleopatra) Turner (Topping!).

Delmore's enthusiasm was echoed by his friends. One night at a dinner party given by the Schwartzes, everyone was shouting tumultuous praise of Stevenson to the accompaniment of Dwight Macdonald banging a chair on the floor. "I don't want Stevenson to be President," Berryman shouted, "I want him to be King." When Stevenson lost by a landslide, Delmore was inconsolable.

•

It was Delmore's unhappy fate to be at once iconoclastic, irascible, egalitarian, and to find himself yearning for acceptance from the very society he so vociferously criticized. Where men like Trilling and Harry Levin could accommodate themselves to academic life, Delmore lacked a certain social grace. He had no patience with manners or polite conversation, perhaps because these things bewildered him; and so he flaunted a bellicose bohemianism in their presence. Behind this pose, however, lay a genuinely democratic spirit and a spontaneous affinity with popular culture. In this, he was the opposite of Trilling, who cultivated a deliberately mandarin voice in his criticism. Their differences made them incompatible socially, but it was not until some years after the publication of Trilling's essay "Manners, Morals, and the Novel" in 1948 that Delmore decided to challenge him in public. "The Duchess's Red Shoes,"* a controversial two-part article published in *Partisan Review* during 1953, constituted his answer to Trilling's critique of the "liberal imagination."

Trilling's essay was a measured, intelligent discussion of the novel in its relation to society, a relation which he found the American novel to have been deficient in exploring. Trilling defined manners, in a well-known phrase, as "a culture's hum and buzz of implication," the often indistinct values and ideas which articulate the character of society. Money, snobbery, "the shifting and conflict of so-

---

* The title refers to an episode in Proust's novel where the Duchesse de Guermantes responds to Swann's announcement that he is dying with a callous deliberation over what shoes to wear that evening.

cial classes" were the true subjects of the novel, Trilling argued, and it was through the revelation of manners that the novelist penetrated the social world. He faulted American novelists for their naïveté—by which he meant they had no "interest in society"—and lamented the absence in their work of a trait he described as "moral realism." Since they lacked an imaginative idea of how society really worked, it followed that they were incapable of illuminating what he referred to variously as "moral passions" and the "moral imagination," those arbiters of conduct which rule the life of society.

These formulations were all rather general, and their subsequent influence derives perhaps more from their authoritative tone than from their substance, for which there exist numerous literary precedents (such as Madame de Staël's *De la littérature* or Lukács' notion of "critical realism"); and it was just this tone of "suavity and fluency" that Delmore found objectionable. Trilling, he noted, was perhaps overly "sensitive to all points of view, so conscious [was he] of others and opposition, so active and ingenious at formulating his own view in such a way that it does not seem to disturb but rather to accommodate and assimilate itself to other points of view." Moreover, "society" in Trilling's definition implied "high" or "polite" society, Delmore claimed, calling attention to Trilling's solemn concentration on the themes of money and snobbery. What Delmore found most oppressive was Trilling's exclusive concern with "the ideas and attitudes and interests of the educated class, such as it is and such as it may become: it is of this class that he is, at heart, the guardian and the critic." This was the essence of Delmore's critique, and no more shrewd summation has ever been made of Trilling's particular bias.

Unfortunately, Delmore's critical intelligence, which had always possessed the fine edge of malice that enlivens literary criticism, was in this instance laden with a hostility only thinly disguised by the heavy-handed jocularity that had lately crept into his writing. "Good manners are very pleasant and literary criticism is often very inneresting [*sic*]," his essay began, and the anecdotal digressions that followed further detracted from the gravity of his argument. The second part of his essay, which dealt with a letter published in *Partisan Review* by the critic John Aldridge expatiating on Trilling's concept of "manners," was even more mocking in tone; but it must be said that Aldridge's fatuous remarks deserved the dismissive treatment they received at Delmore's hands.*

Delmore notified Trilling in advance that his article was to appear, and invited him to publish a reply. Trilling promised to respond with "reciprocal aggressiveness" (it is a pity that he never did), which in turn provoked Delmore to draft an ill-tempered, even paranoid letter denouncing Trilling's "tendency to police comments on [his] work." Other, more unpleasant allegations followed, involving quarrels difficult to sort out in the absence of Trilling's side of the correspondence; gossip, rumors, innuendo, "bad faith," and the loyalties of *Partisan*'s other editors were among the topics of debate.

> Finally [Delmore's letter ended], and to omit several other points of fact in a letter already too long, your letter sounds as if you felt entirely justified in your actions. Perhaps you were; but surely you will not think me entirely guilty of "hostility" if I say that your actions, justified or justifiable, may—or seem to my inspection—to have had unfortunate consequences in the recent past & present, consequences unfortunate not only to you personally but to the values which I presume you are interested in furthering. For there is not only an obsession with goodness and probity in your work, but there is also an emphasis upon "inner motives," moral propriety, and nobility which is badly affected when such stories get about.

•

Delmore's absorption in his own suffering and his struggle to be "good"—a word he often used—required him to

---

* In his communication to *Partisan Review*, "Manners and Values" (May 1952), Aldridge displayed the very sort of mandarin snobbishness Delmore objected to in Trilling. The failure of the American novel, Aldridge asserted, was to be attributed to "a loss of our sense of social class." Only Faulkner, Marquand, and Robert Penn Warren were writing novels of importance now, he went on, and those three only because of "the good fortune of birth and cultural heritage which made one of them a New Englander and the other two Southerners." There were no "manners" anywhere else; the rest of the country was "a sort of infinite Midwest." It is not hard to see how Delmore would have become impatient with such gross deference to the idea of literature as an exclusively aristocratic province.

draw others into its web. Only by goading those closest to him to relinquish their affection could he verify its existence—and in the course of validating his relationships by means of strenuous and impossible accusations, he often forfeited them. "Soon he succeeded in putting everyone in the wrong, the one art learned from his mother," he noted in his journal. More than ever, he felt betrayed on all sides. When Robert Macgregor, an editor at New Directions, rebuked him for not coming to the office for weeks at a time, Delmore replied with a three-page letter of refutation. The fact was that he had been neglecting his responsibilities there, and he was aware that Laughlin had offered him the job to subsidize "an old friend and aid a New Directions author and his wife, also a New Directions author." But to lose the $25 a week he was paid for reading manuscripts would mean having "to go to the bank and borrow money in order to pay my bills, something which I have had to do twice during the fall." Delmore insisted that the "dominant cause" of his rages was poverty, forgetting the moods of suspicion and frustration that had provoked him to violent tantrums ever since adolescence. Elizabeth was more patient and forgiving than Gertrude had been, but her initial resistance to marrying him caused Delmore to wonder if, like Gertrude, she "did not love him enough"; and when she tried to convince him that she did, he complained to Dr. Gruenthal that she was "a very clever liar."

Delmore continued to see Dr. Gruenthal during the years in Baptistown, but he tended to break off treatment whenever he was discouraged. There were times when the psychiatrist himself acknowledged that "little or nothing could be done," although he seemed to hold out hope for Delmore's eventual recovery. In keeping with the Freudian eclecticism Dr. Gruenthal proclaimed as his method, he agreed to take on Elizabeth as a patient, hoping to mediate between them. Elizabeth had problems of her own, and confided to Dr. Gruenthal that she had hoped to acquire confidence in herself by marrying an established literary figure. But it was becoming evident that, far from providing her with emotional support, Delmore had virtually exhausted her patience.

His gathering fury erupted in an ugly scene at one of the Blackmurs' Christmas parties, when he accused Elizabeth of flirting with Ralph Ellison, who had offered to light her cigarette. Delmore grabbed her by the arm and hustled her into another room, where he began a loud harangue audible to the embarrassed guests. On another occasion, Elizabeth insisted on driving home from a party because Delmore was drunk, and got out of the car when he refused. Delmore drove off alone, then decided to return for her, but couldn't find his way back and ended up in Princeton, where the police arrested him for drunken driving. Blackmur arrived at the station to bail him out and found Delmore shouting, "Punish me, I'm guilty!"

.

In the spring of 1953, Delmore's fortunes momentarily improved; he was invited to teach at the American School in Salzburg (an offer he turned down because he hated to travel) and awarded a grant of one thousand dollars by the National Institute of Arts and Letters which, "coming at a time of much stress and strains," he wrote in a letter of acknowledgment, was "like a benediction." Delmore, the citation read, had been "perhaps the first to formulate poetically the consciousness of his own generation in America." But he was by this time beyond such consolations, and had in mind a bizarre scheme by which he hoped to obtain what he coveted more than literary honors: the security of a tenured professorship at Princeton. "You know how much I want, after thirteen years, to have the feeling that I belong in and to a university," he wrote Carlos Baker, the chairman of the English Department; and toward this end he applied the genius for intricate plots bequeathed him by his mother.

The extraordinary story of Delmore's bid for a professorship at Princeton has been told in *Humboldt's Gift* substantially as it occurred, apart from a few fictional embellishments. "*Saul Bellow* (primed by *Carlos Baker*) visited me yesterday," Delmore reported to Laughlin in April, "to tell me that Princeton through the good offices of *Carlos Baker* and *Lawrence Thompson* [the biographer of Robert Frost] and *Dean Brown* wants me as a permanent resident lecturer. I really want the job very much. Can you help? Don't you think I ought to get the offer in writing as soon as possible?!" Here Delmore had conveniently reversed the sequence of events, for it had been he who "primed" Bellow to serve as his emissary to Baker. Bellow's novel pro-

vides a vivid chronicle of this mad, inventive plot. Stalking
about his decaying rural manor, drinking gin straight from
a jam jar, expounding on "machinery, luxury, command,
capitalism, technology, Mammon, Orpheus and poetry, the
riches of the human heart, American civilization," Delmore unveiled his curious plan. Once he had tenure, he
calculated, he could ask the Ford Foundation to underwrite
a chair in the English Department—Delmore to be the first
appointee. "Since one of the purposes of the Ford Foundation is to *spend* rather than to *make* money," he wrote
Laughlin, "I can't imagine that there would be any objection on the Foundation's part or any difficulty for you whatever." A week later he announced triumphantly: "As a
result of deliberations in which everyone was consulted except the College of Cardinals, the Board of Health, and
Oscar Williams, Princeton has decided that I would be a
valuable addition to the faculty."

"Brilliant, haughty, neurotic, valetudinarian, much given
to enormous tears that streaked his cheeks until flicked
away by long and delicate fingers on which the nails had
been chewed to the quick"—in Baker's description—Delmore made impossible demands on the department, implor-
ing, wheedling, cajoling. The appointment he envisaged
would be "the equivalent of being a don in an English
university," the conditions to be tenure and a salary of five
thousand dollars a year—"to be increased *only* in terms of
the cost of living as it applies to the entire university," he
added magnanimously. Once Baker had endorsed this bizarre proposal—and the surprising thing is that he did—it
was only a matter of prevailing upon Robert Hutchins,
then the powerful associate director of the Ford Foundation, to provide the funds for Delmore's chair. In his impatience, he called up Hutchins in Pasadena to discuss the
matter, but found him "not at all optimistic," despite Delmore's recital of such precedents as the support given R. P.
Blackmur and I. A. Richards by the Rockefeller Foundation. If only Delmore could see Hutchins in person! He
offered to go out to Pasadena, or meet him in Chicago, so
that they could talk it over.

A week later, he followed up their conversation with a
letter.

What has happened so far may amuse you as a
veteran of the academic life. After a brief talk with

the chairman of the English department, I wrote to
Jay [Laughlin] asking him if he and you could help
me, and assuming quite wrongly that help would be
understood as financial support. Probably my own
warped view of academic propriety, protocol, and indirection made me think that it would be coarse to
specify help as money, and my understanding was
magnified by my notion of the largesse of founda-
tions; while Jay for his part apparently assumed that
help meant a letter of recommendation. On the basis
of this double misunderstanding, everything went
forward at Princeton: my character, competence,
heterosexuality, and the like were submitted to the
labyrinthine gauntlet with which you must be very
familiar, and I emerged as entirely acceptable to the
full professors, the deans, and the President, and finally as the delighted object of much unofficial con-
gratulation. Since all my experience and all that I was
told made me suppose that the truly difficult obstacle
was Princeton itself, Jay's message naturally left me
with the feeling that I might suddenly turn out to be a
new Captain Cook or a 1953 species of confidence
man.

This letter was so inappropriate, so painfully self-effacing,
so deluded, and so lacking in self-assurance about his
"heterosexuality," among other things, that one wonders
what Hutchins thought of it. That Baker had encouraged
the proposal was remarkable enough, but Delmore's failure
to comprehend the remote and magisterial workings of the
Ford Foundation testifies to his capacity for naïveté and
self-deception—and to his infinite faith in the efficacy of
schemes. When word reached him through Laughlin that
"a firm, negative answer" had come down from Hutchins,
Delmore reported the verdict to Baker in "extreme aston-
ishment and dismay": "I can't be certain as to precisely
what went wrong, since all communication has been at one
remove since I was given the green light in March, before
coming to see you, when my only anxiety—which, as you
remember, was considerable—was Princeton's willingness
to accept the arrangement which had been proposed." As
far as he could tell, "the mysterious internal workings of a
new foundation" were responsible for what had happened.
Disappointed but undaunted, Delmore looked elsewhere

for an academic appointment. Arthur Mizener mentioned the possibility of a job at Cornell, and the chairman of the English Department at Rutgers wrote inviting him to teach there. He also had in mind Brandeis, N.Y.U., Columbia, and the New School, but nothing came of them, and the summer of 1953 found him nervously computing his earnings over the past few years. For the current year, there was an advance from Schocken, another from Holt, $1,800 from Laughlin; all in all, he could count on $3,225 in 1953. He tried to get work as a book reviewer for *Time*, and they were at first "fairly hopeful of being able to offer [him] a regular reviewing job," a possibility Delmore frantically pursued, calling up daily and dropping in at their offices whenever he was in New York; but the result was, to echo *The Waste Land*, "Nothing again nothing."

For all the complaints about not writing Delmore registered almost daily in his journal, he had not lost his talent for literary journalism. During the 1950's he contributed a competent, scholarly introduction to the Modern Library edition of Turgenev's *Fathers and Sons*, and he regularly turned out essays and reviews of the highest order for *Partisan Review*, *The New Republic*, and *The New York Times Book Review*. His front-page review in the *Times* of Jarrell's first collection of essays, *Poetry and the Age*, remains one of the most perceptive critiques ever written of Jarrell's pious attitude toward literature. No one had more reverence for poetry than Delmore, but he possessed a more sophisticated conception of its relation to society than did Jarrell, for whom poetry was "one of the most important things in the world, as it should be," but for whom it was too often "the *most* important thing in the world, which is surely too close to poetry as the *only* important thing in the world." Just as, some years before, he had taken issue with the "thinness and abstractness of texture and reference" that vitiated Jarrell's poetry, Delmore now found him guilty of a sort of willful innocence in his prose, which occupied itself too exclusively with the question "How can any human being in his right mind disregard the power and the glory of poetry?"

The distinguishing feature of Delmore's criticism, even in his later years, was an ease of generality and an attention to the values of literature. "One cannot be a poet and a critic without being a human being to whom nothing is alien and to whom every human being is in some degree a matter of response and responsibility," he observed in the course of a review of Tate's *The Forlorn Demon: Didactic and Critical Essays*. Delmore himself never relinquished this trait of curiosity and openness to experience, which operated in him long after he had ceased to believe in his powers as a poet.

The stories Delmore was publishing during the 1950's had little in common with *The World Is a Wedding*. "The Fabulous Twenty-Dollar Bill," which John Crowe Ransom accepted for *Kenyon*, was a parody of academia in the manner of Mary McCarthy's *Groves of Academe* and Jarrell's *Pictures from an Institution*, in which a nervous professor who bore an obvious resemblance to Delmore was called upon to entertain a visiting Italian writer. To be sure, Professor Robbins, who drinks too much, trusts no one, is full of self-doubt, and "conscious and not spontaneous too often in dealing with his students and his colleagues," is a character out of Delmore's gallery of self-portraits, while the dialogue has that deliberately simplified, self-conscious tone adopted by the hapless intellectuals of *The World Is a Wedding*. But the story's bland irony seemed peculiarly in conformance with the "tranquilized fifties," and lacked the subversive edge that had given clarity to his portraits of life in the Depression.

Another story published in the 1950's, "Tales from the Vienna Woods," was even less characteristic, consisting of maudlin conversations between ordinary people at a bar. Delmore's gift for the demotic did not, unfortunately, extend to a wide range of characters; it was the speech of intellectuals that he had mastered, and the pointless, rambling talk of these shadowy figures possessed none of the subtle complication of the Goodman circle or the *Partisan Review* crowd depicted in his earlier stories. Aware that he had ventured far from his authentic voice, Delmore scribbled on the back of a list of stories written during the early 1950's: "Almost four years have passed—or is it almost five, since the notations on the reverse side of the page / It can certainly be said that I have learned a good deal: the knowledge of sadness."

.

"The poet of 40 years will never be old though he must suck the marrow of his mind." Delmore came up with this rather gruesome image late in 1953, when he was called upon to contemplate once again the meaning of a significant birthday. He was tired of introspection, and compared his thoughts to "caravans of camels lurching slowly across the seemingly endless Sahara."

At times, though, Delmore enjoyed "the pleasant rural post-Bohemian domesticity" of Baptistown, where the landscape was "intent on imitating Brueghel." "I like to live here because I can discuss myself with myself freely & interminably & without encouraging others to do the same," he noted in his journal. And to his old friend Oscar Handlin he wrote cheerfully: "I can't think of a better situation for anyone who wants to write books." Living in New York had become "a pointless drain of energy," while in the countryside he and Elizabeth could devote themselves to "staring at [their] typewriters." In the solitude of the countryside, he concentrated on reform: "To smoke only pipes, and to get up at eight o'clock—and to take vitamins, join a gym, buy new clothes, answer mail."

By 1954, Delmore's various sinecures had dwindled to nothing. He had resigned from *Partisan Review*, lost his job at *Perspectives* when the Ford Foundation curtailed its budget, and no longer had any prospects at Princeton. Always resourceful, he now had other projects in hand, among them a textbook to be written in collaboration with Saul Bellow on "What the Great Novelists Say about Writing the Novel" and an offer to guest-edit an issue of *Perspectives*; these projects, like so many others, were eventually abandoned.

While Delmore toiled fruitlessly, Elizabeth's popular novel had been issued in a paperback edition that sold a quarter of a million copies. Surprisingly, Delmore was pleased by her success, which he hoped would bring in a lot of money; "in which case I will retire to devote myself to what really interests me, psychiatric literature, major league baseball, and military strategy." For the moment, however, they were still penniless; Elizabeth's royalties had been "more or less confiscated by our publisher and benefactor," Delmore hinted darkly to Dr. Gruenthal, referring to Laughlin, whom he had once again begun to accuse of all sorts of malfeasance.

When the University of Chicago invited him to teach there for a term, Delmore accepted without hesitation, and in March 1954 he and Elizabeth went to live in Hyde Park. He found Chicago "terrific," he reported to Bellow; "it's very strange, after two years, to be living day in and day out in a big city: roller skates scraping the sidewalk sound exotic." Exhibiting his best satiric style, he summarized a "weird excursion" he was writing entitled "The Yogurt and the Halvah," "which takes up the well-supported view that Dwight is a cigarstore Indian, Bowden Broadwater [Mary McCarthy's husband] and Lionel Abel are English gentlemen, and Clem's [Greenberg] secret ambition in life is to open a shoe store on Staten Island." But he soon grew restless in Chicago, and was relieved when the term ended and he could return to the seclusion of New Jersey. Teaching at the university had been "very nice, up to a point—reached after the first four weeks," he wrote Arthur Mizener later in the year.

Delmore was by now so poor that he couldn't manage the expense involved in coming to New York. He worried that his friends would think he was avoiding them, or suppose he was "brooding over some slight." The truth was that "a trip to New York costs $5 and to have people here costs even more," he explained to Laughlin, "so it's impossible to do anything about it very often on an income which averages $25 a week." They had no money to keep up the house, which would have to be sold in any event if things continued as they were. Delmore tried to make a wan comedy of his troubles, and predicted he would end up fleeing to Guatemala pursued by creditors. Finally, just after New Year's, he was appointed the poetry editor and regular film critic of *The New Republic*.

Delmore at his best was a first-rate film reviewer, comparable to James Agee. A fanatical absorption in the movies that dated from his forlorn youth, when the darkened theaters on upper Broadway had been a second home to him, and his familiarity with popular culture made Delmore particularly responsive to Hollywood's version of reality. He tended to write about movies from a literary and self-consciously intellectual point of view, characterizing Mary Pickford's beauty by some lines from Keats,

citing Yvor Winters on "the fallacy of pseudo-reference,"
or examining the discrepancies between films and the
books from which they had been adapted; but he was also
capable of discussing the technical aspects of the films
themselves, and the methods of various directors. The movies had so transfixed Delmore over the years that he had
come to regard them as one of life's most irresistible temptations, and he struggled against their power just as he did
against alcohol; but it was this very awareness of their
appeal to those who desired escape that made him such a
perceptive critic of the optimism that dominated American
films. Objecting to the false gaiety of *The Seven Year Itch*,
he suggested a new role for Marilyn Monroe.

Miss Monroe plays Eve, the serpent (Raymond
Massey) comes along with the apple, which is turned
down by Miss Monroe as Eve who declares that she is
getting along fine with Adam, is happily married, and
needs no fruit; and then either the serpent is sent
away like an obstreperous salesman or Eve uses all of
her female wiles to seduce the serpent into eating the
apple himself, thus eliminating Satan, purging the
universe of evil, and bringing about the most over-
whelming, total, and conclusive of all the happy end-
ings Hollywood has ever filmed.

The fragments of stories written during these years,
while diffuse and rather labored, were not quite as disastrous as his unpublished essays—exercises full of pointless
whimsy and a disconcerting garrulity—but they too
showed how far Delmore had strayed from his early mastery of autobiographical fiction. Here were the same
themes he had written of so many times before: his childhood, summer camp, the child's confusion about sex, his
parents' marriage; and not only did he dwell obsessively on
the same themes but on the very same episodes that had
occupied him over the years in one abandoned draft after
another. It was as if the whole of his experience had been
distilled, reduced to a series of significant moments by
which his entire subsequent life could be interpreted.
"Every stage of life aspires to the condition of childhood,"
he once wrote, echoing Pater's formula, "All art constantly
aspires towards the condition of music." The clandestine

visit to a prostitute in Harlem; his mother's cruel rejection
of his offer to explicate the opera to her; negotiations with
lawyers from his father's estate; the girl in his apartment
building who died of influenza: these, together with perhaps a score of other scenes, formed a sort of code; each
contained within itself a part of his life's essence. Given
Delmore's overwhelmingly determinist and world-historical
view of his own life, it was natural for him to discern in
these childhood episodes the mythic material by which
they could be made universal fables of the age. But by the
mid-1950's he still had not discovered either the literary
form or the emotional resources necessary to produce a
sustained work of art about his childhood, and it was becoming increasingly evident that he never would.

There is evidence of what can only be called madness in
these manuscripts, in particular "The Nun's Prayer," a
work of more than a hundred pages of weird raving that
reveals, if nothing else, the disastrous effects of Dexedrine
on Delmore's mind. Sentences so long one descends them
with apprehension as to whether they will ever end, clotted
discourses on "poetry as ontology," elaborate philosophical
disquisitions and "Kantian manoeuvres": it was as if Delmore's burdened mind had overheated to the point where
all his insights ran together in an incomprehensible blur.

.

In July 1955, an impatient Pascal Covici, the editor at
Viking who had contracted for a textbook by Delmore and
Bellow, wrote to ask why they had not turned in a manuscript; it was now six months overdue. Delmore had a gift
for eliciting advances from publishers, and managed not
only to evade the question of when the textbook would be
completed but to procure still another advance, this one for
a "Portable Heine" in Viking's series of selections from
famous authors. "I don't want any more advances," he told
Covici once the new stipend was in his pocket; "they're
demoralizing and useless, since they neither pay the bills nor
help the work get done."

Delmore complained of illness throughout most of 1955;
first there was "an abscessed jaw which makes me look like
a sagging pigskin," then a virus, then a mysterious condition which he described as "glandular." Jogging heavily
along the dusty dirt roads of his run-down rural estate, he

tried to keep in shape; but it was a losing battle against alcohol, insomnia, Dexedrine, barbiturates, and cigarettes. "At the moment I'm so exhausted that I feel like cutting my throat," he wrote Laughlin during the year, "so the next news may well be that I am across the river and under the trees: what is the meaning and purpose of life? death."

For years now, Delmore had been subjecting Elizabeth to what could only be called a reign of terror. She always kept some money hidden in a stocking, in case she was forced into sudden flight. In his journals, he wondered how long their marriage would last. Then, late in the autumn of 1955, Elizabeth left him, as he had long feared she would. Writing to Covici, Delmore pretended that she had gone to Woodstock because both her mother and sister were ill. Alone in the farmhouse, he was at work on a story suggested by a news item headlined JEALOUS MAN KILLS WIFE AND SELF.

15

"Verse is pouring out of my fingers," Delmore announced to Clement Greenberg one day in the late 1950's. And it was, in a profusion of sprawling romantic lyrics that provide a strange contrast to the increasing squalor of his life. For over a decade, he had struggled with fiction while his poetry languished; now he seemed to be in the midst of a renewal of imaginative energies. Delmore's eager perusal of the journals, letters, and memoirs of writers, which in the 1940's had inspired him to compose such marvelous abbreviated biographies in his verse journals, now gave way to a series of poems about Sterne, Swift, Hölderlin, Baudelaire, and characters from the Bible (others, of which only the titles survive, were "Dorothy Wordsworth's Midsummer Night's Dream," "To Walt Whitman in 1952," and "Hegel in New York"). Delmore had an intuitive sense of what was significant in the lives of his favorite authors, conveyed in this instance by monologues drawn almost entirely from their writings; but they lacked the brilliant ease with which he had animated in a few lines the sensibilities of his earlier subjects. At least they were coherent, a virtue notably absent from the other poems he was writing. Delmore may well have been justified in complaining so bitterly about the poet's estrangement from society, but it is a tribute to the loyalty of editors and to his own enduring reputation that some of these poems ever saw print at all. "I'd bleed to say his lovely work improved / but it is not so," wrote Berryman in one of his commmemorative Dream Songs.

In the celebrated selection of his poems published in 1959 under the title *Summer Knowledge*, Delmore chose to devote over a hundred pages to haphazard, euphonious, virtually incomprehensible effusions. Perhaps more than any poet of his generation, Delmore possessed a natural genius for poetry, a fluency that redeemed even his worst poems from bathos; and a few of these late poems are as moving as any he ever wrote. But too many of them are empty symphonies of sound; while not without a peculiar beauty, they verge on being devoid of any sense whatever.

A tattering of rain and then the reign
Of pour and pouring-down and down,
Where in the westwind gathered and filming gown
Of grey and clouding weakness, and, in the mane
Of the light's glory and the day's splendor,
   gold and vain,
Vivid, more and more vivid, scarlet,
   lucid and more luminous,
Then came a splatter, a prattle, a blowing rain!
And soon the hour was musical and rumorous:
A softness of a dripping lipped the isolated houses,
A gaunt grey somber softness licked the glass of hours.

Sure are the limitations of resonance for its own sake. Imitative of Hopkins, Yeats, Shelley ("The mind is a city like London, / Smoky and populous"), and himself (" 'Is it a dream?' I asked . . . Dream or the last resort / Of reality, it is the truth of our minds"), Delmore's late poems ignore the demand he reiterated in his journals: "To look toward the particular fact, seeking to generalize from it." His greatest gift was for dramatizing history by means of episodes drawn from his own life, vignettes at once vivid and ordinary. Now, still in quest of the sublime utopia he had always hoped to enter through poetry's divine auspices, Delmore turned away from a terrible existence in search of a purer Mallarméan mode.

•

In January 1956, Delmore abandoned the farm and moved to the seedy Hotel Marlton on West Eighth Street, where he lived in virtual isolation. Haunting Greenwich Village bars, studying *Finnegans Wake*—which he even annotated while sitting in the stands at the Polo Grounds— scribbling florid verses, he became the tortured figure in his poem "The Dread and Fear of the Mind of Others."

They thought I had fallen in love with my own face,
And this belief became the night-like obstacle
To understanding all my unbroken suffering,
My studious self-regard, the pain of hope,
The torment of possibility . . .

Delmore continued to see Elizabeth on Saturday nights, but he had also taken up again with Eleanor Goff, who still lived in the apartment where he had often visited her in 1945, a single immense room divided by ingenious lofts and crannies on East Tenth Street. Eleanor had since married and divorced the writer Seymour Krim, danced for a time in Martha Graham's company, and taught at various universities around the city. Delmore's separation from Elizabeth was by no means final, but he told Eleanor he would soon be divorced and talked of marriage. He wanted to take her to the New Jersey farm and raise chickens—an unlikely scenario. Still, Delmore had apparently come back into Eleanor's life at a propitious time, for she welcomed his strange proposal. They never got to New Jersey, but he remained in her apartment for several months, unwilling to see his old friends and only going out to the movies or for a walk in Washington Square. He was "tired and unhappy," he told Eleanor, and she found him a different person from the frenetic celebrity of a decade before. Later on that spring, he returned to the New Jersey farm without a word of explanation.

During this troubled year, Delmore continued in his public role of critic and man of letters. In April, *The New York Times Magazine* featured a clever "Survey of Our National Phenomena" in which he examined the myth of prominence in American life and wrote engagingly about his favorite mass-culture heroes—Kinsey, Marilyn Monroe, Adlai Stevenson, Hemingway, and Lindbergh, on whom his dreams of world fame had been modeled in youth. Delmore's interest in the products of the popular mind, while in part motivated by a desire to ally himself with a wider public than was ordinarily available to poets, had none of the moralizing condescension characteristic of Dwight Macdonald's famous essay "Mass-Cult and Mid-Cult" or Harold Rosenberg's disapproval of kitsch; it was a natural expression of his own affinities with all that was American, affinities derived from his early infatuation with

baseball, tabloids, the movies, and whatever else he
thought animated the drama of history. It was true that
Delmore owed his fame in part to the zeal with which he
had taken up the defense of high culture when he was
starting out in the thirties; and he never forfeited his role
as a proselyte of Modernism and the intellectual's necessary alienation from society. But he found a place in his
pantheon for baseball players and movie stars as well as for
Joyce, Eliot, and Yeats. Nor was his adulation of them self-
conscious. He was genuinely democratic—it was this that
attracted him to Joyce—and as the literary influence of
Modernism waned in concert with Delmore's reputation as
one of its leading American exhibits, he began to find his
new journalistic identity both expedient and congenial.

It is unfortunate that Delmore never finished the Heine
project, for the many pages that survive—he claimed to
have produced 1,500, an estimate that may not have been
exaggerated—reveal a thorough familiarity with Heine's
life and work. For years, he labored over translations of
Heine's poems, corresponding with Dr. Gruenthal's German wife about the merits of the various extant versions
and vowing to assemble a complete text, "barring the un-
foreseen, which I have failed to bar for some time"; but in
his journal, he noted ominously: "Obsession and compulsion irresistible & interminable—and this is why I've failed
to finish the Portable Heine or any other thing." Finally, in
1959, the doggedly optimistic editor at Viking wrote demanding the return of his advance, and there the matter
ended.

Always an enthusiastic correspondent, Delmore was
turning out letters that grew stranger every year. The rambling, inappropriately personal drafts of letters that survive
among his papers—to the British novelist Angus Wilson, to
the fiction editor of *Playboy* (who had included one of
Delmore's stories in the *Playboy Annual*), and to the editor of a disreputable magazine called *Dude* ("Looking at
copies of The Dude, it occurred to me that the present
story might be too long for periodical publication")—share
one trait in common: a painful uncertainty about the value
of his work. In his eagerness to reassure himself, he once
again resorted to chronicling praise: "[Jason] Epstein: so
good"; "[Elizabeth] Hardwick: it's wonderful"; "[Helen]

Frankenthaler: staggeringly beautiful"; "Ransom: very impressive."

·

Delmore and Elizabeth were reconciled in the spring, and returned together to the farm in Baptistown, but all was not well between them. Their quarrels reminded Delmore of the violent arguments with his mother that had embarrassed him as a child. In his journal, he acknowledged—citing Coleridge on Iago—"a motiveless malignity."

When Elizabeth was away, Delmore would call on the novelist Josephine Herbst, who lived across the border in Bucks County, and deliver fabulous commentaries on history, literature, politics, and American culture. "He was no tiresome monologist at all," Herbst recalled. "His talk was marvelous and he liked to be interrupted." Late at night, he would retire to his room, where the light burned until dawn. But in the morning he was energetic, explicating with tireless invention the books he had pulled randomly from the shelves and perused all night. Delmore was never too exhausted to start in on what he called "a long cadenza"; it was as if his fund of lore reposed in some involuntary mechanism that had only to be set in motion.

The University of California at Santa Barbara had invited Delmore to teach there for the spring term of 1957, then suddenly "called the whole thing off," he reported to Henry Rago, when Hugh Kenner objected to his presence on the faculty. (The problem with this interpretation was that Kenner was out of the country that year, and knew nothing about the matter.) Daunted but still hopeful, he applied for and was awarded a Fulbright Fellowship to teach at the Free University of Berlin the following autumn. But the prospect left him less than enthusiastic.

Just between us [he wrote his old friend William Van Keuren] the thought of going to Berlin or going anywhere is a tiring one, but perhaps it is time for me to stop avoiding the external world. As you know, it is more of an effort than it should be for me to depart from one room to go to another and the precept which used to get me out of bed, hangover and all, in

Cambridge—il faut tenter de vivre—has now become
—il faut get out of the pajamas every other day.

So great was his despondency that at one point he marveled in his journal: "This is the night of the 13th of
February 1957, and I am still alive!"

After an uneasy summer at Yaddo, Delmore and Elizabeth stopped off in Tivoli to visit Saul Bellow on their way
back to New York, then checked in at the Hotel St. George
in Brooklyn; they were scheduled to sail for Germany on
September 10. The next morning, Elizabeth left Delmore a
note announcing that she had no intention of going with
him, and went to her mother's apartment a few blocks
away. Hilton Kramer, at the time an editor of *Arts* magazine, had invited her to review some art shows, she said in
her letter, and she wanted to take advantage of this opportunity. She wouldn't see Delmore unless he entered a hospital.

In a panic, Delmore drove out to the farmhouse and
went through Elizabeth's things in search of evidence that
she had been unfaithful. Armed with what he thought were
incriminating documents, he wired the Fulbright Commission to cancel his fellowship, then returned to New York
and checked in at the Chelsea Hotel on West Twenty-third
Street. He was desperately in need of someone to blame
and fixed on the innocent Hilton Kramer—an unlikely victim, since Elizabeth's reference to him in her terse note
constituted the only evidence Delmore had for the claim he
now made: namely, that Kramer was in the midst of an
adulterous affair with his wife.

Once this conviction had lodged itself in his mind, Delmore made the first of a long series of phone calls to
Kramer, who happened also to be living at the Chelsea; he
was worried, Delmore explained, because Elizabeth's psychiatrist had told him she shouldn't be alone. Did Kramer
happen to know where she was? Before too long, these
polite inquiries had turned to threats delivered in "old
movie language," and Kramer, who barely knew Elizabeth,
was charged with planning to leave his own wife in order
to marry her. (He had never been married.)

Elizabeth, meanwhile, had vanished. Afraid of Delmore's violent temper, she remained well beyond his reach,
secreted in a friend's apartment. In the heat of August,

Delmore sat in his cramped hotel room, amid a sea of manuscripts, bottles, clothes, and crumpled papers, consulting lawyers, harassing Kramer, and writing aggrieved letters. To Stephen Spender, who had accepted some of his poems for publication in *Encounter*, he poured out a long complaint about his problems and demanded to know why the poems had not yet appeared in print. But literary difficulties were of little consequence beside Delmore's obsession with Hilton Kramer. Finally, on a Saturday night over the Labor Day weekend, he pounded on Kramer's door and threatened to break it down. Kramer opened the door a crack, leaving the chain locked, and, claiming to have glimpsed a gun in Delmore's hand, summoned the desk clerk in alarm. When the clerk came up, Delmore asserted that his wife was hiding in Kramer's room, and refused to leave until it had been searched.

Unnerved by Delmore's persistent siege, Kramer was by this time in a state of terror. After spending the night with a friend in Hoboken, he returned to the city and called Bellow, pleading with him to intervene. Bellow suggested he obtain a restraining order, so Kramer went to the local precinct station and persuaded a detective to accompany him back to the Chelsea. Delmore was called down to the lobby, where he denied threatening Kramer and informed the detective, "My psychiatrist tells me that I'm not crazy, I'm just angry." When asked the name of his psychiatrist, he said he had forgotten, and went off to his room on the pretext of looking it up. After a while, it became evident that Delmore wasn't coming back, so the detective went up and knocked on the door. "You have no right to come in here without a search warrant," Delmore bellowed, but then emerged from his room and agreed to go down to the station for further questioning. Once there, he lost control of himself and began shouting at the officers, at which point he was handcuffed, put in an ambulance, and committed to Bellevue. Like Bellow's Humboldt, "rushed off dingdong in a paddy wagon like a mad dog, arriving foul, and locked up raging," Delmore had descended to the depths.

.

Bellow's testimony is significant, for he soon found himself caught up in the web of Delmore's accelerating mania, and his novel can be read in part as a justification of his role in the ensuing events. It was obvious that Delmore needed medical care, but the notorious Bellevue was hardly the place for him, so Bellow and Catharine Carver, who had worked for *Partisan Review* during the 1940's, decided to collect funds to pay for treatment at the Payne-Whitney Clinic. Many of Delmore's friends contributed, including Laughlin, to whom Delmore had not spoken for over a year; only Rahv, who referred to their efforts as Delmore's "scholarship fund," refused. Fearing that Delmore would simply make off with the money, Bellow placed it in escrow and designated that it was to be used only for expenses incurred at Payne-Whitney.

Delmore, meanwhile, was in a sorry condition. Arriving at Bellevue "excited, hyper-active, and nervous"—according to a physician's report—he had suffered several seizures during the night, possibly brought on by acute alcohol withdrawal. The medical report was somber indeed; Delmore was variously diagnosed as having "acute brain syndrome," "diffuse brain disease," and "psychomotor retardation" due to severe intoxication from a combination of alcohol, Dexedrine, and other drugs. Over the next few days, while Bellow was raising money for his release, Delmore's condition deteriorated further; at one point he was completely out of control, and had to be placed in what were ominously referred to as "full restraints." His hands trembled, his speech was slurred, and his version of the events that had landed him there was incoherent. The habits of twenty years had finally caused irreversible damage.

From Bellevue, Delmore stepped up the program of intimidation and revenge that had begun with Elizabeth's flight, even hiring a private detective named Vincent Stanzioni to investigate her alleged affair with Kramer. The only way now to win anyone's allegiance to Delmore's view of matters was to pay them, and Stanzioni was turning a substantial profit; in August alone, he received four hundred dollars from his client. When he learned from a psychiatrist that Bellow was raising money on his behalf, Delmore put Stanzioni on Bellow's trail, convinced he had acted in concert with Kramer to have him committed. Resorting again to menacing phone calls, Delmore intimated to Bellow that he had suffered a heart attack at Bellevue and demanded the money be turned over directly to him so that he could live on it while he wrote poetry. Besides, he

insisted, some of the checks Bellow had received were
made out to Delmore and were thus rightfully his, a claim
he tried to enforce through Stanzioni. "Delmore's got it in
his mind that I'm one of his ill-wishers, detractors, slander-
ers," Bellow complained to Laughlin, employing the hard-
boiled idiom of Augie March.

> . . . he phoned me in the middle of the night using
> techniques the GPU might have envied, threatening to
> sue me for slander and frightening my poor wife. I
> made an effort to get rid of the private detective he
> had hired at enormous cost, but the guy wouldn't be
> shaken and in the end prevailed with Delmore. God
> knows he found plenty of purchase inside Delmore's
> head. We raised a little dough to help him. . . . I
> imagine the detective, Stanzioni, is still sucking
> around him, and anybody who wants to do Delmore a
> good turn will push this guy into the Hudson.

No great significance can be attached to Delmore's
choice of Bellow as a prominent figure in the conspiracies
he perceived, for he had by this time become indiscrimi-
nate in his suspicions; the mere fact that Bellow had been
involved at all was enough to indict him. Justifiably aggrieved, Bellow was still defending himself a decade later.
"I suffered when the police laid hands on him," he protested in *Humboldt's Gift*, "it threw me into despair." His
fictional portrait of Delmore, recognizable to everyone who
knew him, depicts a "hero of wretchedness" intent on set-
tling ontological scores through more practical instru-
ments: "He consented to the monopoly of power and interest held by money, politics, law, rationality, technology
because he couldn't find the next thing, the new thing, the
necessary thing for poets to do." Nothing ever written
about Delmore has been as shrewd as Bellow's insight into
the conflict between this worldliness and the empyrean
realm of poetry that had dominated Delmore's imagination
since his high-school days, when he dreamed of founding
the True Republic. But there is a certain bitterness in Bellow's portrait of Von Humboldt Fleisher that leads him to
exaggerate Delmore's vindictive qualities. Even in his de-
rangement, he was capable of remorse. "How many have
been disaffected by direct personal attacks?" Delmore
wondered in his journal, and went on to list his two wives,

William Barrett, R. P. Blackmur, and Laughlin. "But then
there are those who like me very much despite these destructive actions"—among whom he included Bellow—"&
those who accept them for a long time, only to become
totally disaffected." All the same, it was not entirely his
own fault, Delmore insisted, that so many of his friendships ended in estrangement.

> One important difficulty which I almost always for-
> get is that the weakness or viciousness, or rivalry or
> jealousy or resentment or desperation of others may
> always be present and when any of these tendencies
> become intensely active, my own way of reacting—
> direct attack—leads to temporary or lasting disaffec-
> tion—the assumption or expectation is that others will
> be good to me—e.g. truthful, generous, noble—and
> when they fail to be—e.g. Saul—I become very angry.

Delmore's expectations of others were impossibly high; and
yet, where in public he could only blame his friends, in
private he mourned the consequences of his own vindictive
conduct. Having always aspired to be "truthful, generous,
noble," he saw those elusive virtues recede from his life,
relegated along with his literary ambitions to an ideal beyond recovery.

.

As it happened, Bellow's "scholarship fund" for Delmore turned out to be unnecessary, for at this point the
best-selling novelist James Jones, who had met Delmore at
a party during the summer and been fascinated by his tales
of wrongdoing, showed up and paid his hospital bill. Delmore was then transferred to the Payne-Whitney Clinic,
where what Bellow called his "tuition" had been deposited.
Still in an agitated state, he was tentatively diagnosed as
"paranoid schizophrenic," but at least had no more violent
episodes. Elizabeth still dominated his thoughts; he denounced her in psychiatric interviews, belittled her writing,
and worried that she was ruining his career by reporting
on his condition to friends and publishers. A week after his
arrival, Delmore signed out against the doctors' advice,
pocketing the balance of his "scholarship."

PART THREE
1958-1966

———•———

There hope was, and the hopes, and the years past,
The beings I had known and forgotten and half-
*   remembered or remembered too often*
—How could I have known that the years and the
*   hopes were human beings hated or loved,*
Or known that I knew less and more than I supposed
*   I supposed?*
(So I questioned myself, in a voice familiar and
*   strange.)*
There they were, all of them, and I was with them,
They were with me, and they were me, I was them,
*   forever united*
As we all moved forward in a consonance silent and
*   moving*
*   Seated and gazing,*
*   Upon the beautiful river forever.*

16

—————•—————

"WHEN DRUNK, I make them pay and pay and pay," F.
Scott Fitzgerald once said; and it was Delmore's self-con-
fessed intention to make his friends—and his wife—pay
for what he regarded as their treachery. In a litigious
mood, he consulted a series of lawyers, and finally managed to persuade the firm of Surowitz and Ruskin to take
on his case. Delmore's poetical gifts may have deserted
him, but his imaginative powers flourished in detecting
conspiracies. Complaints and lawsuits blossomed forth.
First he proposed to sue Bellow for having made off with
funds intended for Delmore's care, and the lawyers, titil-
lated by the celebrity of their client and the supposed
plaintiff, believed his mad stories. "The theoretical climate
of their offices stimulated him," Bellow remarked in a
retributive but exact account of Delmore's legal adventures.

Lawyers didn't often meet writers. How was any
lawyer to know what was going on? A famous poet
calls for an appointment. Referred by so-and-so. The
entire office is excited, the typists put on make-up.
Then the poet arrives, stout and ill but still handsome
pale hurt-looking terrifically agitated, timid in a way,
and with strikingly small gestures or tremors for such
a large man. Even seated he has leg tremors, his body
is vibrating. At first the voice is from another world.
Trying to smile, the man can only wince. Odd small
stained teeth control a trembling lip. Although thick-
set, really a big bruiser, he is also a delicate plant, an
Ariel, and so on. Can't make a fist. Never heard of
aggression. And he unfolds a tale—you'd think it was
Hamlet's father: fraud, deceit, betrayal of pledges;
finally, as he slept in his garden, someone crept up
with a vial and tried to pour stuff into his ear.

In his journal, Delmore noted his pleasure when he called for an appointment and the secretary "went into an ecstatic 'what' as if I were really very famous." The tales of malfeasance he unfolded were so convincing that, a decade after his death, one lawyer still expressed incredulity that none of them was true.

Delmore was comprehensive in his accusations. One affidavit he submitted read: "Case of Delmore Schwartz versus Hilton Kramer, Elizabeth Pollet, James Laughlin, Marshall Best [an editor at Viking who had turned down his novel and demanded the return of his other advances], Saul Bellow, The Living Theatre, William Styron, Perry Miller, Harry Levin"; and there was an even longer list of those to be subpoenaed, including Anatole Broyard, Milton Klonsky, and the anthologist Oscar Williams. "Other names will be added when an investigation has occurred, or perhaps sooner," he noted darkly.

But the focus of the investigation soon narrowed down to Kramer, against whom Delmore filed a suit that dragged on for years. Demanding $150,000 in compensation (it was never quite clear for what), he cited Kramer's "illicit relationship" with Elizabeth Pollet and charged him with false arrest in connection with the Bellevue episode. The suit was "a model of uncertainty and ambiguity," as Kramer's lawyers pointed out, but once the wheels of justice had been set in motion, the innocent defendant found it difficult to extricate himself, and briefs flowed back and forth between the opposing lawyers' offices.

In November 1957, after moving from one hotel to another, Delmore retrieved his belongings from the farm and rented a shabby apartment in the Village. He had lost his cat, and used to call up a Princeton friend, Patricia Hartle, asking her to drive him out to the farm, where he would wander about in the fields for hours, plaintively calling its name. Otherwise he saw almost no one. He felt his "psychic energy used up by unconscious conflicts—half-unconscious frustrations of sexual desire / or anger," and wondered, "How long is it since I did a sustained piece of work?" It seemed to him as if the years of living in the countryside "had the effect of intensifying the tendency to withdraw from others," a tendency further aggravated by his illness. December 8, his forty-fourth birthday, was "a somber day outside & *within*."

Elizabeth, meanwhile, had gone out to Reno and obtained divorce papers, which were served on Delmore in mid-October. Alone in his room, he drafted endless letters to his ex-wife, setting forth evidence of her infidelity and accusing her of "a conspiracy to defraud and defame" as well as "grand larceny"—a reference to alleged improprieties in removing funds from their joint account. Delmore took pleasure in the vocabulary of the law, its tone of importance and elaborate language. With oracular sonority, he spoke of "the unquestionable outcome of the legal actions I must now take." In his journal, he transcribed passages from *Ulysses* that referred to Leopold Bloom as a cuckold, and examined his own predicament, which always returned to the subject of Elizabeth.

> What reason, what conclusive reasons have I to suppose that all my life is concluded, that hope is ended, that nothing better, nothing even as good— now that hope has perished—can be expected? The failure of self-control is now more serious. . . . Addictions exert an attraction which I allow to increase day by day, as for four years I have surrendered to them more and more; they are rooted in impatience as well as lifelong anxiety—lifelong fear—how shall I suppose that the years to come will be other than they have been—you don't know for certain—you are not sure hope has perished—but it is fear-ridden, silenced, made to seem an illusion by an emptiness of mind which is not what the worst of the old kinds of emptiness was since it is, at least in part, an obsession with what has happened to which the mind, wasting itself, constantly returns and turns—the subject which has obsessed me—what will happen to E. in the near future—what I can do to make matters difficult for her—until she is willing to give me full title to the house.

This confession affords a remarkable glimpse into Delmore's rapid vacillation between a piercingly accurate awareness of his desolate condition and the vengeful irrationality that issued forth to conceal it.

It was out of sheer desperation that he concentrated on such matters as the New Jersey house, which now stood

abandoned and vandalized. When asked by Dr. Gruenthal
if he still loved Elizabeth, Delmore responded "strongly
and spontaneously" that he did not; in his journal, he
wrote down the words: "marriage / carriage / carnage /
pillage." But it was urgent nevertheless that justice be done,
and toward this end he applied all his efforts, hoping by
means of the law to redress the humiliations and sorrows
of a lifetime. These negotiations too dragged on for well
over a year, until it was learned that foreclosure proceedings were being instituted on the now-derelict property, at
which point Dwight Macdonald managed to arrange a settlement by persuading Delmore to let him sell the farmhouse, the proceeds (some $6,000, once the mortgage had
been paid off) to be divided between Delmore and Elizabeth.

.

Delmore still enjoyed brief periods of approximate sanity. In February 1958 he went to Washington to give a
lecture at the Library of Congress, where he was interviewed by Randall Jarrell and *The Washington Post*. "Five
Jobs in Fifteen Months," read the *Post*'s headline. "The
public is at least interested in poets, if not poetry," Delmore told the reporter, avowing that he "preferred that to
total oblivion." In his talk "The Present State of Modern
Poetry," he elaborated on these remarks, returning to the
grievances expressed in his lecture before the MLA some
twenty years earlier, "The Isolation of Modern Poetry."
It was on the whole a sensible and lively talk, rehearsing
familiar ideas—the international character of modern poetry, the absence of a significant audience for it, the influence of Pound and Eliot—but in a retrospective context
based on Delmore's own experience as a poet and teacher.
It was true that he had never been able to sustain himself
as a poet, he admitted, and that the American public remained largely ignorant of poetry; all the same, he found
"the present state of poetry in America superior to what it
has ever been in the past." The revolution brought about
by Modernism had been throughly assimilated—perhaps
too thoroughly, since "what was once a battlefield has become a peaceful public park on a pleasant summer Sunday
afternoon." Because the new poets no longer had to contend
with the bewildering inventions of Pound and Eliot that

had overshadowed Delmore's generation, they were "tame and sedate" by comparison. Rebellion for its own sake, as practiced by those whom Delmore called the San Francisco Howlers—Ginsberg and the "Beat" movement—however unpalatable, at least served to confirm the adversary character of American literature.

The leading motive of classical American literature and of twentieth century writing has been a criticism of American life. Sometimes the criticism has had a native basis: the actuality of American life has been criticized from the exalted point of view of the American Dream. And sometimes, in expatriate writers like Henry James and T. S. Eliot, the actuality of American life has been criticized by being compared with the culture of the Old World. But since the Second World War and the beginning of the atomic age, the consciousness of the creative writer, however detached, has been confronted with the spectre of the totalitarian state, the growing poverty and helplessness of Western Europe, and the threat of an inconceivably destructive war which may annihilate civilization and mankind itself. Clearly when the future of civilization is no longer assured, a criticism of American life in terms of a contrast between avowed ideals and present actuality cannot be a primary preoccupation and source of inspiration. For America, not Europe, is now the sanctuary of culture; civilization's very existence depends upon America, upon the actuality of American life, and not the ideals of the American Dream. To criticize the actuality upon which all hope depends thus becomes a criticism of hope itself.

Delmore was perhaps overly zealous in his espousal of an apocalyptic view of history, which he tended to identify with his own suffering; it was an axiom of his that "anyone who is not disturbed in the fearful and apocalyptic 20th century has something wrong with him." But he had reason to feel that his generation possessed a deeper experience of history than their successors did; Stalin had shattered once and for all their "faith in a wholly new society that had been implicit in the revolutionary ideal," as Alfred Kazin put it in his passionate memoir, *Starting Out in the*

Thirties. But Modernism, that other legacy of the period, had survived the death of their political hopes, and Delmore still considered himself its heir, as he made clear in his closing remarks: "The consciousness that experience is international, panhistorical, and multilingual is explicit and intense to a greater degree than ever before." For all his recent ventures in the field of popular culture, Delmore remained to the end a proponent of the great cultural experiment that had enlivened his early years as a poet. It is a striking testament to the vigor of his faith in that experiment that he managed, in the midst of illness and decline, to produce such a fervent account of what he and his generation had accomplished.

·

The last decade of Delmore's life was dominated by a struggle against encroaching madness. "Alone, in a hotel room, almost penniless—in the 44th year of his age—his second wife having taken flight after eight years of troubled and quarrel-racked marriage"—as he put it in his poignant way—he moved from one hotel and boarding-house to another, drifted through a few casual affairs with young, admiring women, and took to spending long hours in the White Horse Tavern on Hudson Street, a bar made notorious by Dylan Thomas in the years before his death. There, surrounded by an assortment of writers, Village regulars, and "an attentive supply of girls," two steins of beer before him, Delmore would hold forth on politics, baseball, the *Partisan Review* days, or pull out one of his tattered, annotated copies of *Finnegans Wake* and read a few pages aloud; he was rumored to have once talked for eight hours straight. Delmore could be "as lively, quick, droll, inventive and wonderfully broad in his allusions as he ever was," Dwight Macdonald recalled, especially when he had an appreciative audience. Norman Mailer, however, who was perhaps less given to appreciation than some of Delmore's younger sycophants, found him "more or less drunk and more or less ordinary," and Delmore offered a melancholy spectacle of decline to those who had known him in better days. But to many others, for whom Delmore's reputation and expansive talk created an aura of oracular intelligence, he still possessed a heroic dimension. Only the subject of Elizabeth could turn his entertaining loquacity into a darkly obsessive harangue. That Delmore genuinely believed the wild assertions he made is evident from his journals, where as late as 1964 he was insisting on their validity.

7.22.64

It is now seven years to the day since my wife, Elizabeth Pollet, left me suddenly at the Hotel St. George in Brooklyn. The man for whom she left me —after many preparations over a period of two years designed to conceal the real motives of her actions was *Nelson Rockefeller*. His great wealth, his status as a married man, and his political ambitions were all very much involved in her effort to conceal the real reasons for her actions.

But Delmore's paranoia was never "self-aggrandizing or deadly (except to himself)," in Macdonald's view. "His aggressions against old friends always seemed to me more a despairing cry than an accusation." His episodes of madness were occasional and unpredictable, a desperate uncontrollable response to the fear of betrayal; and until the very end, he was intermittently aware of how damaging his conduct had become. He once lured the poet Leonard Wolf to New York on the pretext of a mysterious proposal to advance his reputation, then accused him of having had an affair with Elizabeth at Yaddo and threatened to kill him. "But we spent the rest of the day alternately communing with each other on the ugly turn that the world had take or, when his illness seized him, my reassuring him that his suspicions were unfounded; after which we went back to our very warm mutual brooding."

Even in his worst moments, Delmore labored to produce an effect of sanity. To Howard Moss, the poetry editor of *The New Yorker*, who invited him over on occasion for drinks, he still seemed sensible and amusing. Jean Stafford, who was there one afternoon with her third husband, A. J. Liebling, recalled that he looked "grimy, sallow, and undernourished" in a rumpled white suit. Nevertheless, he was "charming and affectionate," she recalled, and it wasn't until afterward that she realized he was "stark, staring mad." Alfred Kazin, too, remarked Delmore's capacity for transcending his madness; visiting him one Saturday morning in the late 1950's, Kazin found him "insatiably bitter," but "the face was still as remarkable, and in a relaxed moment still as noble," as it had looked to him thirty years before.

He sat in his squalid little box of a room on Greenwich Avenue, railing against a friend, against several friends. The room was surely the room that Raskolnikov had holed himself in to dream out his plot against the pawnbrokeress. Poverty could not account for such a room; it was not so much an uncomfortable room, a bad room, a tiresomely damp, dark, and constricted room; it was the kind of room that could have been chosen only by someone with an extraordinary knowledge of all the murderously bad rooms put aside and carefully preserved by the heartless state for poets to die in. It was such a room as only a writer with a long experience of Greenwich Village hand-me-downs could have found. It needed remarkable self-knowledge, long practice in disaster, even to discover a room like that. And there he was, buried alive up to his fine eyes in "betrayal," yet not so much talking as spilling over in that reedy voice, that headlong rush of words, that seemed to engage every muscle behind the surface of his face as he twisted and spat in the rage of his unhappiness.

Delmore's trouble, Kazin shrewdly observed, was that he did not possess "the saving grace of madness" conferred upon Blake; his madness was too intellectual. There was an element of calculation in Delmore's bizarre interpretation of reality, a conviction that logic was at work in the world, and it was this idea that made him so tenacious in his lawsuits. Until his very last years, he continued to put forth new evidence of conspiracy, entrapping whoever had the misfortune to cross his path in the web of his widening prosecution.

In his dreary apartment on Greenwich Avenue, Delmore contemplated the ruined past, mourning over his "dead youth and devastated life." On the back of a letter from Howard Moss he scribbled a few lines.

The years pass and the years pass
& still I see only as in a glass
darkly and vaguely—
waiting, in "grinding misery"
for the fountains of poetry
to flow and overflow once again

Still hoping for the discipline and inspiration that would
enable him to transform his obsession with the past into
literature, Delmore began one story after another, each
abandoned in despair. Awkward fables, fragments of autobiography, rehearsals of incidents exhaustively told in
Genesis, and a draft of a novel entitled *An American
Dream* collected in his room. In a manuscript entitled
"Love Stories," Delmore obliquely revealed what he
thought of these efforts.

> I myself am a teacher of English and an unsuccess-
> ful writer—and the latter fact, that I am a writer but
> an unsuccessful one, is something to which I cannot
> get accustomed or resigned, although I have tried very
> hard. The torment of disappointed hope becomes a
> brutality to oneself, if one is unable to surrender one's
> hope. In other less important realms of desire and
> ambition, one gets used to *not* being what one wants
> to be. . . . But I have passed the thirtieth year of my
> age, and I have become used to the disappointment
> and the forgetting of most of the hopes and ambitions
> of adolescence and young manhood: but I have not in
> the least become used to being a poor or mediocre
> writer. I know that it is more and more unlikely that I
> will ever be the kind of writer I want so much to be,
> or that I will even appear in print very often. Why
> *me*? Why does this desire seem inseparable from the
> very sense of being alive, since it is the cause, year
> after year, of disappointment and pain.

Delmore did manage to produce a few stories of sufficient merit to be published in periodicals and paperback
anthologies, so matters were not as desperate as may seem
from the mass of manuscripts he left unfinished. These
stories, some of them novella-length, were so strikingly
different from *The World Is a Wedding* that a reader fa-

miliar with the earlier stories would hardly believe them to
be by the same author. Irving Howe, reviewing *Successful
Love*, the volume in which these stories eventually appeared, noted Delmore's "quizzical wonderment at the
powers of the American innocent"; in writing about the
sexual education of a typical adolescent girl in the 1950's,
the fortunes of a brilliant scholar whose idiosyncrasies include a refusal to sleep with his young wife, or an idealistic
college girl who kidnaps a baby adopted by her liberal
parents and then rejected because it has a trace of Negro
blood, Delmore employed a whimsical, optimistic mode—
Philip Rahv characterized it as "child's English"—that had
little in common with the self-conscious, ironic voice so
distinctive in his fine autobiographical stories. Just as his
poetry tended to sound more lyrical and effusively romantic the more sordid his life became, Delmore's stories radiated the benevolence and bland tolerance of the Eisenhower era at the very moment when he was enduring his
most profound agony; it was as if he hoped to restore a lost
innocence to his life by dwelling on suburban families and
teenage girls, themes so alien to his own experience that
one wonders how he managed to write about them as well
as he did.

A few of the late stories were respectable, particularly
those in which Delmore echoed the moods and perplexities
of the Depression, or wrote about bewildered young men
reminiscent of the characters in "The World Is a Wedding." But the only story among them that can be considered in any way distinguished is "The Track Meet." First
published in *The New Yorker* in 1958, the story remains a
tribute not only to Delmore's persistence in the face of
madness and disintegration but also to the editorial talents
of William Maxwell. Like so many editors, Maxwell encouraged Delmore out of respect for his past accomplishments, and was deluged with illegible typescripts that
showed little promise. "The Track Meet," which Maxwell
managed to salvage from Delmore's confused submissions,
was a bizarre fable perhaps too derivative of Kafka, in
which a young man is awakened early one morning by a
strange Englishman named Reginald Law, who escorts him
to a track meet. At the stadium, Law reads aloud from the
newspaper various accounts of lurid tragedies, while the
narrator witnesses a sinister progression of events on the
field, culminating in a disorderly race in which his five

brothers, named after the crowned heads of Europe—his own name, he confides, "was actually Franz Joseph, not Frank"—fight among themselves and people in the crowd hurl bottles at their heads. When the narrator protests against these brutal tactics, Law replies: "You are interested in platitudes, but I am interested in reality." The fantastic scenario closes with the murder of his brothers by five girls "dressed as drum majors," who draw forth pistols and shoot them in cold blood, "as if they were shooting horses." In a familiar denouement that inevitably recalls "In Dreams Begin Responsibilities," the narrator wonders if he is dreaming. "It is worse for you—it is far worse for you if it *is* a dream," Law admonishes him. "If what has occurred on the field were merely imaginary and unreal and merely your own private hallucination, then the evil that has terrified you is rooted in your own mind and heart." The story ends with a recognition scene virtually identical to that of "In Dreams."

> I tried once more to stand up, and awoke, and found myself standing up, staring, in the sweat of confusion and dread, not at the sky but at the looking glass above the chest of drawers next to my dishevelled bed. The face I saw was livid and swollen with barbarous anger and unbearable shame.

While Delmore languished in his apartment or in Washington Square Park, his literary career advanced on its own. His stories were anthologized, his poems appeared everywhere, and in 1958 he entered into negotiations with Doubleday for the publication of a *Selected Poems*. Editors were magnanimous and deferential to his reputation. Henry Rago at *Poetry* encouraged him to submit verse and paid for it in advance (an unprecedented gesture for *Poetry*); both William Maxwell and Howard Moss at *The New Yorker* isolated what was publishable from the disorderly manuscripts he submitted; and the quarterlies regularly accepted his work, whatever its quality. "During the past six months I have had more prose and verse accepted for publication than at any other time and more than I would in the past have thought either possible or desirable," he boasted to Maxwell.

Uncertain as he was about the value of his work, Delmore tended to belittle his earlier stories. He thought *The World Is a Wedding* "no good at all," and was annoyed at the attention his famous early poems received. It is natural for an author to be most interested in what he is writing at any given moment, but Delmore was equally indifferent to the fate of his current work. He could never have managed to assemble a collection of his poems without the assistance of his friend Elizabeth Reardon, whom he employed to sort out and type the manuscripts he brought to her house one day crammed into two enormous suitcases. He never even glanced at her selections, preferring to deliver a three-hour lecture on the Dreyfus case while she typed away.

Summer Knowledge, Delmore's title for this new collection, was issued in 1959 to considerable acclaim. Babette Deutsch in *The New York Times*, M. L. Rosenthal in *The Nation*, Stanely Kunitz in *Harper's*, and Kimon Friar in the *Saturday Review* all praised it, as did John Hollander and Anthony Hecht, among others, in the literary quarterlies. And it was acclaim the book deserved, despite the prolix, repetitive lyricism of some of the later work. Virtually the whole of *In Dreams* was reprinted, along with a brief passage from *Genesis* and three poems from *Vaudeville for a Princess*. Few of the later poems were particularly distinguished, but a series of dramatic monologues on Biblical characters—Abraham, Jacob, and Sarah—surely rivaled Delmore's early poems in their meditative eloquence. The poem about Jacob was a terse utterance of remorse and prayer in which Jacob tells of his rivalry with Esau and contemplates his son Joseph's favored status.

The gift is loved but not the gifted one.
The coat of many colors is much admired
By everyone, but he who wears the coat
Is not made warm. Why should the gift be the cause of pain,
O thou unspeakable? Must the vivid coat
Of eminence elect the favored favorite
As scapegoat or turncoat, exile or fugitive,
The loved of mother and God, and by all others
Shunned in fear or contempt?
                    I knew what it was,
When Joseph became my favorite: knew the sympathy
Of the long experience of the unasked-for gift:

Knew the nature of love: how many colors
Can a coat have? What should we wish, if
We could choose? What should I desire,
—Not to have loved my son, the best of sons?
Rejected the choice of love? Should I have hidden
My love of him? Or should he have concealed the self
I loved, above all others, wearing the coat
Which is customary, the coat his brothers wore?
To how many coats can a color give vividness?
How can the heart know love, and not love one the more?
Love is unjust: justice is loveless.

The "gift" in this instance was of course Delmore's poetic
genius, "the cause of pain"; and while the failure to love or
be consoled by love was more a predicament of Delmore's
than of Jacob's, the comparison of Jacob's special status
among the people of Israel to his own sense of being at
once chosen and an "exile or fugitive" remains perhaps
Delmore's most evocative image of his condition.

The other notable poem in *Summer Knowledge*—apart
from those originally published in *In Dreams*, which, as
Stanley Kunitz observed, had "lost none of their lustre after
a score of years"—was "Seurat's Sunday Afternoon along
the Seine." Delmore's meticulous account of the painting
poignantly emphasized his own distance from the pastoral
idyll of the bourgeoisie depicted by Seurat, a world in
which children, lovers, and contented families drift
through the sunlight which

> shines equally and voluptuously
Upon the rich and the free, the comfortable, the *rentier*,
> the poor, and those who are paralyzed by poverty.

In luxurious, casually rhymed and flowing lines orches-
trated by a stately cadence, Delmore brooded over every
detail of the painting.

The sunlight, the soaring trees and the Seine
Are as a great net in which Seurat seeks to seize and hold
All living being in a parade and promenade of mild, calm
    happiness:
The river, quivering, silver blue under the light's variety,
Is almost motionless. Most of the Sunday people

Are like flowers, walking, moving toward the river, the sun,
   and the river of the sun.

Envious of their freedom from "the teething anxiety, the
gnawing nervousness / Which wastes so many days and
years of consciousness," the poet contemplates the vivid
scene with a disturbing awareness of "the uncontrollable
blaze of time and of history" that promises eventually to
destroy it. This vision of arcadian pleasure, which Delmore
had only known fleetingly as a child, and yet had always
celebrated and aspired to possess, was all the more tragi-
cally remote now that he realized it would never be his.
Like Kafka, who often quoted Flaubert's jealous cry, "Ils
sont dans le vrai"—prompted by a visit with his niece to a
normal middle-class family—Delmore suffered from the
sacrifices he felt he had made to his art, and the closing
lines of this poem represent in a sense his farewell to the
long-deferred dream of happiness and tranquillity.

            Far and near, close and far away
Can we not hear, if we but listen to what Flaubert tried to
   say,
Beholding a husband, wife and child on just such a day:
Ils sont dans le vrai! They are with the truth, they have
   found the way
The kingdom of heaven on earth on Sunday summer day.
Is it not clear and clearer? Can we not also hear
The voice of Kafka, forever sad, in despair's sickness trying
   to say:
"Flaubert was right: *Ils sont dans le vrai!*
Without forebears, without marriage, without heirs,
Yet with a wild longing for forebears, marriage, and heirs:
They all stretch out their hands to me: but they are too far
   away!"

                      .

   Delmore's world was as far from the placid existence
captured by Seurat as one could imagine. Virtually penniless as always, he was forced to depend on what little he
could earn from his articles and poetry. Meyer Schapiro,
who remained his loyal friend until the very end of his life,
had arranged for a grant of a thousand dollars to be donated by the philanthropist J. M. Kaplan and presented by

the New School, but within a few months, Delmore was appealing to Kaplan again, intimating that a number of hitherto undisclosed "facts" required him to write. At once rancorous and apologetic, he offered a peculiar appraisal of his situation: "While writing, I kept thinking of a proverb I read last summer: 'If you don't have a dog, you must do your own barking.' " It was hardly the sort of letter to win over a potential patron.

Meyer Schapiro agreed to sponsor a bank loan, which Delmore defaulted on when the first payment was due. To relieve his guilt, Delmore convinced himself that Schapiro was "involved in the failure to get [him] out of Bellevue," and avoided his old friend and teacher after that unfortunate transaction. It was the same with Dwight Macdonald, who submitted Delmore's work to *The New Yorker*— where he was a staff writer at the time—arranged for the sale of the New Jersey house, and recommended him to the Ford Foundation for a grant. Delmore, meanwhile, was noting in his journal that Macdonald had "allowed my books to be stolen."

"Had I but known that I would be alone / At forty-five—what, in all truth, would I have done?" he wondered sadly in his customary commemoration of a birthday. Only his mother remembered the day:

Dec. 6, 1958

Dear Delmore:

By chance I came across the Commentary magazine

I hope these letter will reach you.

I read the poems in June issue, also the story in November issue.

The story is very good
on the 8th is your birthday
I don't remember how old you are.

Tell every-one-here you advised me against entering a home

It's not to believe how I exists here.

If I fell into a well and looking up to get out
no one comes to take me out.

I have something for you dont know about
Remeber I am certain you do let me know
It's by Clara [Delmore's aunt]

I am in no position to write clearer and therefor not satisfied with my letter /

Dont phone Clara until you dont get in touch with me, she no doubt will deny everything.

No harm if you write to me.

God health and where are you.

> Love,
> Mother

In the spring of 1959, Delmore was evicted from his apartment for non-payment of rent, and a new friend from the White Horse, Marshall Allen, financed another apartment for a time. Delmore always managed to land in the dreariest lodgings imaginable; one that Meyer Schapiro recalled was in "a dilapidated old house at the edge of the old city near abattoirs or wholesale meat-storage quarters." From there, after quarrels with the landlord and other tenants, Delmore fled to still more disreputable apartments and hotels, leaving his manuscripts scattered all over the Village.

In his journals, Delmore recorded his disintegration in despairing poems and notations on what he wryly called "the Daily Noose" that he felt tightening about him; on a June day in 1959, he observed:

> It is full summer in Washington Square & a sunny warm weekend: everyone & his dog is outdoors: and most of the human beings in the park seem pleased or at least appeased or at any rate not as troubled as I am by any feeling of emptiness . . . the grey feeling of being forty five years of age—today sixteen dex have hardly induced even the kind of nervousness which comes of taking so much; the old nostalgia does not come to me at all anymore, not now & not when I am high . . . the bleakness of the future—it is the boarding up of the gallery of memory which makes it so difficult for me to begin—and when I merely write down names something—some vibration of feeling, however faint—returns

It was the theme of "Seurat's Sunday Afternoon along the Seine" repeated, and with considerable eloquence. A month later, echoing Job, he entered in his journal the most devastating cry of all: "Away! Away! Let the day perish that I was born."

By the end of the 1950's Delmore had withdrawn more and more into a strange world of solitude and memories. Recalling again the significant events of his childhood, copying out passages from "Lycidas" interspersed with paranoid accusations, he found it difficult to concentrate for more than a few moments at a time. ("Only a very unfavorable review of one of Levin's books kept mind & eye from skipping distractedly," he noted once, temporarily revived by the deflation of an old enemy.) Robert Lowell's sonnet "In Dreams Begin Responsibilities" provides a sad portrait of these bleak, isolated years.

> Your dream had humor, then its genius thickened,
> you grew thick and helpless, your lines were variants,
> unlike and alike, Delmore—your name, Schwartz,
> one vowel bedevilled by seven consonants . . .
> one gabardine suit the color of sulphur,
> scanning wide-eyed the windowless room of wisdom,
> your notes on Joyce and porno magazines—
> the stoplights blinking code for you alone
> casing the bars with the eye of a Mongol horseman.

Ashamed of his condition, Delmore deliberately chose to avoid his friends, preferring to take up with young women half his age and people who hadn't known him in his celebrated youth. There were perhaps a few casual affairs, but for the most part he complained of "complete chastity," and it was to this condition that he attributed his anxiety. When he did see old friends, it was not a very rewarding experience for them. Visiting William Phillips, Delmore complained of hearing voices and intimated that he was being poisoned. When Dwight Macdonald called up to find out how he was, Delmore derided him as a "fucking Yalie" and tore the telephone from the wall. William Barrett's last encounter with Delmore was harrowing. It was in a Village restaurant; Barrett was dining with friends when Delmore entered in the company of a young woman. They nodded politely, and as Delmore was leaving, Barrett invited him over to their table for a brandy. For a while he talked with amiable restraint, until suddenly, Barrett recalled, "there burst forth a Delmore I'd never seen or heard, not even in his most agitated moments." His voice reverberated through the restaurant, a torrent of "yells, grunts, groans" that rose to a "wrathful and incoherent bellow."

At uptown literary parties, he paraded an ostentatious bohemianism. Once he reproached Hannah Arendt for what he called her "German" views; on another occasion he displayed his tattered trousers to Robert Lowell, and whined, "See how poor I am." He pressed Dr. Gruenthal to attend a party at Norman Podhoretz's, then made a scene when the doctor showed up. A birthday party the Macdonalds gave for Delmore ended unhappily for the host (to the hostess, Delmore was charming and warm, as he always was toward the wives of his friends), when the guest of honor brought along a coterie of raucous Village friends and made Macdonald the subject of an evening's malicious monologue.

Early in 1961, Delmore attended a notorious party given by Norman Mailer in which he was not, for once, the instigator of chaos. It was on this occasion that Mailer stabbed his wife. Some two hundred people attended, and Delmore figured only in the guest list published in the newspapers as part of their zealous coverage of this incident. All the same, he was convinced that the party "may have been—probably was—a set-up," and that Mailer's only motive was to embarrass him. It was a case of "guilt by association," he claimed. But what really infuriated him was that he had been identified by the press as a critic when, as everyone knew, he was a poet.

In 1960 Delmore was awarded the prestigious Bollingen Prize, the youngest poet ever to win it. He gave a reading at Yale, where he had a reunion with Cleanth Brooks; back in New York, he lunched with Robert Penn Warren, who had served on the selection committee, at the Century Club. But he seemed to Warren "ill and depressed," and was long past taking any consolation in such literary achievements. Not long afterward, *Successful Love* was brought out by Ted and Eli Wilentz, proprietors of the Eighth Street Bookshop and publishers of Corinth Books. When *The World Is a Wedding* was reviewed in *Time*, Delmore had eagerly calculated the number of copies he thought it would sell; now, when he no longer cared, both *Time* and *Newsweek* reviewed his new book, accompanied by a somewhat deranged-looking photograph. The review in *Time* was mildly disapproving, but *Newsweek* praised the stories' "vitality," while David Boroff in *The New York Times Book Review* paid homage to Delmore's high place in the American literary establishment, calling him "that rare and indispensable thing—a gifted man of letters." But it was R. W. Flint, writing in *Commentary*, who proved to be the most sensitive critic of Delmore's fiction. "Something is missing," he noted, "and it is neither skill nor acuteness of perception or humor." What these new stories lacked was "simply a theme to match the theme or themes of *The World Is a Wedding*." Delmore had repudiated "his doctrinaire past," convinced that it belonged to "the general climate of innocence" in which he had come of age, and in so doing forfeited the world he knew best in favor of commentaries on the "general vacancy" of the fifties.

.

As always, Delmore experienced occasional manic days when he was "riding high" and could hold forth for hours whenever he had an audience; "that guy'll talk your head off," complained Casey Lee, owner of a Village restaurant Delmore frequented and one of his many patrons. Delmore seemed to take a certain grim pleasure in his litigious activities, drafting briefs and sending summonses to friends. "I master my fears by facing, by finding them out," he gloated, "by testing them through the explicit articulation of them in front of other human beings or here upon the typewriter." In these exuberant moods, he would flood the periodicals with his work, often submitting the same poem to several editors at once.

Diffuse, eerie, on occasion strikingly lyrical, Delmore's last poems suffered from an excessive spontaneity. Some were simply awful, especially the lyrics from "Kilroy's Carnival":

"—I'll kiss you wherever you think you are poor,
  Wherever you shudder, feeling tiny or skinny, striped or
    barred,
  Feeling you are bloodless, cheerless, chapless or
    marred . . ."

Some were grotesque:

And hence the poet must seek to be essentially anonymous,
   He must die a little death each morning,
      He must swallow his toad and study his vomit
         as Baudelaire studied *la charogne* of Jeanne Duval.

Still others reproduced puns and bad jokes that had first
appeared in letters: "A horse divided against itself cannot
stand"; the poet must be "Professor Tenure, and Dizzy the
Dean and Disraeli of Death." The strangest performance
of all was a "Poetic Prologue for TV" in which Delmore
impersonated a disc jockey on a late-night program, field-
ing improbable questions from his audience. Interspersed
with these queries were passages of weird, uncanny raving.

    To those who have tuned in on this program for the
   first time, it is necessary to say as I have said before:
   the Creation occurs every morning at dawn and all
   day long. The world is a fire, a great fire, a bonfire, a
   wild fire, a stupendous conflagration: it must be sustained continually by a new supply of fuel—I almost
   said fool or fowl— Hence it must be apropriate to cite
   once again the incidental views and comments which
   occurred on the very first day that God made heaven
   and earth:
    A Throne said: Wow!
    A Power exclaimed: Anything for a laugh!
    A Domination remarked: This is pure virtuosity!

Not all his late poems were so hopeless, and some, in the
expansive, meditative mode of "Seurat," were quite moving. Elegies for his early discipleship to the Muse, whom he
felt had now traduced and deserted him, these poems re-
capitulate the arduous struggle to restore hope that occupied the last twenty years of Delmore's life; perhaps its
fullest expression is to be found in a poem reminiscent of
his youthful masterpieces.

   The world was warm and white when I was born:
   Beyond the window pane the world was white,
   A glaring whiteness in a leaded frame,
   Yet warm as in the hearth and heart of light.
   Although the whiteness was almond and was bone
   In midnight's still paralysis, nevertheless

The world was warm and hope was infinite
All things would come to me and be my own,
   all things would be enjoyed, fulfilled and known.
How like a summer the years of youth have passed!
—How like the summer of 1914, in all truth!—
Patience, my soul, the truth is never known
Until the future has become the past
And then, only, when the love of truth at last
Becomes the truth of love, when both are one:
When Eden becomes Utopia, and is surpassed:
For then the dream is knowledge and knowledge knows
Motive and joy at once wherever it goes.

But the most revealing poem of all was one entitled "All
Night, All Night," a terse, controlled account of riding on
a train and observing a bird fly parallel to the tracks.

Looked out at the night, unable to distinguish
Lights in the towns of passage from the yellow lights
Numb on the ceiling. And the bird flew parallel and still,
As the train shot forth the straight line of its whistle,
Forward on the taut tracks, piercing, empty, familiar—

The poem's closing lines evoke Delmore's disillusion and
fear of death with a passion so direct and unrelieved as to
call forth a profound pity in those who know the circumstances of his last years.

And then the bird cried as if to all of us:

   O your life, your lonely life
   What have you ever done with it,
   And done with the great gift of consciousness?
   What will you ever do with your life before death's knife
   Provides the answer ultimate and appropriate?

As I for my part felt in my heart as one who falls,
Falls in a parachute, falls endlessly, and feels the vast
Draft of the abyss sucking him down and down,
An endlessly helplessly falling and appalled clown:

This is the way that night passes by, this
Is the overnight endless trip to the famous unfathomable
   abyss.

Apart from ominous letters intimating the dangers that threatened him, Delmore wrote less and less after 1960. And what he did write was often an exercise in character assassination. There was a bitter portrait of F. O. Matthiessen, whose radicalism he depicted as the infatuation of a spoiled child from a privileged background; another, abandoned after a few sentences, disposed of the eminent Columbia professor Jacques Barzun: "It is entirely fitting that the Master of Ceremonies this evening should be Professor Jacques Barzun. The perfection of his social manner is equalled only by the insincerity of his utterances . . . few authors have written so much and understood so little." A review for *Commentary* arrived with some unpublishable remarks about "the retarded conscience of Arthur Miller, the ballplayer for whom Marilyn Monroe consented to be circumcised."

Delmore did, miraculously, manage to produce a few coherent pieces during these years: reviews of Herbert Gold's first novel and of the late Isaac Rosenfeld's collection of essays, *An Age of Enormity*; a generous estimate of Roethke; and an uneven but well-argued appraisal of Pound's most recent *Cantos*, "Thrones de Los Cantares." But by 1961 he was a ruined man. With his grimy hands, his worn, rumpled suits, and his "greenish-bronze pallor," he had come very far from the handsome, animated poet of twenty years before, "flagrant," as Berryman recalled him at Harvard, with "young male beauty."

.

One consequence of Delmore's transient existence was that he failed to receive an invitation to attend President Kennedy's inauguration on January 21, 1960, until four months after the event. Fifteen other poets had been invited to celebrate what was to become a brief romance between intellectuals and the Kennedy Administration, an alliance Delmore had fervently wished for when Stevenson was a candidate. Delmore and Robert Lowell were the youngest of those invited, the others being men of an older generation, among them Auden, Tate, William Carlos Williams, and of course Robert Frost, who gave a memorable reading that day. Only a decade before, Delmore would have been overwhelmed by this evidence of his great stature. Moreover, he had conceived an enthusiasm for Kennedy that rivaled his admiration for Stevenson, and was elated to have caught a glimpse of him in a motorcade passing through Washington Square. But now he simply regarded the invitation's delayed arrival as yet another manifestation of the conspiracy closing in on him.

In the spring of 1961, the University of California invited Delmore to teach a summer term there, and that June he went out to Los Angeles, where he took a room at the Holiday House in Malibu Beach. On the first day of classes, Delmore asked one of his students, a pretty red-headed freshman of seventeen named Victoria Bay, to rent a car on his behalf and drive him back to Malibu. She ended up living with him the entire summer—except for those nights when he slept in a park on campus, rising in the morning to stand before his class in a grass-stained suit—and when he returned to New York that autumn he asked Victoria to come with him. She was only seventeen, but Delmore was fortunate in her devotion, for over the next two years she took care of him intermittently, even when he reviled her as a "stooge" of various imaginary agents.

When, after much hesitation, Victoria followed him to New York, he announced that he didn't want to see her again, so she went to live in another hotel, found a job as a typist, and didn't see Delmore for several months. Then, one night in October, Delmore went on a rampage and smashed every window in his apartment. The police arrived to find him standing nude in the middle of the room with a lamp in his hands. Brought in handcuffs to Bellevue, he raved on about his legal rights, contended he was a victim of the two most powerful law firms in New York, accused Norman Mailer, James Laughlin, and Hilton Kramer of nefarious deeds, and demanded to see a judge. When he had calmed down, he explained that he had been asleep and awakened suddenly "panic stricken and afraid." Delmore could be very sly about his illness, and while he refused to concede to the physicians who interviewed him that his conduct was in any way aggressive or strange, he became charming when other strategies failed. "The only violent thing I've done was to give beef kidney to my cat," he claimed.

Marshall Allen arranged for Delmore to be transferred to a private hospital, but he walked out the following day. Allen then managed to get him admitted to Columbia

Presbyterian, but Delmore managed to lose his benefactor on the way, and hid out at the Albert Hotel in Greenwich Village. His behavior grew more unpredictable by the day; there were telegrams to Dr. Gruenthal, threatening phone calls to Gruenthal's wife, to whom he intimated that the FBI would want to know about her associations with Brecht, and a fist fight on a Village street. Just before Christmas, however, he was reconciled with Victoria, and together they moved in with some friends on Gansevoort Street. This arrangement was followed by a succession of hotels and, from May to September, a dark apartment on Bank Street.

When the ever-loyal Meyer Schapiro heard of his difficulties, he appealed to Syracuse University to offer Delmore a full professorship. Both Lowell and Bellow supported his recommendation (without, of course, letting Delmore know that they had done so), as did Donald Dike, of the Syracuse English Department, who had sponsored Delmore's visits there in the past. The administration was at first wary, but pressure from Dike, William Wasserstrom, and others in the newly formed creative-writing program persuaded the Vice-Chancellor of the university, Frank Piskor, to offer him a temporary appointment. He was to teach Milton, a course on Eliot and Yeats, and a graduate seminar entitled "The Philosophy of Fiction." So in August 1962, Delmore went up alone to the university where he was to spend the next three years; Victoria decided to remain in New York. A few days later, he called up Dike—from the Syracuse county jail.

17

—————•—————

DURING HIS LAST YEARS, the Delmore who threatened and abused his friends dominated the Delmore loved by so many people, but he never succeeded in destroying their loyalty. Despite his refusal to see them, despite his having taxed their friendship to the very limits, Dwight Macdonald and Meyer Schapiro revered his genius and tried until the end to help him, as did John Berryman, Robert Lowell, Saul Bellow, and a great many others. And he inspired the same unquestioning loyalty in more recent acquaintances: Marshall Allen, Donald Dike, the young women who lived with him at various times. Even in his ruined state, Delmore somehow remained impressive. No matter how ill he was, he always managed "to convey dignity with that noble head," recalled a student of his at Syracuse. "Delmore exerts a moral force just when he paces the hall," observed the poet Philip Booth, his colleague in the Syracuse English Department. An aura of tragedy surrounded Delmore during his years at Syracuse, one that even his increasingly violent and unpredictable behavior could not reduce to squalor.

Delmore's arrival on the campus was inauspicious; he had damaged his hotel room, been "beaten up by police while drunk & alone in bed"—a claim supported by the black eye Dike noticed when he came to bail him out—and was required to appear in court. When the judge learned that Delmore was an eminent writer, he invited him into his chambers, which were stocked with confiscated copies of *Tropic of Cancer*. What was his opinion of this book? the judge wanted to know. Delmore had the sense to give an evasive reply, and the case was dismissed.

In September, he moved into the Skyline Apartments, a high-rise building near the campus, and edged uneasily into his new academic career. Teaching was more of an effort than ever, and he often read aloud from Eliot or *Ulysses* to pass the time. But there were days when he could still summon up the energy to discourse animatedly about his favorite subject: the private lives of writers as revealed in their work. When he taught Eliot, it was invariably in terms of the complicated biographical scheme he had worked out to prove that Eliot's poems constituted a sexual confession. This approach was no mere eccentricity of Delmore's; in concentrating on anecdotes and biography, he meant to reveal the lived experience that informed any literary work, "to convey," in the words of one of his students, "a sense of the works as personal, rather than purely literary statements."

Delmore's profound affinity with Joyce was based in part on his appreciation of Joyce's realism—for it was in this way that he read *Ulysses*—and he would tell his students, "If you want to know Dublin, walk around Syracuse." He himself derived an odd pleasure from the vistas of filling stations and vacant lots around the university, proclaiming their splendor without a trace of irony. He liked to dwell on what one of his graduate students, David Zucker, described as "the broad recognizability of reality." His genuine reverence for the authors whose works he taught never prevented him from observing their human failings, and it was this egalitarian spirit that he tried to communicate to his students, who appreciated his informality and candor. It was a good thing Maude Gonne hadn't yielded to Yeats, he would tell them, because "he wouldn't have known what to do"; and he confided gleefully that Wallace Stevens was an abusive drunk.

But teaching was generally a terrible ordeal, and Delmore was lonely in Syracuse, which he thought of as a form of exile from New York. Victoria joined him in October, and he seemed reasonable for a time. Then, a few weeks later, still another violent scene occurred, at the National Poetry Festival in Washington, D.C. Delmore's reading was an ominous portent; at first, "he seemed to have a new kind of delivery," Richard Eberhart recalled, "normal for a while, then way high, very loud, strident, blatant, eerie." But it soon became evident that this "moving new aesthetic device" was in fact a sign of madness, a verdict confirmed that night when Delmore "hurt his hotel room"—to borrow Richard Wilbur's expressive summation of events. In a characteristic fit of rage, he pulled the telephone from the wall; later on, when he wanted to use it, his earlier misdeed provoked him to renewed frustration and he smashed the phone to splinters, then proceeded to tear up the room. The police were called, and Victoria, who was too young to sign for his release, located John Berryman at a party Robert Frost was giving in a different hotel. Berryman, Richard Wilbur, and Victoria went down to the station, where they found Delmore in a wild mood. "Everything I am doing," he shouted, "I am doing on the orders of the Chief Executive!" He grabbed for Victoria's handbag, asserting that she had taken his money, and insulted Berryman when he tried to intercede; then, just as Wilbur and Berryman were completing the forms for his release at the front desk, Delmore ran out the door and occupied their waiting taxi, locking all the doors. "Berryman, you've taken every woman I ever had!" he shouted enigmatically as the taxi drove off, leaving the forlorn trio stranded on the curb.

•

Back in Syracuse, Delmore suffered through classes and kept apart from the faculty, except for an occasional party where he would hold forth like a "famously Jewish Frost." Once Nelson Algren visited his writing class, and they spent the whole hour gossiping about Simone de Beauvoir, with whom Algren had had a much-publicized liaison. But such moments of animation were rare. For the most part he was more despondent than ever. Then, late that autumn, his mother died. Delmore had not seen her in over a year, and refused to attend her funeral; his only gesture was to send flowers with an altered quotation from Joyce's poem, "Ecce Puer": "Oh mother forsaken, forgive your son" (in the original, the father is addressed). But a closer parallel is to Dedalus in *Ulysses*, refusing to kneel beside his mother's deathbed and pray. "I'm a bad son," Delmore would moan, life once again imitating art as he heard in Buck Mulligan's condemnation of Dedalus—"There is something sinister in you"—a reproach of his own neglect. Delmore's hatred of his mother had always been tempered by pity, a feeling she herself had labored to produce in him ever since he was a child. Now he felt as if he had committed the ultimate betrayal, and he allowed it to torment him for months.

Victoria was finding Delmore impossible to live with,

since he subjected her to the emotional and, some have
said, physical violence reserved for those he loved most. He
was proud of Victoria's youth and beauty, and liked to
introduce her as his fiancée. "Making love to her," he
boasted, "was like Grant taking Richmond"; but his affection was invariably converted by his illness into rage. She
had often thought of leaving him, only to be dissuaded
when Delmore, intuitively sensing what was on her mind,
would plead, "I don't know what I'd do without you."
Finally, in January 1963, he called up from Cambridge to
warn her that "someone was coming to kill her," at which
point she summoned Donald Dike; and while Sanford
Meech, the chairman of the English Department, kept
watch in the lobby to make sure Delmore didn't show up,
they hastily packed up her belongings and drove off to the
airport.

·

Left alone, Delmore lapsed into a severe paranoid state,
the imagined plot against him by Rockefeller and his
agents reaching new levels of implausibility. He now believed that he had been lured to Syracuse so that Rockefeller
could carry on his affair with Elizabeth unhindered in New
York. President Kennedy was implicated as well in Delmore's undoing, along with the Pope and other notables.
His salvation lay in England, where T. S. Eliot and Sieg-
fried Sassoon were in possession of vital information about
a mysterious million dollars that awaited him in Rome. So
Delmore went to New York to make arrangements for a trip
abroad. But instead he registered at the Hotel Earle and
began sending telegrams to Adlai Stevenson at the United
Nations and harassing friends over the telephone. One day
he left a stray cat in the offices of New Directions. A few
weeks later, Delmore returned to Syracuse, where Donald
Dike arranged for his commitment to the Twin Elms Hospital, a private sanatorium near the university.

Despite his fanatical devotion to Freud, Delmore had
remained an intransigent patient through his many years of
therapy, and took a fatalistic view of his condition, which
he had come to consider hereditary. "I won't have anything
to do with them, psychiatrists, psychoanalysts," he once
told William Wasserstrom, citing the experience of Van
Wyck Brooks, who he was convinced had been "brain-
washed" in the course of a mental breakdown. "They ruin

you. Not Freud but the others, the epigones, they iron you out and there's nothing left but to fold." Delmore sensed he was beyond recovery, but defended the idea—loosely adapted from Freud—that paranoia induced heightened insights. "Suppose psychosis clarifies things?" he speculated, invoking Poe as a famous literary instance. Then he would be off on a tirade about conspiracies: "Right this minute I know what's going on, down in Albany . . ." At Twin Elms, he liked to expound Freud to the psychiatrists, militant in his conviction that he had nothing to learn from them. When Dike tried to console him, he was irate: "It's a free country. Who says everyone has to be happy?" It perplexed him to hear other inmates rejoice over having been spared whenever a hearse passed by on the way to a funeral parlor down the road. He "seemed almost to envy the dead," Dike recalled.

After his release in June, Delmore moved into a desolate apartment that featured on the living-room wall a primitive mural of orange trees beside a highway. Sometimes he slept on a sofa in the Hall of Languages, from which he would rise groggily to teach. "He would come to class most often looking tormented, sallow, bloated, shuffling," and read aloud in a passionless voice, stalling for time and glancing repeatedly at his watch. Even then, "beneath the depression and boredom would be the attention to what he was reading," David Zucker recalled, but "he read badly," and the few comments he made were usually "lame, obvious ones."

Alone in his room, Delmore took to poring over his life's work, in some instances annotating and correcting it. From his very earliest poems to the stories he wrote in the fifties, virtually every manuscript bore signs of his agitated scrutiny in the form of dates, strange hieroglyphics, and exclamation marks. On occasion, he would enter a name or brief explanatory note beside some incident drawn from life and thinly fictionalized. It was a melancholy enterprise, for in reading his old manuscripts he was in a sense reading his autobiography. The same crucial events that had obsessed him all his life, events that had doomed him—in that alarming refrain from *Genesis*—to "lie in the coffin of his character," returned again to haunt him in his miserable room devoid of furniture, where the wind rushed in through the windows, open in all weather, scattering his manuscripts about like old newspapers in a city park.

"Don't be like me, Hershey," he scrawled on the last page of *Genesis*; "forgive & live."

.

Even during his worst sieges of depression, Delmore continued to read eagerly, filling the margins of his books with observations and reminiscences. He had collected and dispersed several libraries in the course of his chaotic life, but he could always remember where and on what date he had first purchased a book, information he would meticulously enter in the front of any new acquisition. Kafka, Rilke, Joyce, and Eliot, the great masters of Modernism who had always dominated his consciousness, were the authors he returned to most often, and it was clear from his animated annotations that books could still excite him; he filled his copies of Baudelaire, Valéry, and Rilke with provisional translations, read *The Penguin Encyclopedia* in its entirety, and even commented on the advertisements in the back, checking off the books he had read. On the last page of *The Brothers Karamazov*, a novel with which he identified perhaps more than with any other, he penciled in a single word of praise: "Hurrah!"

Nor did Delmore ever cease to write. The last piece he published was a halting, kindly introduction to a pamphlet of poems by his students, and even that required a prodigious amount of labor; but to the very end, he continued to fill scores of spiral notebooks with a virtually illegible script. ("Beware / to read the meanings which these scribbles bear," he warned on the cover of one.) Here again were the familiar themes: his parents, Mary McCarthy, the *Partisan Review* crowd, and a young man "who had become famous as the boy wonder of the publishing world at the age of twenty-five." *The Lyceum Idea*, a novel that occupied several notebooks, rehearsed the years when he had taught at Harvard. The non-tenured lectureship to which his protagonist had been appointed would have required "a miracle to rescind the terminal appointment's pronouncement of slow suspended but inevitable doom." Moreover, he believed "the fear of genius was universal," and that Lyceum—Delmore's name for Harvard—hired "a certain number of geniuses" (of which he was one) only to preserve the university's prestige. Perhaps his most significant grievance had to do with "being a Jew at Harvard" (Delmore was too involved with his own experience at this point even to change the name). In the last months of his life, he was still protesting the injustices, both real and imagined, of that traumatic period, injustices which represented to Delmore the fatal estrangement he had endured both as a poet and as a Jew.

"No desire for publication," he noted in his journal, and he no longer made any attempt to type up or revise his work. But he was too exacting not to notice its very obvious failings. "All this is not at all necessary or useful," he would note beneath a digressive passage, or simply "not very good." The real problem, however, was one that had always plagued him: "the tendency for memory to act when invention fails."

.

Toward the end of 1964, the manic-depressive roller coaster rose in a sudden steep ascent. "After so many years, at last with much joy for the first time!" he exclaimed over Rilke's poems. And in his journal he marveled: "How much has changed—teaching without emotional blindness, drinking, sleeping, the need for others —all under almost complete control." He had acquired a following of devoted students—"he was a regular Pied Piper," one recalled—who gathered around him in the shabby Orange Bar off campus. Talking for hours without a pause, gesticulating frantically, drinking shots of bourbon and paying for them with hundred-dollar bills, Delmore would elaborate on the anecdotes perfected through many years of practice: his marriages, the sex life of T. S. Eliot, his lost inheritance, and the years at George Washington High School, where he had been "the brightest person ever tested," interspersed with Hollywood gossip and Giants' batting averages. And there were some new exotic variations tailored to the demands of a college audience, including a notable account of how Queen Elizabeth had traveled to the Orient to learn secret techniques of fellatio, which involved introducing rare herbs into her mouth— and had then returned to England, where the first beneficiary of these recondite practices was none other than Danny Kaye. With his pigeon-toed walk, immense stomach, and rumpled clothes, Delmore was by now more or less confined to the vicarious pleasure of talking about sex. He envied his young friends' "healthy appetite" for women, and liked to dwell on his own past exploits. All he wanted now was to marry "a deaf and dumb Italian woman who could cook and loved to fuck."

Delmore felt more comfortable with these students than with the faculty, and they in turn revered him; to Lou Reed, who later formed a famous band, The Velvet Underground, and dedicated a song to Delmore, he was a "spiritual godfather." Eventually Delmore quarreled with most of his friends on the Syracuse faculty, and during his last years there he tended to avoid everyone but the Orange Bar circle. The day after Kennedy's assassination, he wandered through the streets, "staggering in unbuckled galoshes, dazed and purplish"; and when a colleague approached to offer comfort, he lurched away with a look of "criminality." He had now begun to resort once again to intimidation, terrorizing secretaries and threatening to sue the university. Delmore had obviously learned from Ivan Karamazov to "revel in his resentment till he [felt] great pleasure in it," a remark he underscored in his copy of the novel.

Pursued by creditors, he had long since given up answering his mail and no longer even opened it. Dr. Donald Boudreau of the Twin Elms Hospital was particularly irate over Delmore's failure to pay his bill: "Our services saved your professional career as you have said or implied and [saved] you from a state hospital," the doctor reminded him, but to no avail. Delmore—in a draft of a letter he never sent—insisted he was broke, even though his bank account showed almost four thousand dollars.

•

On New Year's Eve, 1964, he met the last of the devoted young women who helped him through these years, Elizabeth Annas, an undergraduate who at twenty had been married and divorced and had a one-year-old son, Blake. At the party where they met, rumors circulated that a famous guest was present, but Delmore's name meant nothing to Elizabeth; unlike so many of the young women who fell for Delmore in his later years, she was drawn to him not by his reputation but by the sheer force of his personality. That night they returned to her house and talked for hours. For a time, they spent many long evenings together, drinking whiskey in Delmore's apartment out of the only glass he owned. It was a sign of Delmore's power that, for all his madness and infirmities, Elizabeth thought of him as a "proper Jewish man," dignified and gentle. In a grotesque display of affection, he once presented her with a bouquet of flowers appropriated from a neighbor's garden, roots and clumps of earth still dangling from their stems.

By the close of 1965, Delmore's condition had deteriorated to the point where he could leave Elizabeth's apartment wearing only one shoe and not even notice it. Exhausted by the demands of their relationship, she ended up in a santorium, where Delmore visited her one day and accused her of being a spy for Rockefeller. He never spoke to her again, and when she left a Christmas tree outside his door as a gesture of reconciliation, he doused it in the bathtub, convinced the tree was wired with explosives.

By this time Delmore had ceased to teach at all. He roamed about the East in an agitated state, and once hired a taxi to drive him from Cambridge all the way to Syracuse. On another occasion, he arrived at John Berryman's house in Providence at eight in the morning, having taken a taxi from Cambridge. As Berryman recalled it in a Dream Song:

> He walked my living-room & did not want breakfast
> or even coffee, or even a drink.
> He paced, I'd say Sit down,
> it makes me nervous, for a moment he'd sit down,
> then pace. After an hour *I* had a drink.
> He took it back to Cambridge,
>
> we never learnt why he came, or what he wanted.
> His mission was obscure. His mission was real,
> but obscure.

The English Department at Syracuse remained loyal to Delmore despite his erratic performance as a teacher, and in the autumn of 1965 unanimously recommended him for tenure. But he was an obvious liability to the university, and the administration had every reason to be hesitant. Tenure had always been a sensitive issue for Delmore, and he was wounded by what he took to be their "prevarication." Whether because of this issue, or simply because "his mission was obscure," Delmore left Syracuse for the last time in January 1966, without informing anyone, and returned to New York, where he took a room at the Hotel Dixie in Times Square.

18

———•———

EVIDENCE OF DELMORE'S former distinction followed him to his last sordid refuge. While he sat alone in his room perusing the *Daily News* and magazines with such names as *Whisper, Stare*, and *Tattler*, letters from the editors of *Eminent Americans* and *Who's Who*, having been forwarded from his publishers to Syracuse to the Hotel Dixie, remained unopened. As late as 1963, M. L. Rosenthal was proclaiming on the front page of *The New York Times Book Review*, "We've an American poetry now and the heirs of its creators are thriving in their season." With the deaths of Frost, William Carlos Williams, and e. e. cummings, a new "space" had opened up, Rosenthal observed, to be occupied by the generation now in its ascendancy. Photographs of Delmore, Randall Jarrell, Robert Lowell, John Berryman, and Theodore Roethke, among others, graced this optimistic cover story, soon to be so cruelly betrayed by events; for within a few years, four members of that generation would be dead, two by premature heart attacks and two by suicide. Delmore's splendid translation of Valéry's sonnet "To Helen," published in *The New York Times* in February 1962, could well have represented the grandeur of their early promise and Delmore's tragic farewell to its blandishments:

I hear the profound horns and the trumpets of war
Matching the rhythm, swinging of the flying oars:
The galleys' chant enchains the foam of sound:
And the gods, exalted at the heroic prow,
E'en though the spit of spray insults each smiling brow,
Beckon to me with arms indulgent, frozen, sculptured,
and dead long long ago.

For months Delmore saw virtually no one, preferring the anonymity of Cavanaugh's Irish Bar in Chelsea to his old haunts in the Village. Occasionally, he would meet Rosalie Netter, one of the young women who had befriended him in the late 1950's, and together they would go to a movie or have dinner at the Egyptian Gardens on West Twenty-ninth Street. But few people even knew where he was, and those who did try to see him, such as his former student Lou Reed, were turned away. Once, he consented to have a drink with another Syracuse student, Erin Clermont, but the evening ended disastrously. Sitting with her in the Plantation Lounge of the Dixie, huddled in a stained black raincoat, Delmore poured forth a tale of perfidy involving everyone at Syracuse; even the filling-station attendants on West Onondaga Street were implicated. Later on, at P. J. Clarke's, Clermont had the temerity to accuse Delmore of "megalomania," where upon he exploded, called her a whore, and sent her away in a taxi. Not long afterward, he moved to another hotel, the Columbia, on West Forty-sixth Street near Sixth Avenue.

A number of friends glimpsed Delmore on the street during those months, a frightening apparition. To Matthew Josephson, who encountered him outside the White Horse, Delmore explained: "You didn't recognize me because the whole shape of my head has changed." When David Diamond observed him trundling along with his shoelaces untied, Delmore managed a feeble wave; but Saul Bellow, who pronounced his pallor "East River gray," was too unnerved to approach his old friend. In *Humboldt's Gift*, Bellow elaborated on this scene, noting the disparity between Citrine's prosperous appearance and Humboldt's, "gray stout sick dusty."

Not long after his arrival in New York, Delmore heralded yet another manic phase: "With the New Year, a consciousness of powers unknown before and the very control and patience longed for for so long!" His tenacious hope still unextinguished, he sat in the Main Reading Room of the New York Public Library filling one notebook after another with incomprehensible novels. In his hotel room, he read with a nervous, consuming attention: *Pilgrim's Progress*, the *Kama Sutra*, a book about the Dead Sea Scrolls, and appropriately enough, the poems of Hölderlin. Still struggling with the inhibited sexuality that had tormented him all his life, he crumpled up his "girlie" magazines (far less explicit in those days than now) as if agitated by their vague allure.

On July 11, a Mrs. Kruger in room 506, just beneath Delmore's, called the desk clerk at three in the morning to complain that "Mr. Schwartz was dropping and throwing things again." Delmore promised the desk clerk he would quiet down. Then he decided to take out the garbage, which meant going down to the lobby. Unshaven, the elbows of his shirt torn, he felt ill as he waited for the elevator, and got off on the fourth floor, where he fell down and tore open his shirt and trousers in an effort to breathe. There he lay for over an hour, until Mr. Kleinman in room 406 called the desk to report a man "making strange noises outside his door." The police arrived at 4:15 in the morning, summoned an ambulance, and started for Roosevelt Hospital, but ten minutes later Delmore was dead of a heart attack.

.

"At the morgue there were no readers of modern poetry," Bellow noted in *Humboldt's Gift*, and so for two days Delmore's body lay unclaimed. Finally, Milton Klonsky, who knew he had been living at the Columbia Hotel, called up to notify him that a check was arriving from Marshall Allen, only to learn from an alarmed desk clerk that Delmore had died two days before. But by this time, a reporter routinely reading over the morgue lists had recognized his name, and on July 14 the *Times* ran a lengthy obituary, accompanied by a late photograph. His body lay still unclaimed at Bellevue, the article reported.

Delmore's aunt Clara, alerted by a family friend, went down to the morgue that afternoon and claimed the body, while Dwight Macdonald arrived at the hotel with a *New Yorker* editor, William Knapp, to collect his belongings. William Buckler, dean of N.Y.U.'s Washington Square campus, offered to pay for the funeral from an emergency Undesignated Fund, and Stanley Saplin, N.Y.U.'s director of community relations, made the final arrangements in an atmosphere of wrangling and dissension. The chaos of Delmore's life pursued him even in death. Clara was suspicious of everyone and demanded that a limousine be sent up to Washington Heights to collect her; rumors circulated that N.Y.U. was trying to appropriate Delmore's manuscripts; some of the official documents listed the name of the deceased as Delmar Schwartz. At the Schwartz Funeral Home on Second Avenue and Tenth Street, a marquee over the doorway proclaimed Delmore's family name, as if his death were a theatrical event—which, in a sense, it was.

Only Elizabeth Annas, in the company of a friend, had come to sit beside Delmore's open coffin on the nights before the funeral, but nearly two hundred people showed up for the service itself. Macdonald and F. W. Dupee spoke of Delmore in his *Partisan Review* days, M. L. Rosenthal said a few words about his poetry, and telegrams from Meyer Schapiro and Robert Lowell were read. Afterward, two cars followed the hearse out to Cedar Park Cemetery in Westwood, New Jersey. Macdonald, Clara Colle, Elizabeth Annas, Victoria Bay, and Peter Locke, a student of Delmore's from Syracuse, reminisced about Delmore on the way. "Our house wasn't Jewish in dishes, or in always going to *shul*," Clara remarked. "Jewish is heart. Delmore was Jewish."

•

Delmore, who derived such pleasure from the incongruous, would have made much of the bizarre events that followed in the wake of his death. A Sister St. Joan Delmore wrote to Macdonald from Minnesota to say that she had been drawn to Delmore's poetry by his name. A chance encounter in a bar between one of Macdonald's sons and the proprietor of the moving company that had stored away a vast cache of Delmore's papers led ultimately to their recovery. But he would have been most amazed by the subsequent revival of his reputation. Through William Barrett's memoirs and others by Macdonald and Philip Rahv, Berryman's vivid *Dream Songs*, and an article by Louis Simpson in *The New York Times Magazine*, Delmore has returned, as he used to predict he would, to haunt the living. And he would perhaps have been surprised to find himself the subject of a best-selling novel by his old friend Saul Bellow. Delmore's photograph in *Newsweek*, his name on the front page of *The New York Times*: and all because Bellow, tormented by the dead, was compelled to resurrect an image of "that grand erratic handsome person with his

wide blonde face, that charming fluent deeply worried man
[who] passionately lived out the theme of Success."

Delmore's family has been dispersed by time and circumstance: his brother is an industrial engineer in Gautier,
Mississippi, while his aunt and uncle live in the same modest apartment in Washington Heights they have occupied
for half a century. What survives is the memory of an
uncanny personality whose genius touched all who knew
him.

> The spirit & the joy, in memory
> live of him on, the young will read his verse
> for as long as such things go:

wrote Berryman, who thought Delmore "the most under-
rated poet of the twentieth century"; and another friend
cited in his behalf Roethke's line, "What's madness but
nobility of soul at odds with circumstance?" And Delmore's literary style was no less influential than his personality. Surely his terse, ironic stories suggested a great
deal to Saul Bellow, while as a poet he had an incalculable
effect on Robert Lowell, who once observed, "I think I've
never met anyone who has somehow as much seeped into
me." He was "*the* genius of the old Partisan group," Alfred
Kazin emphasized; and in that capacity, too—as a luminous intellectual presence—Delmore presided over his generation.

"Into the Destructive Element . . . that is the way,"
Delmore scrawled on a bank-deposit envelope found in his
last hotel room. It was his conviction that the self-immolat-
ing powers of the imagination would lead him to some
purer realm; and it is a measure of the lethal character of
that myth that he died alone in a midtown Manhattan
hotel. But his life, tragic as it was, possessed a demonic
intensity, a fabled agony, that made him memorable. Many
of Delmore's poems will last, and his vivid, strange,
mythologized existence will not be easily forgotten.

Notes

———•———

VIRTUALLY all of Delmore Schwartz's own papers are in the American Collection of the Beinecke Library at Yale. They are by no means complete, the most significant lacuna being letters written to Schwartz, few of which appear to have survived. These papers include stories, poems, unfinished book manuscripts, journals, drafts and copies of letters, and other miscellaneous documents. (Another significant collection of Schwartz's papers, which I examined at Syracuse University, has now been transferred to Yale.) Since so much of my book is based on this collection, I have referred to it only when a particularly valuable source is in question, and the reader may assume that any unattributed evidence has been drawn from there. I have also relied heavily on John Berryman's journals, William Barrett's two memoirs in *Commentary*—cited in the notes to my preface—and on letters Schwartz wrote to James Laughlin, Julian Sawyer, and Gertrude Buckman, citing them only where the source is ambiguous in the text. Schwartz's copiously annotated library is divided between the Department of Special Collections, U.C.L.A., and the George Arents Research Library at Syracuse. Unless otherwise noted, Schwartz's letters are in private hands. On the assumption that his published works are at least potentially available to interested readers, specific page references to them have not been cited here.

PREFACE

ix   "If a life . . . memory": Rambler #60; quoted in James Boswell, *The Life of Dr. Johnson* (London: 1933), 10.

ix   "a toothless . . . nature": Anatole Broyard, *The New York Times* (August 14, 1975), 23.

ix   "deficient . . . life": Philip Rahv, "Delmore Schwartz: The Paradox of Precocity," *The New York Review of Books* (May 20, 1971), 20.

ix   "told . . . other": William Barrett, "The Truants:

Partisan Review in the 40's," *Commentary* (June 1974), 49.

ix   "The stockmarket . . . Wall Street": William Barrett, "Delmore: A 30's Friendship and Beyond," *Commentary* (September 1974), 41.

x   "the only . . . Eliot": Letter to DS from Allen Tate, January 5, 1939. Beinecke Library, Yale.

x   "its most . . . prophet": Morris Dickstein, "Cold War Blues: Notes on the Culture of the Fifties," *Partisan Review* #1 (1974), 35.

x   "the idea . . . Schwartz": Irving Howe, "The New York Intellectuals," *Decline of the New* (New York: 1970), 242.

xi   "intricate . . . labor": Rahv, op. cit., 20.

PART ONE 1913–1945

CHAPTER I

4   "the poet . . . America": Letter to James Laughlin, August 21, 1941.

4   "a beautiful . . . Delmore": Telephone interview with Rose K. Lieberman, 1976.

6   "Tall, dark, dynamic": Ibid.

7   "my Harry, my Harry": Ibid.

8   "She spoke . . . upon it": *The World Is a Wedding* (Norfolk, Conn.: 1948), 107.

9   "decided . . . poet": Author Information Sheet, New Directions office files, 1951.

10   "Tartar blood": Letter to author from Rosemary Mizener, 1975.

10   "unseen and all-seeing": Robert Lowell, "My Last Afternoon with Uncle Devereux Winslow," *Life Studies* (New York: 1959).

14   "shyness . . . social life": Letter to James Laughlin, undated.

15   "an intimate . . . goodness": "The Child Is the Meaning of This Life," *The World Is a Wedding*, 178.

15   "Baba . . . my professor": Interview with Clara Colle, Deutsch Papers.

15   "a means . . . wealth": Clement Greenberg, "Under Forty," *Contemporary Jewish Record* #7 (February 1944), 33.

16   "old-fashioned": Colle interview.

17   "pale . . . life": Telephone interview with Joseph Lotterman, 1975.

18   "The third . . . subway strike": "The Saturday Show," *The Poconola* (August 21, 1926), 10.

18   "That Socrates . . . Napoleon": Joseph Lotterman,

"Pocono Broadcastings," *The Poconola* (August 7, 1926), 2.

20   "learn . . . language": Greenberg, op. cit., 14.

20   "of the lower : . . inheritance": Ibid.

20   " 'philosophical' discourse": Telephone interview with Julie Salomon, 1975.

21   "a cruel . . . man": John Berryman, Journal, March 7, 1943.

21   "a peculiar boy": ibid, February 1, 1943.

25   "an Irish . . . temper": Letter to author from Gertrude Buckman, 1976.

25   "T. S. Eliot . . . prophet": Interview with William Roerick, 1976.

25   "members . . . 1927–1931": *The Poet's Pack*, edited by Mary J. J. Wrinn (New York: William Edwin Rudge, 1932).

25–6   "I am . . . world": Julian Sawyer papers.

26   "like someone . . . self": Letter to author from Gertrude Buckman, 1976.

CHAPTER 2

33   "The aroma . . . bolshevism": Maurice Zolotow, "Bohemia on the Campus," *The American Mercury* (December 1939), 471–6.

39   "i.e. country . . . born": Transcript of application to the University of Wisconsin.

41   "voluble and dogmatic": Schwartz, "An American Fairy Tale," *Successful Love* (New York: 1961), 101.

CHAPTER 3

45   "Shake-Shake": Interview with Stanley Saplin, 1976.

47   "I am . . . make": Letter to Julian Symons, December 6, 1938. Berg Collection.

47   "He sounded . . . Dealer": Interview with Sidney Hook, 1975.

47   "Don't worry . . . nothing": Sidney Hook, "Delmore Schwartz as a Student," unpublished manuscript.

48   "the Catholic . . . arts": *The Memoirs of the Life of Edward Gibbon* (London: 1900), 69.

49   "hoi polloi . . . cynical wit": Interview with Norman Jacobs, 1975.

49–50   "studious . . . poetry": Ibid.

50   "Where's the can?": Letter to James Laughlin, undated.

50   "the poetic . . . demonic": Jacobs interview.

51   "the Odyssey . . . poetry": "Just Off the Press," *Washington Square College Bulletin* (March 8, 1934), 3. N.Y.U. archives.

51 "What Eliot . . . words": *Washington Square College Bulletin* (February 15, 1934), 3.

52 "only served . . . critic": "The Present State of Poetry," *Selected Essays of Delmore Schwartz*, edited by Donald A. Dike and David H. Zucker (Chicago: 1970), 32.

52–3 "In the year . . . intellectuals?": "An Argument in 1934," *Kenyon Review* (Winter 1942), 62.

54 "with a social . . . aesthetic": *Mosaic* (Autumn 1934), 2. Princeton University Library.

54 "devastating attack": *Washington Square College Bulletin* (October 29, 1934), 3.

55 "mastery . . . understanding": "The Stars of Joseph Gordon Macleod," *Mosaic* (Spring 1935), 15.

55 "bourgeois gypsy": Quoted from "A Memoir and Appreciation" by George Dennison, in Paul Goodman, *Collected Poems* (New York: 1973), xiii.

56 "unpublished reputation . . . behind him": Barrett, "Delmore," 45.

56 "That he seemed . . . private": Letter to author from Arnold Canell, 1974.

56 "sacrificial lamb": Interview with Raymond Rosenthal, 1974.

56 "living . . . means": Canell letter.

57 "as intently . . . market": Barrett, "Delmore," 45.

58 "It would be . . . levels": Rorschach interpretation by Benjamin J. Murawski, Peter Bent Brigham Hospital, Boston, Massachusetts.

59 "terribly innocent": Interview with Sigmund Koch, 1976.

59 "When you take . . . orgasm": Interview with Maurice Zolotow, 1975.

60 "a poor . . . 'successful,' ": Buckman letter.

60 "it was always . . . sort": Ibid.

60 "Mrs. Fine's . . . husband": "New Year's Eve," *The World Is a Wedding*, 72.

60 "tough and sardonic and hard": Rosemary Mizener letter.

61 "I was being . . . articulate": Letter to author from Gertrude Buckman, 1977.

62 "The self . . . hot": Quoted in Lila Lee Valenti, "The Apprenticeship of Delmore Schwartz, *Twentieth Century Literature* (July 1974), 205.

62–3 "The blueness . . . understood": Ibid.

64 "a sacred . . . universe": Koch interview.

CHAPTER 4

71 "professional philosopher": Letter to Gertrude Buckman, March 7, 1936.

71 "I am . . . delightful": Letter to Paul Goodman,
     October 1, 1935; published in *Antaeus*, #23 (Au-
     tumn 1976), 181.

71 "I'm at Harvard . . . friends": Interview with Ben
     Hellman, 1976.

72 "Prolegomena . . . Poetry": Letter to Gertrude Buck-
     man, January 18, 1936.

72 "You're wrong . . . matters": Letter to Maurice
     Zolotow, January 19, 1936. U.C.L.A.

72 "inevitable self-consciousness": Letter to Goodman.

72 "He was . . . people": Interview with Arthur Berger,
     1974.

73 "a *laideur* . . . Epstein": Harry Levin, "Delmore's
     Gift," unpublished manuscript.

73 "His eyes . . . listened": Letter to author from Gerson
     Brodie, 1976.

73-4 "That I . . . Remind me' ": Letter to Goodman.

75 "with a . . . mineral!": Berryman, Journal, undated.

75 "devouring . . . weeks": Letter to Gertrude Buckman,
     undated.

75-6 "Wolfson . . . class": Letter to Zolotow.

76 "in enemy territory": Letter to Richard McDougall
     from Harry Levin, undated.

76 "Both of them . . . students": Levin, "Delmore's
     Gift."

76-7 "systems . . . Existence": Letter to Zolotow.

77 "The price . . . hate": Letter to Gertrude Buckman,
     January 4, 1936.

78 "now, alone . . . will": Quoted in a letter to Gertrude
     Buckman, February 16, 1936.

78 "prescribed minutes . . . especially": Letter to Ger-
     trude Buckman, undated.

79 "Old age . . . die": "Old Man in the Crystal Morning
     after Snow," *Poetry* (February 1937), 252-3.

80 "Now . . . distance": *Choosing Company, The New
     Caravan*, edited by Alfred Kreymborg, Paul Rosen-
     feld, and Lewis Mumford (New York, 1936), 271.

80 "sensitiveness . . . literature": William Phillips, "Mark-
     ing Time," *New Masses* (December 26, 1936), 23.

81 "It is in . . . future": P. M. Jack, "The *New Caravan*'s
     Wide Diversity," *The New York Times Book Re-
     view* (January 17, 1937), 2.

81 "In seeking . . . beliefs": "Poetry and Imitation,"
     Bowdoin Prize Essay, 1936. Harvard University
     archives.

82 "Mirror . . . society": "A Note on the Nature of Art,"
     Marxist Quarterly (January–March 1937), 307.

83 "Miserere Me": Interview with Lincoln Reis, 1975.

84   "none . . . so many": Letter to Gertrude Buckman, September 19, 1936.

CHAPTER 5

85   "to finance . . . novel": Letter to Gertrude Buckman, August 9, 1936.

85   "did not . . . book": Letter to author from Clifton Fadiman, 1976.

85   "In the end . . . concerned": Letter to Arthur Berger, March 24, 1937.

86   "The vision . . . you!": Letter to DS from William Barrett, September 13, 1942. Yale.

88   "I am . . . mislaid": Letter to Arthur Berger, April 15, 1937.

88   "charming": Interview with Solomon Surowitz, 1975.

89   "young writers . . . follows it": Richard Ellmann, *James Joyce* (New York: 1959), 263.

90   "Europeanization . . . literature": Philip Rahv, "The Cult of Experience in American Writing," in *Literature and the Sixth Sense* (Boston: 1970), 37.

90   "was born . . . radicalism": Leslie Fielder, " 'Partisan Review': Phoenix or Dodo?" *Perspectives* #15, 85.

91   "had the sense . . . masterpiece": Dwight Macdonald, "Delmore Schwartz 1913–1966," *The New York Review of Books* (September 8, 1966), 14; reprinted in *Selected Essays of Delmore Schwartz*.

91   "extreme precocity . . . possessed him": Rahv, "Delmore Schwartz: The Paradox of Precocity," 21.

92   "Philip does . . . Slav": Barrett, "The Truants," 49.

93   "violet . . . child": Telephone interview with Mary McCarthy, 1976.

93   "day-long epic account": Letter to author from Arthur Mizener, 1976.

94   "immense charm . . . erudition": Interview with F. W. Dupee, 1974.

94–5   "Delmore was . . . reaches": Macdonald, op. cit., xvi.

97   "All I ask . . . wonderful": Letter to Arthur Berger, undated.

97   "You're throwing . . . department": Reis interview.

97   "one had to . . . poet": Interview with Harold Rosenberg, 1974.

97   "friend of . . . et al.": Letter to Berger.

98   "He seated . . . movies": "Screeno," *Partisan Review*, Fall 1977.

100   "the conscious . . . psychic life": "The Two Audens," *Kenyon Review* (Winter 1939), 34–45; reprinted in *Selected Essays of Delmore Schwartz*.

100–1   "the *representation* . . . attitude": "Primitivism and

Decadence," *Southern Review* III, #3 (1938), 28–39; reprinted in *Selected Essays of Delmore Schwartz*.

101   "it is only . . . age": Rahv, "Delmore Schwartz: The Paradox of Precocity," 22.

102   "if you want . . . you": Letter from James Laughlin to DS, January 15, 1938. Yale.

104   "Suppose . . . suit": Quoted in letter to Pound from DS, April 9, 1938; published in *Antaeus*, #23, 86. Yale.

104–5   "This is only . . . whole": Ibid.

106   "NEXT/ . . . contrast": Ibid.

106–7   "And your unawareness . . . sense": Letter to Pound from DS, May 19, 1938; published in *Antaeus* #23, 188. Yale.

110   "The river . . . disease": Galleys of *Vaudeville for a Princess*. Houghton Library, Harvard University.

CHAPTER 6

111   "Everything . . . needed": Letter to F. W. Dupee, July 6, 1938. Columbia.

112   "My lord . . . came": Buckman letter, 1976.

114   "suspicion . . . with him": Letter to James Laughlin, undated.

114   "sensitive . . . mastery": Letter to F. W. Dupee, August 24, 1938. Columbia.

114   "great deal . . . opinions": Letter to John Crowe Ransom, September 24, 1938. Kenyon College archives.

115   "the Lord . . . gluttony": Interview with William Barrett, 1974.

116   "How could . . . home?": Interview with Elizabeth Pollet, 1974.

118   "They don't know . . . poet": Rosenberg interview.

118   "after . . . asylum": Letter to James Laughlin, August 17, 1941.

118–9   "Put . . . Tom": Interview with James Laughlin, 1974.

119   "Get hot . . . morning": Letter to James Laughlin, undated.

119   "obviously tense": Letter to author from Allen Tate, 1975.

120   "I am . . . letter": Letter to Arthur Berger, October 10, 1938.

120   "a great . . . writer": Review of W. C. Williams, *Collected Poems: 1906–1938, Common Sense* (February 1939), 24.

120   "no editor . . . happen": Letter to Selden Rodman, November 2, 1938.

121   "could use . . . id": Diary of Selden Rodman, March 21, 1939.

121   "Your book . . . parallel": Letter to DS from Allen Tate, January 5, 1939. Yale.

121-2   "I shall . . . generation": Letter to DS from George Marion O'Donnell, January 9, 1939, Yale.

122   "liked . . . book": Letter to DS from Kenneth Schwartz, Syracuse University Archives; quoted in "The Present State of Poetry," *Selected Essays of Delmore Schwartz.*

122   "as good . . . generation": Mark Van Doren, "Music of a Mind," *Kenyon Review* (Spring 1939), 282.

123   "the one . . . America": George Marion O'Donnell, "Delmore Schwartz's Achievement," *Poetry* (May 1939), 107.

123   "since . . . meaning": F. W. Dupee, "The Book of the Day," *The New York Sun* (March 13, 1939), 24.

123   "an inexhaustible . . . reveal": R. P. Blackmur, "The Poet's Responsibilities," *Partisan Review* (Spring 1939), 118.

123   "Modern . . . directness": Louise Bogan, "Young Modern," *The Nation* (March 25, 1939), 353-4.

124-5   "the deepest . . . outsider": "The Isolation of Modern Poetry," *Kenyon Review* (Spring 1941), 211; reprinted in *Selected Essays of Delmore Schwartz.*

127   "the values . . . fruition": Letter to Seldon Rodman, undated.

130   "to develop . . . international": Letter to Robert Hivnor, November 3, 1940.

131   "the I . . . action": Letter to James Laughlin, undated.

132   "the sing-song . . . anti-rhetoric": Irving Howe, *World of Our Fathers* (New York: 1976), 592.

132   "the poet . . . England": Irving Howe, "Delmore Schwartz—a Personal Appreciation," *The New Republic* (March 10, 1962), 26.

CHAPTER 7

134   "You ought . . . Broadway!": Rodman diary, April 17, 1939.

134   "immense . . . manner": Alfred Kazin, "Delmore Schwartz, 1913–1966," New York *World Journal Tribune Book Week* (October 9, 1966), 1.

134   "slovenly . . . tense": Saul Bellow, *Humboldt's Gift* (New York: Viking, 1975), 11.

135   "to insist . . . anthology": Letter to Robert Hivnor, September 8, 1939.

136   "Casuistry . . . to be so": Letter to John Berryman, May 29, 1939.

136   "Everything . . . bought": Letter to James Laughlin, January 16, 1939.

137   "There is . . . mind": Letter to John Crowe Ransom, February 21, 1939. Kenyon College archive.

137   "ethical-logical": John Crowe Ransom, *The New Criticism* (Norfolk, Conn.: 1941), 212.

137   The letters from Prall, Van Doren, and Hook are in the Beinecke Library at Yale.

138   "the creative . . . wife": Letter to Mark Van Doren, April 4 ,1939. Columbia.

139   "one of . . . simplicities": Letter to John Berryman, May 29, 1939.

140   "With the advent . . . itself": "A Man in His Time," *Partisan Review* (Summer 1944), 350.

141-2   "a way . . . life": Letter to Mark Van Doren, September 16, 1939. Columbia.

142   "By this time . . . another": Letter to F. W. Dupee, November 1, 1939. Columbia.

142   "I might . . . light": Letter to Arthur Mizener, May 7, 1940.

145   "intelligence . . . possible": "The Criterion, 1922–1939," *Kenyon Review* (Autumn 1939), 438.

145   "I feel . . . *Responsibilities*": Letter from T. S. Eliot to DS, October 26, 1939. Houghton Library.

147-8   This account of Delmore's visit with Auden is drawn from the diary of Robert Hivnor, December 18, 1939.

148   "eastern . . . Protofascists": Letter to author from Arthur Mizener, 1975.

149   "with almost . . . issues": Ibid.

149   "His complexion . . . ramified": Rosemary Mizener letter.

149-50   "the sensibility . . . association": "The Isolation of Modern Poetry," 7.

150   "eloquent . . . either of us": Letter to Mark Van Doren, January 29, 1940. Columbia.

150   "very self-conscious about herself": Rosemary Mizener letter.

151   "as a result . . . life": Letter to F. W. Dupee, November 1, 1939. Columbia.

152   "This has excited . . . soon": Letter to John Berryman, January 28, 1940.

CHAPTER 8

153   " 'indifference' . . . principle": Levin, "Delmore's Gift."

154   "My mother . . . looking at": Letter to R. P. Blackmur, February 18, 1943. Princeton.

154–5   "Dear Mr. Pound . . . Schwartz": Letter to Ezra
        Pound, March 5, 1939; published in *Antaeus* #23,
        189, Yale.

155   "a new basis . . . years": 'H.H.' [James Laughlin]
        and S.D. [Delmore Schwartz], "Notes on Ezra
        Pound's Cantos: Structure and Metric," a pamphlet
        bound into review copies of Ezra Pound, *Cantos
        LII–LXXI* (Norfolk, Conn.: 1940); reprinted in
        Ezra Pound: The Critical Heritage (London, 1973).

156   "There too . . . Jew": Greenberg, op. cit., 12.

156   "refugees . . . Jews": Berryman, Journal, March 7,
        1943.

156   "Fuck the Jews!": Letter to R. P. Blackmur, May 3,
        1942.

156   "My ancestors . . . something": "A Bitter Farce,"
        The World Is a Wedding, 103.

157   "a central . . . view": Greenberg, op. cit., 33.

157   "the alienation . . . beg": Letter to Dwight Macdonald,
        undated. Sterling Library, Yale.

157   "I never . . . poet": Rosenberg interview.

157   "a dandy . . . Bostonian": Matthew Josephson, "Im-
        proper Bostonian: John Wheelwright and His
        Poetry," *Southern Review* (Spring 1971), 509.

158   "The people . . . catalogue": Letter to F. W. Dupee,
        April 24, 1940. Columbia.

159   "As you probably . . . sentiment": Ibid.

159   "The result . . . read": Letter to Arthur Mizener,
        March 7, 1940.

159   "something like a sacrilege": Justin O'Brien, "A
        Mystic in the Raw," *Kenyon Review* (Spring 1940),
        232.

159   "unfortunately . . . language": Philip Blair Rice,
        "The Rimbaud Mystery Clarified," *Poetry* (May
        1940), 97.

160   "ignorant . . . stones": Paul Rosenfeld, "Rimbaud in
        Two Translations," *Saturday Review of Literature*
        (January 20, 1940), 16.

160   "evolving . . . language": Mary Colum, "Experiment
        and Evaluation," *Book Forum* (March 4, 1940),
        130.

160   "fairly good": Letter to James Laughlin from T. S.
        Eliot, February 16, 1940. Yale.

160   "Schwartz's . . . matter": Letter to Leonard Van
        Geyzel from Wallace Stevens, May 24, 1940; *Let-
        ters of Wallace Stevens*, edited by Holly Stevens
        (New York: 1966), 356.

160   "surprisingly . . . original": Herbert Gorman, "Arthur
        Rimbaud's 'Season in Hell,'" *The New York Times
        Book Review* (January 28, 1940), 5.

160–1   "an adequate pony . . . edification": Letter to Arthur Mizener, April 2, 1940.

160   "sheer perverseness": Roger Shattuck, "The Brother of Us All," *The New York Review of Books* (June 1, 1967), 10.

161   "What happened . . . before": Letter to John Berryman, February 26, 1940.

161   "I trusted . . . dictionary": Letter to James Laughlin, April 18, 1952.

161   "The history . . . life": *A Season in Hell* (Norfolk, Conn.: 1939), xii.

162   "the last . . . poetry": *A Season in Hell*, 2nd ed. (Norfolk, Conn.: 1940), 12.

162   "Maybe the Old . . . mind": Letter to Laughlin from Eliot.

162   "tiresome . . . Jewish": Letter to James Laughlin, March 7, 1940.

162   Delmore's letters to Macdonald are in the Sterling Memorial Library at Yale.

163   "ontological contradiction": Barrett interview.

165   "in the middle . . . literature": Letter to Robert Hivnor, October 13, 1940.

165–6   "made . . . end": Letter to John Berryman, March 7, 1940.

166   "Sometimes . . . obsessions": Letter to Arthur Mizener, May 7, 1940.

166   "to get . . . texture": Ibid.

170   "The function . . . way—": "Paris and Helen," *New Directions in Prose and Poetry* (Norfolk, Conn.: 1941), 207.

170   "coward . . . view of him": Philip Rahv, "Souvenir and Experiments," *Kenyon Review* (Spring 1942), 239.

174   "But you . . . down": Letter to author from Lionel Abel, 1975.

175   "I have . . . idea": Letter to R. P. Blackmur, October 23, 1941. Princeton.

177   "put no . . . work": Rahv, "Delmore Schwartz: The Paradox of Precocity," 19.

177   "a Washington . . . country": "The Fiction of William Faulkner," *Southern Review* VII, #1 (1941), 149; reprinted in *Selected Essays of Delmore Schwartz*.

178   "in preparation": Cf. frontispiece to John Berryman, *Stephen Crane* (New York: 1950).

178–9   "The poet . . . overconcentration": "The Poetry of Allen Tate," *Southern Review* V, #3 (1940), 431; reprinted in *Selected Essays of Delmore Schwartz*.

179   "The inside . . . ideas": "Poetry and Belief in Thomas Hardy," *Southern Review* VI, #1 (1940), 71; re-

printed in *Selected Essays of Delmore Schwartz*.

180   "moralistic . . . type": Interview with Milton Klonsky, 1974.

181   "utterly disgusted": Rosemary Mizener letter.

CHAPTER 9

182   "not even . . . asked": Letter to R. P. Blackmur, undated. Princeton.

183   "ran with . . . De Voto": Letter to author from Wallace Stegner, 1974.

183   "talking pessimistic . . . mask": Levin, Delmore's Gift," and an undated letter from Levin to Richard McDougall.

183–4   "Goodka . . . back": Ibid.

184   "mesmerized": McCarthy telephone interview.

184   "the most . . . far": James Joyce, *Letters* III, edited by Richard Ellmann (New York: 1966), 468.

186   "considerable profundity": Mary Colum, "The New Books of Poetry," *The New York Times Book Review* (November 30, 1941), 5.

186   "undistinguished": Babette Deutsch, "Poets and New Poets," *The Virginia Quarterly Review* (Winter 1942), 134.

186   "adolescent . . . humorless": Edna Lou Walton, "Names and Symbols," New York *Herald Tribune Books* (November 23, 1941), 33.

187   "an original . . . imagination": *Poetic Drama: An Anthology of Plays from the Ancient Greek to the Modern American*, ed. Alfred Kreymborg (New York: 1941), 842.

187   "separate entities": Letter to Robert Hivnor, December 12, 1940.

187   "keen . . . brother": Barrett interview.

187   "Jews don't drink": Interview with Eileen Simpson, 1974.

190   "experiment . . . sake": Letter to Gertrude Buckman, October 7, 1943.

190   "the prison-house of English A": Letter to James Laughlin, undated.

191   "no political . . . abstraction": Letter to Dwight Macdonald, August 30, 1943. Sterling Library, Yale.

191   "trimming . . . issues": Letter to DS from Dwight Macdonald, September 30, 1943; copy in Sterling.

192   "You have . . . hopes": Letter to William Carlos Williams, August 20, 1943; published in *Antaeus*, #23, 191. Yale.

193   "no energy . . . anyone": Letter to James Laughlin, September 4, 1942.

193   "I was drunken . . . summer": Letter to R. P. Black-
        mur, September 10, 1942. Princeton.

193   "for the last . . . Cambridge": Letter to R. P. Black-
        mur, October 18, 1942. Princeton.

193   "set pieces . . . painting": Macdonald, "Delmore
        Schwartz," xviii.

193-4   "that gratification . . . eyes": Letter to Gertrude
        Buckman, July 2, 1943.

194   "the great . . . necessity": Letter to Robert Hivnor,
        October 25, 1939.

194   "William . . . ambiguity": Letter to Gertrude Buck-
        man, November 23, 1943.

194-5   "I've felt . . . glory": Letter to Robert Hivnor,
        October 13, 1940.

195   "You said . . . were": John Berryman, *The Dream
        Songs* (New York: 1969), 171.

195   "His taste . . . dead": Robert Lowell, "For John
        Berryman," *The New York Review of Books*, April
        6, 1972, 3.

195   "complicated . . . scheme": Letter to John Berryman,
        May 8, 1940.

196   "Let's join . . . small": Quoted in a preface by Saul
        Bellow to John Berryman, *Recovery* (New York:
        1973), ix.

197   "to let . . . look at it": Quoted in John Haffenden,
        "Berryman in the Forties: A Biographical Passage
        I," *The New Review* III, #30, 10.

197   "electrical . . . love": Berryman, *The Dream Songs*,
        174.

197   "Deep . . . head": Berryman, "At Chinese Checkers,"
        Short Poems (New York: 1967), 40.

198   "but you . . . city": Quoted in Haffenden, "Berryman
        in the Forties II," *The New Review* III, #31, 26.

198   "Living . . . month": Letter to Mark Van Doren,
        March 22, 1942.

198-9   "My own . . . with him": Ibid.

201-2   "I have . . . drought": Letter to Mark Van Doren,
        March 22, 1942.

204   Auden's letter, dated August 26, 1942, is in the
        Beinecke Library; for the complete text, see *Antaeus*
        #23, 194-7.

210   "All poet's . . . will—": Letter to R. P. Blackmur,
        January 22, 1943. Princeton.

CHAPTER 10
211   "I must . . . powers": "A Poet's Notebooks," edited
        by Lila Lee Valenti, *New York Quarterly* (Spring
        1972), 117.

211 "as a Modernist . . . Jew": Letter to Gertrude Buckman, undated.

213 "inept . . . visitor": Letter to Kenneth Henry, April 27, 1943.

214 "First . . . this!": Interview with Oscar Handlin, 1975.

216 "a harmonious . . . art": Richard Eberhart, "Beginning of a Beginning," *The New Republic* (June 14, 1943), 803.

216 "a compelling . . . things": Dudley Fitts, "Among Recent Books," *Accent* (Summer 1943), 244.

216 "a positive . . . sensibility": Frank Jones, "Ourself When Young," *The Nation* (August 14, 1943), 187.

216 "The whole . . . profound": Northrop Frye, "Books of the Month," *Canadian Forum* (June 1943), 69.

216 "when completed . . . novel": Gustav Davidson, *The New York Times Book Review* (June 6, 1943), 6.

216 "Apart from . . . mid-ocean": Letter to Dwight Macdonald, August 30, 1943. Sterling.

216 "unreadable . . . commentary": Letter to DS from Dwight Macdonald, July 21, 1943.

216 "inner . . . year": Letter to Dwight Macdonald, undated. Sterling.

216–7 "It is difficult . . . gloom": Paul Goodman, "What a Poet Remembers," *The New Leader* (May 22, 1943), 3.

217 "more critical . . . live up to": F. O. Matthiessen, "A New York Childhood," *Partisan Review* (May–June 1943), 293.

217 "A poet . . . newspaper": "Poetry and Imitation," 17.

220 "involved . . . society": "The Sick City and the Family Romance," *The Nation* (January 12, 1946), 47.

222 "Posthumously": Letter to author from David Kerner, 1976.

223 "day . . . collapse": Letter to R. P. Blackmur, October 18, 1943.

223 "a great . . . pleasant": Letter to James Laughlin, undated.

223 "When asked . . . language": Letter to W. H. Auden, November 16, 1943. Yale.

224 "Everyone . . . parties": Letter to R. P. Blackmur, August 11, 1943. Princeton.

224 "When Mike . . . *staff!*": In the possession of Dwight Macdonald.

225 "Coleridge-like": Interview with Aileen Ward, 1974.

225 "in an indirect way": Ibid.

226 "Today . . . as it is": Letter to John Berryman, December 8, 1943.

230 "the paradigmatic . . . craved": Rahv, op. cit., 22.

230 "He's a . . . poet": Handlin interview.

231 "specious adultery": Letter to Gertrude Buckman, November 23, 1943.

231-2 "This was . . . woman": William Barrett to author in conversation, 1976.

232 "as if contemptuous of life": Letter to DS from James Laughlin, reporting on the impressions of Robert Hivnor, undated.

232 "You have . . . reasons": Letter to Helen Blackmur, undated.

PART TWO 1945-1957

CHAPTER 11

237 "individual integrity": Quoted in Alan Wald, "Revolutionary Intellectuals: Leon Trotsky and *Partisan Review* in the 1930's," *Occident* (Spring 1974), 131.

237 "It was a case . . . country": Bellow, op. cit., 12.

238 "anxious . . . adopted": Howe, "The New York Intellectuals," 218.

238 "it wasn't . . . cards": Quoted in Barrett, "The Truants," 61.

239 "intellectual's chorus girl": Telephone interview with Milton Klonsky, 1977.

239-40 "There was a large . . . space": Elizabeth Pollet, "Cold Water Flat," *New World Writing* (New York: 1953), 67.

240 "In the pages . . . Williams": Interview with Patricia Eden, 1975.

240 "Well, I . . . months": Barrett interview.

241 "Delmore . . . business": Quoted in Barrett, "Delmore," 50.

241 "He invariably . . . himself": "Delmore Schwartz: The Paradox of Precocity," 20.

242 "You've got . . . Philip": Quoted in Barrett, "Delmore," 49.

242 Delmore's remarks on Theodore Spencer and Allen Tate are in letters to R. P. Blackmur and James Laughlin.

242 "exhausts . . . sympathy": Letter to Robert Lowell, December 15, 1945. Houghton Library, Harvard.

242 "in a croaking voice": Interview with Robert Lowell, 1975.

242 "Everything . . . forth in him": *Writers at Work: The Paris Review Interviews, Second Series* (New York: 1965), 362.

242   "loyal but thoughtless friend": Interview with Clement Greenberg, 1975.

243   "The idea . . . itself": "The Noble Voice," *Sewanee Review* (October–December 1947), 707.

243   "lived . . . promise": Allen Tate, *Recent American Poetry and Poetry Criticism* (Washington, D.C.: Library of Congress, 1943), 17.

243   "promise . . . achievement": Horace Gregory and Marya Zaturenska, *A History of American Poetry, 1900–1940* (New York: 1946), 495.

243   "ablest . . . poetry": John Berryman, review of Randall Jarrell, *Poetry and the Age, The New Republic* (November 2, 1953), 17; reprinted in *Randall Jarrell 1914–1965*, edited by Robert Lowell, Peter Taylor, and Robert Penn Warren (New York: 1967).

244   "His books . . . expression": "He Too Has Lived in America," *Partisan Review* (Winter 1945), 128.

244   "What . . . untrue": Ibid., 130.

244   "believed . . . poetry": Kazin, "Delmore Schwartz, 1913–1966," 18.

245   "The Jewish . . . theme": Greenberg, op. cit., 13.

246   "If you can't . . . mention": Letter to R. P. Blackmur, undated. Princeton.

246   A copy of this letter to Elizabeth Pollet is in the Beinecke Library.

248–9 "One might . . . phonograph": Letter to Helen Blackmur, February 2, 1946.

250   "I've never . . . gladness": Letter to Robert Lowell, April 12, 1959. Houghton.

250   "We got . . . milk": Interview with Jean Stafford, 1976.

251   "with a fearful . . . audibility": Letter to author from Richard Wilbur, 1974.

251–2 "I've been . . . cans": Letter to William Barrett, January 27, 1946.

252   "If it is not . . . possible?": Letter to Elizabeth Pollet, March 26, 1946.

253   "to give . . . ulcers": Letter to James Laughlin, undated.

253   "green-faced . . . dishevelled": Interview with Morton Margolis, 1976.

253   "the image . . . poet": Quoted in "Kenneth Koch: 'I Like Writing,'" by William Zavatsky, *The New York Times Book Review* (April 10, 1977), 27.

254   "The Literary Dictatorship of T. S. Eliot," *Partisan Review* (February 1949), 119–37.

255   "melancholy and unavailable": Letter to author from Leslie Fiedler, 1975.

CHAPTER 12

256   "Everything . . . manage not to": Letter to F. W. Dupee, June 2, 1947. Columbia.

258   "To be . . . parents": Greenberg, op. cit., 14.

259   "the definitive . . . Depression": R. W. Flint, "The Stories of Delmore Schwartz," *Commentary* (April 1962), 337.

261   "among . . . writers": "Stories Through a Plate Glass," *Time* (August 9, 1948), 86.

262   "handsome . . . old ones": Galleys of *Vaudeville for a Princess*. Houghton.

262   "coarsened . . . weight": Simpson interview.

262   "Anyone . . . work": Ibid.

263   "I got married . . . crime": "A Poet's Notebooks," 117.

CHAPTER 13

265   "every modern . . . over-simplifications": "Views of a Second Violinist," *Partisan Review* (December 1949), 1251, 1254.

265   "Existentialism . . . you": "Does Existentialism Still Exist?" *Partisan Review* (December 1948), 1362.

265   "the most lucid . . . life": Quoted in *Current Biography*, 1943, 1249.

266   "As things . . . mass": "Our Country and Our Culture," *Partisan Review* (September–October, 1952), 596.

267   "Yet from . . . magnanimous": "There'll Be Others but None So for Me," *Vaudeville for a Princess* (New York: 1950), 75.

268   "a rare . . . wonder": "The Reynolds Girls," *Time* (November 20, 1950), 112.

268   "delicacy and perception": Review by Ray Pierre, *Saturday Review* (December 30, 1950), 37.

270   "a traffic . . . Styx": Letter to Randall Jarrell, October 4, 1950. Berg Collection.

270   "destroyed . . . hero-worship": "Fun with the Famous, Stunned by the Stars," *Vaudeville for a Princess*, 29–33.

272   "You couldn't . . . Jew": Interview with Edward T. Cone, Deutsch Papers.

272   "notes . . . places": Mark Shechner, "Isaac Rosenfeld's World," *Partisan Review* #4 (1976), 536.

273–4   "with his big . . . Barsetshire": Letter to author from George Lanning, 1975.

277   "banality": Louise Bogan, "Verse," *The New Yorker* (June 9, 1951), 94.

277   "the extreme . . . music-hall": David Daiches, "Some Recent Poetry," *The Yale Review* (Winter 1951), 357.

277　"Dear Delmore . . . Stevens": Letter to DS from Wallace Stevens, October 9, 1950, in *Letters of Wallace Stevens*, 693.

278　"I'm not . . . print": Letter to Wallace Stevens, October 11, 1950. Huntington Library, San Marino, California.

278　"We are printing . . . for you": Letter to DS from Karl Shapiro, September 13, 1951; copy in the *Poetry* magazine papers, University of Chicago Library.

278　"The unbelievable . . . burden": Hugh Kenner, "Bearded Ladies & the Abundant Goat," *Poetry* (October 1951), 50–53.

279　"Rahv . . . drove": Interview with Robert Fitzgerald, 1975.

279　"Bored . . . disorganized": Interview with Irving Howe, 1974.

279　"Pistils and stamens!": Rosemary Mizener letter.

CHAPTER 14

280　"Burdocks . . . fields": Bellow, op. cit., 22.

280　"landed . . . trash": Letter to Oscar Handlin, February 4, 1953.

280　"after extorting . . . friend": Letter to James Laughlin, January 29, 1952.

281　A copy of this letter to Van Wyck Brooks is in the Beinecke Library.

284　"By then . . . spook": Quoted in William Wasserstrom, *The Legacy of Van Wyck Brooks: A Study of Maladies and Motives* (Carbondale, Ill.: 1971), 9.

284　"buckshoe humanists": Howe interview.

284　"Delmore . . . cash": Broyard, op. cit., 23.

285　"In the unpredictable . . . survives": "The Vocation of the Poet in the Modern World," *Poetry* (July 1951), 231.

288　"What perplexes . . . rate": Letter to Roger Straus, March 2, 1952.

289　"He still . . . clerk": Hayden Carruth, "Delmore, 1913–1966," *Texas Quarterly* (Summer 1967), 45.

291　"a real . . . education": Monroe Engel, "An Educational Incident," *The Harvard Advocate* (Spring 1969), 18.

292　"knock his block off": Cone interview.

292　"Listen . . . Aristotle": Ibid.

292　"a sanctuary . . . ass-kissing": Bellow, op. cit., 128.

292　"I was told . . . critic": Author Information Sheet, New Directions office files, 1951.

293　"I don't . . . King": Eden interview.

293 Trilling's essay is to be found in *The Liberal Imagination* (New York: 1950); Delmore's essay in *Partisan Review* (January and May, 1953). Reprinted in *Selected Essays of Delmore Schwartz*.

295 "reciprocal aggressiveness": A phrase quoted in the draft of a letter to Trilling from DS. Yale.

295 "Finally . . . get about": Ibid.

296 "an old . . . during the fall": A copy of this letter is in the Beinecke Library.

297 "Punish me, I'm guilty!": Interview with Helen Blackmur, 1974.

297 "coming . . . benediction": Letter to Mrs. Matthew Josephson; files of the National Institute of Arts and Letters.

297 "perhaps . . . America": National Institute files.

297 "You know . . . university": Letter to Carlos Baker, April 17, 1953.

298 "machinery . . . civilization": Bellow, op. cit., 118.

298 "Brilliant . . . quick": Carlos Baker, "Bellow's Gift," *Theology Today* (January 1976), 411.

298 "not at all optimistic": Letter from James Laughlin to DS, May 3, 1953.

298–9 "What has happened . . . man": A copy of this letter is in the Beinecke Library.

299 "extreme . . . foundation": Letter to Carlos Baker, June 10, 1953.

300 "one of the most . . . world": Review of Randall Jarrell, *Poetry and the Age, The New York Times Book Review*, August 16, 1953.

300 "thinness . . . reference": Review of Randall Jarrell's *Little Friend, Little Friend, The Nation* (December 1, 1945), 19.

301 "One cannot . . . responsibility": "Sympathy and Insight," *The New York Times Book Review* (April 5, 1953), 6.

302 "I can't think . . . typewriters": Letter to Oscar Handlin, February 4, 1953.

302 "in which case . . . strategy": Letter to James Laughlin, January 4, 1953.

302 "more or less . . . benefactor": Letter to Max Gruenthal, January 28, 1953.

303 "terrific . . . Island": Letter to Saul Bellow, March 31, 1954. University of Chicago Library.

303 "very nice . . . weeks": Letter to Arthur Mizener, October 27, 1954.

304 "the fallacy of pseudo-reference": Review of Elia Kazan's movie *East of Eden, The New Republic* (April 25, 1955), 22.

304   "Miss Monroe . . . filmed": *The New Republic* (August 8, 1955), 23.

305   "I don't . . . done": Letter to Pascal Covici, December 15, 1955.

305   "an abscessed . . . pigskin": Letter to Catharine Carver, December 3, 1953. *Partisan Review* archive, Rutgers University.

CHAPTER 15
307   "Verse . . . fingers": Greenberg interview.

309   "They thought . . . possibility": "The Dread and Fear of the Mind of Others," *The New Republic* (February 2, 1959), 18.

309   "tired and unhappy . . . written evidence": Interview with Eleanor Goff, 1975.

310   "barring . . . time": Letter to Lola Gruenthal, July 13, 1956.

311   "He was no tiresome . . . interrupted": Letter from Josephine Herbst to Dwight Macdonald, September 26, 1966.

311   "called . . . off": Letter to Henry Rago, January 21, 1957. *Poetry* magazine papers, University of Chicago Library.

311-2 "Just between . . . day": Letter to William Van Keuren, undated; copy in Beinecke.

312   "old movie language": Interview with Hilton Kramer, 1975.

313   "My psychiatrist . . . warrant": Ibid.

313   "rushed . . . raging": Bellow, op. cit., 155.

314   "scholarship fund": Interview with Saul Bellow, 1974.

314   This account of Delmore's condition is drawn from the medical records of Bellevue Hospital.

315   "Delmore's got . . . Hudson": Letters to James Laughlin from Saul Bellow, October 27, 1957.

315   "I suffered . . . poets to do": Bellow, op cit., 155.

PART THREE 1958–1966

CHAPTER 16
319   "When drunk . . . pay": Letter from F. Scott Fitzgerald to John Peale Bishop, undated. Princeton.

319   "The theoretical . . . ear": Bellow, op. cit., 160.

320   "Case of Delmore . . . sooner": Legal documents among Delmore's papers at Syracuse University.

320   "a model . . . ambiguity": Ibid.

322   "The public . . . oblivion": *The Washington Post*, January 31, 1958, 17.

323 "The leading . . . hope itself": "The Present State of Poetry," published in *American Poetry at Mid-Century* (Washington, D.C.: Library of Congress, 1958); reprinted in *Selected Essays of Delmore Schwartz.*

324 "an attentive . . . girls": Marlene Nadle, "Delmore Schwartz 1913–1966," *The Village Voice*, July 21, 1966, 6.

324 "as lively . . . ever was": Letter from Dwight Macdonald to Meyer Schapiro, July 28, 1966.

324 "more or less . . . ordinary": Letter to author from Norman Mailer, 1975.

325 "self-aggrandizing . . . accusation": Macdonald letter to Schapiro.

325 "But we spent . . . brooding": Letter to author from Leonard Wolf, 1975.

325 "grimy . . . mad": Stafford interview.

326 "He sat . . . unhappiness": Kazin, "Delmore Schwartz, 1913–1966," 1.

328 "quizzical . . . innocent": Howe, "Delmore Schwartz —a Personal Appreciation," 26.

328 "child's English": Letter from Philip Rahv to William Phillips, undated. *Partisan Review* archive, Rutgers.

329 "I tried . . . shame": "The Track Meet," *The New Yorker* (February 28, 1959), 34.

329 "During . . . desirable": Letter to William Maxwell, October 11, 1958.

330 "no good at all": Ibid.

331 "lost . . . years": Stanley Kunitz, "Process and Thing: A Year of Poetry," *Harper's* (September 1960), 100.

333 "While writing . . . barking": Letter to J. M. Kaplan, December 28, 1958.

334 "a dilapidated . . . quarters": Letter from Meyer Schapiro to Dwight Macdonald, August 8, 1966.

335 "Your dream . . . horseman": Robert Lowell, *History* (New York: 1973), 136.

335 "complete chastity": Letter to Howard Moss, undated.

335 "fucking Yalie": Interview with Elizabeth Oldham, 1976.

336 "See how poor I am": Lowell interview.

336 "ill and depressed": Letter to author from Robert Penn Warren.

337 "vitality": "Golden Satire," *Newsweek* (December 4, 1961), 90.

337 "that rare . . . letters": David Boroff, "The Theme Is Innocence," *The New York Times Book Review* (December 10, 1961), 5.

337   "Something . . . general vacancy": R. W. Flint, op. cit., 337.

337   "that guy'll . . . off": Rosenthal interview.

337   "—I'll kiss . . . marred": "Two Lyrics from Kilroy's Carnival, a Masque," *Sewanee Review* (Winter 1962), 12.

338   "And hence . . . Duval": "Apollo Musagete, Poetry, and the Leader of the Muses," *Poetry* (October–November 1962), 109.

338   "To those . . . virtuosity!": "Kilroy's Carnival: A Poetic Prologue for TV," *The New Republic* (December 1, 1958), 16.

339   "The world . . . goes": "Sonnet: The World Was Warm and White When I Was Born," *Kenyon Review* (Summer 1958), 441.

339   "Looked . . . abyss": "All Night," *The New Republic* (March 21, 1960), 18.

340   "greenish-bronze pallor": Interview with David Diamond, 1974.

341   "panic . . . to my cat": Records of Bellevue Hospital.

CHAPTER 17

343   "to convey . . . head": Letter to author from David Zucker, 1974.

343   "Delmore . . . hall": Ibid.

344   "to convey . . . statements": Letter to author from Jay Meek, 1976.

344   "If you want . . . Syracuse": Interview with David Zucker, 1975.

344   "he wouldn't have known what to do": Zucker letter.

344   "he seemed . . . device": Letter to author from Richard Eberhart, 1974.

344–5   This account is based on a letter to the author from Richard Wilbur.

345   "famously Jewish Frost": Letter to author from Philip Booth.

345   "Oh mother forsaken your son": Telephone interview with Victoria Bay Knight, 1975.

345   "I'm a bad son": Interview with Sanford Meech, 1975.

346   "Making love . . . Richmond": Letter to author from Robert Mason, 1975.

346   "I don't . . . kill her": Knight interview.

346–7   "I won't have . . . Albany": Wasserstrom, op. cit., 10.

347   "It's a free . . . dead": Interview with Donald Dike, 1974.

347   "He would come . . . obvious ones": Zucker letter.

348   "Don't be . . . live": This copy of *Genesis* belongs to Irwin Cohen.

349   "he was . . . Piper": Quoted in Macdonald, op. cit., xxi.

349   "the brightest . . . tested": Interview with Peter Locke, 1975.

349   "healthy appetite . . . loved to fuck": Ibid.

350   "spiritual godfather": Letter from Lou Reed to DS, undated. Syracuse.

350   "staggering . . . criminality": Letter to author from David Goldknopf, 1975.

350   "Our services . . . hospital": Letter from Donald Boudreau to DS, undated. Syracuse.

351   "proper Jewish man": Letter to author from Elizabeth Annas Leyh, 1975.

351   "He walked . . . obscure": Berryman, *The Dream Songs*, 174.

CHAPTER 18

352   "We've an American . . . season": M. L. Rosenthal, "New Singers and Songs," *The New York Times Book Review* (June 30, 1963), 1.

352   "I hear . . . ago": "To Helen," *The New York Times* (February 6, 1962), 18.

353   "megalomania": Telephone interview with Erin Clermont, 1976.

353   "You didn't recognize . . . changed": Letter to author from Matthew Josephson, 1975.

353   "East River gray": Bellow interview.

354   "Mr. Schwartz . . . again": Quoted in Nadle, op. cit., 1.

354   "making . . . door": Ibid., 6.

354   "At the morgue . . . poetry": Bellow, op. cit., 16.

355   "Our house . . . Jewish": Nadle, op. cit., 25.

355–6 "that grand . . . Success": Bellow, op. cit., 6.

356   "The spirit . . . go": Berryman, *The Dream Songs*, 175.

356   "the most . . . century": *Writers at Work, The Paris Review Interviews, Fourth Series* (New York: 1976), 308.

356   "I think . . . seeped into me": *Writers at Work*, Second Series, 362.

356   "*the* genius . . . group": Letter to author from Alfred Kazin, 1974.

356   "Into the Destructive . . . way": In the possession of Dwight Macdonald.

Works By
Delmore Schwartz

Acknowledgments

———————•———————

Leon Edel once claimed that biography is "the costliest of all labors on this earth," and my own labors would have proved more costly still had it not been for the assistance and encouragement of many friends, both Delmore Schwartz's and mine. Were it not for Dwight Macdonald, Delmore Schwartz's literary executor, this book could not have been written, for it was he who recovered Schwartz's papers and arranged for their transfer to Yale. Moreover, he put in much labor on the various drafts I showed him, and his brilliant, copious annotations had a profound influence on my style and ideas. Thomas A. Stewart, my first editor, started me on this project and contributed a great deal to its design. Robert Giroux provided crucial advice and sympathy later on, and guided me through the complexities involved in preparing a book for publication. Anna Fels devoted many hours to revising a late draft, and improved it immeasurably. Justin Kaplan, Katha Pollitt, Jean Strouse, and Jonathan Galassi were generous enough to read the finished manuscript and offer suggestions informed by their considerable literary experience. Many others supported me over the last three years in various ways, but I am especially grateful to Elizabeth Glassenberg, R. D. Rosen, David Zucker, Sam Schulman, Christina Rago, my parents, my brother Stephen, David Bloom, who accompanied me through the unfamiliar South on a visit to Schwartz's brother; Andrew Loewinger of Farrar, Straus and Giroux; and my research assistant, Sara Binder. Raymond Rosenthal and Taylor Stoehr, Paul Goodman's biographers, shared with me the results of their research, as did Richard McDougall, author of a book on Schwartz published by Twayne; Edward Mendelson, W. H. Auden's executor; Alan Wald, an authority on the politics of the 1930's; John Haffenden, John Berryman's biographer; and Merrill Leffler, who loaned me his comprehensive bibliography of Schwartz. Dwight Macdonald turned over to me various invaluable papers in his possession. Schwartz's brother Kenneth generously ensured that I had access to various sources of information. James Laughlin, who has done as much as anyone to preserve the memory of his friend, encouraged this project from the start and made available to me his vast and entertaining correspondence with Schwartz. I must also thank Stephen Berg, the editor of *American Poetry Review*, who published an essay of mine on Schwartz which led to the writing of this book, and Daniel Halpern, the editor of *Antaeus*, who published with great enthusiasm a selection of Schwartz's letters. Andreas Brown, the proprietor of the Gotham Book Mart, allowed me to consult and quote from his remarkable collection of letters from Schwartz to Julian Sawyer. Selden Rodman went to the trouble of sending me relevant entries from his journals of the period. Dr. Sanford Gifford offered a number of valuable psychoanalytic insights, and Benjamin D. Murawski contributed a thorough interpretation of Schwartz's Rorschach. R. H. Deutsch was kind enough to share with me transcripts of his interviews with some of Schwartz's friends (known as the Deutsch Papers). Kate Berryman provided me with copies of Schwartz's letters to John Berryman. Curtis Harnack and the staff of Yaddo answered a great many troublesome queries. Dr. Arthur Zitrin made available to me relevant medical records from Bellevue Hospital in New York. I must also thank Lynn Warshow, my copy editor at Farrar, Straus and Giroux, for having devoted such close attention to the finished manuscript.

Many people enhanced my portrait of Schwartz by granting interviews: Sherry Abel, Mrs. Newell Alford, Marshall Allen, Carlos Baker, William Barrett, Saul Bellow, Arthur Berger, Ann Birstein, the late Helen Blackmur, John Malcolm Brinnin, Anatole Broyard, Gertrude Buckman, James Burnham, Erin Clermont, Clara Colle, Robert Gorham Davis, David Diamond, Donald Dike, F. W. Dupee, Mrs. Murray Eden, Monroe Engel, Albert Erskine, James T. Farrell, Rose Feitelson, Francis Fergusson, Robert Fitzgerald, Eleanor Goff, Clement Greenberg, Lola Gruenthal, Oscar Handlin, Robert Hanlon, Ben Hellman, Robert Hivnor, Sidney Hook, Tessa Horton, Irving Howe, Norman Jacobs, Alfred Kazin, Milton Klonsky, William Knapp, Victoria Knight, Kenneth Koch, Sigmund Koch, Hilton Kramer, Seymour Krim, Harry Levin, the late Meyer Liben, Mrs. Rose K. Lieberman, Peter Locke, the late Robert Lowell, Mary McCarthy, Morton Margolis, Sanford Meech, Theodore Morrison, Howard Moss, Benjamin Nelson, Rosalie Netter, Elizabeth Oldham, Anthony Ostroff, the late George A. Palmer, the late Norman Holmes Pearson, William Phillips, Norman Podhoretz, Elizabeth Pollet, the late Philip Rahv, Lincoln Reis, Rosetta Reitz, William Roerick, Harold Rosenberg, Stanley Saplin, Harold Schapero, Meyer Schapiro, the late Mark Schorer, Oscar Shaftel, Harvey Shapiro, Eileen Simpson, Louis Simpson, Harry

Smith, Dr. Bertram Spira, Jean Stafford, Roger W. Straus, Jr., Saul Touster, Diana Trilling, the late Lionel Trilling, Aileen Ward, Eli Wilentz, Theodore Wilentz, Dennis Wrong, Dr. Arthur Zitrin, Charlotte Zolotow, Maurice Zolotow, Dr. Howard D. Zucker.

Many others took the time to write down their recollections: Philip Booth, Gerson Brodie, Cleanth Brooks, Mary Breen, Hayden Carruth, Rose Dickson, Richard Eberhart, Richard Entin, Leslie Fiedler, Matthew Josephson, George Lanning, Elizabeth Leyh, Robert Mason, Jay Meek, Arthur and Rosemary Mizener, Melvin Rosenberg, George Schloss, Harry Schwartz, Wallace Stegner, Allen Tate, Richard Wilbur, Leonard Wolf, David Zucker.

I owe a particular debt to Mr. Donald Gallup, Curator of the American Collection of the Beinecke Library, Yale University, which contains the most important archive of Schwartz's papers; Thomas B. Greenslade, the Kenyon College Archivist; Amy Doherty, University Archivist for the George Arents Research Library at Syracuse University; Mary Janzen Wilson, Manuscripts Research Specialist at the Joseph Regenstein Library of the University of Chicago; the late Herman Kahn, Associate Librarian for Manuscripts and Archives, Sterling Memorial Library, Yale University; the Berg Collection of the New York Public Library; Houghton Library, Harvard University; Brooke Whiting, Curator of Rare Books in the Department of Special Collections, Research Library, University of California, Los Angeles; and Kenneth A. Lohf of the Columbia University Library, for the letters to Mark Van Doren and F. W. Dupee.

For permission to publish the letters to Ezra Pound and William Carlos Williams, acknowledgments are made to the American Collection of the Beinecke Library, Yale University; to Kenneth Schwartz; to Mrs. Mary de Rachewiltz; and to James Laughlin, acting in behalf of the Estate of William Carlos Williams. The letters to Paul Goodman are published with the permission of Taylor Stoehr, Goodman's literary executor. Letters to R. P. Blackmur belong to the R. P. Blackmur papers at Princeton, and are published with the permission of Joseph Frank.

Index